Stupid Web Tricks

Jim Buyens

PUBLISHED BY
Microsoft Press
A Division of Microsoft Corporation
One Microsoft Way
Redmond, WA 98052-6399

Library of Congress Cataloging-in-Publication Data
Buyens, Jim
    Stupid Web Tricks / Jim Buyens.
      p. cm.
    Includes index.
    ISBN 1-57231-922-4
    1. Web sites—Design.   2. Web publishing.   I. Title
  TK5105.88.B895   1998
  005.7'2—dc21   98-19055
                                       CIP

Printed and bound in the United States of America.

3 4 5 6 7 8 9 WCWC 3 2 1 0 9 8

Distributed in Canada by ITP Nelson, a division of Thomson Canada Limited.

A CIP catalogue record for this book is available from the British Library.

Microsoft Press books are available through booksellers and distributors worldwide. For further information about international editions, contact your local Microsoft Corporation office or contact Microsoft Press International directly at fax (425) 936-7329. Visit our Web site at mspress.microsoft.com.

For Microsoft Press
    Acquisitions Editor: Kim Fryer
    Project Editor: Jenny Moss Benson

For LightSpeed Publishing, Inc.
    Project Editor: Joel Fugazzotto
    Editor: Scott J. Calamar
    Production: Cecelia Morales
    Technical Editor: Cheryl Kirk

Contents

This book is dedicated to the homeless mentally ill persons of America. Why, for this one illness, do we condemn its victims to the gutters and jails?

Acknowledgments

Many thanks to my wife, Connie, and my children, Lorrill, Justin, and Lynessa, for putting up with all the time I spent writing this book and for their support. Thanks as well to my parents, my brothers, and their families: Harold, Marcella, Ruth, Dave, Connie, Michael, Steven, Rick, Jenny, Matt, and Claire. What a bunch we are.

At Microsoft I'd like to thank Kim Fryer—who I guess now qualifies as my mentor—Lucinda Rowley, Jenny Benson, Bill Teel, and anyone else I may have dealt with and stupidly forgotten.

Thanks as well to the people at LightSpeed Publishing for transforming a draft manuscript into the book you're holding today: Joel Fugazzotto, Scott Calamar, and Cheryl Kirk.

Thanks to Interland, Inc., and in particular to Ken Gavranovic and Jason Peoples, for their assistance in providing the *www.interlacken.com* Web site.

Most of all, thanks to you, the readers, who make an effort such as this both possible and worthwhile. I hope the book meets your expectations and that we meet again.

About This Book

A few years ago my Dad asked me why, if processors, operating systems, and applications were really getting better and better, computers weren't getting any easier to use. Instinctively I knew the answer, but it took me two days to put it into words. "Dad," I said, "For every difficult thing that becomes easy, two impossible things become difficult."

So it is with Web pages. Not so long ago, producing a Web page consisting of some headings, some body text, a few images, and some hyperlinks required a major learning effort. Now, advances in HTML editors, image editors, and other tools make producing such pages a simple chore.

Web pages are curious animals, though; an unusual mix of artistic design and arcane computer programming. The more artistic and interactive you want your page to be, the more technology you have to deal with. Trends in Web design certainly provide no relief; today's cutting-edge Web page is nothing less than a new and exciting, mind-expanding, multimedia experience complete unto itself yet hooked into the world.

Knowing basic HTML isn't enough to produce a competitive Web site these days, or even one that attracts much attention. To provide state-of-the-art appearances and features, Web authors must use server-side scripting, browser-side scripting, Cascading Style Sheets, Dynamic HTML, and additional techniques, each with its own syntax and requirements. You can call these crass gimmickry, stupid tricks, advanced technology, or cutting-edge communication, but one thing seems sure: they're the stuff of the Web to come.

Keeping up-to-date with all these techniques is more than a lot of Web authors can absorb, especially if the only learning aids available are abstract technical descriptions and dry, comprehensive references. *Stupid Web Tricks* shortens the learning curve by concentrating on practical examples. There's no attempt to be excruciatingly comprehensive; instead, the emphasis is on concrete examples and how they work.

Once you get the mind-set—the overall sense of what goes into today's best Web pages—filling in the details is something you can easily do on the Web, in newsgroups, or from one of those abstract technical books. *Stupid Web Tricks* is an eminently practical book about how today's trendy Web pages work, and therefore about how yours can work as well.

Who This Book Is For

This book is written for Web authors who have basic HTML skills but lack the time, interest, or aptitude to learn advanced techniques in any sort of theoretical or comprehensive way. You want clear examples you can copy to your own pages, and clear explanations for modifying and debugging the results. In short, if you're better at starting with a piece of well-explained, working code than trudging through a ton of technical treatises, this is your book.

There are two caveats. First, despite the obligatory screen shots, this is basically a lines-of-code book. You should be capable of reading and entering HTML, at least enough to poke around in your editor's "raw HTML" mode. Second, making things happen automatically inevitably requires small bits of program-like code. We're not talking rocket science here: a bit of syntax, some *if* statements, and some simple loops are about as tough as it gets. Honest.

Objectives of This Book

Stupid Web Tricks uses practical examples to get you up to speed on Web tricks. It features techniques both old and new, often obscure, but always useful. Most of the topics covered are capabilities new to Microsoft Internet Explorer 4, Netscape Navigator 4, or both. (The book will emphasize Internet Explorer and Microsoft Internet Information Server, but it addresses compatibility with Netscape Navigator and with other Web servers as well.) This, of course, is the trendy new stuff everyone at parties is talking about (well, at Webhead parties, anyway).

There are some older topics too, mostly based on questions that keep coming up years after the corresponding browser capabilities appeared. In every case, though, you'll see the capability used and explained in a practical, nearly real-world example without unnecessary embellishments.

As to instructional techniques, the emphasis is on:

- Visual demonstration, with concise, highly focused instructions.

- Quick results rather than deep understanding. You can always get more detail from the Web, from newsgroups, or from other books.

How This Book Is Organized

Principally there are 15 numbered chapters corresponding to 15 useful tricks. An unnumbered introduction precedes these and provides a quick overview of the various technologies used.

The 15 numbered chapters each illustrate one major technique—that is, one trick—in the context of one or more examples. Discussion of each example begins with a screen shot, followed by a brief discussion of page layout strategy, and in some cases, how a Web visitor would operate the page. Next come explanations of any special techniques—HTML, style sheets, scripts, and so forth—and finally a complete, fully annotated HTML listing.

Most of the Web pages actually demonstrate several techniques. First and foremost, of course, each example demonstrates the topic of the trick in which it appears. Don't make the mistake of thinking each example contains plain-jane HTML with one enhancement, though. I've tried to make each page interesting, attractive, and representative of the real world, and that means using a variety of techniques in concert. Not to worry, however; the text for each example explains *all* the special techniques used, not just the subject of the current trick.

About the Web Pages

Unlike the sample pages in many Web authoring books, those in this book actually resemble something you'd create in real life. They're attractive and functional, but not so laden with other content and formatting that the point of the example is obscured.

The examples differ from real life in several ways:

- All the pages, characters, places, and critters are fictional.

- You won't find many hyperlinks on the sample pages, just text or images where hyperlinks might be. This keeps each example simple, self-contained, and focused. Creating hyperlinks is something you're already supposed to know.

- The fonts and images are probably a bit larger than you'd use in a real Web page. There seemed little point in loading up the example pages with lots of small text.

- With one exception, the HTML forms are dummies; clicking the Submit button simply displays a dialog box. For one thing, variations among Web server configurations mean the chances of client-server applications running straight off the CD are minimal. So I decided to give you a nice, demo-oriented dialog box instead of an ugly error message. For another, this is a book about realizing up-to-date Web page designs in code, not about the hookup between browsers and Web servers, and not about back-end processing.

I do provide general guidance in making the connection between HTML forms and Web servers, in case you decide to make this happen. This requires no more customization than if I'd supplied the examples configured to work in my lab.

I tested the examples with Microsoft Windows 95 and Microsoft Windows NT 4.0, both with Internet Explorer 4.01 and Netscape Navigator 4.05. These were the current versions at the time. Given the current rate of software development there's an excellent chance you'll be using subsequent versions, particularly of the browser software, but that can't be helped; retesting the examples, revising the text, and printing new books every couple of months simply isn't practical. Hopefully, all the pages will be upward compatible, and if not, I'm sure you'll let me know.

Differences among browsers (and browser versions) are a fact of life that eventually affect all Web page authors. A common solution, and one shown often in this book, is to test the browser version with code and configure the page differently based on the result. In most cases, the examples simply test for IE or

Netscape Navigator and presume the version number is 4. This simplifies the examples, making them easier to read and understand, but in real life you'll probably need to test the version number as well. Trick 2, "Generating Tables Dynamically," shows how to do this.

You can install Internet Explorer 4.01 on your computer by running the setup program in the \ie401 folder of the companion CD.

Using the Files on the CD

You can access all the Web pages in this book from the CD cleverly affixed to the back cover, from your own hard disk (once you've copied them from the CD), or from the Internet.

- On the CD, the Web pages are stored in a folder called *tricks*, and there's a home page at *\tricks\default.htm*. To locate a Web page on the CD, find its URL in the figure in the book that references it, remove the prefix *http://www.interlacken.com*, and you've got the CD location. Figure 1-1, for example, shows this URL in the browser's Address field:

  http://www.interlacken.com/tricks/trick01/nature.htm

  If your CD-ROM drive is drive D, you can find the corresponding HTML file as:

  d:\tricks\trick01\nature.htm

- To copy the files from the CD to your hard disk, you can either drag the \tricks folder to the desired location or run the CD's setup program. Then locate the Web page on your hard disk as described above.

- To access the Web pages from the Internet, enter the URL exactly as shown in the appropriate figure in the book, starting with *http://www.interlacken.com* There's also a home page at:

  http://www.interlacken.com/tricks/

Internet Explorer displays the home page as an expanding outline; click on any chapter heading to display the files for that chapter. Netscape Navigator, which has fewer Dynamic HTML features, displays all the choices all the time.

ASP files and Perl programs won't display correctly unless you copy them from the CD to a Web server and mark the Web server location as executable. These kinds of files actually execute on the Web server, you see, and not on your computer or the one running the browser.

Marking a server location executable is something the Web server's system administrator must do. In you're not the system administrator, contact whomever is. If you are the system administrator, consult your Web server's documentation. The area that needs to be executable is *tricks/exec* and all its subfolders (assuming you've copied the whole */tricks/* folder off the CD and to some server location).

There are two more prerequisites to running the ASP and Perl files:

- To run an ASP file, the Web server must be (1) Microsoft Internet Information Server 3.0 or above, running on Windows NT Server, or (2) Microsoft Peer Web Server 3.0 or above, running on Windows NT Workstation.

- To execute a Perl program, the Web server needs a copy of Perl. Again, this is something the server administrator must install.

Permission to run ASP pages or Perl programs on the server is relatively common on commercial Web sites and intranets, much less so for $20 per month ISP subscribers. (An ISP is an Internet service provider.) For $20 a month most providers simply aren't ready to supply the extra CPU time and support associated with user-written programs. Still, each ISP has its own policies and it never hurts to ask.

Introduction

Web pages have come a long way since they emerged in 1992 from a physics lab in Switzerland. The first Web pages had no color, no fonts, no pictures, and almost no page layout. Not only that, but they were all about boring scientific stuff like, um, physics. Yech.

To keep Web pages and their creation simple, the Web pioneers designed a low-end, deliberately crippled document format called Hypertext Markup Language (HTML). Nowadays, most Web designers view the original simplicity of HTML as a nuisance rather than a strength. They want their pages to be attractive, compelling, and downright amazing, and they target the mass market, not just scientists, technicians, and other geeks. Purity of HTML is not an issue. The original "Simpler is better" crowd must be in tears. Oh well.

Unfortunately, the ordinary trooper just trying to produce a competitive Web page is probably in tears as well. The latest browsers support more complex and gimmicky HTML than ever before. To make matters worse, they also support a number of features that aren't HTML at all but get mixed in just the same—style sheets and program code, for example. Together these features can transform any static Web pages into a freestanding, interactive, multimedia show. They can also transform the unsuspecting Web author into a muttering lunatic.

This book short-circuits the learning curve for all the latest Web gizmos by using simple, focused examples and offering clear explanations of how they work. There are no long, technical explanations of every possible option and feature; those books have their place but they don't get you up and running quickly.

What You'll Need

Note: The accompanying CD contains all the HTML code, images, programs, and related files for all the examples you'll see in this book.

As complex as Web pages have become, the tools that create them are still relatively cheap and simple. Often, they are free. This section describes the tools you'll need to view and create all the Web pages in this book in full animation and color.

Hardware

Creating Web pages generally doesn't require a high-end, high-speed, state-of-the-art, financially crippling computer, nor does viewing them. If you're satisfied with the performance of your computer for word processing and other general productivity applications, you'll probably be satisfied with its performance for Web applications as well.

If you're going to spend a little extra for Web authoring, aim for video. A 17-inch color monitor and a 4-MB video card are wonderful to own; together, they provide plenty of screen space for lots of open windows (1024 by 768 pixels) and 24-bit color (enough to render any color without graininess).

They say you can never be too rich or too thin. Well, you can never have too much RAM, either. If you find yourself with lots of open windows, misbehaving applications, and system halts, consider upgrading to 32 or 64 megabytes of RAM. It's cheap these days.

Assuming you intend others to view your Web pages, you'll also need a network connection. This could be a dial-up connection to an ISP (Internet Service Provider), a LAN connection in your building or office, or one of the new high-speed connections like ISDN (Integrated Services Digital Network), cable modem, or ADSL (Asynchronous Digital Subscriber Loop). Faster is better here; what more is there to say?

Browser Software

Programs that display Web pages are called *browsers*, so unless you're planning to simply imagine how your pages will look, you'll need a browser of your own.

The wonderful thing about browsers is that they're improving all the time. New versions (counting beta releases) seem to arrive every couple of months. This provides a never-ending stream of glitzy new features you can add to your pages. The discouraging part is that many of your Web visitors won't upgrade, and therefore won't see your glitzy new pages as you intend.

Usually, browser manufacturers try to design new features so that older browsers simply ignore the "extra" HTML and display some kind of scaled-back version. With each new browser version, though, this approach grows less and less realistic. For one thing, the technological differences between the newest version and the oldest version keep increasing. For another, more and more new features are not only cosmetic, but interactive. It's one thing for an old browser to display text in a default font rather than a custom font and color, but it's quite another when the user sees a badly formatted mishmash instead of fancy push buttons or time-sequenced content.

There are no easy answers to the problem of multiple browser versions and nonuniversal features. You can ignore the new features and develop for older browsers. You can design for new browsers only and place "Best Viewed With" warnings on each page. You can test and debug each page with a jillion browser versions. You can design pages that modify their own HTML depending on the browser version, or that display completely different pages based on the user's browser. This book will explain all these techniques. When it comes to designing your own pages, however, the choice is completely yours.

The browsers used in this book are Microsoft Internet Explorer 4.01 and Netscape Navigator 4.03, both running on Windows 95. I suppose that by the time you read this, newer versions of each will have appeared. This can't be helped, because the time to develop and release a browser version is apparently less than the time to write, print, and distribute a book. Sigh.

HTML Editors

Despite the growing use of images and other Web page objects, HTML, style definitions, and script statements still consist of plain text. To create Web pages you're going to need a plain text editor, even if it's a very simple one, and in the Microsoft Windows environment this means the Notepad program. You can edit and debug every Web page in this book with two windows open on your

Note: Syntax has nothing to do with government collections on tobacco, alcohol, or any other commodity. In computer terms, syntax is the set of rules that define how program statements or commands can be formatted. In effect, a syntax is a notational system. HTML, Cascading Style Sheets, JavaScript, Microsoft Visual Basic, Perl programs, and Active Server Pages each have their own syntax—that is, their own rules governing what constitutes a valid statement.

 Hyperlink: You can download Textpad from:

http://www.textpad.com/

 Note: Be sure to pay for any shareware you download and continue to use.

 Hyperlink: You can download Paint Shop Pro from:

http://www.jasc.com

screen: Notepad to enter the HTML and your browser to view it. Notepad offers no features to help you with the syntax of HTML, but neither does it have anything to get in the way. If you prefer a gut simple, minimalist approach, Notepad is your program. You can also dig your own well, fell your own timber, and make your own soap.

A step above Notepad are shareware and commercial text editors. These can open larger files than Notepad, open multiple files at once, and perform additional functions like search/replace and spell checking. Some have macro features you can program, and offer hot keys and toolbar buttons that create HTML code automatically. One such program is Textpad, from Helios Software Solutions.

At the top of the food chain are dedicated HTML editors like Microsoft FrontPage, the scaled-back FrontPad that comes with Internet Explorer, Netscape Composer, HomeSite, HoTMetaL Pro, Adobe Page Mill, and others. I'm not going to kid around here; this book is from Microsoft Press, and if you're going to buy one of these editors, we're going to recommend FrontPage. FrontPage also has a wonderful reference guide available, *Running Microsoft FrontPage 98* by, uh, me. But again, the final choice is yours.

One disadvantage of dedicated HTML editors is that they usually lag behind browsers in supporting new features. The browser folks invent doodads and the editor crowd runs to catch up; that's just the way it is. For certain advanced pages in this book, an HTML editor will only get in the way. For others, it can be a tremendous boon. Raw HTML remains the common denominator of all editors, though, so that's what this book will show.

Image Editors

Images are a major component of today's Web pages, so it stands to reason you'll need an editor that supports all the common formats. Some popular editors used on Windows are:

- **Paint Shop Pro**, a shareware program from JASC Incorporated.

- **Microsoft Image Composer**, which comes bundled with Microsoft FrontPage, Microsoft Publisher, and some versions of Microsoft Office 97.

- **Adobe Photoshop**, a high-end commercial editor popular with graphics professionals and leading Web page designers. There's also a Lite version with enough capabilities for most Web work.

Hyperlink: For a list of HTML editors, translators, and resources, browse:

http://www.primenet.com/~buyensj/ htmledit.html

This book isn't about image editing; it just assumes you have a way to do it and that you're comfortable with it. If you're not an artist, a large clip art library is a wonderful thing to have. Most of the images in this book are clip art supplied with Microsoft FrontPage or Microsoft Office, converted to Web formats. There are also many Web sites that offer free graphics for your HTML pages.

Web Sites

You can view your own Web pages by pointing your browser at a hard disk location, but you'll need to put your pages on a Web server for others in your company or around the world to see them.

Individuals working from home usually get Web space from an Internet service provider. Each designer controls what appears in his or her own Web space by uploading only that content.

At the office, network administrators provide access to Web servers on the Internet or on internal networks. These administrators usually enact stringent controls to keep Internet users from accessing internal servers and employees from putting unauthorized content on external servers.

Web servers deliver ordinary Web pages exactly as you upload them, adding only a few standardized and necessary headers. For some purposes, though, it's extremely useful if the Web server does some additional processing for you. For example:

- You may want the Web server to check the user's browser type and deliver different pages accordingly.

- You may want the Web server to read data from a file or database and make it part of the Web page.

- You may want the Web server to take action based on a Web page request, such as sending mail, writing data to a file, counting accesses to a page, or updating a database.

This book will show several examples of such applications, but to run these examples you'll need access to the right kind of Web server, with the right features, and with the right permissions.

To obtain processing capability on your ISP's or company's Web server, contact the appropriate system administrator. Access to server-side processing is usually controlled more tightly than simple Web page delivery, because a poorly written or malicious program can do a lot more damage than the worst Web page.

 Hyperlink: To obtain Web servers for Microsoft Windows 95 or Microsoft Windows NT, browse:

http://www.microsoft.com/iis

Browser Document Languages

This section begins a high-level overview of the document and scripting languages used in the rest of the book and, for that matter, on the World Wide Web. This is only to establish mindset and terminology; it doesn't attempt to be comprehensive. You can get more information from other books, from newsgroups, or from the Web.

If you start falling asleep, skip ahead, read through a few tricks, and return only as necessary. I won't be offended. Much.

HTML

Hypertext Markup Language is a system for "marking up" blocks of plain text with formatting commands. Anything enclosed in <angle brackets> is called a *tag*, considered a command, and isn't displayed.

Some commands require beginning and ending tags, such as <I> *to start italics and* </I> to stop them. Others, such as
 (line break), stand alone. The tag identifiers aren't case sensitive;
 and <br> are interpreted in exactly the same way.

The following six lines appear in virtually all Web pages:

```
<HTML>
<HEAD>
</HEAD>
<BODY>
</BODY>
</HTML>
```

- <HTML> and </HTML> mark the beginning and end of the page.
- <HEAD> and </HEAD> mark the beginning and end of the header, an area the browser never displays. The header is useful for information like the page title, browser commands, style sheets, and script code that'll be used elsewhere.
- <BODY> and </BODY> mark the displayable area of the Web page.

Note: Because HTML tags aren't case sensitive, you can use whatever capitalization scheme you want. In this book, we'll use uppercase to make HTML tags stand out in body text, but lowercase in code listings (where you already know it's HTML). Some tag attributes (values) *are* case sensitive, though, and these will always appear in the correct case.

When a tag has multiple parameters (settings), they're separated by spaces, tabs, line endings, or any combination. Here's an example:

```
<IMG SRC="picture.gif">
```

The first parameter specifies the type of tag: *IMG* makes this an *image* tag. *SRC="picture.gif"* supplies the URL of an image file. The browser will display this file in place of the image tag. A space separates *IMG* and *SRC*.

Here's a slightly more complex tag:

```
<font face="Arial Narrow" size=2 color=#FF0000>
```

The browser will display everything between this tag and a closing </FONT> tag in the Arial Narrow font, in a relatively small size, and in red. Note that to treat Arial Narrow as one value, it had to be enclosed in quotes. Without the quotes, the browser would set the <FONT> tag's FACE attribute to Arial and discard Narrow as something it didn't understand.

The cryptic string #FF0000 means *red* because each pair of hexadecimal digits controls the intensity of red, green, and blue, respectively. FF (which means 255 in decimal notation) is the most of a color you can have; 00 is the least.

Hexadecimal Conversions

Instead of a units (ones) place and a tens place, hexadecimal numbers have a units place and a sixteens place. Counting in hexadecimal therefore looks like this:

0, 1, 2, 3, 4, 5, 6, 7, 8, 9, A, B, C, D, E, F, 10, 11, 12.

Hyperlink: The following sites provide full documentation on all the features of HTML:

Microsoft:
http://www.microsoft.com/workshop/ author/default.asp

Netscape:
http://developer.netscape.com/library/ documentation/communicator/

World Wide Web Consortium:
http://www.w3.org/MarkUp

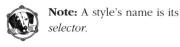

Note: A style's name is its *selector.*

Hexadecimal Conversions *(continued)*

To convert a hexadecimal number to decimal, multiply the sixteens digit by 16 and then add the units digit:

$$2B = (2 * 16) + 11 = 43$$

$$B2 = (11 * 16) + 2 = 178$$

To convert a decimal number (255 or less) to hexadecimal, first divide by 16. Then put the quotient into the sixteens place and the remainder into the units place:

$$185 / 16 = 11 \text{ r } 9 = B9$$

The Calculator program supplied with Windows can also convert between decimal and hexadecimal. Choose Scientific from the View Menu, click Hex or Dec depending on what system you're converting *from*, and then type the number. Clicking Dec or Hex will then display the same value in the alternate system.

Cascading Style Sheets

Even with tags like <B> (bold), <I> (italic), and <FONT>, HTML provides relatively limited control over the appearance of text. For years, Web page designers have been clamoring for more control over text, and Cascading Style Sheets (CSS) have finally given it to them. So there.

The goal of a style sheet is to describe a particular format once, give it a name, and then apply it elsewhere, probably in several places. In HTML, you define a style like this:

```
<style>
<!--
  .warning { font-family: Arial Narrow, sans-serif;
             font-size: 10pt;
             color: rgb(255,0,0) }
-->
</style>
```

This defines a style called *warning* that will appear either in the Arial Narrow font or, if Arial Narrow isn't available, in whatever sans serif font the browser can find. The text will appear in 10-point type, and will be bright red (255 on a scale of 0 to 255).

Notice that specifying CSS is quite a bit different from HTML:

- The <STYLE> and </STYLE> tags tell the browser to stop interpreting HTML and start interpreting a style sheet.

- <!-- and --> are HTML comment tags. If an older browser doesn't understand the <STYLE> and </STYLE> tags, it will treat everything between <!-- and --> as comments.

- The name of the style has no parameter name; CSS knows that *.warning* is a style name based on its position.

- The style parameters are enclosed by {curly braces} rather than <angle brackets>.

- Style parameters are separated by semicolons instead of spaces.

- Style values are set by colons instead of equal signs.

In addition to the <STYLE> tag, CSS adds two parameters to almost every other HTML tag:

- The CLASS attribute invokes a predefined CSS style. The following line of HTML, for example, would apply all settings from the *warning* class to a paragraph:

```
<P CLASS="warning">
```

- The STYLE attribute specifies CSS attributes for the range of the tag. The following code would surround a paragraph with a border one pixel thick:

```
<="border: 1px solid">
```

Cascading Style Sheet properties are subject to multiple overrides before the browser displays your text. At the highest level, the browser has default style properties for each HTML tag. These can be overridden on a property-by-property basis, though; first by style properties in a Web page's <HEAD> section, then

Note: CSS style names (selectors) that begin with a period are user-defined names called *classes*. Selectors that begin with a letter are called *types* and override the appearance of built-in HTML styles such as P (paragraph) and B (bold).

Tip: The CLASS attribute applies a style by name—generally, a name you assigned to some properties between the <STYLE> and </STYLE> tags. The STYLE attribute applies individual CSS properties to the tag that contains it.

Note: *Inheritance* provides another example of CSS cascading. This means that some built-in selectors, such as TD, inherit most of their style properties from other selectors, such as P. Therefore, changing the style properties of the P type will affect the TD type as well.

Hyperlink: The following sites provide documentation on the features and use of Cascading Style Sheets:

Microsoft:
http://www.microsoft.com/workshop/author/default.asp

World Wide Web Consortium:
http://www.w3.org/Style/

by attributes assigned to *containers* such as spans, divisions, tables, and paragraphs, then by attributes assigned to individual tags. This is the *cascading* idea in Cascading Style Sheets.

CSS provides a wide variety of measurement units: px for pixels, pt for points, in and cm for inches and centimeters, % for percent, and so forth.

Recent additions to CSS control not only typography, but position. The following style properties position the enclosed text 50 pixels from the top of a Web page and 100 pixels from its left edge:

```
<span style="position: absolute; top: 50px; left: 100px;">
I'm lost. Where am I?
</span>
```

A Word About Fonts

Fonts were never a problem during my college and early career days; mainframe printers had one font, all uppercase, and it came out on 11 × 14 green bar paper. The choice, such as it was, was like it or lump it.

Fonts were a joy when my first PC offered them, but they quickly became a burden when I started supporting other users. Word processors and the early releases of Windows let users specify fonts not installed on their system, and those users complained long and loud when the specified font didn't appear in their output. Fonts were the bane of my existence.

That changed, of course, when Microsoft added TrueType fonts to Windows. The font dialogs listed only the fonts you could print, and Windows could print any size you specified. Life was good.

Cascading Style Sheets provides tremendous flexibility for specifying and controlling fonts. Unfortunately, just putting font names in your Web pages doesn't ensure that Web visitors will have those fonts installed on their systems. In short, we're back to specifying fonts that exist on input but not on output. Fonts are once again the bane of my existence.

The Web desperately needs a way for Web designers to put font files on their Web sites, and for visitors to download them as needed. Designers could stop converting text to graphics, download times would decrease, and Web visitors would see pages as their designers intended. The only losers would be the font companies, who prefer the current system of selling fonts over any new system that involves free downloads.

Someday, hopefully, we'll have a generally accepted way to download font files, just as we do for images today. Until then, keep an eye on the following Web locations:

- *http://www.microsoft.com/opentype* is Microsoft's home page for Web typography. OpenType is a joint initiative of Microsoft and Adobe that will produce a single, downloadable font format compatible with both PostScript and TrueType systems.

- *http://www.truedoc.com/* is the home page for TrueDoc, an invention of Bitstream Inc., the digital type house. Web designers convert font files on their own systems into TrueDoc files (a process called *burning*) and put the TrueDoc files on their Web site. Remote browsers download the TrueDoc files and use them to display pages from that site.

Whenever you create a TrueDoc font file, you have to specify either a site name (like *http://www.whatever.com*) or a path (like */~whoever/*). This makes the TrueDoc file unusable on any other site or path. Bitstream added this restriction so each Web site has to buy any fonts they use. Unfortunately, if a user visits several sites that deliver the same font via TrueDoc, the font will be downloaded multiple times.

Bitstream provides a number of free TrueDoc fonts—free, that is, if you don't mind coding Bitstream's site as your font location. Their site also provides an ActiveX control that adds TrueDoc functionality to Internet Explorer.

- *http://www.netscape.com/communicator/version_4.0/dynfonts/* describes Netscape's approach to downloadable fonts. Basically, Netscape has adopted TrueDoc and built it into Navigator 4.0 and above.

- *http://www.hexmac.com/index2.html* is the home location for Typograph, a utility that converts fonts on your system to TrueDoc format. (Be aware, however, that not all fonts have licenses that permit this.)

The Web pages in this book use a variety of fonts, most of which come with Windows or with Internet Explorer, and additionally specify a generic font as fallback.

Browser Scripting Languages

HTML and Cascading Style Sheets are both relatively static. You specify what you want and, hopefully, that's the way it'll look. This is all well and good, but occasionally you'll want to do more.

JavaScript

For sophisticated state-of-the art Web pages, you'll often want to:

- Display variable data, such as the current time or date.

- Program different content depending on the date, the user's browser, or other variables.

- Change the appearance of Web page elements as the user clicks or hovers the mouse over them.

Anything that involves decisions or responses made at browse time will require programming of some kind and, I hear you saying, it had better be simple. This is the purpose of browser-side scripts—simple little bits of programming interspersed with your HTML and CSS code. Yet another syntax to learn. Oh goodie.

Scripts reside in the same file as your Web page and they require no compilation. The most widely supported script language, known currently as JavaScript, was invented by Netscape. Both Netscape Navigator and Microsoft Internet Explorer now support JavaScript, although Microsoft likes to call it JScript. Here's a simple example:

```
<script language="JavaScript">
<!--
document.write("URL=" + document.location);
// -->
</script>
```

The <SCRIPT> tag tells the browser to expect JavaScript code instead of HTML. The </SCRIPT> tag does the reverse. The <!-- and --> tags tell browsers that can't interpret the <SCRIPT> and </SCRIPT> tags to view the lines of script code as comments. The two slashes (//) in front of the --> tag are a JavaScript comment indicator; without them, JavaScript would interpret the --> as an erroneous statement.

Document.write is a method that writes HTML into the Web page as if it were originally hand-coded. The text written is the string *URL=* followed by the location property of the current document: (that is, the URL of the current Web page).

A semicolon must appear at the end of every JavaScript statement. Forgetting the semicolon is the leading cause of JavaScript errors, at least for this punctuationally challenged author. Logical expressions are enclosed by parentheses, and blocks of statements by curly braces. An *if* statement thus appears as follows:

```
If (navigator.platform == "Win32") {
    document.write("Windows");
    winplat = "y";
}else{
    document.write("Other");
    winplat = "n";
}
```

This code executes lines 2 and 3 if the platform property of the *navigator* object equals *Win32*, and executes lines 5 and 6 in any other case. JavaScript uses the double equal sign for comparison and the single equal sign to assign values. Attempting to compare two items with a single equal sign is the number two cause of JavaScript errors, at least for you-know-who.

Note that in line 3, simply mentioning the variable *winplat* causes it to be defined. No error message results if you misspell a variable name; instead, JavaScript creates a new variable with the misspelled name. This is the number three cause of JavaScript errors, especially because JavaScript variable names are case sensitive. To Java Script, the variable names *Cool* and *cool* are as different as *cool* and *kewl*.

There are no strong data types in JavaScript; variables take on the characteristics of whatever you store in them. If you store a number, you can use the variable numerically or as a string. Values containing non-numeric characters, of course, can only be used as strings.

To create objects more complex than simple variables, JavaScript requires statements such as this:

```
curDt = new Date();
```

Tip: If you forget a semicolon, JavaScript will usually supply one at the end of the line. You'll have fewer problems, though, if you supply your own semicolons and don't require JavaScript to guess where they should be.

Note: Strong data typing means each variable you define has one and only one data type that can't be changed: once an integer, always an integer; once a string, always a string; that sort of thing. Weak data typing, as used in JavaScript, means you can put any kind of value in any variable, and the variable takes on the required data type.

This creates a date object initialized to the current date. Such objects inherit a variety of useful methods. For example, the following *getDay* method obtains the *curDt* object's day of the week:

```
curDay = curDt.getDay();
```

Hyperlink: The following sites provide complete JavaScript documentation:

Microsoft:
http://www.microsoft.com/jscript/

Netscape:
http://developer.netscape.com/library/documentation/communicator/

Although both Netscape Navigator and Microsoft Internet Explorer support JavaScript, minor but extremely irritating differences tend to show up just where you least expect them. In addition, new JavaScript features appear with each new browser version. Adding new features to solve old nuisances is great, but only until someone using an old browser version comes along and the new script code fails. Should Web page creators stay two or three releases behind the current version, or should they exclude users who haven't upgraded their browsers? This is a difficult problem with no obvious answer.

VBScript

Microsoft's answer to JavaScript is a version of their popular Visual Basic programming language. Basically (sorry), VBScript in the browser does the same things as JavaScript, except that the code is very much like Visual Basic. It differs from JavaScript in that:

- There are no semicolons at the ends of statements.

- The equal sign is used both for assigning values and for comparing.

- Blocks of statements are indicated not with curly braces, but with keyword pairs like *if...endif, do...loop,* and *while...wend.*

As in JavaScript, variables are self-defining and self-typing. VBScript supports almost all the built-in functions anyone familiar with Visual Basic would expect.

In a Web page, VBScript looks like this:

```
<script language="VBScript">
<!--
document.write("URL=" + document.location)
-->
</script>
```

The <SCRIPT> and </SCRIPT> tags are pretty much the same as before, except that the language is specified as VBScript. The <!-- and --> tags are also the same, except that the // JavaScript comment prefix isn't required on the --> tag.

VBScript happens to support the *document.write* method in exactly the same way as JavaScript, except that the trailing semicolon isn't required.

The primary drawback to VBScript is that only Internet Explorer supports it. This eliminates all hope of being able to deliver the same page to both Netscape Navigator and Internet Explorer users. For this reason alone, use of browser-side VBScript has been limited.

Hyperlink: For detailed information about VBScript, browse:

http://www.microsoft.com/ vbscript/

Dynamic HTML

Until version 4.0 of Internet Explorer and Netscape Navigator, scripts could change the content and appearance of a Web page only by using the *document.write* method while the page loaded. Any script that ran later could issue commands to the browser, such as asking it to load a new page, display an alert box, or change the value of a form field. But once the page was loaded, a script couldn't change the displayed HTML code. A pity, wouldn't you say? How can Web pages be interactive if they can't change in response to the user?

Dynamic HTML, implemented to some extent in Netscape 4 and more so in Internet Explorer 4, eliminates this restriction. With Dynamic HTML, a script can insert entire blocks of HTML, delete them, replace them, or change the properties of objects *while the page is on display*. The browser adjusts automatically to display the new properties, the new HTML, or both.

Dynamic HTML involves two important concepts:

- **The Document Object Model** (a name only a mother or a model could love) describes how the various objects in the browser and in the Web page are organized and named. It also controls which objects and properties can be modified and what values are acceptable.

- **The Event Model** (a name only Don King could love) describes how a script can receive control; that is, what actions can trigger a script.

See Also: Trick 1 shows how to examine the Document Object Model in greater detail.

Hyperlink: For more details on Dynamic HTML, consult these Web sites:

Microsoft:

http://www.microsoft.com/workshop/ author/dhtml

Netscape:

http://developer.netscape.com/library/ documentation/communicator/ dynhtml/index.htm

With Internet Explorer, almost any object on the screen—hyperlinks, images, paragraphs, whatever—can respond to a rich variety of events. Netscape Navigator, by contrast, honors fewer events—and then pretty much only for hyperlinks and form objects.

The real pity of Dynamic HTML is that Internet Explorer and Netscape Navigator differ greatly in both their document and event models. To some extent this is fallout from the browser wars, and to some extent it's because the browsers appeared at different times. Either way, the end result is that developing a Dynamic HTML page that works both under Netscape and IE (my shorthand for Internet Explorer) is very tricky. Enough so to warrant writing books about it, I suppose.

Web Server Scripting Languages

As useful as browser-side scripting can be, there are times when scripting on the Web server is the best or the only way to get a job done. Server-side scripts can access files, databases, and other resources stored on the server, and they can access centralized services like electronic mail and fax.

A consistent and controlled environment is another advantage of server-side scripting. Your code only needs to run on one version of one server, not multiple versions of multiple browsers. (The resulting HTML still has to work with multiple browsers, though. You don't get off so easily.)

There are three main drawbacks to server-side scripting:

- Running server-side scripts generally requires special permission from your Webmaster or system administrator. This is because a haywire server script can impact the entire Web server.

- To interact with a server-side script, the user must click a hyperlink or button and then wait for the server to run the script and transmit the resulting Web page. Interaction with a Dynamic HTML script is much faster.

- To test a server-side script before uploading it requires running your own Web server, preferably the same type as your public (production) server.

Because of these drawbacks, most HTML authors use browser-side scripting wherever possible. Following that trend, most of the tricks in this book are browser-side as well. Some of the tricks *do* run on the server, though, so here's a rundown on the languages we'll use.

Active Server Pages

Internet Information Server, Microsoft's Web server for Windows NT, provides a server-side version of VBScript called Active Server Pages (ASP). This permits intermixing blocks of VBScript code and HTML code. Each block of VBScript executes on the server, doesn't get transmitted to the remote user, and gets replaced by any generated HTML.

ASP provides built-in objects for the incoming request, the outgoing response, the user session, the application, and the server itself. Specifically:

- **The Request object** tells you about the user's browser, the URL submitted, any form fields, and so forth.

- **The Response object** receives the outgoing HTML, status codes, and certain commands. With status codes, for example, you can force the user to enter a username/password combination known to the server. Commands can refer the user to another URL, for instance.

- **The Server object** provides information about the server: its name, the software it's running, the version, and so forth.

- **The Session object** saves information about each user from one interaction to the next. It identifies transactions from the same user by sending a cookie to the user's browser, and then watching for that cookie in incoming requests.

- **The Application object** stores information common to all users of a given application. (An application means all ASP pages in a given directory tree.)

Perl

This ancient language dates prior to the Web; its acronym stands for Practical Extraction and Report Language. Larry Wall invented Perl because, according to legend, his boss told him to write a reporting program and no existing language made the job easy enough to suit Larry's taste. Perl is covered by the GNU software agreement, and therefore it's always free and it's always being enhanced.

Note: A cookie is a small block of data that a Web server sends to a visitor's browser. The browser sends the cookie back, unchanged, the next time it submits a request to the same URL, folder, or server.

Hyperlink: For more information about Active Server Pages, consult the "Scripters Reference" section at:

http://www.microsoft.com/iis/Support/ iishelp/iis/misc/documentation.asp

On a Web server, Perl scripts operate as CGI (Common Gateway Interface) programs. When the Web server receives the URL for a Perl program, it fires up the Perl interpreter, tells the interpreter what Perl program to run, and supplies information about the incoming request in two ways:

- **As standard input**—that is, as if the server were redirecting input into an MS-DOS command.

- **As environment variables**—the items you see listed after typing SET at the DOS prompt.

The Perl program writes HTML to standard output, like a MS-DOS program writing to the screen. The Web server captures this output and sends it back to the remote user.

Perl, like JavaScript and VBScript, has self-defining variables that change automatically from numeric to string. Simple variables have names beginning with a dollar sign ("$"), and arrays have names beginning with an "at" sign ("@").

As with JavaScript, Perl statements end with a semicolon; {curly braces} denote blocks. An equal sign ("=") assigns a value; for comparisons, you must use "==" or "eq". If $a == $b performs a numeric comparison, $a eq $b performs a string comparison. The operator "<=" is numeric, "le" is alphabetic, ad infinitum. Mixing up these operators is even easier than forgetting semicolons and double equal signs.

Perl programs often require minor modification when moved between systems. On UNIX systems, for example, the first line of a Perl program usually has to specify the location of the Perl interpreter, as in:

```
#!/usr/bin/perl
```

The exact location will vary, of course, from system to system.

On Windows NT systems, the opening #! line isn't required at all. Instead, your system administrator must associate the Perl interpreter (perl.exe) with the .pl filename extension in the Web server's configuration.

And now, let the tricks begin.

 Hyperlink: To obtain Perl for Windows NT, browse Active State Tool Corporation's site at:

http://www.activestate.com/

For general information about Perl, browse:

http://www.perl.net/

Designing with Grids and Styles

The entire World Wide Web was originally flush left. No, this had nothing to do with Uncle Elmo's poker game, return drainage, hot flashes, or minor daily embarrassments. It meant that every heading, every paragraph, and every list was crammed against the left margin. This was ugly, boring, and dangerous; the entire Internet began listing to port.

The first big Web innovations were centered text and right-aligned images. This set off a flurry of creative activity by designers desperate for any sort of feature that actually let them, well, design. People in those days were not only desperate but easily satisfied; they embraced these innovations despite serious limitations. Centered text is hard to read, because every time the eye moves to a new line, it has to search for the starting point. Right-aligned images broke up the monotony of universal left alignment, but hardly provided the flexibility needed for high-end graphic design work like laundry detergent and tractor pull advertising.

No, the tool that really opened the Web to page layout was the HTML table. Almost every Web page in this book uses tables for page layout, so it seems reasonable to talk about this technique first. Specifically, we'll look at three Web pages that use tables for page layout and explain how they work. Along the way we'll also begin looking at Cascading Style Sheets, which basically bring typography to the Web. (One of you drummers out there, please give me a pish-boom.)

The Nature Page

Figure 1-1 shows the first example in this trick: The Nature Page, a Web page whose design occupies a table with three columns and two rows. Images completely occupy the top-left, top-right, and bottom-center cells.

Table Fundamentals

Browsers go through a very complex process to optimize the width of table columns. I suspect that only a few programmers at each browser company really understand all the rules, but in general the browser tries to make the table as short as possible. This means:

FIGURE 1-1. *A table measuring three cells wide by two cells high provides this page's basic design.*

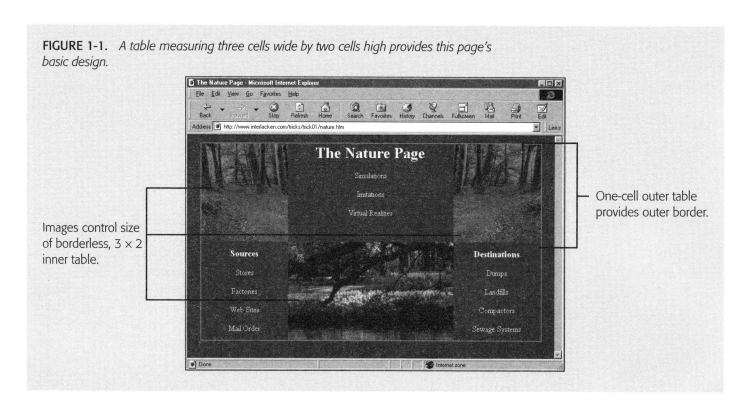

Images control size of borderless, 3 × 2 inner table.

One-cell outer table provides outer border.

Tip: Browsers have no compunctions about making tables (and Web pages) longer than the browser window, but they do almost anything to fit them within the width.

 Tip: The space available for table cells is the width of the table. When specifying column widths as percentages, make sure they don't add up to more than 100 percent. Whatever a particular browser does in this situation, it's probably not what you want and certainly not reliable. (Likewise but sideways for heights: think about it.)

 Tip: The available space for a table is the height and width of whatever surrounds it: the browser window, a cell in another (larger) table, or whatever.

- Given a choice between making a table wider or longer, the browser always chooses wider. However, it never willingly makes a table wider than the available, visible space (for instance, the browser window or whatever else encloses the table).

- The browser adjusts column widths to minimize total white space within the table.

- If a column contains a lot of white space, the browser makes that column narrower. This provides more horizontal space for other columns.

- If a column contains little white space, the browser makes it wider. Given more horizontal space, the same content generally requires less vertical space.

The more you work with tables, the more you'll swear that browsers have a mind of their own when it comes to sizing table columns. There's no substitute for experience here; you just need to develop a feel for the way columns get wider (forcing other columns to become more narrow) as you add content to them. As columns widen, the table gets wider and wider until it runs out of screen space, and then it starts getting longer and longer.

The end result of all these sizing calculations is usually a good-looking table, but occasionally you'll want to override the browser. To provide more control, HTML provides two ways to control the height and width of individual cells or the entire table. The most straightforward method is to code WIDTH=, HEIGHT=, or both within the <TD> or <TH> tag for the cell you want to control, or within the <TABLE> tag for the table you want to control. If you specify WIDTH= or HEIGHT= as a number, the browser sets aside that many pixels. If you specify a percentage, the browser allocates that much of the available space.

An Incredibly Brief Introduction to HTML Tables

Here are the basic facts you need to construct tables out of HTML code:

- Tables begin and end with <TABLE> and </TABLE> tags.
- <TR> and </TR> tags mark the beginning and end of each row.
- Within each row, <TD> and </TD> tags mark the beginning and end of each cell.

Hyperlinks: For a definitive guide to all aspects of HTML, including tables, browse the following Web sites:

Microsoft:
http://www.microsoft.com/workshop/author/default.asp

Netscape:
http://developer.netscape.com/library/documentation/communicator/

World Wide Web Consortium:
http://www.w3.org/MarkUp

The trouble with coding HEIGHT= and WIDTH= in the HTML for a table is that a browser considers these settings only as suggestions. Suppose you code WIDTH=50% for two adjacent cells, but the left cell contains much more content than the right. To avoid a lot of blank space in the right cell, the browser automatically widens the left cell in spite of your carefully coded instructions.

Using images to control column widths and row heights is a much more reliable method. The browser always makes columns wide enough to display the widest image they contain, and rows tall enough to display the tallest image.

The three large images in Figure 1-1 determine the height and width of the rows and columns. Note the symmetry of this design; arranging the three images and the three blocks of text in a checkerboard pattern is far more interesting than, say, a bulleted list. Making the center column wider than the rest adds emphasis to the heading text and breaks up monotony. Making both outer columns a uniform width provides balance and symmetry.

From Paste-Up to Mark-Up

All good page layouts begin with a well-chosen two-dimensional pattern. For years, page designers working in print cut their various content items into strips or pieces, then pasted them onto cross-ruled layout sheets. Aligning pictures or strips of text along strict vertical or horizontal lines provides a sense or order, organization, and professionalism. When several items are aligned together, the reader assumes they're related. When they're disjointed, the reader infers independence. Like alignment means like items; unlike alignment means unlike items. This is page layout, not nuclear physics.

Nowadays we do page layout with software like Microsoft Publisher, Microsoft FrontPage, or even (ugh!) Notepad. Be that as it may, time-tested principles of page layout and design continue to apply. Align your major items of content in a two-dimensional grid, lining up like items and separating unlike ones.

Page Layout Details

Figure 1-1 also shows one table within another. There's a border around the entire composition, but no visible borders between cells. How, you gasp, can this occur? Especially since giving a non-zero value to the BORDER= attribute of any table draws borders around each cell as well as around the entire table.

Fortunately, there's an easy answer. Phew. The Nature Page's border comes from a one-row, one-column table that surrounds the two-row, three-column table. The outer table has a border and the inner table doesn't. It's as simple as that.

Complete HTML Listing

Here's the HTML for The Nature Page, with annotations and feeling:

The variables *bgcolor* and *text* specify background and text colors—two hexadecimal values.

Within the <table> tag, *align* positions the entire table as a unit on the page.

The *cellspacing* attribute reserves space between cells. The *cellpadding* attribute reserves space around the inside of each cell.

```
<html>
<head>
<title>The Nature Page</title>
</head>
<body bgcolor="#006600" text="#FFFF99">
<table border="1" bordercolor="#999900" align="center"
          cellspacing="0" cellpadding="0">
<tr>
  <td>
```

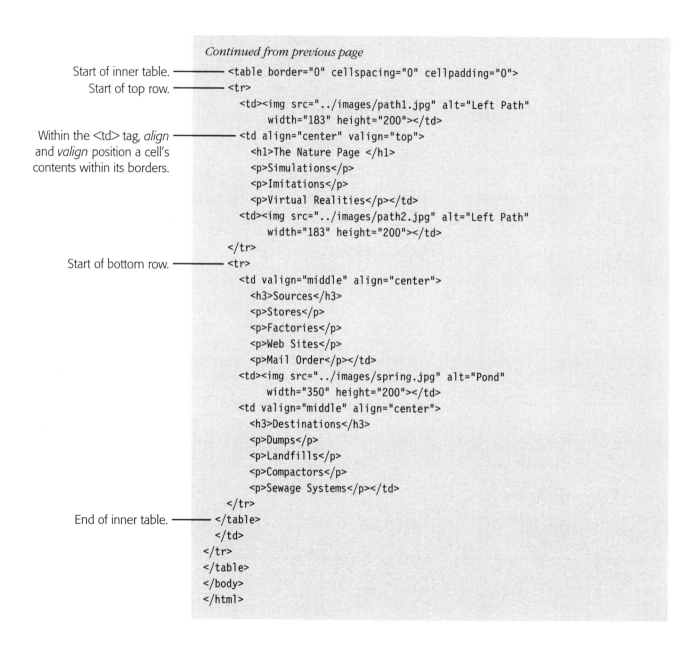

Continued from previous page

Start of inner table. ——— `<table border="0" cellspacing="0" cellpadding="0">`
Start of top row. ——— `<tr>`
```
        <td><img src="../images/path1.jpg" alt="Left Path"
            width="183" height="200"></td>
```
Within the <td> tag, *align* ——— `<td align="center" valign="top">`
and *valign* position a cell's
contents within its borders.
```
          <h1>The Nature Page </h1>
          <p>Simulations</p>
          <p>Imitations</p>
          <p>Virtual Realities</p></td>
        <td><img src="../images/path2.jpg" alt="Left Path"
            width="183" height="200"></td>
      </tr>
```
Start of bottom row. ——— `<tr>`
```
        <td valign="middle" align="center">
          <h3>Sources</h3>
          <p>Stores</p>
          <p>Factories</p>
          <p>Web Sites</p>
          <p>Mail Order</p></td>
        <td><img src="../images/spring.jpg" alt="Pond"
            width="350" height="200"></td>
        <td valign="middle" align="center">
          <h3>Destinations</h3>
          <p>Dumps</p>
          <p>Landfills</p>
          <p>Compactors</p>
          <p>Sewage Systems</p></td>
      </tr>
```
End of inner table. ——— `</table>`
```
      </td>
    </tr>
  </table>
  </body>
</html>
```

The Society to Suppress Obstructionism

By now you're ready to eat Web pages like The Nature Page for breakfast. (Please be sure to print them out with child-safe ink on edible paper, though.) So, let's try something more interesting: Figure 1-2 shows a Web page with *two* tables inside a larger one. Also, it doesn't use the browser's standard fonts.

Page Layout Details

This page shows how tables can easily control margins and alignment. Although both the heading and detail sections are centered, the page as a whole avoids

FIGURE 1-2. *The heading area and the three-column area of this page are each HTML tables. A third, larger table surrounds them and organizes the entire page.*

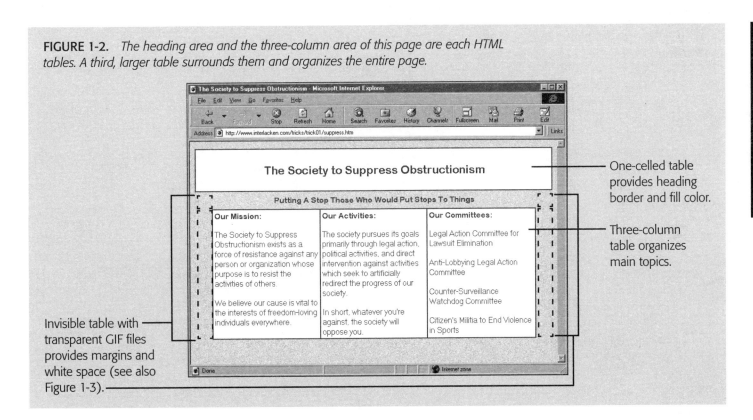

One-celled table provides heading border and fill color.

Three-column table organizes main topics.

Invisible table with transparent GIF files provides margins and white space (see also Figure 1-3).

Tip: White space isn't necessarily white. For years, page designers have used the term white space to mean any background space that separates the elements of a layout. Although solid white is the most common background, especially in print, any background color or pattern can be white space.

Tip: Never make the mistake of assuming blank space is worthless or wasted. Just as placing two items close together tells the viewer they're related, separating them tells the viewer they're distinct. Separating two items, of course, means putting blank space between them.

Caution: You can specify both COLSPAN and ROWSPAN for the same cell, but you can only define rectangular areas. The same cell can't span one column in row 3 and two columns in row 4, for example.

Tip: Assuming your image editor permits, always set a GIF file's color resolution as low as possible. If a file actually contains only one or two colors, saving it in two-color format results in a much smaller file than saving it in 256-color format.

irregular text margins (that is, content areas with jagged edges). The centered heading is only one line, eliminating any difficulty locating the start of a subsequent line. Also, the heading is surrounded by plenty of white space. The three sections of detail text are each left justified, even though the entire block of three is centered. This provides a certain symmetry without making the page hard to read.

The rectangle containing the heading is a one-cell table with a border and a solid background color. The boxes labeled Our Mission, Our Activities, and Our Committees are three cells in a second table that, like the heading table, has just a single row. Both of these tables are contained in the invisible 3 × 3 table shown in Figure 1-2. (If you can't see it, you've forgotten to put your invisible glasses on.)

The invisible layout table has three rows and three columns because:

- It needs three rows to contain the heading, subheading, and detail text, respectively.

- It needs three columns to provide a left margin, content area, and a right margin for the subheading and detail text areas. To avoid these margins for the heading area, we'll merge that row's three cells into one.

The tag that merges the three cells in the first row is <TD COLSPAN=3>. *COLSPAN* extends a cell across multiple columns; *ROWSPAN* extends it along multiple rows.

In the layout table's second row, the three cells contain (respectively) a transparent GIF file, the subheading text, and another transparent GIF file. Transparent GIF files (sometimes called spacers) are wonderful for blocking out white space and sizing tables. The browser reserves space for transparent files just as it does for visible images, but of course neither you nor your Web visitor can see them. Spooky. It's very common to use a very small GIF file for this sort of thing; a 1-pixel by 1-pixel two-color file, for example. You can always make the browser stretch the invisible image larger by specifying a height and width in the HTML. Loss of resolution isn't a problem for invisible images.

FIGURE 1-3. *This is the same Web page shown in Figure 1-2. In this illustration, however, the borders of the outermost table are visible.*

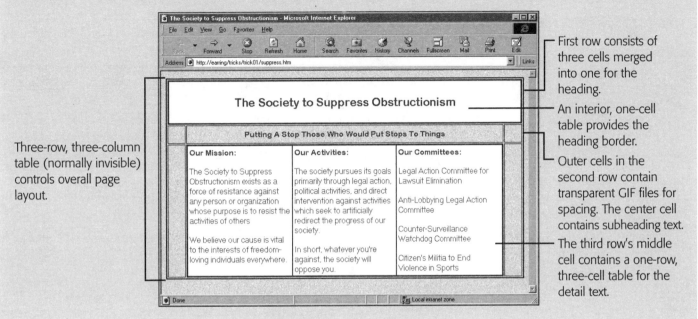

First row consists of three cells merged into one for the heading.

An interior, one-cell table provides the heading border.

Outer cells in the second row contain transparent GIF files for spacing. The center cell contains subheading text.

The third row's middle cell contains a one-row, three-cell table for the detail text.

Three-row, three-column table (normally invisible) controls overall page layout.

As it does for many other tags, HTML supports HEIGHT and WIDTH attributes for the <TABLE>, <TD>, and <TR> tags. To specify dimensions in pixels, supply integer values. To specify dimensions relative to the element's *container*, specify numbers from 1 to 100 followed by a percent sign. WIDTH=50 means 50 pixels; WIDTH=50% means half the size of the object's container.

Note: In terms of page layout, an object's container is whatever surrounds it and limits its size.

All three tables in the Society to Suppress Obstructionism page make use of HEIGHT attributes in their <TABLE> tags:

- The large outer table—the transparent one that organizes the entire page— has no container other than the browser window. (That is, it isn't inside anything else that limits its size.) Its <TABLE> tag specifies WIDTH=100% so this table fills the entire window.

Note: HTML tables (and cells) normally shrink around their contents, first to minimize the table's height and then to minimize its width. Coding WIDTH=100% or HEIGHT=100% reverses this behavior; that it, it makes the table (or cell) as wide or as tall as possible, within the available space.

Caution: Netscape Navigator ignores the HEIGHT= setting for tables.

- The attribute WIDTH=100% also appears within the <TABLE> tag for the one-celled heading table. Otherwise, the border around the heading (which is really a table border) won't fill the entire top row. It would only be as wide as the heading text.
- The three-celled table titled Our Mission, Our Activities, and Our Committees also has WIDTH=100% coded within its <TABLE> tag. This not only makes the table fill the entire available area (that is, the full width of the table's container), but also creates a sort of outward pressure that forces its container to become as wide as possible.

  When resizing the transparent layout table, the browser won't make column two so wide that it can't display the transparent GIFs in columns one and three. It addition, it makes sure the entire table isn't too wide to fit inside the browser window.

Two tables in the Society to Suppress Obstructionism page also contain HEIGHT attributes in their <TABLE> tags:

- Specifying HEIGHT=100% for the outermost, transparent table makes it occupy the entire height of the browser window, even if you make the window larger than the table's contents.

- Specifying HEIGHT=100% for the Mission-Activities-Committees table likewise makes that table (as well as its container—the middle cell in the bottom row of the transparent layout table) as tall as possible. If you make the window longer than needed to display its content, the Mission-Activities-Committees table also gets longer. Making the table get visibly longer and shorter as you resize the page is much cooler than showing extra margin.

Style Sheet Usage

This Web page contains our very first Cascading Style Sheet, something definitely worth examining. Here it is:

```
<style>
<!--
TD { color: rgb(102,51,51); font-family: sans-serif; }
-->
</style>
```

See Also: To review the syntax of CSS statements, please refer to the "Cascading Style Sheets" section of the Introduction.

Tip: Browsers that understand Cascading Style Sheets will ignore any comment tags that appear within <SCRIPT> and </SCRIPT> tags.

Tip: Whenever possible, use RGB color values of 0, 51, 102, 153, 204, or 255 for Web designs. These are the only color values the browser can display on 256-color video equipment without dithering or substitution. The corresponding hexadecimal values are 00, 33, 66, 99, CC, and FF.

The <STYLE> and </STYLE> tags mark the beginning and end of the style sheet. The <!-- and --> tags are for browsers that don't understand CSS; they tell such browsers to ignore whatever appears between them as comments.

Line three is the guts of this style sheet: it applies two properties—*color* and *font-family*—to the type selector TD:

- The *color* property has a value of *rgb(102,51,51),* which means intensities of 102 for red, 51 for green, and 51 for blue, all on a 0–255 scale. This produces a medium brown color.

- The *font-family* property has a value of *sans-serif.* This tells the browser to display text in its default, sans serif font (usually Arial or Helvetica).

Text Pointers—Serif vs. Sans Serif

Serifs are those pointy little endings that appear in some fonts. Serif fonts like Times New Roman have serifs; sans serif fonts like Arial don't.

Serifs add a horizontal flow to lines of text, making it easier for the reader to stay on track. You can prove this to yourself by finding a page in this book that's full of body text, holding the right or left edge of the page near your eye, and sighting down the lines of text. The bodies of the lowercase letters will look almost like railroad tracks.

Because sans serif fonts lack this horizontal guidance, they make it harder for the eye to stay on track. To compensate, provide extra white space between lines when using a sans serif font.

The style name TD is a *type* selector because it begins with a letter. A type selector overrides the properties of the corresponding HTML tag: (<TD> in this case). Unless overridden again (and it isn't), everything on this page within <TD> and </TD> tags will appear in brown sans serif type. Our luck must be good because *all* content on this page lies within <TD> and </TD> tags, and that's what we want. We're done.

Complete HTML Listing

Here's the HTML for the Society to Suppress Obstructionism page:

Define a simple Cascading Style Sheet. On this page, anything within <TD> and </TD> tags will be brown and appear in the browser's default sans serif font.

Make the outer table occupy the entire browser window. Make a cell that spans three columns.

Start of heading table.

The <font> tab sets typography via HTML.

End of heading table.

Row 2, column 1 contains a transparent GIF.

Row 2, column 2 contains the subheading.

Row 2, column 3 contains a transparent GIF.

```html
<html>
<head>
<style>
<!--
TD { color: rgb(102,51,51); font-family: sans-serif; }
-->
</style>
<title>The Society to Suppress Obstructionism</title>
</head>
<body background="../images/bkgrnd01.gif">
<table border="0" cellpadding="0" cellspacing="0"
        width="100%" height="100%">
<tr>
 <td colspan="3">
   <table border="1" cellpadding="0" cellspacing="0"
           width="100%" bordercolor="#663333" bgcolor="#FFFFFF">
    <tr>
     <td width="100%" align="center">
       <font size="5"><strong> <br>
       The Society to Suppress Obstructionism<br>
        </strong></td>
    </tr>
   </table>
 </td>
</tr>
<tr>
 <td valign="middle" align="center">
   <img src="../images/trans5x5.gif"
        width="35" height="35"></td>
 <td valign="middle" align="center"><strong>Putting A Stop
   Those Who Would Put Stops To Things</strong></td>
 <td valign="middle" align="center">
   <img src="../images/trans5x5.gif"
        width="35" height="35"></td>
</tr>
<tr>
```

Make row 3 consume as much
vertical space as possible. This keeps
rows 1 and 2 from growing taller as
the window grows.

Start of Mission-Activities-
Committees table.

Our Mission.

Our Activities.

Our Committees.

End of Mission-Activities-
Committees table.

Continued from previous page

```
<td height=100%></td>
<td valign="top">
<table border="1" cellpadding="3" cellspacing="0"
       width="100%" height="100%"
       bordercolor="#663333" bgcolor="#FFFFFF">
<tr>
<td width="33%" valign="top"><strong>Our Mission:</strong>
<p>The Society to Suppress Obstructionism exists as a
   force of resistance against any person or organization
   whose purpose is to resist the activities of others.</p>
<p>We believe our cause is vital to the interests of
   freedom-loving individuals everywhere.</td>
<td width="33%" valign="top"><strong>Our Activities:</strong>
<p>The society pursues its goals primarily through legal
   action, political activities, and direct intervention
   against activities which seek to artificially redirect
   the progress of our society.</p>
<p>In short, whatever you're against, the society will
   oppose you.</td>
<td width="34%" valign="top"><strong>
   Our Committees:</strong>
<p>Legal Action Committee for Lawsuit Elimination</p>
<p>Anti-Lobbying Legal Action Committee</p>
<p>Counter-Surveillance Watchdog Committee</p>
<p>Citizen's Militia to End Violence in Sports</td>
</tr>
</table>
</td>
<td></td>
</tr>
</table>
</body>
</html>
```

See Also: For more CSS information, refer to the "Cascading Style Sheets" section in the Introduction.

Note: Cascading Style Sheets force a change in the way you use the <P> (paragraph) tag. Before CSS, most people never used the <P> tag at the beginning of a paragraph; they only used it *between* paragraphs. Also, they *never* used the closing </P> tag. With CSS, each paragraph needs to be enclosed within a <P>…</P> tag pair. The opening <P> tag can then specify any desired style information.

An Incredibly Brief Introduction to Cascading Style Sheets

CSS is a language that expresses typographical formats in terms of *rules*. The general format of a CSS rule is:

```
selector { properties }
```

The selector identifies the rule and controls where it's applied. The properties specify how the Web page elements covered by the rule will look. There are three basic kinds of selectors:

- **Type Selectors** override the default appearance (determined by the user's browser) of standard HTML tags like <H1> and <P>. The style sheet below, for example, defines a rule that makes all paragraph text (that is, all text governed by <P> tags) green. CSS knows P is a type selector because it begins with a letter. The last line in this example shows a paragraph marked by <P> and </P> tags, and the second line shows a CSS rule that will make its text (and all other paragraph text) green:

```
<style>
 P {color: green; }
</style>
</head>
<body>
<p>This text would be green.</p>
```

Type selectors, like HTML tags, aren't case sensitive.

- **Class Selectors** aren't tied to specific HTML tags; you can apply a class to any tag you want by coding CLASS=*selector* within the tag. The following style sheet defines a class selector named *.panic,* and the subsequent HTML applies this class to one paragraph. CSS knows the selector is a class because its name begins with a period. You must omit the period when using the class, though (that is, when coding the CLASS= attribute within an HTML tag), as shown in the last line of the example:

```
<style>
 .panic {color: red; }
</style>
</head>
<body>
<p class="panic">Watch out!</p>
```

This example defines a class called *.panic* with one property, *color: red*. Coding CLASS="panic" within a <P> tag makes all text in that paragraph red. We could code CLASS="panic" within any tags we wanted, <P> or not, and all text under control of those tags would be red.

The CSS specification is unclear as to the case sensitivity of class selectors. Therefore, you should always use consistent case when defining and using class selectors.

- **ID Selectors** define properties for individual elements on the page. The selector name begins with a pound sign when you define the style rule, but not when you define the ID. In the following example, the attribute ID="tulip" identifies the paragraph on the last line, and the selector defined on line two specifies CSS properties for that paragraph:

```
<style>
 #tulip {color: yellow; }
</style>
</head>
<body>
<p id="tulip">Here's tiptoeing to you!</p>
```

As with class selectors, it's best to assume IDs and ID selectors are case sensitive.

I give it a 73.2 percent probability that you're confused about the difference between class selectors and ID selectors. Well:

- **A type selector** is the name of an HTML tag. If you code a CSS rule with a type selector as its name, the rule will affect all content governed by the corresponding tag. The rule *P { color: green: }* makes any text between the <P> and </P> tags green.

- **A class selector** is the name of a style. Any number of page elements, such as paragraphs, can refer to the class and thereby take on its appearance. The rule *.panic {color: red; }* applies to any tag containing a STYLE="panic" attribute.

- **An ID** is the name of one specific page element, and an ID selector supplies CSS properties for that one element. You can't give two different elements (paragraphs, images, hyperlinks, whatever) the same ID without wreaking major havoc. The rule *#tulip {color: yellow; }* applies to the one tag containing an ID="tulip" attribute.

Hyperlinks: For more information about Cascading Style Sheets, browse these Web sites:

Microsoft:
http://www.microsoft.com/workshop/author/default.asp

World Wide Web Consortium:
http://www.w3.org/Style/

An Incredibly Brief Introduction to Cascading Style Sheets *(continued)*

There are several additional kinds of selectors: Combined, Contextual, Pseudo-Class, and Pseudo Element. These are beyond the scope of this book, but you can look them up on the Web. Check out the margin note for hyperlink locations.

TABLE 1-1. Common CSS Properties

Property	Description	Typical Values
font-family	The font used for displaying text.	*Arial, sans-serif*
font-size	The size in which text will appear.	*24pt*
font-style	A style variant applied to the font: normal, italic, or oblique.	*italic*
font-weight	The stroke weight for displaying the font. This can be either a number between 0 and 999 or the keyword *lighter, normal, bold,* or *bolder.* 400=normal and 700=bold.	*bold*
color	The foreground (text) color or an object. The following forms are equivalent: *rgb(255,204,204), #ffcccc,* and *#fcc.* Certain names like black, white, and red are also acceptable.	*rgb(255,204,204)*
background-color	The background color of an object.	*#FFFFCC*
margin	Space reserved between an object's contents and its border.	*3px*
border-width	The width of an object's border. If zero, no border is visible.	*1px*
border-style	The type of border that should surround an object. Can be none, dotted, dashed, solid, double, groove, ridge, inset, or outset.	*solid*
padding	Space reserved between an object's border and other objects.	*4px*

Tip: Style sheet property names aren't case sensitive. However, it's best to assume that property values, such as font names, are case sensitive.

 Tip: Although Internet Explorer seems to have an occasional problem with cascading styles, Netscape seems to have more. You'll generally find that Netscape requires you to specify styles in more places, and more specifically, than does Internet Explorer.

An Incredibly Brief Introduction to Cascading Style Sheets *(continued)*

To assign a CSS property, type the property name, a colon, the value you want, and then a semicolon. You can repeat this pattern for as many properties as you want.

Table 1-1 lists a few of the most common CSS properties. Complete descriptions of all CSS properties are clearly beyond our scope; there are dozens of properties, hundreds of possible values, and a myriad of lurking restrictions, caveats, and downright gotchas. This book is chock full with examples, though, and using CSS properties really isn't hard once you get the mindset. You can get more information from any number of reference books, or from the Web locations noted on page 34.

Containers, Inheritance, Parentage, and Style Sheets

The cascading aspect of Cascading Style Sheets refers to the way CSS properties are over-ridden (often several times) on their way from browser defaults to on-screen display. For example:

- The browser initializes styles for the <H1> tag.

- One or more rules in <STYLE>...</STYLE> sections could easily override that appearance.

- A particular <H1> tag could inherit more properties from an HTML container—a <BODY>, <DIV>, <SPAN>, or <TABLE> tag, for example.

- Individual <H1> tags can include CLASS= and STYLE= attributes that override the same or different properties.

Inheritance occurs on a property-by-property basis. This means that no matter where (or how often) an override occurs, only the properties you discretely specify will change. Consider:

```
<style>
 H1 { font-size: 20pt; font-family: Arial; }
 H1 { font-size: 24pt; color: rgb(0,102,0); }
</style>
```

Coding two rules for the same selector is no error; it merely results in two overrides. The first rule overrides the *font-size* and *font-family* properties, while the second overrides *font-size* and *color*. The result, by the way, will be 24 point dark green Arial.

Style sheets make special use of the *container* concept. The body of a Web page is the largest container, but other containers may be nested within it: areas enclosed by <DIV> and </DIV> or <SPAN> and </SPAN> tags, for example. Tables and rows can also be containers.

Here's another example of style sheet cascading:

```
<div style="font-family: sans-serif; color: green">
  This text will be sans serif green.
  <span style="color: red">
    This text will be sans serif red.
  </span>
This text will be sans serif green.
</div>
```

The STYLE= attribute in the <DIV> tag makes the entire division green sans serif type. The STYLE= attribute in the <SPAN> tag overrides the *color* property but not the *font-family*. The <SPAN>…</SPAN> area inherits its *font-family* property from the <DIV>…</DIV> tags that contain it.

Unfortunately, what's considered a container it isn't always obvious or well documented, particularly with regard to pre-CSS elements like tables and forms. Furthermore, it varies from browser to browser. Be prepared to experiment; grin, and bear it.

Tip: Is <G> the HTML tag for grin? No browser to date supports this function; instead, each user must supply the function manually. (OK, facially, but why quibble?)

SWAT Team Pest Control

Figure 1-4 features another example of page layout using tables. This Web page uses two tables: a two-by-two table provides margins and frames the detail area, and a four-row by two-column table presents the detail information.

Page Layout Details

Note the interesting contrast between the diagonally opposed dark and light area; on a color monitor, these are light and dark shades of roughly the same hue

FIGURE 1-4. *In this page, a two-by-two table provides the top and left border. A four-row, two-column table lays out the detail.*

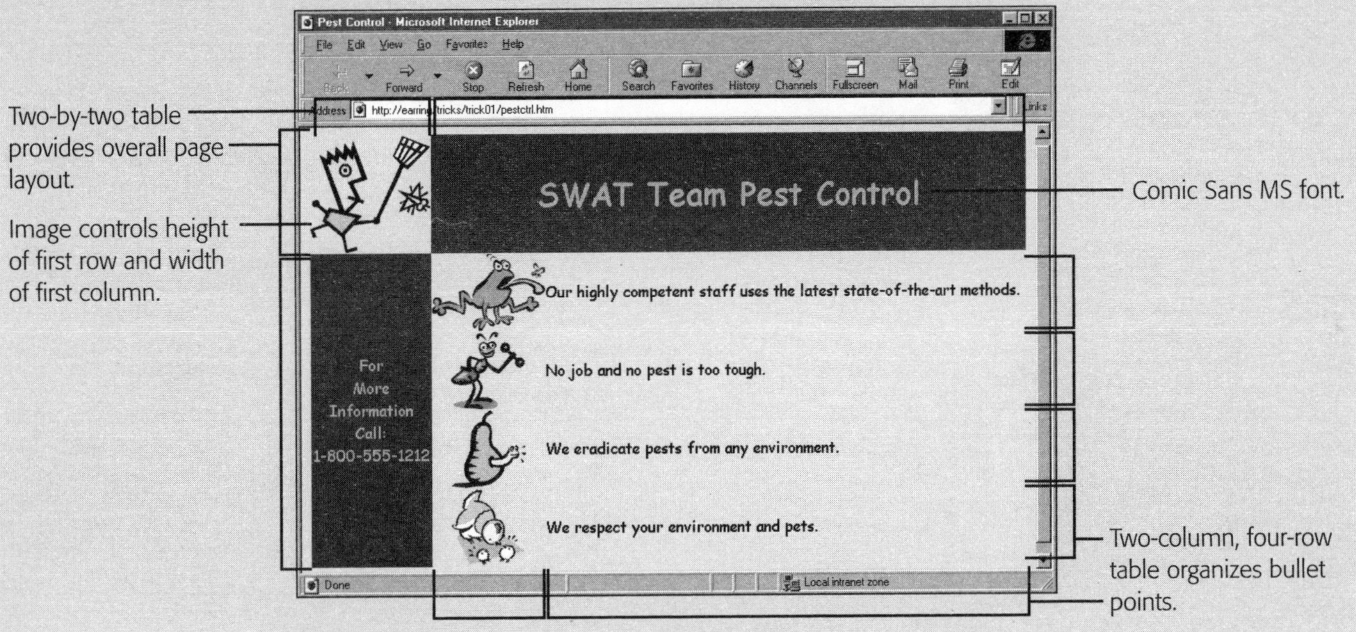

Two-by-two table provides overall page layout.

Image controls height of first row and width of first column.

Comic Sans MS font.

Two-column, four-row table organizes bullet points.

(green). The graphic in the top-left corner not only provides interest, but also sets lower bounds on the height of row 1 and the width of column 1. The cell that contains the *SWAT Team Pest Control* heading has a width of 99 percent, which makes the entire right column as wide as possible.

Using a second table for the detail text has two benefits. First, all the text lines up at the same left margin position, even though the various images have slightly different widths. Second, if the Web visitor narrows the window so much that the text wraps to multiple lines, the text will always wrap to the same margin, and never under the corresponding image.

Style Sheet Usage

Once again the style sheet consists of a single rule:

```
TD { font-family: Comic Sans MS, sans-serif }
```

This sets the default font for table details to Comic Sans MS or, if that isn't available, to the browser's default sans serif font. Whenever you call for a font by name, it's a good idea to specify a generic font as well. After all, it's quite likely that at least some Web visitors won't have the same fonts on their system that you have on yours. Table 1-2 lists the generic fonts defined within CSS.

TABLE 1-2. Generic CSS Font Families.		
font-family	**Description**	**Example**
serif	A normal text font with serifs	Times New Roman
sans-serif	A normal text font with no serifs	Arial
monospace	A font where all the characters have the same width	Courier New
cursive	A font that resembles handwriting	French Script MT
fantasy	An extremely decorative font	Braggadocio

Complete HTML Listing

Here's the HTML that produces the SWAT Team Pest Control page:

```
<html>
<head>
<title>Pest Control</title>
<style>
<!--
TD { font-family: Comic Sans MS, sans-serif }
-->
</style>
</head>
```

Defines style sheet for this page.

Continued from previous page

Start of outer table. ——

The *width=99%* setting makes the
right column as wide as possible. The
bgcolor setting makes the cell's
background dark green.

Start of Detail Information table. ——

```html
<body bgcolor="#CCFFCC">
<table border="0" cellpadding="0" cellspacing="0" width="100%">
<tr>
  <td><img src="../images/flychase.gif"
          alt="SWAT Team Pest Control"
          width="126" height="121"></td>
  <td width="99%" bgcolor="#006600" align="center">
      <font size="6" color="#66FF66"><strong>
      SWAT Team Pest Control</strong></td>
</tr>
<tr>
  <td bgcolor="#006600" valign="middle" align="center">
      <font color="#66FF66">
      For<br>
      More<br>
      Information<br>
      Call:<br>
      1-800-555-1212</td>
  <td>
    <table border="0" cellpadding="0" cellspacing="0">
      <tr>
        <td align="center"><img src="../images/frog4.gif"
            alt="Our Staff" width="119" height="80"></td>
        <td>Our highly competent staff uses the
            latest state-of-the-art methods.</td>
      </tr>
      <tr>
        <td align="center"><img src="../images/ant1.gif"
            alt="Tough Bug" width="78" height="80"></td>
        <td>No job and no pest is too tough.</td>
      </tr>
      <tr>
        <td align="center"><img src="../images/pearworm.gif"
            alt="Go Anywhere" width="79" height="80"></td>
        <td>We eradicate pests from any environment.</td>
      </tr>
```

Trick 1

Designing with Grids and Styles   **39**

Continued from previous page

```
       <tr>
         <td align="center"><img src="../images/chicks.gif"
            alt="Respect Environment"
            width="78" height="80"></td>
         <td>We respect your environment and pets.</td>
       </tr>
```

End of Detail Information table. ⟶ `    </table>`

```
     </td>
   </tr>
```

End of outer table. ⟶ `   </table>`

```
   </body>
   </html>
```

You should consider using a grid for every Web page you plan. The proof is all around you: newspapers, magazines, brochures, posters, even this book. Grid layouts are the basis for professional page designs of all kinds. Put the most important topics at the top; align body text flush left; line up similar items similarly and dissimilar items differently; and balance the right side of the page with the left.

Typography is another major graphic design tool, and Cascading Style Sheets bring it to the Web in a major way. Style sheets separate format from content, making both easier to read during page construction. Applying styles by reference guarantees again that similar items look alike.

Creating all these tables is fine, but sometimes, especially for lengthy displays of data, it's easier to create tables with programming than by hand. This is the innocent, unsuspecting subject of the next trick.

Generating Tables Dynamically

U sing tables for Web page layout can produce quite a rush—well, my pulse quickens, anyway—but using tables to display rows and columns of data remains one of their first and best uses. This is the aspect of tables we'll examine in this chapter.

The tricky part about our examples is that, when we create the page, we won't know how many items the tables will contain. So we'll have to write simple program code that custom-generates and fills the correct number of rows on the fly.

We'll also take a first look at the kinds of information you, or anyone else on the Internet, can surreptitiously learn about Web visitors. Both of these topics will be very useful in later tricks. Trust me on this; I have an inside informant named Boris.

The Bitwise Psychic Hotline

The Web page in Figure 2-1 displays the properties of three useful browser objects. These are:

- *Navigator*—an object that describes the current browser software
- *Window*—an object that controls the current browser window
- *Document*—an object that contains the Web page currently on display

Knowing something about the *navigator, window,* and *document* objects will come in handy for some of the tricks later in this book. For now, though, we're only looking to see what information's available—just browsing, so to speak.

FIGURE 2-1. *This Web page shows information about the current browser (navigator), the current browser window, and the current document on display. The window and document information are out of view.*

A browser script writes a variable number of table rows depending on the number of available properties.

These are typical values for Internet Explorer.

Bitwise Psychic Hotline - Microsoft Internet Explorer

File   Edit   View   Go   Favorites   Help

Back   Forward   Stop   Refresh   Home   Search   Favorites   History   Channels   Fullscreen   Mail   Print   Edit

Back to Stupid Web Tricks

Address   http://www.interlacken.com/tricks/trick02/bitprops.htm   Links

The Bitwise   Psychic Hotline

The JavaScript Master divines the following information about your visitation.

navigator Properties:

Property	Value
userAgent	Mozilla/4.0 (compatible; MSIE 4.0; Windows 95)
userLanguage	en-us
userProfile	undefined
appCodeName	Mozilla
appMinorVersion	0
appName	Microsoft Internet Explorer
appVersion	4.0 (compatible; MSIE 4.0; Windows 95)
cookieEnabled	true
cpuClass	x86

Done   Internet zone

What This Page Does

Tip: Programmers at Netscape invented the navigator object to describe and control their browser—Netscape Navigator. To provide Netscape compatibility, all browsers now support this object and—again in the spirit of compatibility—they all call it *navigator*.

Only a portion of the *navigator* object is visible in Figure 2-1; to see the entire listing for all three objects, load the *bitprops.htm* page into your browser directly from the accompanying CD, from a copy on your hard disk, or from your Web server, and then scroll down. The figure shows Internet Explorer displaying the page.

Figure 2-2 shows Netscape Navigator displaying the same Web page (see Trick 3 if you're curious about the Mozilla moniker). For each of the three objects, Netscape provides different properties and, even for like properties, different values. If this seems less than convenient, you win the astuteness award of the day. Buy yourself a cup of coffee at the regular price.

FIGURE 2-2. *This is the same Web page shown in Figure 2-1, this time displayed by Netscape Navigator. Note the different number of properties, the different property names, and the different property values.*

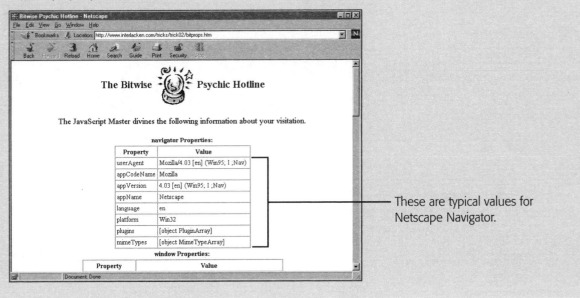

These are typical values for Netscape Navigator.

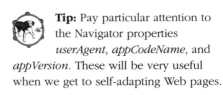 **Tip:** Pay particular attention to the Navigator properties *userAgent, appCodeName,* and *appVersion.* These will be very useful when we get to self-adapting Web pages.

 Note: A browser's Document Object Model describes how the browser internally stores information about itself and the current Web page.

You may also wonder why Internet Explorer and Netscape Navigator display different results from the same HTML file, and then how the same table can have a different number of rows. The answers lie in the Document Object Model for each browser and two special JavaScript statements.

Scripting Techniques

HTML is a *page description* language; it describes how the page should look. However, you can't program *if-then-else* statements, loops, or most real-time actions in HTML.

In a general sense, scripting refers to a crude but effective programming language used in concert with an application. For Web pages, JavaScript is the most common scripting language.

Trick 2

Note: Script languages are usually a bit more capable, more flexible, and more program-like than macros, but they're far less rigorous than formal languages like C and Pascal. Most script languages require no compilation; instead, a run-time interpreter compiles and executes source code at run time.

Browser Scripting Languages

Netscape Navigator was the first browser to provide a scripting language, which Netscape called JavaScript. This language really doesn't have much to do with Java, though; the differences are many and major. Choosing the name JavaScript was more an accident of timing and marketing spin than of technology.

Internet Explorer supports two scripting languages: JScript and VBScript. JScript is essentially JavaScript. VBScript is a derivative of Visual Basic.

Because Netscape Navigator doesn't support VBScript, JavaScript is the language of choice for most browser scripting.

The code for adding a script to a Web page looks like this.

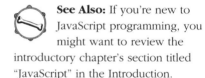

Your script goes here.

```
<script language="JavaScript">
<!--

// -->
</script>
```

The <SCRIPT> and </SCRIPT> tags mark the beginning and end of the script. LANGUAGE="JavaScript" is the default; if you omit it, the browser assumes JavaScript. For VBScript you would specify LANGUAGE="VBScript"; no great surprise here, right?

Stripped to its barest essentially, the JavaScript code we need for this trick is:

```
for (props in navigator){
    document.write (props + "=" + navigator[props] + "<br>");
    }
}
```

See Also: If you're new to JavaScript programming, you might want to review the introductory chapter's section titled "JavaScript" in the Introduction.

Hyperlinks: If you want to get down and dirty writing hard-core JavaScript code, you can either settle down with a couple of good books or consult the following Web sites:

Microsoft:
http://www.microsoft.com/jscript

Netscape:
http://developer.netscape.com/library/ documentation/communicator

Navigator, you probably recall, is one of the objects whose properties we're trying to examine. The *for...in* statement runs a loop once for each element in an array or collection—in this case once for every property of the *navigator* object. Curly braces "{}" mark the beginning and end of the loop. The *props* variable receives the current property name for each execution of the loop. There's nothing special about the name *props*; we could have called this variable *thingie, gadget,* or anything else that seemed amusing (or not).

Tip: The *for...in* loop only works with the 4.0 versions (or above) of Internet Explorer and Netscape Navigator.

Note: Remember, *document.write* works only *while the Web page is loading*. Once the page is on display, you can't document.write more HTML into it.

See Also: Trick 14, "Interacting with Tables," shows how to modify tables already on display.

The *document.write* statement writes HTML into the Web page as if you had coded it by hand. Wherever the script appears in the HTML code, your visitor will see output produced by your *document.write* statements. In the preceding example, we're writing the property name, an equal sign, the property value, and a line break tag into the HTML.

With only slight embellishment, the same loop can generate a variable number of table rows. All we need to do is change the *document.write* statement to:

```
document.write ("<tr>");
document.write ("<td>" + props + "</td>");
document.write ("<td>" + navigator[props] & " </td>");
document.write ("</tr>");
```

This could easily have been one long statement instead of four short ones; I used four statements only for clarity.

The * * code in line 3 tells the browser to display a nonbreaking space; a space the browser isn't allowed to suppress. In this case, it ensures that every cell of the generated table has at least *some* content. Some browsers don't display cell borders for empty cells, giving the table a non-uniform appearance. The answer is to buy insurance (using the * * code) against empty cells.

To add one last complication, let's list the properties of the *navigator* object out of sequence. The *userAgent*, *appName*, and *appVersion* properties are particularly interesting (well, they quicken *my* pulse), so let's list all properties beginning with *use* first, then all those beginning with *app*, and then all the others. Here's the code to list all the *use* properties:

```
for (props in navigator){
  if (props.substring(0,3) == "use"){
    document.write ("<tr>");
    document.write ("<td>" + props + "</td>");
    document.write ("<td>" + navigator[props] & " </td>");
    document.write ("</tr>");
  }
}
```

The expression *props.substring(0,3)* extracts three characters, starting at position zero, from the value of *props*. Position zero is the first character; position

Tip: The values returned by *for (props in navigator)* appear in the Property column under *navigator* Properties.

Tip: Don't count on JavaScript to treat the end of a line as the end of a statement; always end your statements with a semicolon. However, statement blocks enclosed in curly braces don't need an ending semicolon.

Note: One of the most common mistakes of JavaScript programming is using a single equal sign for comparisons. The expression *if (A = B)* copies the value of *B* to *A*, returning *true* if the operation worked.

one is the second character, and so forth. Don't yell at me; this wasn't my decision. I don't know who decided one was zero, but I often wonder if they give away one dollar bills for nothing. Oh well.

Note the general form of the *if* statement, illustrated below. The condition appears within parentheses, while curly braces group statements appearing before and after the *else*. Table 2-1 lists the permissible relational operators.

```
if (condition) {
    block of statements
} else {
    different block of statements
}
```

TABLE 2-1. JavaScript Relational Operators.

Operator	Description
==	Equal
!=	Not equal
<	Less than
<=	Less than or equal
>	Greater than
>=	Greater than or equal
&&	And
||	Or

Complete HTML Listing

Here's the complete HTML listing for the Bitwise Psychic Hotline page:

```
<html>
<head>
<title>Bitwise Psychic Hotline</title>
</head>
```

Continued from previous page

```
<body>
<p align="center"><strong><font size="5">The Bitwise
<img src="../images/crystbal.gif"
     alt="Crystal Ball" align="absmiddle"
     width="89" height="91">
Psychic Hotline</font></strong></p>
<p align="center"><font size="4">
The JavaScript Master divines the following
information about your visitation.</font></p>
<div align="center"><center>
<table border="1" cellpadding="3" cellspacing="0">
<caption><strong>navigator Properties:</strong></caption>
<tr>
  <th>Property</th>
  <th>Value</th>
</tr>
<script language="JavaScript">
<!--
for (props in navigator){
  if (props.substring(0,3) == "use"){
    document.write ("<tr><td>" + props + "</td><td>");
    document.write (navigator[props]);
    document.write (" </td></tr>");
  }
}
for (props in navigator){
  if (props.substring(0,3) == "app"){
    document.write ("<tr><td>" + props + "</td><td>");
    document.write (navigator[props]);
    document.write (" </td></tr>");
  }
}
for (props in navigator){
  if ((props.substring(0,3) != "app") &&
      (props.substring(0,3) != "use")){
```

Display heading.

Heading for *Navigator* table.

Start *Navigator* script.

Display Navigator properties beginning with "use".

Display *Navigator* properties beginning with "app".

Display *Navigator* properties not beginning with "use" or "app".

Trick 2

Generating Tables Dynamically   **47**

Continued from previous page

```
    document.write ("<tr><td>" + props + "</td><td>");
    document.write (navigator[props]);
    document.write (" </td></tr>");
    }
  }
  // -->
</script>
</table>
</center></div>
<div align="center"><center>
<table border="1" cellpadding="3" cellspacing="0">
<caption><strong>window Properties:</strong></caption>
<tr>
  <th>Property</th>
  <th>Value</th>
</tr>
<script language="JavaScript">
<!--
for (props in window){
  document.write ("<tr><td>" + props + "</td><td>");
  document.write (window[props]);
  document.write (" </td></tr>");
}
// -->
</script>
</table>
</center></div>
<div align="center"><center>
<table border="1" cellpadding="3" cellspacing="0">
<caption><strong>document Properties:</strong></caption>
<tr>
  <th>Property</th>
  <th>Value</th>
</tr>
<script language="JavaScript">
```

End of Navigator script.

Heading for Window table.

Start of Window script.

End of Window script.

Heading for Document table.

Start of Document script.

Continued from previous page

```
<!--
for (props in document){
  document.write ("<tr><td>" + props + "</td><td>");
  document.write (document[props]);
  document.write (" </td></tr>");
}
// -->
</script>
</table>
</center></div>
</body>
</html>
```

End of Document script.

This example showed how to use variable-length tables, a great way to present repeating data when you don't know ahead of time how often the data will repeat. Along the way we also learned about the *navigator, window,* and *document* objects, which provide scripts with valuable information about the browser environment they're running in. Finally, we looked at our first browser-side script, learned something about JavaScript syntax, used the *for...in* construct and the *document.write* statement, and learned how to incorporate JavaScript into HTML. Is that gnarly or what?

Little Egypt ASP Information Pit

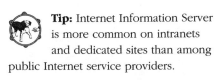

Tip: Internet Information Server is more common on intranets and dedicated sites than among public Internet service providers.

If your Web server is Microsoft Internet Information Server version 3.0 or above, you can use Active Server Pages to program variable-length tables at the server. That is, you can have the Web server, rather than the browser, create customized on-the-fly HTML. This is very handy if the multiple rows of data are coming from something on the server—a file or a database, for example.

An Active Server Page strongly resembles an ordinary Web page, except that it has one or more sections of VBScript designated with <%...%> tags. These tags identify the code that will execute on the server. Neither the <%...%> tags nor

Trick 2

See Also: For an example of server-side scripting that doesn't require Internet Information Server, skip ahead to the third part of this trick, "Perl Transaction Values."

 Note: Actually, you can write ASP scripts in any language installed on the Web server for that purpose. VBScript, however, is by far the most common. To use JavaScript, for example, you would code <SCRIPT LANGUAGE= "JScript" RUNAT="SERVER">, then the script, then a closing </SCRIPT> tag.

 See Also: For a further introduction to Active Server Pages, refer to the section by that title in the Introduction.

 Note: Just as browsers have a wealth of information they don't normally transmit to servers, servers have large amounts of information they don't normally send to browsers. Aside from privacy and security issues, the volume of data in both directions would simply be too great. To obtain browser-side data, write a browser-side script. To obtain server-side data, write a server-side script.

the VBScript code get transmitted to the browser, but the result *of executing* the VBScript code *does* get transmitted. Here's a rather boring piece of ASP code:

```
<% = "Boar."%>
<% = "Ring."%>
```

ASP interprets any line of code beginning with an equal sign as data it should write to the browser. You can enclose each line of VBScript code in <%...%> tags, as shown above, or enclose an entire block of code in one pair of tags. The following code is exactly equivalent to the first example:

```
<% = "Boar."
   = "Ring."%>
```

Figure 2-3 shows an Active Server Page displayed by a browser. Note the filename extension .asp in the URL. This page displays information obtained in real time from the server, much of which isn't available any other way to the browser.

Running and Viewing Active Server Pages

If you try browsing the *egyprop.asp* page directly from the accompanying CD, or from a file copied to your hard disk, what you get won't look anything like Figure 2-3. The figure shows output from a program that can only execute on a Web server. The requirements for running an Active Server Page are:

- It must reside on a Web server running Microsoft Internet Information Server, version 3.0 or above. (Equivalent personal Web servers are available for Windows 95 and Windows NT Workstation.)

- It must have a filename extension of .asp.

- It must reside in a folder designated for running scripts.

An ASP script requires nothing special on the browser assuming, of course, that the script produces correct HTML. A wonderful advantage of server-side scripting is that your script only needs to run in one environment—the server's—and not on fifty jillion browser versions.

FIGURE 2-3. *This table was generated by VBScript code embedded in the HTML and executed on the Web server.*

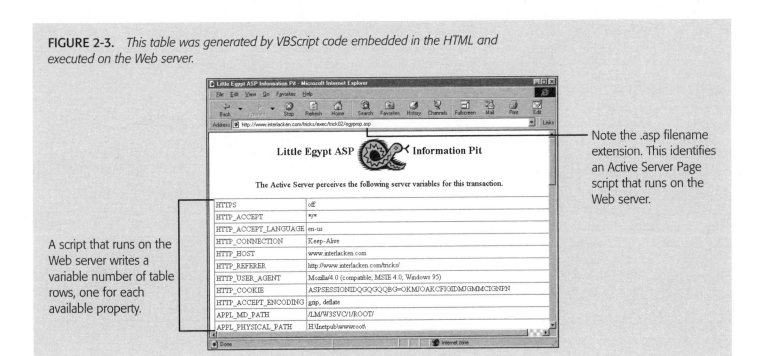

Note the .asp filename extension. This identifies an Active Server Page script that runs on the Web server.

A script that runs on the Web server writes a variable number of table rows, one for each available property.

Tip: Note the similarity between the HTTP_USER_AGENT field on this page and the *userAgent* field in Figure 2-1. This must be an interesting morsel of information because it keeps showing up everywhere, eh? We'll examine the *userAgent* field more closely in Trick 3.

Scripting Techniques

The information we'll display in this example is part of the *Request* object: specifically, a collection called ServerValues. This collection provides a variety of information about the browser, the server, and the remote user's request. The loop to dump the entire collection looks like this:

```
<% for each key in Request.ServerVariables %>
<% val = Request.ServerVariables(key)      %>
<tr>
<td valign="top"><% =key %></td>
<td valign="top"><% =val %>  </td>
</tr>
<% next                                    %>
```

Note: Because ASP scripts consume more of the Web server's CPU time than ordinary pages, and because a badly written ASP script can do much more damage than the worst possible HTML file, Webmasters usually control script folders more tightly than ordinary Web page folders. If you want to run ASP scripts, you may have to contact your Webmaster for access.

 Hyperlinks: To obtain ASP-capable Web servers for Windows NT Server, Windows NT Workstation, or Windows 95, browse:

http://www.microsoft.com/iis

For more information about Active Server pages, consult the "Scripters Reference" section at:

http://www.microsoft.com/iis/Support/ iishelp/iis/misc/documentation.asp

For more information about VBScript, browse:

http://www.microsoft.com/vbscript/

Note the Visual Basic syntax: there are no semicolons at the ends of lines and no curly braces to denote blocks. The *next* statement terminates the range of the *for each* loop. In lines 4 and 5, the VBScript portion occupies only part of the line.

As with the browser's *navigator* object, some elements in the *Request.Server Variables* collection are more interesting than others. In order, we'll display:

- Those whose names begin with HTTP.

- Those whose names begin with something other than ALL and HTTP, and which have non-empty values.

- Those whose names begin with ALL.

- Those whose names begin with something other than ALL and HTTP, and which have empty values.

To filter each group requires code such as the following:

```
<% for each key in Request.ServerVariables         %>
<% val = Request.ServerVariables(key)              %>
<% if ((left(key,4) = "HTTP") and (val <> "")) then %>
  <tr>
    <td valign="top"><% =key %></td>
    <td valign="top"><% =val & " "%></td>
  </tr>
<% end if                                          %>
<% next                                            %>
```

Note the *if* in line 3 and the *end if* in line 8. The *for each* loop repeats the lines between these statements (provided the *if* statement is true) even though they don't appear within <%...%> tags. The *end if* statement terminates the *if* statement just as the *next* statement terminates the *for each*.

Complete HTML Listing

Here's the complete HTML listing for the Little Egypt ASP Information Pit page:

Display page heading.

Display non-blank HTTP variables.

Display non-blank, non-ALL variables.

```html
<html>
<head>
<title>Little Egypt ASP Information Pit</title>
</head>
<body>
<p align="center"><strong><font size="5">
Little Egypt ASP
<img src="../../images/snakcoil.gif"
     alt="Snake Coil" align="middle"
     width="121" height="72">
Information Pit</font></strong></p>
<p align="center"><font size="4">
The Active Server perceives the following
server variables for this transaction.</font></p>
<table border="1" cellpadding="3" cellspacing="0">
<% for each key in Request.ServerVariables        %>
<% val = Request.ServerVariables(key)             %>
<% if ((left(key,4) = "HTTP") and (val <> "")) then %>
  <tr>
    <td valign="top"><% =key %>
</td>
    <td valign="top"><% =val & " "%>
</td>
  </tr>
<% end if                                         %>
<% next                                           %>
<% for each key in Request.ServerVariables        %>
<% val = Request.ServerVariables(key)             %>
<% if ((left(key,3) <> "ALL") and _               %>
<%      (left(key,4) <> "HTTP") and _             %>
<%      (val <> "")) then                         %>
  <tr>
    <td valign="top"><% =key %>
</td>
    <td valign="top"><% =val & " "%>
```

Continued from previous page

```
</td>
  </tr>
<% end if                                                   %>
<% next                                                     %>

<% for each key in Request.ServerVariables                  %>
<% val = Request.ServerVariables(key)                       %>
<% if (left(key,3) = "ALL") then %>
  <tr>
    <td valign="top"><% =key %>
</td>
    <td valign="top"><% =val & " "%>
</td>
  </tr>
<% end if                                                   %>
<% next                                                     %>

<% for each key in Request.ServerVariables                  %>
<% val = Request.ServerVariables(key)                       %>
<% if ((left(key,3) <> "ALL") and (val = "")) then   %>
  <tr>
    <td valign="top"><% =key %>
</td>
    <td valign="top"><% =val & " "%>
</td>
  </tr>
<% end if                                                   %>
<% next                                                     %>
</table>
</body>
</html>
```

Display ALL variables.

Display blank, non-ALL variables.

That's all there is to generating variable-length on-the-fly tables using ASP.

Perl Transaction Values

Server-side scripting is such a proven and popular technique that it's available in some form on virtually all Web servers. The most widely supported language is called Perl.

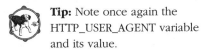

Tip: Note once again the HTTP_USER_AGENT variable and its value.

Perl was originally developed for generating reports on UNIX-based computers. On a Web server, Perl programs use an interface called CGI—Common Gateway Interface. The Web server pipes input data, such as form fields, into the Perl program's standard input. The server also, in a series of environment

FIGURE 2-4. *This Web page comes from a Perl program that runs on the Web server and creates HTML on the fly. Note the filename extension .pl in the URL.*

A Perl program that runs on the Web server writes a variable number of table rows.

You can tell that a Perl program created this page from the filename extension.

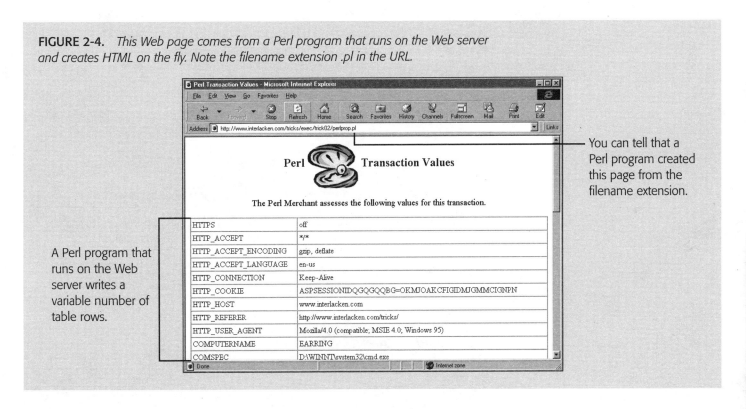

Trick 2

Note: If you're a Windows user, standard input, standard output, and environment variables may seem like carryovers from the glory (or gory) days of the MS-DOS prompt. Nevertheless, UNIX systems used these concepts long before there was such a thing as MS-DOS, and continue to use them heavily today.

variables, supplies various information about the remote browser and the local Web server. The Perl program writes HTML to standard output, which the Web server intercepts and sends to the remote user.

Scripting Techniques

Perl sees the data we want to display as a table called *%ENV*. The following code dumps this table as rows in an HTML table:

```
for $key (sort keys %ENV) {
    print "<tr><td>$key</td><td>$ENV{$key}</td></tr>\n";
}
```

This takes all the keys in the *%ENV* array, sorts them, and then runs a block of statements once for each key. Note that *%ENV* and *$ENV{$key}* refer to the same table in different ways:

- *%ENV* refers to the entire table, without regard to individual entries or keys.

- *$ENV{$key}* refers to the value of one entry in *%ENV*—the entry whose key is the value in the variable *$key*.

Table 2-2 explains these variable name prefixes a little more.

TABLE 2-2.	Prefixes for Variable Names in Perl.	
Operator	**Type**	**Description**
$	Scalar	A variable containing a single value
@	Array	A series of values indexed numerically.
%	Associative Array	A series of values indexed by an arbitrary key.

An Introduction to Perl Syntax

Here are a few tips to help you get started with the syntax of Perl:

- Perl statements end with a semicolon. Forgetting the semicolon is the number one cause of Perl errors.

- As in JavaScript, curly braces "{ }" denote blocks.

- An equal sign ("=") assigns a value.

- Two equal signs ("==") compare two values numerically. The same is true for "!=", ">", "<=", and so forth. Coding comparisons with a single equal sign is the number two source of Perl problems.

- Alphabetic operators like *eq* compare two values as strings. The same is true for *ne*, *gt*, *le*, and so forth. Comparing string values with "==" is the third most popular cause of Perl problems.

- Perl has some extremely powerful and cryptic string matching functions. Consider each such line of code an adventure to be fully relished. The following code, for example, searches the variable *$fkey* for this pattern: a percent sign, then one of 22 characters (a, b, c, d, e, f, A, B, C, D, E, F, 0, 1, 2, 3, 4, 5, 6, 7, 8 ,9), then one of those same 22 characters again. For each such pattern found, it treats the second and third characters in the pattern as hex digits and converts the two-digit hex expression to the corresponding ASCII character.

```
$fkey =~ s/%([a-fA-F0-9][a-fA-F0-9])/pack("C", hex($1))/eg;
```

This example isn't as far-fetched as it might first appear. Percent sign, hex digit, hex digit is the convention used for putting normally prohibited characters in a URL. The statement above converts *%20* to a space, *%3F* to a question mark, and *%2F* to a slash, for example.

Complete Perl Listing

The Perl program that produced the Web page in Figure 2-4 follows. The most common statement by far is *print*, which writes to standard output. The string "\n" means new line. As before, we favor the HTTP keys by displaying them first. The expression:

```
(substr($key,0,4) eq "HTTP")
```

is true if the first four characters of $key are HTTP and false in any other case.

Trick 2

Print Content-type header and a blank line.

Start creating HTML.

```
print "Content-type: text/html\n";
print "\n";
print "<HTML>\n";
print "<HEAD>\n";
print "<TITLE>Perl Transaction Values</TITLE>";
print "</HEAD>\n";
print "<BODY>\n";
print "<p align=center><font size=5><strong>Perl ";
print "<img src=../../images/pearl.gif ";
print " width=105 height=91 align=middle>";
print " Transaction Values</strong></font></p>";
print "<p align=center><font size=4>";
print "The Perl Merchant assesses the following ";
print "values for this transaction.</font></p>";
print "<table BORDER=1 cellspacing=0 cellpadding=3>\n";
```

Print *ENV* entries whose keys begin with HTTP.

```
for $key (sort keys %ENV) {
  if (substr($key,0,4) eq "HTTP"){
    print "<tr><td>$key</td><td>$ENV{$key}</td></tr>\n";
  }
}
```

Print *ENV* entries whose keys don't begin with HTTP.

```
for $key (sort keys %ENV) {
  if (substr($key,0,4) ne "HTTP"){
    print "<tr><td>$key</td><td>$ENV{$key}</td></tr>\n";
  }
}
print "</table>\n";
print "</BODY>\n";
print "</HTML>\n";
```

Running Perl Programs via CGI

Perl programs, like Active Server Pages, must reside in an executable folder on your Web server. This means that to run them, you'll need a folder on the Web server marked *executable* by the administrator.

The Web server will also need to have a copy of Perl itself available; this is something the server's system administrator must install. On a Windows NT system, the administrator also needs to associate the .pl filename extension with the interpreter. On a UNIX system, you may need to identify the Perl interpreter by adding a special line to the top of each Perl program. That line will look something like this:

```
#!/usr/bin/perl
```

The Web pages in this trick change automatically every time a user requests them. This is quite a powerful concept, and what's more, the changing content certainly isn't limited to tables. By using *document.write* and additional techniques we'll discover throughout this book, the old, static Web page can become quite a flexible and interactive display. Let's motor.

Determining the Browser Version

Microsoft Internet Explorer and Netscape Navigator have different objects, properties, values, and capabilities, and this can be a real nuisance. It means Web pages you develop for Netscape Navigator may not work in Internet Explorer, and pages developed for Internet Explorer may not work in Netscape Navigator. To overcome this, you can either confine yourself to the limited set of features common to both browsers, or create pages that tailor themselves to whatever browser displays them. You'll probably use the second approach at least part of the time, and that means you'll need this trick.

Four examples will show how to obtain the current browser properties using JavaScript, Active Server Pages, and Perl. The point of these examples really isn't their visual appearance, although the first example is so simple that we'll spend some time juicing it up. Rather, we're concentrating on obtaining information we'll use in later tricks when different browsers require different code.

Your Browser Is...

For the first example of this trick, we'll build a Web page that uses JavaScript to detect and display the browser type—that is, its product name and version. As well you might suspect, the browser's name and version are properties of the *navigator* object. Some typical *navigator* property values appeared in Figure 2-1 and Figure 2-2, and they appear again in Table 3-1.

Browser	**TABLE 3-1.** Typical Values of the *navigator* Object.	
	navigator **Property**	
	appName	**appVersion**
Internet Explorer	Microsoft Internet Explorer	4.0 (compatible; MSIE 4.0; Windows 95)
Netscape Navigator	Netscape	4.03 [en] (Win95; I ;Nav)

In JavaScript, you can test the values of any object with code such as the following:

```
if (navigator.appName == "Microsoft Internet Explorer ") {
    document.write("This is IE.");
}
```

If you're not into typing long names like Microsoft Internet Explorer, you can shorten the comparison with code like this:

```
if (navigator.appName.substring(0,9) == "Microsoft") {
    document.write("This is IE.");
}else{
    if (navigator.appName == "Netscape") {
        document.write("This is Netscape.");
    }else{
        document.write("This is something else.");
    }
}
```

For most purposes, the entire *appVersion* string is too much of a good thing; all you need is the first number. JavaScript has a built-in function that does this—the *parseInt* function. Here's an example:

```
if (parseInt(navigator.appVersion) == 4){
    document.write("Version Four.");
}else{
    document.write("Some other version.");
}
```

A basic working example of these properties and functions involves little more than code than we've already seen. The resulting display is decidedly boring and mundane, though, so I've tricked up the typography a bit. The result appears in Figure 3-1 and Figure 3-2.

Style Sheet Usage

The HTML code that displays the text "Your Browser Is…" appears below. Note the STYLE= setting in the <P> tag; this supplies Cascading Style Sheet properties that apply to this paragraph only:

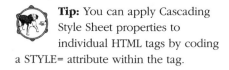

Tip: You can apply Cascading Style Sheet properties to individual HTML tags by coding a STYLE= attribute within the tag.

```
<p style="font-family: Verdana, sans-serif;">
<strong><font size="6"><em>
Your Browser Is...
</em></font></strong></p>
```

FIGURE 3-1. *This Web page determines and displays the browser version each time it's loaded.*

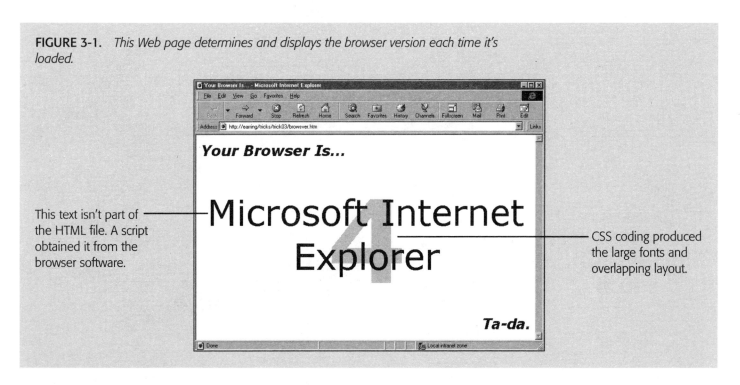

This text isn't part of the HTML file. A script obtained it from the browser software.

CSS coding produced the large fonts and overlapping layout.

FIGURE 3-2. *Here's exactly the same Web page shown in Figure 3-1, this time displayed by Netscape Navigator*

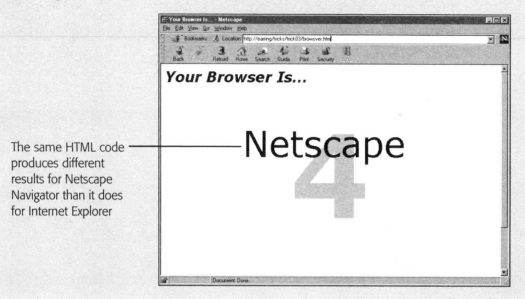

The same HTML code produces different results for Netscape Navigator than it does for Internet Explorer

 Tip: Browsers that don't support Cascading Style Sheets simply ignore them. The result is usually text displayed in the browser's normal font.

The <STRONG>, <FONT SIZE=>, and <EM> tags are traditional HTML. Traditional tags work with a wider range of browsers, but CSS properties are much more powerful and flexible. If you can't make up your mind which to use, you can always mix and match.

Weighing Markup Tags vs. CSS Properties

There are basically three alternatives for controlling typography in Web pages:

- Using traditional HTML tags like <FONT> for font, <B> for bold, <I> for italic, and so forth. Because these tags appeared long before CSS, many older browsers support them.

CSS Positioning

Here's the HTML code that writes the large version number shown in Figure 3-1 and Figure 3-2.

```
<div align="center"
     style="position: relative;
            font-family: Verdana, sans-serif;
            font-size: 190pt; font-weight: bold;
            color:#CCC;">
<script language="JavaScript">
<!--
document.write(parseInt(navigator.appVersion));
// -->
</script></div>
```

The <DIV>...</DIV> tags in the Your Browser Is page mark our first use of *CSS Positioning*.

The *position: relative* style setting (in the second line of code) tells the browser to position this division relative to the current screen location; that is, wherever it would normally appear. The *top* and *left* properties default to 0.

To display the browser's *navigator.appName* property on top of the version number, the HTML code specifies *position: absolute, align: center,* and *top: 120*. This centers the *navigator.appName* value on the displayed page, 120 pixels from the top. This code appears in the complete HTML listing.

An Incredibly Brief Introduction to CSS Positioning

CSS Positioning gives designers real control over the placement of content. This involves six key concepts:

- Two pairs of tags that specify the content to be positioned:

  - <DIV> and </DIV> mark everything between them as a block element—that is, as content that's preceded and followed by a line break.

  - <SPAN> and </SPAN> mark everything between them as an inline element—that is, as content that flows normally, as if the <SPAN> and </SPAN> tags weren't present.

- Two CSS properties that control placement of the positioned element:

  - The *top* property specifies the vertical distance between a starting point and the element's top edge. Positive values are below the starting point and negative values are above.

  - The *left* property specifies the horizontal distance between a starting point and the element's left edge. Positive values mean positions to the right of the starting point; negative values mean positions to the left. You can use any of the standard CSS units of measure: px for pixels, a percent sign for percentage of container width, and so forth.

- A position property that specifies the starting point for the top and left measurements:

  - If you specify position: absolute, the top and left measurements are relative to the upper-left corner of the element's container. (Unless the browser is IE and the <DIV> or <SPAN> lies within some other container, this will be the upper-left corner of the browser window.)

  - If you specify position: relative, the top and left measurements are relative to the top left corner of wherever the content would naturally appear.

- Two properties, height and width, that control the element's size.

  - If you don't specify these, the browser makes the element just large enough to display its contents.

See Also: Tricks 5, 6, and 10 show how to manipulate divisions and spans. For example, you can make them visible or invisible, move them around the page, and change their contents while displayed.

See Also: Tricks 5, 6, and 10

An Incredibly Brief Introduction to CSS Positioning *(continued)*

- If you specify a height or width that makes the element too small to display all its contents, the *overflow* property tells the browser what to do. With overflow: visible (the default), the excess contents spill outside the element's borders. With overflow: hidden, the excess contents don't appear at all. Specify overflow: auto to provide scroll bars that appear and disappear as needed, or overflow: scroll to provide scroll bars that are always visible.

- A *z-index* property that controls the ordering of overlapping elements. Given the ability to position things anywhere you want on a Web page, it's obviously possible to position two elements so they overlap. And you—control freak that you are—probably care which of them appears to be on top. If so, z-index is your tool. Elements with larger z-index values appear on top, those with smaller values appear beneath. Normal, unpositioned content has a z-index value of zero, by the way; elements with negative z-index values therefore appear behind normal content.

- A visibility property that controls whether the element appears at all. In IE, the permissible values are visible, hidden, and inherit. In Netscape, they're show, hide, and inherit. How convenient. The default is inherit, which means the element's visibility is the same as its container.

Complete HTML Listing

This example started off by demonstrating a simple way of getting two properties from the user's browser: its name and its version. Then it went crazy with CSS style and positioning statements to display those properties in an interesting way. Whether or not this Web page's appearance is worth all the extra work, at least we learned something.

Anyway, here's the complete HTML for the Your Browser Is page.

```
<html>
<head>
<title>Your Browser Is...</title>
</head>
```

Continued from previous page

```
<body>
<p style="font-family: Verdana, sans-serif;">
<strong><font size="6"><em>
Your Browser Is...
</em></font></strong></p>
```
Lay out text in upper-left corner.

```
<div align="center"
        style="position: relative;
                font-family: Verdana, sans-serif;
                font-size: 190pt; font-weight: bold;
                color:#CCC;">
<script language="JavaScript">
<!--
document.write(parseInt(navigator.appVersion));
// -->
</script></div>
```
Display browser version.

```
<div align="center"
        style="align: center;
                position: absolute; top:120;
                font-family: Verdana, sans-serif;
                font-size: 60pt;">
<script language="JavaScript">
<!--
document.write(navigator.appName);
// -->
</script>
</div>
```
Display browser name.

```
<p align="right"
style="font-family: Verdana, sans-serif;">
<strong><font size="6"><em>
Ta-da.
</em></font></strong></p>
</body>
</html>
```
Lay out text in lower-right corner.

Paranormal Browser Detection

The most detailed information about the browser version is the *navigator.user-Agent* property. The Paranormal Browser Detection Web page shows how to pick apart the fields within this property so you can examine them individually.

Here are a couple of typical *navigator.userAgent* values. The first is from Internet Explorer, the second from Netscape Navigator:

```
Mozilla/4.0 (compatible; MSIE 4.0; Windows 95)
Mozilla/4.03 [en] (Win95; I ;Nav)
```

There's useful information buried within these strings: the browser type, browser version, platform and, in the case of Netscape Navigator, the spoken language and processor type.

In case you're wondering, yes, most of this information is also available through properties of the *navigator* object; Table 3-2 provides the correspondence. Unfortunately, some of these properties are unavailable in some browser versions. Fortunately, almost every browser supports the *navigator.userAgent* property. Unfortunately, *userAgent* strings are messy to decode but we're tough and anyway, what glory is there in wimpy, simple examples?

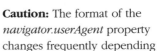 **Caution:** The format of the *navigator.userAgent* property changes frequently depending on the browser type, version, and platform. In almost every case, your code will be subject to fewer problems if you use specific *navigator* properties instead. If you really need information that's available only from *navigator.userAgent,* expect to fiddle with your decoding routine on a fairly regular basis.

TABLE 3-2. Comparing *navigator* Object Properties and *userAgent* Subfields.

Browser Characteristic	Internet Explorer 4		Netscape Navigator 4	
	navigator Property	Included in *userAgent*	*navigator* Property	Included in *userAgent*
Name	*appName*	Yes	*appName*	Yes
Version	*appVersion*	Yes	*appVersion*	Yes
Language	*userLangauge*	No	*language*	Yes
Platform	*platform*	Yes	*platform*	Yes
Processor	*cpuClass*	No	*N/A*	Yes

Scripting Techniques

Frankly, all the punctuation within the *userAgent* value bothers me. Code that depends on data with such complex punctuation tends to break following even minor version changes. Therefore, let's just erase all the punctuation and select the data we want by position. The following code, for example, changes all semicolons in the string variable *ua* to spaces:

```
while (ua.indexOf(";") >= 0) {
  ua = ua.replace(";"," ");
}
```

The first line uses the *indexOf* method to determine if the string has any semicolons. If so, *indexOf* returns the position of the first semicolon; if not, it returns *–1*. If there are semicolons, the second statement uses the *replace* method to replace the first one with a space. The *while* loop then continues until there are no more semicolons.

Regular Expressions in JavaScript

It's often quite handy to search for a pattern of characters rather than single, discrete values. You might, for example, want to replace any number of successive a's with a single z. Not only would *a9* become *z9*, but so would *aa9*, *aaa9*, and *aaaaaaa9*. The term for this is pattern matching—instead of testing whether a string exactly equals something, you test to see if it matches a pattern.

The most common way to specify such patterns, especially in computer languages with UNIX ancestry, is through regular expressions. A regular expression looks like an ordinary string value but its characters represent a pattern rather than the characters themselves. As a regular expression, for example:

- The expression "a*" means any number of *a*'s rather than an *a* followed by an asterisk.

- The expression "(ab)*" means an empty string, a*b*, *abab*, *ababab*, or in fact the letters *ab* repeated any number of times from zero on up.

- The expression "[ab]" means either an *a* or a *b*.

If JavaScript supported regular expressions, we could replace all semicolons, slashes, and parentheses in the *userAgent* string with one statement; specifically, we could replace *[;/)(]* with a space.

In real life, JavaScript's *replace* method provides half of what we want. Netscape Navigator's *replace* method supports regular expressions, but Internet Explorer's doesn't. Because Internet Explorer doesn't support regular expressions, the following statement works just fine: it replaces the first left parenthesis in *ua* with a space.

```
ua = ua.replace("("," ");
```

Netscape Navigator, however, rejects this statement with an error message stating "Unterminated parenthetical." Netscape, you see, thinks the opening parenthesis in "(" is the beginning of a regular expression, and it complains because there's no closing parenthesis. The required Netscape Navigator coding is:

```
ua = ua.replace("[(]"," ");
```

As noted in the sidebar, removing left parentheses from the *userAgent* string requires a different statement in Internet Explorer than it does in Netscape Navigator. This presents a real dilemma, because:

1. I can't determine the browser type until I decode the *userAgent* string, and,

2. I can't decode the *userAgent* string until I determine the browser type.

Is that disgusting or what?

Well, when the going gets tough, the tough cheat. The following code performs a quick check for the string *MSIE* anywhere in the *userAgent* string, and then, if found, executes the Internet Explorer version of the replace-right-parenthesis code. Otherwise, it executes the Netscape Navigator version. So there.

```
if (ua.indexOf("MSIE") >= 0) {
    ua = ua.replace("(", " ");
}else{
    ua = ua.replace("[(]"," ");
}
```

The same kind of logic can change all slashes and parentheses to spaces, and then all multiple spaces to one space. It can also change *Windows* to *Win* so we don't have to worry about whether the browser reports the user's platform as Windows 95 or Win95, Windows NT or WinNT.

The following statements test whether the last (the rightmost) character in the string is a space and, if so, removes it. Remember, if the string contains 20

Tip: In many cases, a quick scan of the *userAgent* string may provide all the information you need and be far less troublesome than a full decode.

characters, they're numbered from 0 to 19. The position of the last character is one less than the string's length.

```
if (ua.substring(ua.length - 1) == " ") {
  ua = ua.substring(0, ua.length - 1);
}
```

Okay, now we've made the following transformation:

Before: `Mozilla/4.0 (compatible; MSIE 4.0; Windows 95)`
After: `Mozilla 4.0 compatible MSIE 4.0 Win95`

The last step is converting the resulting string to an array. The following statements accomplish this nicely:

```
var binfo = new Array();
binfo = ua.split(" ");
```

The first statement creates a new, empty array named *binfo*. In statement two, the *split* method breaks the *ua* string into array elements, using the space character as a delimiter.

Figure 3-3 and Figure 3-4 show all of this in action. The left table shows a minor assortment of *navigator* properties, including the all-important *userAgent* property. The Subfields table shows the *userAgent* property broken into table elements. Note the different Subfield values for IE and Netscape; the only common entries are Mozilla in position zero and the version number in position one.

We'll interpret the subfields in the *userAgent* property as follows, no matter what kind of punctuation separates them:

- Initially, we'll assume the first and second subfields tell us the browser name and version. We'll also assume the browser's platform is unknown.

- We'll scan all the remaining subfields looking for the value MSIE. If and when we do find it, we'll reset the browser name to that value and reset the version number to the next subfield (after, of course, checking that it exists).

- During the same scan, we'll check the first few letters of each subfield for common platform identifiers: Win, Mac, Sun, Linux, OS/2, and so forth. If we find one, we'll save the whole subfield value as the platform value.

FIGURE 3-3. *A script within this Web page splits the* navigator.userAgent *value into subfields and then extracts the browser name, version, and platform.*

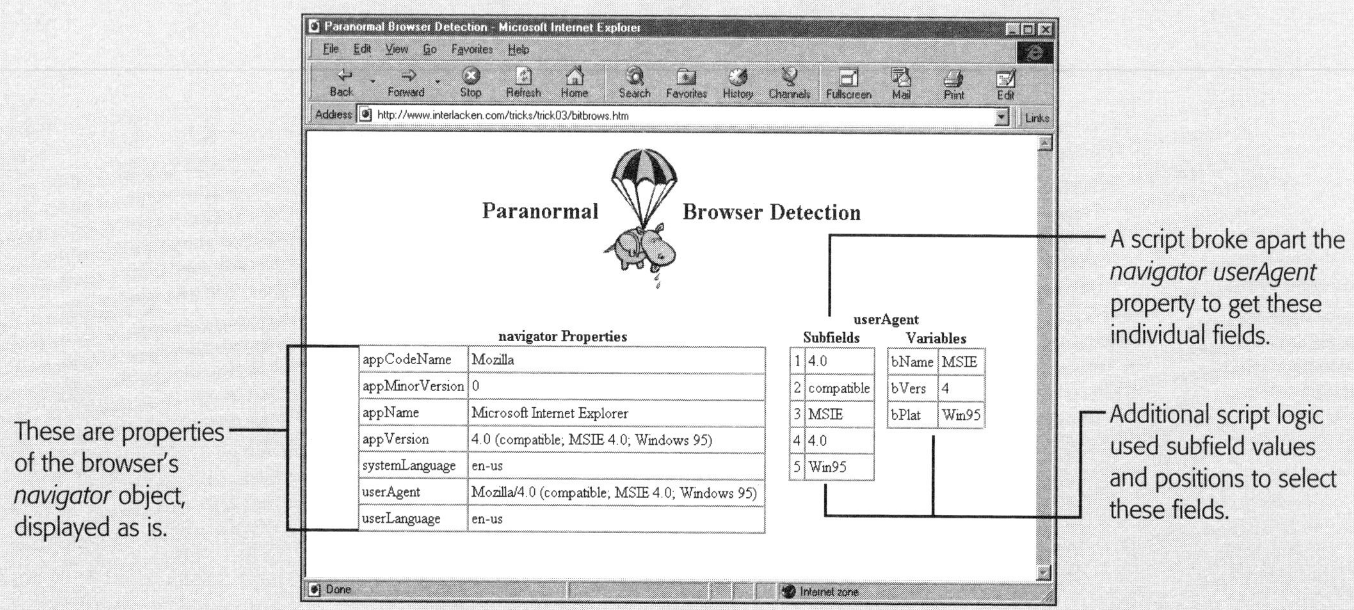
Paranormal Browser Detection - Microsoft Internet Explorer
File Edit View Go Favorites Help
Back Forward Stop Refresh Home Search Favorites History Channels Fullscreen Mail Print Edit
Address http://www.interlacken.com/tricks/trick03/bitbrows.htm
Links
Paranormal Browser Detection
navigator Properties
appCodeName Mozilla
appMinorVersion 0
appName Microsoft Internet Explorer
appVersion 4.0 (compatible; MSIE 4.0; Windows 95)
systemLanguage en-us
userAgent Mozilla/4.0 (compatible; MSIE 4.0; Windows 95)
userLanguage en-us
userAgent
Subfields
1 4.0
2 compatible
3 MSIE
4 4.0
5 Win95
Variables
bName MSIE
bVers 4
bPlat Win95
Done
Internet zone
These are properties of the browser's *navigator* object, displayed as is.
A script broke apart the *navigator userAgent* property to get these individual fields.
Additional script logic used subfield values and positions to select these fields.

Decoding and interpreting the *userAgent* field is a messy business, no doubt, but in some cases there's no other reliable way to get the information it provides.

Complete HTML Listing

Given all the above, we're now ready to read the HTML code for the Paranormal Browser Detection page.

FIGURE 3-4. *This is the same Web page shown in Figure 3-3, this time displayed by Netscape Navigator. Note the differences in the Subfield entries.*

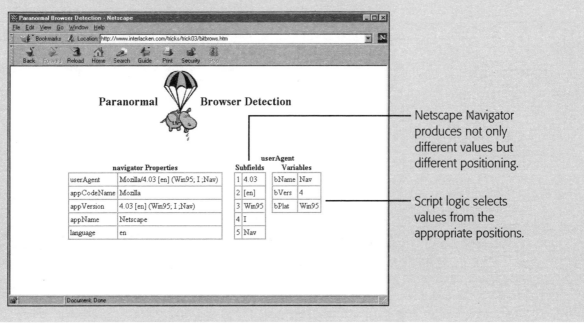

Netscape Navigator produces not only different values but different positioning.

Script logic selects values from the appropriate positions.

Start of *userAgent* decoding script. ———

Replace *Windows⌀* with *Win*. ———

Replace left parenthesis with a space. ———

```
<html>
<head>
<script LANGUAGE="JavaScript">
<!--
ua = navigator.userAgent;
ua = ua.replace("Windows ","Win");
if (ua.indexOf("MSIE") >= 0) {
    ua = ua.replace("("," ");
}else{
    ua = ua.replace("[(]"," ");
}
```

Continued from previous page

Replace right parenthesis with a space. ——
```
ua = ua.replace(")"," ");
```

Replace each slash with a space. ——
```
while (ua.indexOf("/") >= 0) {
  ua = ua.replace("/"," ");
}
```

Replace each semicolon with a space. ——
```
while (ua.indexOf(";") >= 0) {
  ua = ua.replace(";"," ");
}
```

Replace all multiple spaces with one space. ——
```
while (ua.indexOf("  ") >= 0) {
  ua = ua.replace("  "," ");
}
```

Remove trailing space, if any. ——
```
if (ua.substring(ua.length - 1) == " ") {
  ua = ua.substring(0, ua.length - 1);
}
```

Define array and split *userAgent* subfields into it. ——
```
var binfo = new Array();
binfo = ua.split(" ");
if (binfo.length > 1) {
```
—— Verify that the *binfo* table has at least two entries.

Set browser name and platform defaults as the first subfield, second subfield, and blank. ——
```
  bName = binfo[0];
  bVers = parseInt(binfo[1]);
  bPlat = "";
  for (pos = 2; pos < binfo.length; pos++){
```
—— Start of loop to examine the third and all remaining subfields.

```
    inf = binfo[pos];
    if (inf == "MSIE"){
      bName = inf;
```

Check subfield for "MSIE". If found, save the subfield value as the browser name and the next subfield value as the version. ——
```
      if (pos+1 < binfo.length){
        bVers = parseInt(binfo[pos+1]);
      }
    }
```

Check the beginning of subfield for common platform names, saving the complete name if found. ——
```
    if ((inf.substring(0,3) == "Win")
    || (inf.substring(0,3) == "Mac")
    || (inf.substring(0,3) == "Web")
    || (inf.substring(0,3) == "Sun")
    || (inf.substring(0,2) == "HP")
    || (inf.substring(0,3) == "AIX")
    || (inf.substring(0,3) == "BSD")
```

Continued from previous page

```
        || (inf.substring(0,7) == "FreeBSD")
        || (inf.substring(0,3) == "OSF")
        || (inf.substring(0,4) == "IRIX")
        || (inf.substring(0,5) == "Linux")
        || (inf.substring(0,4) == "OS/2")){
        bPlat = inf;
      }
    }
```

End of loop to examine the third ——— `}`
and all remaining subfields.

```
// -->
</script>
<title>Paranormal Browser Detection </title>
</head>
<body>
<p align="center">
<strong><font size="5">Paranormal</font></strong>
<img src="../images/hppochut.gif" alt="Hippo"
    align="center" WIDTH="80" HEIGHT="145">
<strong><font size="5">Browser Detection</font></strong></p>
<div align="center"><center>
<table border="0" cellpadding="0" cellspacing="0">
  <tr>
    <td></td>
    <td></td>
    <td colspan="3" align="center"><strong>userAgent</strong></td>
  </tr>
  <tr>
    <td align="center">
      <strong>navigator Properties</strong></td>
    <td></td>
    <td align="center">
      <strong>Subfields</strong></td>
    <td></td>
    <td align="center">
```

Display heading. ———

Start three-row, five-column
page layout table. ———

Row one contains headings. ———

Row two contains headings. ———

Continued from previous page

```
            <strong>Variables</strong></td>
        </tr>
        <tr>
          <td valign="top">
            <div align="center"><center>
            <table border="1" cellpadding="3" cellspacing="0">
            <script language="JavaScript">
            <!--
            for (props in navigator){
              if (props.substring(0,3) == "app" ||
                  props.substring(0,5) == "userA" ||
                  props.indexOf("ang") > 0) {
                document.write ("<tr><td>");
                document.write (props + "</td><td>");
                document.write (navigator[props]);
                document.write (" </td></tr>");
              }
            }
            // -->
            </script>
            </table>
          </center></div></td>
          <td>      </td>
          <td valign="top">
            <div align="center"><center>
            <table border="1" cellpadding="3" cellspacing="0">
            <script language="JavaScript">
            <!--
            for (bent in binfo) {
              if (bent > 0){
                document.write("<tr><td>");
                document.write(bent + "</td><td>");
                document.write(binfo[bent] + "</td></td>");
              }
            }
```

Row three contains three data tables and two columns of white space.

Start *navigator* properties table.

Loop through all *navigator* properties.

Select properties that begin with "app", "userA", or contain "ang".

Display selected property name and its value.

End *navigator* properties table.

Reserve white space.

Start Subfields table.

Continued from previous page

End Subfields table. ⸺

Start Variables table. ⸺

End Variables table. ⸺
End page layout table. ⸺

```html
        // -->
        </script>
        </table></td>
    <td>   </td>
    <td valign="top">
        <table border="1" cellpadding="3" cellspacing="0">
        <script language="JavaScript">
        <!--
        document.write("<tr><td>bName</td><td>");
        document.write(bName + "</td></tr>");
        document.write("<tr><td>bVers</td><td>");
        document.write(bVers + "</td></tr>");
        document.write("<tr><td>bPlat</td><td>");
        document.write(bPlat + "</td></tr>");
        // -->
        </script>
        </table>
    </table>
</center></div>
</body>
</html>
```

Active Server Browser Menu

Determining the capabilities of the remote user's browser can be very helpful when scripting Active Server Pages. With such knowledge, code on the server can customize the outgoing HTML code so it takes full advantage of (and doesn't exceed) the display capabilities of each user's browser.

Modern browsers transmit the *userAgent* string with every request to a server. That's right—every time you enter a URL, choose an entry from your favorites list, click a hyperlink, or submit a form, your browser transmits the *userAgent* property to the Web server. Many sites capture and analyze this data to see which

Hyperlink: For an example of *userAgent* analysis at a large site, browse the following URL at University of Illinois:

http://www.cen.uiuc.edu/bstats/latest.html

browsers their visitors are using, and thus which browsers they should test their Web pages with.

Scripting Techniques

If you've been studying for the test, you'll remember a Web page in Trick 2 named the Little Egypt ASP Information Pit. This page displayed the *userAgent* value, obtaining it from the *HTTP_USER_AGENT* property of the *request.serverVariables* collection.

We could easily develop some VBScript code to pull the individual fields out of *request.serverVariables*("*HTTP_USER_AGENT*") but Microsoft has already done this work for you. To use the prewritten solution, simply insert the following statement in your ASP page:

```
<% Set bc = Server.CreateObject("MSWC.BrowserType") %>
```

This creates an object named *bc* that has these properties:

- **Browser**—the name of the browser, usually IE or Netscape.
- **Version**—the full version number, such as 4.0.
- **Majorver** — the integer part of the version number, such as 4.
- **Minorver**—the decimal part of the version, such as 0.
- **JavaScript**—whether the browser supports JavaScript (indicated by true/false values).
- **Frames**—whether the browser supports frames (true/false).
- **Tables**—whether the browser supports tables (true/false).
- **Cookies**—whether the browser supports cookies (true/false).
- **BackgroundSounds**—whether the browser can play background sounds (true/false).
- **VBScript**—whether the browser supports VBScript (true/false).

To access these values, just code *bc.property* in your VBScript code, as shown below. (There's nothing special about the name *bc*, by the way. You can use any valid name you want.)

```
<%= bc.browser %>
```

Figures 3-5 and 3-6 show this technique in action. As usual, note the different values for Internet Explorer and Netscape Navigator.

In case you're wondering how this magic works, Active Server Page uses a file named browscap.ini to assign property values based on the *userAgent* string. This is usually located in the following location on the Web server:

\winnt\system32\inetsrv\browscap.ini

FIGURE 3-5. *This server-generated Web page displays a variety of browser properties deduced from the incoming request.*

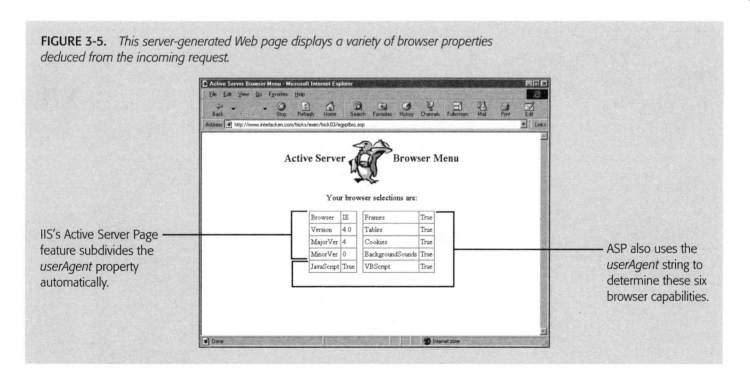

IIS's Active Server Page feature subdivides the *userAgent* property automatically.

ASP also uses the *userAgent* string to determine these six browser capabilities.

FIGURE 3-6. *Here's the same page as shown in Figure 3-5, but with Netscape Navigator submitting the request. Note the differences in values.*

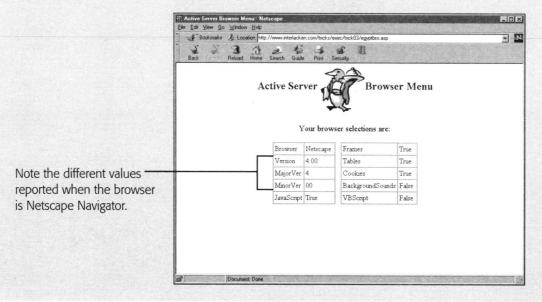

Note the different values reported when the browser is Netscape Navigator.

 Hyperlink: To obtain updated versions of the browscap.ini file, browse the following location on Microsoft's Web site:

http://backoffice.microsoft.com/ downtrial/moreinfo/bcf.asp

You should update this file from time to time, so the IIS Web server provides accurate information about new browser versions.

Complete HTML Listing

Here's the code for the Web pages in Figure 3-5 and Figure 3-6.

```html
<html>
<head>
<title>Active Server Browser Menu</title>
</head>
<body>
```

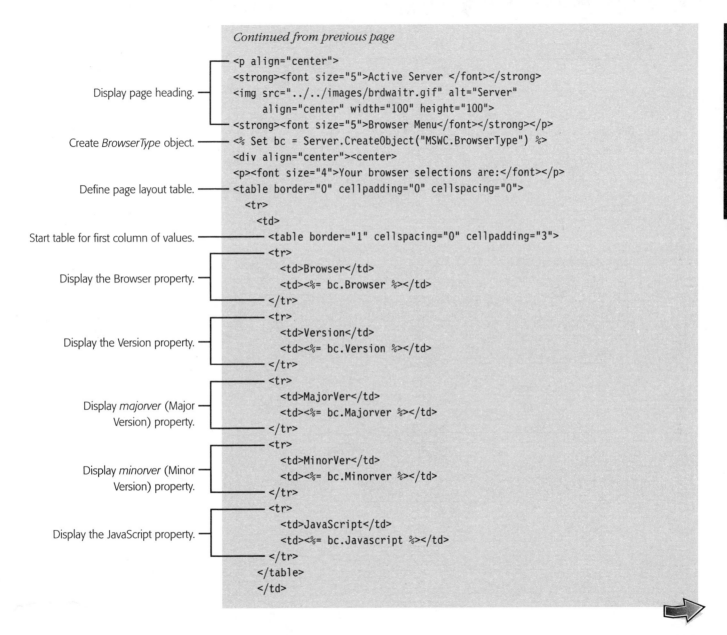

Continued from previous page

Display page heading.

```
<p align="center">
<strong><font size="5">Active Server </font></strong>
<img src="../../images/brdwaitr.gif" alt="Server"
     align="center" width="100" height="100">
<strong><font size="5">Browser Menu</font></strong></p>
```

Create *BrowserType* object.

```
<% Set bc = Server.CreateObject("MSWC.BrowserType") %>
<div align="center"><center>
<p><font size="4">Your browser selections are:</font></p>
```

Define page layout table.

```
<table border="0" cellpadding="0" cellspacing="0">
  <tr>
    <td>
```

Start table for first column of values.

```
    <table border="1" cellspacing="0" cellpadding="3">
```

Display the Browser property.

```
      <tr>
        <td>Browser</td>
        <td><%= bc.Browser %></td>
      </tr>
```

Display the Version property.

```
      <tr>
        <td>Version</td>
        <td><%= bc.Version %></td>
      </tr>
```

Display *majorver* (Major Version) property.

```
      <tr>
        <td>MajorVer</td>
        <td><%= bc.Majorver %></td>
      </tr>
```

Display *minorver* (Minor Version) property.

```
      <tr>
        <td>MinorVer</td>
        <td><%= bc.Minorver %></td>
      </tr>
```

Display the JavaScript property.

```
      <tr>
        <td>JavaScript</td>
        <td><%= bc.Javascript %></td>
      </tr>
    </table>
    </td>
```

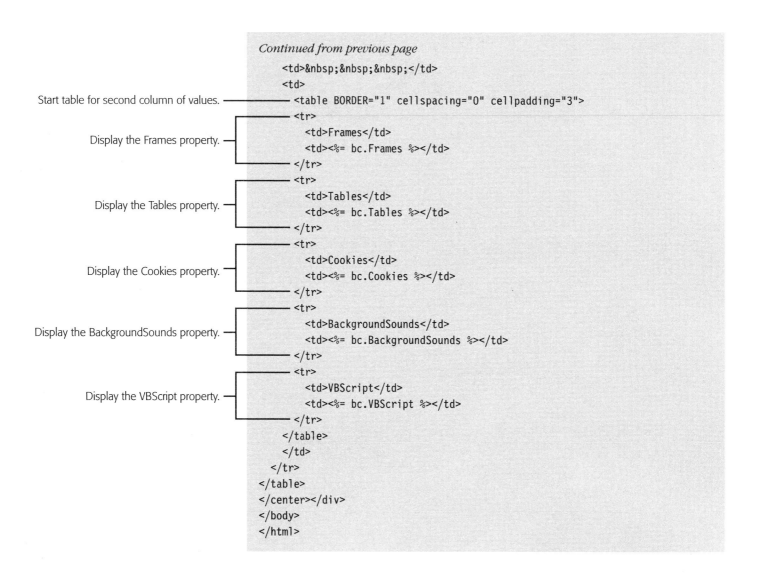

Continued from previous page

Start table for second column of values.

Display the Frames property.

Display the Tables property.

Display the Cookies property.

Display the BackgroundSounds property.

Display the VBScript property.

```html
    <td>   </td>
    <td>
    <table BORDER="1" cellspacing="0" cellpadding="3">
      <tr>
        <td>Frames</td>
        <td><%= bc.Frames %></td>
      </tr>
      <tr>
        <td>Tables</td>
        <td><%= bc.Tables %></td>
      </tr>
      <tr>
        <td>Cookies</td>
        <td><%= bc.Cookies %></td>
      </tr>
      <tr>
        <td>BackgroundSounds</td>
        <td><%= bc.BackgroundSounds %></td>
      </tr>
      <tr>
        <td>VBScript</td>
        <td><%= bc.VBScript %></td>
      </tr>
    </table>
    </td>
  </tr>
</table>
</center></div>
</body>
</html>
```

Browser Information in Perl

If you write server-side scripts in Perl, you can obtain the *userAgent* string from the *%ENV* array we first looked at in Trick 2. The code to do this is:

```
$browser = $ENV{HTTP_USER_AGENT};
```

Scripting Techniques

Remember, Perl variable names beginning with dollar signs are called scalars and contain single values only. There's nothing special about the name *$browser*. As before, we'll change *Windows∅* to *Win*, and remove all the slashes, semicolons, and parentheses. We'll also remove any square brackets. Here's the code that changes *Windows∅* to *Win*:

```
$browser =~ s/Windows /Win/gi;
```

The variable *$browser* is both the source and destination variable in this statement. The =~ operator means pattern matching, and the *s* means substitute. If found, *Windows∅* will be replaced by *Win*. The *g* suffix means all occurrences of *Windows∅* will be replaced; the *i* suffix means the search isn't case sensitive.

```
$browser =~ tr#[]/(;) #        #s;
```

The preceding statement also modifies the *$browser* variable, this time translating each character between the first and second pound signs to the corresponding character between the second and third pound signs; in this case, it translates any square brackets, slashes, parentheses, semicolons, and spaces to spaces. The *s* suffix means that if two successive characters get translated to the same character, that resulting character will appear only once.

The reason for translating a space to a space is that otherwise an existing space and a new space (resulting from translation) would not be combined. Including a space in the translation list makes sure that *all* spaces are translated spaces. The only good space is a translated space. So there.

The following statement splits the space-delimited values from the *$browser* variable into a table called *@brw*.

```
@brw = split(/ /,$browser);
```

As in the JavaScript code for the Paranormal Browser Detection page, we can now query the *userAgent* subfields (as entries in the *@brw* table), determine the browser type, and identify the version and platform. This is exactly the same drill we coded in JavaScript for the Paranormal Browser Detection page. The *int* function built into Perl obtains the integer part of the version number:

```
$Bmaj = int($Bvers);
```

Figure 3-7 and Figure 3-8 illustrate the results of parsing the *userAgent* string this way.

FIGURE 3-7. *A server-based Perl program produced this output based on* userAgent *information supplied by the browser—in this case, MSIE.*

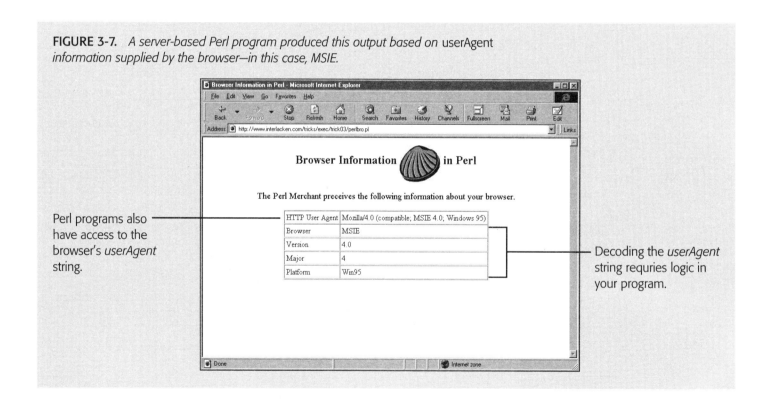

Perl programs also have access to the browser's *userAgent* string.

Decoding the *userAgent* string requries logic in your program.

FIGURE 3-8. *The same URL that produced Figure 3-7 produced this output when Netscape Navigator submitted the request.*

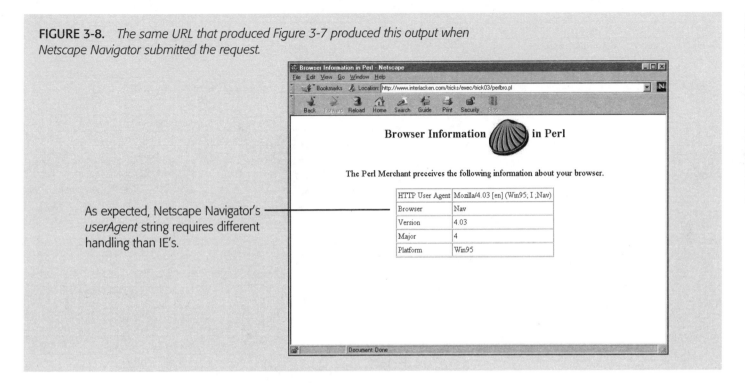

As expected, Netscape Navigator's *userAgent* string requires different handling than IE's.

Complete Perl Listing

The Perl program follows:

```perl
print "Content-type: text/html\n";
print "\n";
print "<HTML>\n";
print "<HEAD>\n";
print "<TITLE>Browser Information in Perl</TITLE>";
print "</HEAD>\n";
print "<BODY>\n";
```

Continued from previous page

Create page heading.

```perl
print "<p align=center><font size=5><strong>";
print "Browser Information ";
print "<img src=../../images/clam1.jpg";
print " width=85 height=75 align=middle>";
print " in Perl</strong></font></p>";
print "<p align=center><font size=4>The Perl";
print " Merchant preceives the following information";
print " about your browser.</font></p>";
```

Define data table to display results.

```perl
print "<table BORDER=1 cellspacing=0 ";
print " cellpadding=3 align=center>\n";
print "<tr><td>HTTP User Agent</td><td>";
print "$ENV{HTTP_USER_AGENT}</td></tr>\n";
```

Display *userAgent* info.

Copy *userAgent* info to *$browser* variable.

Search for *Windows∅* and replace with *Win*.

```perl
$browser = $ENV{HTTP_USER_AGENT};
$browser =~ s/Windows /Win/gi;
$browser =~ tr#[]/(;) #          #s;
```

Translate punctuation characters to spaces, suppressing multiple spaces on output.

Split space-delimited values into *@brw* table.

```perl
@brw = split(/ /,$browser);
if ($#brw > 1) {
```

Verify that the *brw* table has at least two entries.

Set the browser name and platform defaults as the first subfield, second subfield, and blank.

```perl
  $Bname = $brw[0];
  $Bvers = $brw[1];
  $Boper = "";
  for ($pos = 2; $pos <= $#brw; $pos++){
    $inf = $brw[$pos];
    if ($inf eq "MSIE"){
      $Bname = $inf;
      if ($pos+1 < $#brw){
        $Bvers = $brw[$pos+1];
      }
    }
```

Start of loop to examine the third and all remaining subfields.

Check subfield for "MSIE". If found, save the subfield value as the browser name and the next subfield value as the version.

Check the beginning of the subfield for common platform names, saving the complete name if found.

```perl
    if ((substr($inf,0,3) eq "Win")
    || (substr($inf,0,3) eq "Mac")
    || (substr($inf,0,3) eq "Web")
    || (substr($inf,0,3) eq "Sun")
    || (substr($inf,0,2) eq "HP")
    || (substr($inf,0,3) eq "AIX")
```

Continued from previous page

```
        || (substr($inf,0,3) eq "BSD")
        || (substr($inf,0,7) eq "FreeBSD")
        || (substr($inf,0,3) eq "OSF")
        || (substr($inf,0,4) eq "IRIX")
        || (substr($inf,0,5) eq "Linux")
        || (substr($inf,0,4) eq "OS/2")){
        $Boper = $inf;
      }
    }
}
$Bmaj = int($Bvers);
print "<tr><td>Browser</td><td>$Bname</td><tr>\n";
print "<tr><td>Version</td><td>$Bvers</td><tr>\n";
print "<tr><td>Major</td><td>$Bmaj</td><tr>\n";
print "<tr><td>Platform</td><td>$Boper</td><tr>\n";
print "</table>\n";
print "</BODY>\n";
print "</HTML>\n";
```

Obtain major version. — `$Bmaj = int($Bvers);`

Display results as table rows. — `print "<tr><td>Browser</td>..."`

The examples in this Trick show how to obtain information about the user's browser regardless of whether you're working on the browser, in HTML and JavaScript, or on the server, with Active Server Pages or Perl. This will be of use later in the book, or whenever you need to customize your own code so it works correctly on different browsers.

Border Graphics

B ackgrounds and borders are two of the most popular ways to spruce up a Web page. A good background improves both the appearance and readability of your page.

Unfortunately, the garden variety background images that people have been using for years can be overpowering. A large pattern distracts the eye, while a fine pattern obscures the details of fine text. A pattern that complements your content without overpowering it can be extremely difficult to find.

This trick describes two ways of applying background images to parts of a page, namely to the borders, rather than the whole area.

The first example shows how to display a border pattern along the right margin of a page. Web designers have known for some time how to display patterns along the left margin, but the left margin is usually full of content so the border pattern and the content interfere with each other. The right margin is often relatively empty and in dire need of something interesting.

The second example displays images of variable height along the right and left margins. These images have top, bottom, and middle sections, and the middle section grows and shrinks as the user resizes the browser window.

This trick is mostly concerned with visual gimmicks, but these gimmicks have two very real benefits: they divide your page layout into interesting zones, and they provide visual impact without obscuring your text.

Shades of Gray Detective Agency

Figure 4-1 shows a Web page with a fairly traditional background image. The background image appears by itself in Figure 4-2; it's only 10 pixels high, but the browser repeats it (or tiles it) down and across the entire page. (In this case, there's no horizontal repetition because the image is 1200 pixels wide—wider than almost any display window.) The gradient (the shading, that is) occurs only in the leftmost 150 pixels; the remaining 1050 pixels are solid gray.

The HTML to produce this background is:

```
<body background="../images/grade03b.gif"
       bgcolor="#CCCCCC">
```

FIGURE 4-1. *The gradient background interferes with the icons in this Web page. Unfortunately, HTML has no provision for right-aligning background images.*

Left-justified background images often compete with content for attention...

...while the right border remains boring and empty.

FIGURE 4-2. *This is the background image used in the Web page of Figure 4-1. In theory, the browser repeats this image both vertically and horizontally. In practice, it's so wide that horizontal repetition never occurs.*

The BACKGROUND= attribute provides the URL of an image file, and the BGCOLOR= setting specifies a solid color the browser should display (in this case, a neutral gray). The browser displays the solid color until it can download the image, or permanently if the user has images turned off.

The background image and the content icons interfere with each other because they're both at the left. The right side of the page, by contrast (so to speak), is rather empty. Moving the icons to the right wouldn't make much sense, but moving the background to the right has real possibilities. For proof, see Figure 4-3, where the same page appears much better balanced. The icons, appearing against a solid background, attract more attention. Frankenstein is emerging from the gloom rather than walking in a fog.

FIGURE 4-3. *Here's another version of the Web page shown in Figure 4-1. This time, Cascading Style Sheets attributes align the background to the right margin.*

Right-aligned border graphics can balance left-aligned content without interfering.

Style Sheet Usage

The effect in Figure 4-3 requires more properties than just BACKGROUND= and BGCOLOR=. We need to tell the browser it should put the first copy of the background image in the upper-right corner, and then repeat the image only vertically. The HTML that does this is:

```
<body style="background-position: top right;
            background-repeat: repeat-y;
            background-image: url(../images/grade03a.gif); ">
```

Tip: The STYLE= attribute assigns CSS properties to the single tag that contains it. The value you assign to STYLE= is anything you could put between the curly braces of a CSS rule in a <STYLE> section.

The good stuff (as keeps happening, you should note) consists of Cascading Style Sheet properties. We could have defined these properties between <STYLE> and </STYLE> tags in the <HEAD> section, assigning them either to the BODY type or to some class we would name on the <BODY> tag. In this case, however, defining the style inline with the <BODY> tag just seemed simpler.

The *repeat-y* value is the key to tiling vertically only. There are actually five background-related CSS properties; Table 4-1 lists them. By happy accident (or could it be careful planning?), each background property takes unique kinds of values. This allows the following shortcut form of coding:

```
<body style="background: top right
            repeat-y url(../images/grade03a.gif); ">
```

Instead of coding each background property separately, we can just code the property name as background and then specify the values we want. The browser knows that *repeat-y* can only be a *background-repeat* value, that *top right* can only be a *background-position* value, and so forth.

Hyperlink: For a comprehensive chart showing CSS properties supported by each browser version, browse:

http://www.webreview.com/guides/ style/mastergrid.html

Keywords and values listed in the Values column of Table 4-1 are mutually exclusive; for example, you could code *background-color: transparent* or *background-color: gray* but not both. There is one exception: the *background-position* property can specify both vertical and horizontal alignment keywords, as in *background-position: top left*.

The Shades of Gray page uses two CSS rules to control fonts. Here's the code that defines them:

```
.ss { font-family: Verdana, sans-serif; font-size: 14pt; }
H1 { font-family: Verdana, sans-serif; font-size: 32pt;
     font-weight: normal; }
```

Property	Description	Values (Default first)
background-color	A solid color that fills the entire area.	*transparent <color>*
background-image	The URL of an image that will fill the area.	*none <url>*
background-repeat	Determines whether a background image is repeated horizontally only (*repeat-x*), vertically only (*repeat-y*), both (*repeat*), or not at all (*no-repeat*).	*repeat* *repeat-x* *repeat-y* *no-repeat*
background-attachment	Controls whether the image is fixed or movable with respect to the Web page.	*scroll* *fixed*
background-position	Specifies the initial position of a single or repeated background image.	*0 0* *x-units y-units* *top/center/bottom* *left/center/right*
background	Specifies all five properties listed above.	Any/all above

TABLE 4-1. CSS Background Properties.

Trick 4

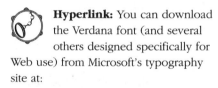

Hyperlink: You can download the Verdana font (and several others designed specifically for Web use) from Microsoft's typography site at:

http://www.microsoft.com/typography/ web/fonts/

This is also an excellent site for information about typography on the Web and in general.

The rule for the *ss* class sets the font to Verdana, a freely distributed sans serif font from Microsoft, and to the default font *sans-serif* if Verdana isn't available. The font size will be 14 points. There's no particular significance to the name *ss*; I used it as an abbreviation for sans serif. All ordinary text objects receive this formatting because I coded CLASS="ss" in the tags that define them.

The rule for the H1 type is pretty much the same except I set the *font-size* to 32 points and turned off bolding. Most browsers default to *font-weight: bold* for the H1 through H5 types.

Scripting Techniques

In a perfect world, every browser would fully and uniformly support all the CSS background tags. You didn't really expect this, though, did you? No. As luck would have it, version 4 was the first release of Microsoft Internet Explorer that fully supported all the background properties as defined in the CSS standard. Netscape Navigator 4 and Internet Explorer 3 both ignored the *background-position: right*

Tip: Heavy use of Trick 3 will continue throughout the book. Brace yourself. If you slept through that lecture, read the textbook during lunch or the 4:00 P.M. cartoons.

Note: The CSS background image is named grade03a.gif; it's 150 pixels wide and a gradient that gets darker to the right. The non-CSS background file, grade03b.gif, is 1200 pixels wide, has gradient only in the first 150 pixels, and the gradient gets lighter to the right. Both these images (and all the images used in this book) are on the accompanying CD in a folder called *tricks**images*.

Tip: Notice how the style sheet property *background-repeat* becomes *backgroundRepeat* in code. The names of CSS elements and their equivalent JavaScript properties are almost always related this way. Wherever you see a hyphen in a CSS property name, bagging it and capitalizing the next letter gets you the JavaScript version.

setting and always displayed background images at the left margin. To solve this dilemma and present the best possible results each browser can display, we'll drag out Trick 3, "Determining the Browser Version."

Here comes the tricky part. First we're going to code:

```
<body background="../images/grade03b.gif"
       bgcolor="#CCCCCC">
```

to provide a solid color and static background image that older browsers can cope with and display. Then, we're going to run a little script that tests the browser version and changes the CSS background properties if and only if the browser is IE4. Here's the script:

```
<script language="JavaScript">
<!--
if ((navigator.appName.substring(0,9)=="Microsoft")
 && (parseInt(navigator.appVersion) > 3)){
    document.body.style.backgroundRepeat="repeat-y";
    document.body.style.backgroundPosition="top right";
    document.body.style.backgroundImage="url(../images/grade03a.gif)";
}
// -->
</script>
```

The first four lines in the preceding JavaScript listing should be old hat; if not, refer back to Trick 3. The next three lines establish the same settings we put inside the STYLE= attribute a little while ago; we're just doing it in JavaScript code, that's all.

Page Layout Details

The rest of the page is largely unremarkable (oxymoron alert):

- The heading text stands alone, modified by a style sheet for type H1 in the <HEAD> section.

- A three-column, four-row, 100 percent–width table organizes the rest of the page. Column 1 contains the icons, column 2 the item text, and column three the Frankenstein image.

- Where Frank appears, the cell in column 3 is three rows high. It spans rows 2, 3, and 4.

- Columns 1 and 2 in row four are merged. The resulting double-width cell contains a two-cell table that's 100 percent wide. The left cell is left-aligned, and contains the text "For More Information…" The right cell is right-aligned, and contains the text "No Case Too Strange."

Complete HTML Listing

Here's the full HTML listing for the page shown in Figure 4-1 and Figure 4-3.

Define styles for the *ss* class and the H1 type.

Define conventional background image and background color.

Test the browser version and, if IE4, modify background properties.

Define the page heading.

```html
<html>
<head>
<style>
<!--
 .ss { font-family: Verdana, sans-serif; font-size: 14pt; }
 H1 { font-family: Verdana, sans-serif; font-size: 32pt;
       font-weight: normal; }
 -->
</style>
<title>Shades of Gray Detective Agency</title>
</head>
<body background="../images/grade03b.gif"
      bgcolor="#CCCCCC">
<script language="JavaScript">
<!--
if ((navigator.appName.substring(0,9)=="Microsoft")
 && (parseInt(navigator.appVersion) > 3)){
     document.body.style.backgroundRepeat="repeat-y";
     document.body.style.backgroundPosition="top right";
     document.body.style.backgroundImage="url(../images/grade03a.gif)";
}
// -->
</script>
<h1>Shades of Gray Detective Agency</h1>
```

Continued from previous page

Define three-column, four-row page layout table.

First row of page layout table.

Second row of page layout table.

The cell containing Frankenstein images spans three rows.

Third row of page layout table.

Last row of page layout table.

The first cell spans two columns.

Define inner layout table containing two cells.

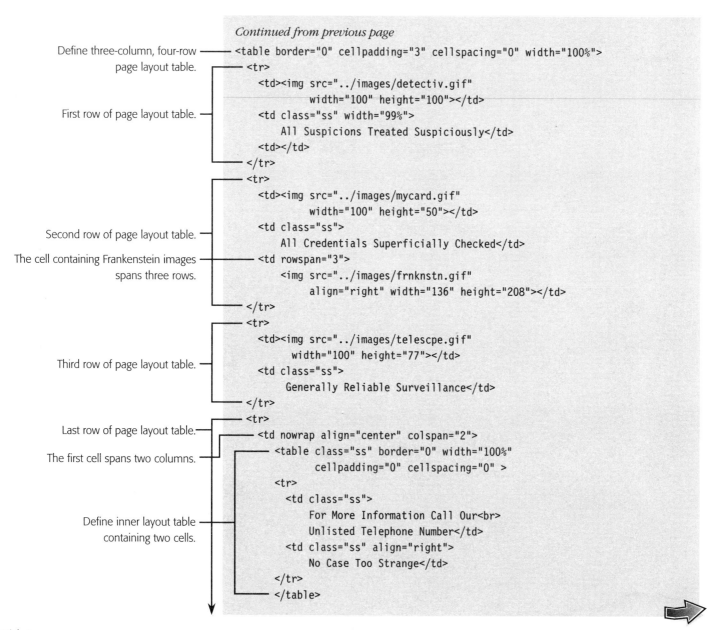

```html
<table border="0" cellpadding="3" cellspacing="0" width="100%">
  <tr>
    <td><img src="../images/detectiv.gif"
            width="100" height="100"></td>
    <td class="ss" width="99%">
        All Suspicions Treated Suspiciously</td>
    <td></td>
  </tr>
  <tr>
    <td><img src="../images/mycard.gif"
            width="100" height="50"></td>
    <td class="ss">
        All Credentials Superficially Checked</td>
    <td rowspan="3">
        <img src="../images/frnknstn.gif"
            align="right" width="136" height="208"></td>
  </tr>
  <tr>
    <td><img src="../images/telescpe.gif"
        width="100" height="77"></td>
    <td class="ss">
        Generally Reliable Surveillance</td>
  </tr>
  <tr>
    <td nowrap align="center" colspan="2">
      <table class="ss" border="0" width="100%"
            cellpadding="0" cellspacing="0" >
      <tr>
        <td class="ss">
            For More Information Call Our<br>
            Unlisted Telephone Number</td>
        <td class="ss" align="right">
            No Case Too Strange</td>
      </tr>
      </table>
```

Continued from previous page

```
    </td>
  </tr>
</table>
</body>
</html>
```

The Shades of Gray page is a precursor to most of the remaining examples in this book. It combines page layout with HTML, font control with Cascading Style Sheets, processing on the user's browser with JavaScript, and a nonsensical theme all working together. Pretty tricky, eh?

Column Up Telephony Services

It may have occurred to you, while striving to balance the left and right sides of the Shades of Gray page, how wonderful it might be to have multiple background images on one page. You might envision, for example, one background image that repeats along the left margin and another along the right. Or one across the top, one across the bottom, and another down the middle. Or dozens of other variations. Unfortunately, even the normally powerful Cascading Style Sheets provide only one background image per page.

Fortunately, you can achieve much the same effect by using a table to lay out page borders, and then assigning different background images to each border cell. This can produce results such as you see in Figure 4-4.

Page Layout Details

There's more to this Web page than you might first suspect. The columns are formed from the separate crown, midsection, and base images as shown here.

coltop.gif   colmid.gif   colbase.gif

FIGURE 4-4. *This page provides variable-height columns by using a repeating background image in table cells that border the left and right edges. Top and bottom aligned images in the same cells provide the crowns and bases.*

The bodies of these columns are made from repeating sections. In IE4, the columns grow and shrink as you vertically resize the page.

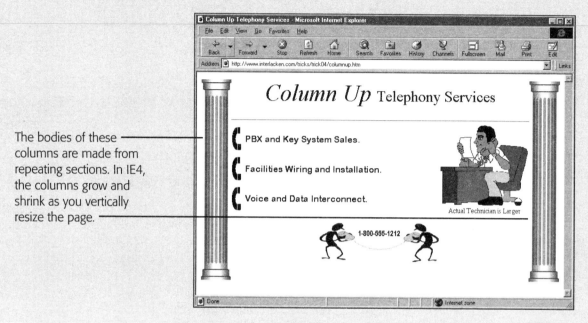

The Column Up Web page uses a page layout table coded WIDTH=100% and HEIGHT=100% so it occupies the entire browser window. This table has three columns and two rows. The middle column is coded WIDTH=99%, making it as wide as possible. This also makes the left and right columns as narrow as possible without obscuring the images. Finally, the two cells in the middle column are joined, spanning both rows and creating one large display area. This layout is shown in Figure 4-5.

FIGURE 4-5. *This diagram shows the main page layout table for the Column Up page.*

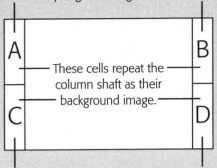

These cells top-align an image of the column head.

These cells repeat the column shaft as their background image.

These cells bottom-align an image of the column base.

To form the columns:

- Cells A, B, C, and D all use colmid.gif as their background image.

- Cells A and B display coltop.gif at the top of the cell.

- Cells C and D display colbase.gif at the bottom of the cell.

The advantage of building the columns this way is that they become adjustable in size. No matter the window size, no matter the user's font settings, the columns will always be long enough to at least match the height of the main content. In IE4 or any other browsers that support HEIGHT=100% for tables, the columns will match the content height or the window height, whichever is larger. Browsers that don't support HEIGHT=100% will simply ignore it, and size the table just large enough to contain its content.

The easiest way to specify colmid.gif as the background image for the four border cells is to use a style sheet. That way, we can define the background scheme once and use it in four places. The code goes in the <HEAD> section and look like this:

```
<style>
<!--
.col { background-image: url(../images/colmid.gif);
        background-repeat: repeat-y; }
-->
</style>
```

The definition for cell A is then:

```
<td class="col" valign="top">
  <img src="../images/coltop.gif"
       width="64" height="64"></td>
```

CLASS="col" pulls in the background style. Cells A and B both specify VALIGN= "TOP", so anything these cells contain (except the repeating background image, of course) appears at the top. Cells C and D both specify VALIGN= "BOTTOM", so their content appears at the bottom. Where coltop.gif and colbase.gif appear, they will overlay colmid.gif—the background image, because that's how background images work.

The heading Column Up Telephony Services, the horizontal rule, and the phone number graphic appear directly within the large, spanned, central page layout cell. A 3 × 3 table arranges the three telephone icons in the left column, the three feature slugs in the middle column, and the technician image in the right column, spanning all three rows.

The technician image and its caption reside within a third table consisting of one column and two rows. The upper cell contains the image, and the lower cell contains the caption.

Figure 4-6 shows another view of the Column Up page, this time with table borders activated. The outer page layout table and the innermost technician table have black cell borders, while the three-bullet table has gray. Adding table borders has offset the column top and bottom images, but not the midsection (background) images. As proven in Figure 4-4, the misalignment disappears when table borders are turned off, which is how a remote user would see it.

Tip: Many HTML editors (and Web designers as well) enclose all HTML attribute values in quotes. This is the safest and most consistent approach. Quotes aren't required, though, if the value consists entirely of letters, numbers, hyphens, and periods. There's no significant difference between WIDTH="64" and WIDTH=64.

FIGURE 4-6. *This is the same Web page as shown in Figure 4-4, this time with table borders made visible.*

Table to organize page layout (including columns).

Table to organize icons, bullet points, and technician image.

A third table organizes the technician image and its caption.

Complete HTML Listing

Here's the complete HTML for the Column Up Telephony Services page:

Style sheet for column background.

```
<html>
<head>
<style>
<!--
.col { background-image: url(../images/colmid.gif);
       background-repeat: repeat-y; }
-->
</style>
```

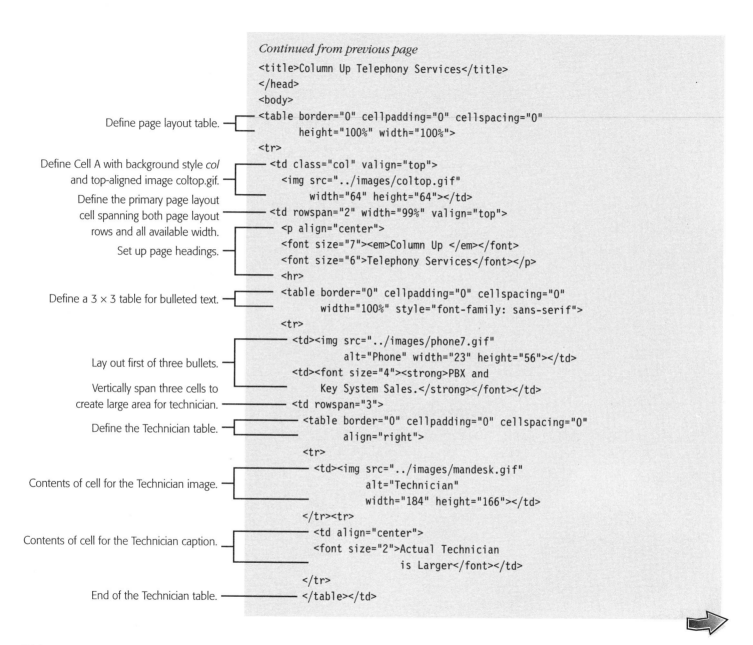

Continued from previous page

```html
<title>Column Up Telephony Services</title>
</head>
<body>
<table border="0" cellpadding="0" cellspacing="0"
        height="100%" width="100%">
<tr>
  <td class="col" valign="top">
    <img src="../images/coltop.gif"
          width="64" height="64"></td>
  <td rowspan="2" width="99%" valign="top">
    <p align="center">
    <font size="7"><em>Column Up </em></font>
    <font size="6">Telephony Services</font></p>
    <hr>
    <table border="0" cellpadding="0" cellspacing="0"
            width="100%" style="font-family: sans-serif">
    <tr>
      <td><img src="../images/phone7.gif"
                alt="Phone" width="23" height="56"></td>
      <td><font size="4"><strong>PBX and
          Key System Sales.</strong></font></td>
      <td rowspan="3">
        <table border="0" cellpadding="0" cellspacing="0"
                align="right">
        <tr>
          <td><img src="../images/mandesk.gif"
                    alt="Technician"
                    width="184" height="166"></td>
        </tr><tr>
          <td align="center">
          <font size="2">Actual Technician
                          is Larger</font></td>
        </tr>
        </table></td>
```

Define page layout table.

Define Cell A with background style *col* and top-aligned image coltop.gif.

Define the primary page layout cell spanning both page layout rows and all available width.

Set up page headings.

Define a 3 × 3 table for bulleted text.

Lay out first of three bullets.

Vertically span three cells to create large area for technician.

Define the Technician table.

Contents of cell for the Technician image.

Contents of cell for the Technician caption.

End of the Technician table.

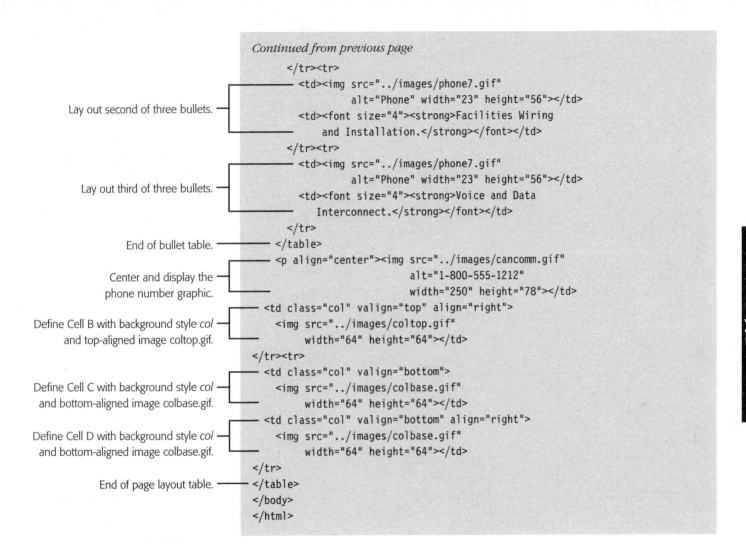

Continued from previous page

```
                        </tr><tr>
                          <td><img src="../images/phone7.gif"
                                   alt="Phone" width="23" height="56"></td>
                          <td><font size="4"><strong>Facilities Wiring
                                and Installation.</strong></font></td>
                        </tr><tr>
                          <td><img src="../images/phone7.gif"
                                   alt="Phone" width="23" height="56"></td>
                          <td><font size="4"><strong>Voice and Data
                                Interconnect.</strong></font></td>
                        </tr>
                        </table>
                        <p align="center"><img src="../images/cancomm.gif"
                                           alt="1-800-555-1212"
                                           width="250" height="78"></td>
                        <td class="col" valign="top" align="right">
                          <img src="../images/coltop.gif"
                              width="64" height="64"></td>
                        </tr><tr>
                        <td class="col" valign="bottom">
                          <img src="../images/colbase.gif"
                              width="64" height="64"></td>
                        <td class="col" valign="bottom" align="right">
                          <img src="../images/colbase.gif"
                              width="64" height="64"></td>
                        </tr>
                        </table>
                        </body>
                        </html>
```

Lay out second of three bullets.

Lay out third of three bullets.

End of bullet table.

Center and display the phone number graphic.

Define Cell B with background style *col* and top-aligned image coltop.gif.

Define Cell C with background style *col* and bottom-aligned image colbase.gif.

Define Cell D with background style *col* and bottom-aligned image colbase.gif.

End of page layout table.

The coolest thing about the Column Up page is that the columns are variable height. If you enlarge the browser window so it's longer than the page's content, the columns automatically get longer as well. If you shorten the browser window, the columns get shorter to match. It's really pretty cool and it doesn't require a bit of programming—not even JavaScript.

Positioning
with Style Sheets

Page layout in HTML is almost a contradiction in terms. Anyone who's created Web pages and tried to make them attractive knows this very well. No other medium provides so little control over page layout. Other media provide control over placement and presentation down to the finest detail; HTML provides tables, left alignment, right alignment, and centering. Oooh, big whoop.

A new aspect of Cascading Style Sheets called *positioning* moves Web-based page layout a giant step forward. Positioning introduces two new properties, *top* and *left*, that control the vertical and horizontal position of any content on the page. It also provides *height* and *width* properties that control the size of displayed objects.

Is there a catch? Of course. Your Web visitors will continue adjusting their browser windows to any size they want, and they'll expect your Web pages to compensate accordingly. This usually means that supplying absolute coordinates when you create the page isn't enough. Instead, you'll need to provide code that calculates positions on the fly. Tricky, eh?

This trick contains three examples. The AERO Message Service page uses CSS positioning to display variable text (some browser properties) superimposed on graphics. As you resize the page, the graphic and the superimposed text change position to match.

The Brickbat Page shows how to allocate part of a Web page as a scrollable area. What's more, this example shows how to display different sets of content within the scrollable area without waiting for new data to arrive from the Web server. It's almost like having a frameset but without the hassle.

The UFO Corner positions four objects on the Web page so they line up exactly with the corners of the browser window. This is trickier than it sounds, because keeping those objects in the corners means moving them up and down, right and left as the user scrolls around the document.

Is there another catch? You betcha. Microsoft Internet Explorer and Netscape Navigator differ drastically in how they support positioning—so drastically that it's almost impossible to develop pages that work properly in both. The answer:

- This trick shows three examples that work only in Internet Explorer.

- Trick 6 shows two examples that work only in Netscape Navigator, and a third example that works in both browsers.

- Trick 8 (yeah, we skipped one: Trick 7 is about timers) shows how a single URL can jump to two different pages, depending on the user's browser.

AERO Message Service (IE)

With normal HTML it's impossible to superimpose one element over another. Web pages like the one shown in Figure 5-1, which displays variable text over a graphic, simply aren't possible. Such is the power of CSS positioning. Well, *I* was impressed…

There are four tables in Figure 5-1—one for each row of content except the heading. You can see the tables more clearly in Figure 5-2.

Page Layout Details

The first and third tables, containing Your Browser and Today's Date, are left justified. The second and fourth tables, Your Platform and Last Updated, are flush right; this means they move right as the browser window grows and left as it shrinks. This keeps the right-facing propellers a constant distance from the right margin.

Each plane and banner is a single image file. Actually there are two such files, one flying left and one flying right, each used twice. A table cell provides a *container* for each image.

Caution: Nowhere do Netscape Navigator and Internet Explorer differ so greatly as in their treatment of positioning, spans, and divisions. The version of the AERO Message Service page described here is incompatible with Netscape Navigator, at least through version 4. A Netscape-compatible version appears in the next trick.

FIGURE 5-1. *CSS positioning superimposes text over each banner graphic in this Web page.*

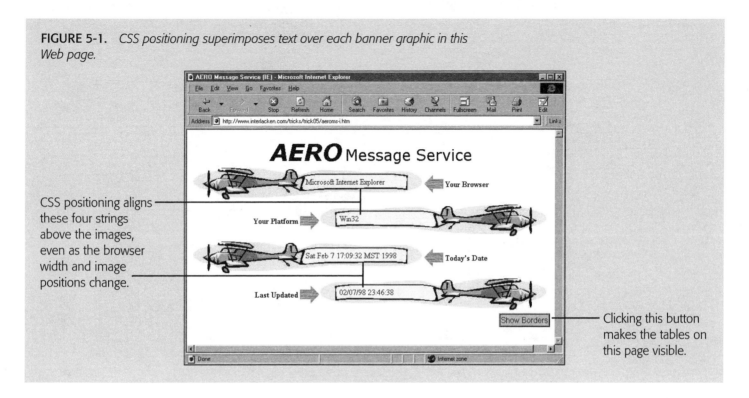

CSS positioning aligns these four strings above the images, even as the browser width and image positions change.

Clicking this button makes the tables on this page visible.

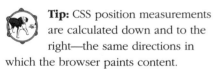 **Tip:** CSS position measurements are calculated down and to the right—the same directions in which the browser paints content.

CSS Positioning

In this trick each table cell that contains an airplane image is defined with a statement like the following:

```
<td style="position:relative;">
```

This code establishes the table cell as a container but, because there are no top or left attributes, it doesn't actually change the position of anything. The next statement within each airplane cell is an ordinary image tag such as the following:

```
<img src="../images/airmsg2.gif" width="481" height="71">
```

Trick 5

FIGURE 5-2. *The four tables used for alignment in Figure 5-1 are clearly visible in this view. The button in the lower-right corner toggles the table borders.*

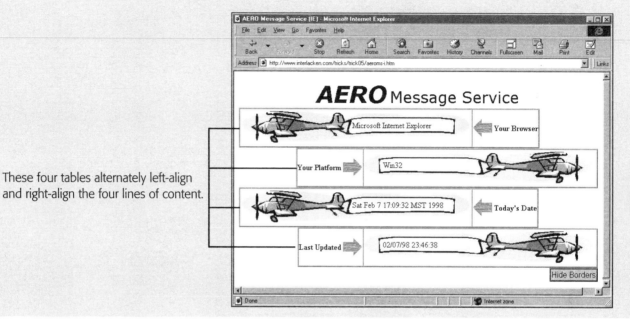

These four tables alternately left-align and right-align the four lines of content.

 Tip: The <SPAN>...</SPAN> and <DIV>...</DIV> are similar in that both mark a block of content on a Web page. The difference is that a break (normally a new line) occurs before and after the <DIV>...</DIV> pair. Unless modified by HTML attributes or style properties, the <SPAN>...</SPAN> pair has no visible effect on the Web page.

Text displayed over the banner portion of this image needs to begin 23 pixels below the top edge and 237 pixels from the left edge. If we wanted to display "Your Ad Goes Here," the coding would be:

```
<span style="position: absolute; top:23; left:237">
Your Ad Goes Here
</span>
```

The <SPAN> and </SPAN> tags mark a section of HTML so you can assign properties to it. HTML within the <SPAN>...</SPAN> tags flows like any other HTML. In this case, marking the text "Your Ad Goes Here" as a span allows CSS positioning to apply to that phrase.

Tip: If you give some image an absolute position of *left=30px top=10px*, the browser will start displaying the image's top-left corner 30 pixels to the right and 10 pixels below its container's top-left corner.

Containers and Positioning

In the exciting milieu of CSS positioning, a *container* is an area whose upper-left corner provides a frame of reference; that is, we measure from the upper-left corner. To position something inside the container, you state how far to the right and how far below the container's upper-left corner you want it to be. This is called *absolute* positioning.

The other kind of positioning is *relative*. Relative positioning describes where all the aunts, uncles, and cousins sit at large dinners (not). Okay, instead of being measured from the container's top-left corner, relative positions are measured from the spot an object would otherwise occupy.

As an example, suppose you have some normal content that, after normal formatting, winds up 100 pixels from the top edge and 100 pixels from the left edge of the document area. The following actions would change its document position as indicated.

	top	left
Normal position	100	100
Enclose with <SPAN> and </SPAN> tags	100	100
Add STYLE="position: relative" to <SPAN> tag	100	100
Change STYLE= attribute to "position relative; top:50; left:50"	150	150
Change STYLE= attribute to "position absolute; top:0; left:0"	0	0
Change STYLE= attribute to "position absolute; top:50; left:50"	50	50

Scripting Techniques

In the AERO Message Service page, a script creates each piece of repositioned text. The entire coding for one cell then comes to this:

```
<td style="position:relative;">
    <img src="../images/airmsg2.gif" width="481" height="71">
    <span style="position: absolute; top:23; left:237">
    <script language="JavaScript">
    <!--
    document.write(navigator.appName);
    // -->
    </script></span></td>
```

The button that turns table borders on and off is the homemade variety; it's actually a one-celled table, not to be confused with an amoeba, a paramecium, a wild west jail, or any other one-celled doohickey. Here's the code:

```
<table align="right" border="2" cellspacing="0"
  bgcolor="#CCCCCC"
  bordercolorlight="#999999"
  bordercolordark="#000000"
  style="font-family: sans-serif; cursor: hand;"
  onclick="toggleBorders()">
<tr><td id="bordButn">Show Borders</td></tr>
</table>
```

The ALIGN=RIGHT clause glues the table to the right margin, and the three color settings, all gray, impart a roughly button-like appearance. Style properties assign the browser's default sans serif font and change the browser's mouse pointer to a hand icon whenever it passes over the button (OK, the table).

Tip: The CSS *cursor* property controls which mouse pointer appears when the mouse is over an object. Table 5-1 lists the permissible values.

TABLE 5-1. Values for the CSS Cursor Property.	
Value	**Description**
auto	The browser determines which mouse pointer to display, based on the context. This is the default.
default	The operating system's default mouse pointer (usually an arrow) will appear, regardless of the context.
hand	The operating system's normal mouse pointer for clickable objects.
wait	A mouse pointer, typically an hourglass or stopwatch, that indicates the user should wait.
text	The normal mouse pointer for text, usually an I-beam.
help	Indicates help is available for the object under the mouse pointer; usually a question mark or balloon.
move	Indicates the user can move an object under the mouse pointer.
crosshair	A mouse pointer that looks like a crosshair aiming device.
xx-resize	Various mouse pointers used for resizing objects, typically double arrows. Replace *xx* with n, s, e, w, ne, se, sw, or nw.

Tip: The World Wide Web Consortium (W3C) officially recommends using the <HEAD> section for script functions, style sheets, and other kinds of behind-the-scenes code. The more of this you keep out of the <BODY> section, the cleaner your content will be.

 Tip: No matter where you define a function, the browser doesn't execute it immediately. The browser merely stores the function for use by other code.

The *onClick* attribute gives the name of a JavaScript function the browser should execute whenever the user clicks the mouse pointer on the current object. The current object in this case is our button-table, because the *onClick* attribute appears within that <TABLE> tag. The browser runs the *toggleBorders()* function whenever the user clicks the table.

The *toggleBorders()* function is defined up in the <HEAD> section. We could've defined this function anywhere in the Web page before we used it, but the <HEAD> section is just a handy place for stuff that isn't part of the visible Web page. Here's the JavaScript code that defines *toggleBorders()* function:

```
<script language="JavaScript">
<!--
function toggleBorders(){
    if (document.all.tab1.border == "2"){
        document.all.tab1.border = "0" ;
        document.all.tab2.border = "0" ;
        document.all.tab3.border = "0" ;
        document.all.tab4.border = "0" ;
        document.all.bordButn.innerHTML = "Show Borders";
    }else{
        document.all.tab1.border = "2" ;
        document.all.tab2.border = "2" ;
        document.all.tab3.border = "2" ;
        document.all.tab4.border = "2" ;
        document.all.bordButn.innerHTML = "Hide Borders";
    }
}
// -->
```

The identifiers *tab1*, *tab2*, *tab3*, and *tab4* are assigned by ID= attributes in the <TABLE> tags of the four airplane tables. If the first table's border width is 2, that means table borders are currently visible; setting all the border widths to 0 makes them invisible. Otherwise, table borders are currently invisible; assigning a non-zero border width—2 in this case—makes them visible.

If your jaw isn't dropping yet, it's about to. Along with turning the table borders on and off from code, we'd like to change the button title so it reads "Show Borders" or "Hide Borders," as appropriate. The code to make the button read "Show Borders" is:

```
document.all.bordButn.innerHTML = "Show Borders";
```

The name *bordButn* identifies the table cell that serves as the button. There's nothing special about this particular name; we could've coded any name we wanted in the following code:

```
<td id="bordButn">Show Borders</td>
```

The *innerHTML* property refers to all the HTML that appears between a matching pair of HTML tags. In this case, *document.all.bordButton.innerHTML* refers to everything between the <TD ID="bordButn"> and </TD> tags. The *innerHTML* property is fully read-write, so we can easily replace Show Borders with Hide Borders and vice versa.

OK, now's the time to whoop all over the place and jump up and down until you get a headache. The *innerHTML* property is an extremely powerful feature. In this example we just used it to replace a simple text string, but the values you put in *innerHTML* can contain any valid HTML: text, hyperlinks, images, tables, forms, whatever. This gives you unprecedented control over the display your users see—without making them wait for the server to send out a new Web page. In addition to the strings "Show Borders" and "Hide Borders," we could have included some image tags, for example.

Complete HTML Listing

Here's the complete HTML listing for the AERO Message Service page:

Tip: Since there's an *innerHTML* property, you might wonder if there's an *outerHTML* property as well. There is. The *outerHTML* property includes the defining tags as well as the content between them, and yes, you can replace the *entire outerHTML* value.

See Also: For a further illustration of the *innerHTML* property, see The Brickbat Page, the next example in this trick.

```
<html>
<head>
<title>AERO Message Service (IE)</title>
<script language="JavaScript">
<!--
function toggleBorders(){
```

Start of function to toggle table borders and button caption.

Continued from previous page

If borders are visible, make them invisible. ─

```
if (document.all.tab1.border == "2"){
    document.all.tab1.border = "0" ;
    document.all.tab2.border = "0" ;
    document.all.tab3.border = "0" ;
    document.all.tab4.border = "0" ;
    document.all.bordButn.innerHTML = "Show Borders";
```

If borders aren't visible, make them so. ─

```
}else{
    document.all.tab1.border = "2" ;
    document.all.tab2.border = "2" ;
    document.all.tab3.border = "2" ;
    document.all.tab4.border = "2" ;
    document.all.bordButn.innerHTML = "Hide Borders";
}
}
// -->
```

End of function to toggle table ─
borders and button caption.

```
</script>
</head>
<body>
<p align="center" style="margin:0; ">
```

Set up page heading. The *margin:0* ─
style setting eliminates the white space
that normally follows a paragraph.

```
  <span style="font-family: Verdana, sans-serif">
  <font size="7"><em><strong>
  AERO</strong></em></font>
  <font size="6">Message Service</font></span></p>
<table id="tab1" border="0" cellspacing="0" cellpadding="0">
<tr>
```

Display the first airplane table. ─

```
  <td style="position:relative;">
    <img src="../images/airmsg2.gif" width="481" height="71">
```

Position script output over image. ─

```
    <span style="position: absolute; top:23; left:237">
    <script language="JavaScript">
    <!--
    document.write(navigator.appName);
    // -->
    </script></span></td>
  <td><img src="../images/arrowlf.gif"
```

Trick 5

Continued from previous page

```
            align="absmiddle" width="41" height="38">
        <strong>Your Browser</strong></td>
</tr></table>
<div align="right">
<table>
<table id="tab2" border="0" cellspacing="0" cellpadding="0">
  <td style="position:relative;">
     <strong>Your Platform</strong>
     <img src="../images/arrowrt.gif" align="absmiddle"
         width="41" height="38"></td>
  <td style="position:relative;">
     <img src="../images/airmsg1.gif" width="481" height="71">
     <span style="position: absolute; top:23; left:40">
     <script language="JavaScript">
     <!--
     document.write(navigator.platform);
     // -->
     </script></span></td></tr></table></div>
<table id="tab3" border="0" cellspacing="0" cellpadding="0">
<tr>
  <td style="position:relative;">
     <img src="../images/airmsg2.gif" width="481" height="71">
     <span style="position: absolute; top:23; left:237">
     <script language="JavaScript">
     <!--
     TodaysDate = new Date();
     document.write(TodaysDate);
     // -->
     </script></span></td>
  <td><img src="../images/arrowlf.gif" align="absmiddle"
         width="41" height="38">
     <strong> Today's Date</strong></td></tr></table>
```

Display the second airplane table. ———

Position script output over image. ———

Display the third airplane table. ———

Position script output over image. ———

Continued from previous page

Display the third airplane table. —

Position script output over image. —

```
<div align="right">
<table id="tab4" border="0" cellspacing="0" cellpadding="0">
<tr>
  <td style="position:relative;">
    <strong>Last Updated</strong>
    <img src="../images/arrowrt.gif" align="absmiddle"
        width="41" height="38"></td>
  <td style="position:relative;">
    <img src="../images/airmsg1.gif" width="481" height="71">
    <span style="position: absolute; top:23; left:40">
    <script language="JavaScript">
    <!--
    document.write(document.lastModified);
    // -->
    </script></span></td></tr></table>
```

Display Show Border / Hide Borders button. —

Set button colors. —

Set the font and mouse pointer. —

Set the mouse-click event handler. —

Display the button caption
and name it *bordButn*.

```
<table align="right" border="2" cellspacing="0"
  bgcolor="#CCCCCC"
  bordercolorlight="#999999"
  bordercolordark="#000000"
  style="font-family: sans-serif; cursor: hand;"
  onclick="toggleBorders()">
<tr><td id="bordButn">Show Borders</td></tr>
</table>
</div>
</body>
</html>
```

CSS Positioning is both a joy and a disappointment. It's a joy because Web designers can finally put things exactly where they want them. It's a disappointment because many aspects of a Web page remain variable—the window size, the font magnification and so forth—and keeping positioned objects positioned correctly often requires custom script code. Well, that's life; deal with it.

The Brickbat Page

This example illustrates more things you can do with the <SPAN> and <DIV> tags, the *innerHTML* property, and the *onClick* event. As the remote user clicks certain hot spots, we'll display changing content in another part of the Web page. The page itself appears in Figure 5-3.

CSS Positioning

In this figure, a two-column, four-row table organizes the icons and titles at the left. Each table row is coded with an *onClick* property that copies associated

FIGURE 5-3. *As the remote user clicks the icon or titles at the left, different content appears in the box at the right. Unlike a frameset, this requires no additional interaction with the Web server.*

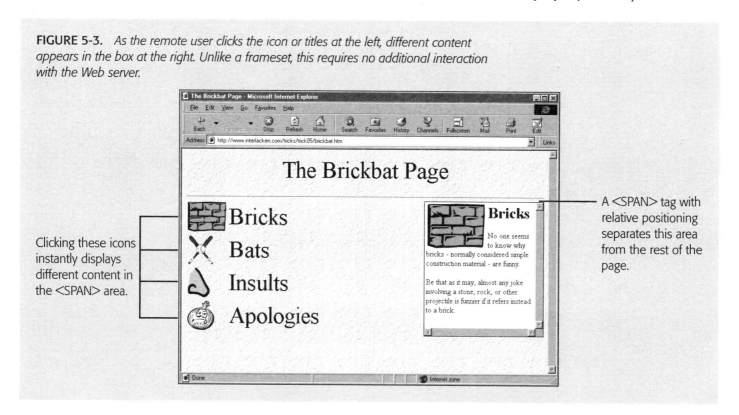

Clicking these icons instantly displays different content in the <SPAN> area.

A <SPAN> tag with relative positioning separates this area from the rest of the page.

content to the box at the right. The box at the right is a span defined by the following code:

```
<span id="descBox"
      style="position: relative;
      float: right;
      width: 250;
      height: 275;
      overflow: scroll;
      padding: 3;
      border: 1px solid black;
      background-color: #FFFFFF; ">
```

This tag does a lot. Specifically:

- The *position: relative* property allows the <SPAN> area to occupy its normal place in the HTML flow.

- Because of the *float: right* property, the span will align to the right margin and any nearby text will wrap around it.

- The *height* and *width* properties control the size of the box in pixels, the default measurement.

- An *overflow* property of *scroll* specifies that any content larger than the span area will be accessible via scroll bars.

- The *padding* property inserts three pixels of blank space between the border and any contents.

- The *border* property surrounds the span with a solid black border, 1 pixel wide.

- The span area will have a white background.

Scripting Techniques

Four different descriptions can appear in the <SPAN> box—one for each choice at the left of the page. The description for the Bricks choice appears directly in the original HTML; that is, it's between the <SPAN> and </SPAN> tags. The other

Trick 5

descriptions are coded inside three invisible divisions using the notation that follows. The style setting *display: none* makes the division invisible:

```
<div id="batBox" style="display: none;">
    <!-- content appears here -->
</div>
```

When the remote user clicks the Bats row, the *onClick* event executes the following statement:

```
descBox.innerHTML = batBox.innerHTML
```

Such a statement appears within the *onClick* attribute of each <TR> tag. This copies whatever HTML lies between the <DIV ID=batBox>...</DIV> tags and replaces whatever currently lies between the <SPAN ID=descBox>...</SPAN> tags. Only the content is copied: the *display: none* property, which is coded within the opening <DIV> tag, isn't copied at all. (Ignore the difference between <DIV> and <SPAN> tags for now; it's not relevant.)

All this leaves only two details: Netscape compatibility and saving the initial Bricks description. Regarding the first, Netscape Navigator, at least through version 4:

- Doesn't support the *innerHTML* property.

- Doesn't support the *onClick* event except for hyperlinks and a certain HTML form elements.

- Supports the <SPAN> and <DIV> tags, but much differently than Internet Explorer.

- Supports *display: none* the same as Internet Explorer.

The net result (so to speak) for our page is that with Netscape Navigator, only the original Bricks content will ever appear within the description box. Netscape can't respond when the remote user clicks on the choices at the left, and even if it could, it can't replace the description box's *innerHTML* contents. The three invisible divisions, however, do remain invisible. For now, at least, that's as compatible as these techniques can be.

A final problem arises if an IE user loads The Brickbat Page, clicks a choice other than Bricks, and then clicks Bricks. The original box contents have long since been overwritten. Shozbot. Putting the Bricks content in a fourth invisible division would be one solution, but then the description box would always be blank with Netscape Navigator. Netscape can't copy the invisible Bricks division's *innerHTML* to the description box's *innerHTML* even once, when the page loads.

Coding the Bricks content directly inside the description box remains the best solution. All we have to do, if the browser is Internet Explorer, is copy the initial Bricks description to some variable. We do this, of course, as soon as the page loads and certainly before the remote user can overwrite the contents we're trying to save. Later, if the user clicks the Bricks choice, we have a copy of the original description. The code for all this is actually simpler than the explanation. In the <BODY> statement we code:

```
<body onload="saveBrickBox();">
```

Then, in the <HEAD section, we add the following script:

```
<script language="JavaScript">
<!--
function saveBrickBox(){
  if ((navigator.appName.substring(0,9)=="Microsoft")
  && (parseInt(navigator.appVersion) >= 3)) {
      txtBrick = descBox.innerHTML;
  }
}
// -->
</script>
```

If the browser is IE3 or later, the script saves the original *descBox.innerHTML* contents in a variable called *txtBrick*. When the user clicks the Bricks choice, we just execute the reverse of line 6 above:

```
descBox.innerHTML= txtBrick;
```

Complete HTML Listing

Lest we stand accused of breaking tradition, here's the complete HTML listing for The Brickbat Page:

```
<html>
<head>
<script language="JavaScript">
<!--
function saveBrickBox(){
  if ((navigator.appName.substring(0,9)=="Microsoft")
   && (parseInt(navigator.appVersion) >= 3)) {
     txtBrick = descBox.innerHTML;
  }
}
// -->
</script>
<title>The Brickbat Page</title>
</head>
<body
  onload="saveBrickBox();"
  background="../images/backgrnd.gif">
<p align="center">
<font size="7">The Brickbat Page</font></p>
<hr>
<span id="descBox"
        style="position: relative;
        float: right;
        width: 250;
        height: 275;
        overflow: scroll;
        padding: 3;
        border: 1px solid black;
        background-color: #FFFFFF; ">
<p><img src="../images/brickwal2.gif" alt="Bricks"
        align="left" width="119" height="91"></p>
<h1>Bricks </h1>
<p>No one seems to know why bricks - normally
considered simple construction
material — are funny.</p>
```

Script to save the contents of the initial description box if the browser is IE3 or later.

Run *saveBrickBox* function when page loads.

Display page heading.

Define span for description box.

Define initial contents of description box.

Continued from previous page

```
<p>Be that as it may, almost any joke involving
a stone, rock, or other projectile is
funnier if it refers instead to a brick.</p>
</span>
<table border="0" cellpadding="3" cellspacing="0">
<tr style="cursor: hand; "
    onclick="descBox.innerHTML=txtBrick">
  <td><img src="../images/brickwal.gif" alt="Bricks"
           width="80" height="61"></td>
  <td><font size="7">Bricks</font></td></tr>
<tr style="cursor: hand; "
    onclick="descBox.innerHTML=batBox.innerHTML">
  <td><img src="../images/bbalbat.gif" alt="Bats
           width="54" height="61"></td>
  <td><font size="7">Bats</font></td></tr>
<tr style="cursor: hand; "
    onclick="descBox.innerHTML=nosBox.innerHTML">
  <td><img src="../images/nose.gif" alt="Insults"
           width="47" height="61"></td>
  <td><font size="7">Insults</font></td></tr>
<tr style="cursor: hand; "
    onclick="descBox.innerHTML=cryBox.innerHTML">
  <td><img src="../images/onion.gif" alt="Apologies"
           width="56" height="61"></td>
  <td><font size="7">Apologies</font></td></tr>
</table>
<div id="batBox" style="display: none;">
<h1><img src="../images/bbalbat2.gif" alt="Bats"
        align="right" width="81" height="91">
    Bats</h1>
<p>Aluminum baseball bats have become very popular at
all levels of the game except Major League Baseball.</p>
```

Table of choices.

The Bricks choice.

The Bats choice.

The Insults choice.

The Apologies choice.

Invisible division for Bats contents.

Trick 5

Continued from previous page

```
<p>Players at the little league, high school, college,
and amateur levels find aluminum bats far more durable
and powerful than their wooden predecessors, but fans at
major league ballparks seem to prefer the satisfying
crack of a wooden bat over the metallic ping of an
aluminum model.</p></div>
<div id="nosBox" style="display: none;">
<h1><img src="../images/nose2.gif" alt="Insults"
        align="left" width="70" height="91">
        Insults</h1>
<p>There are few things in life so enjoyable as
disparaging comments against one's opponent.</p>
<p>This is not to imply any one should harbor or
encourage hatred in their relationships. On the
contrary, a friendly insult is a sure and simple sign
of friendly competition.</p></div>
<div id="cryBox" style="display:none;">
<p align="center">
<img src="../images/onion2.gif" alt="Apologies"
     width="86" height="91"></p>
<h1 align="center">Apologies</h1>
<p>Anyone ready to throw insults should be ready to
offer apologies as well. Offering an apology is seldom
a sign of weakness; instead, it signifies the strength
and willingness to resolve a misunderstanding.</p></div>
</body>
</html>
```

Invisible division for Insults contents.

Invisible division for Apologies contents.

This use of CSS Positioning is simpler than on the AERO Message Page because it doesn't position any content with code. This comes at a price: if you narrow the browser window enough, the scrollable <SPAN> area will overlap the menu choices. Almost any Web page in the world becomes illegible if you narrow or shorten it enough, though; what's important is to test it over a truly practical range.

The technique of displaying rich content inside a scrolling window is an interesting one. I'm sure you can picture it previewing the content of hyperlinks or displaying product information as the user moves the mouse around the page.

The UFO Corner

The third and final example in this trick adds a subtle degree of motion to a Web page. We're going to move four images up and down the Web page whenever the user scrolls the browser window. When the user scrolls down, we'll move the images up just the same amount. We'll do the same in reverse when the user scrolls up. In short, we're going to move so fast it'll look like we're standing still.

Consider, if you will, the Web page shown in Figure 5-4. Pay particular attention to the four images in the corners. You can scroll up and down, right and

FIGURE 5-4. *The four corner images always stay in the corners of the browser window. A script moves them around the Web page precisely as the user scrolls or resizes the window.*

A script moves the four corner images up and down the Web page as fast as the user scrolls the page.

As a result, they seem attached to the window border and not to the Web page.

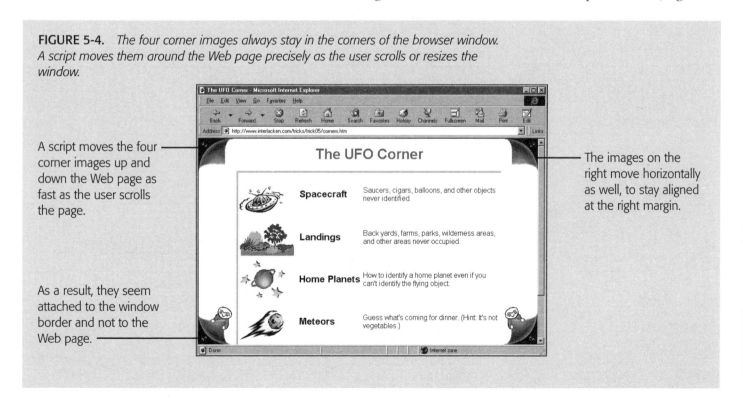

The images on the right move horizontally as well, to stay aligned at the right margin.

left, or resize the window all you want, but the four images will always remain fixed in the corners of the document window. In short , it looks as if the corner images are attached to the browser window and not part of the Web page at all.

Scripting Techniques

This example uses the four *document.body* properties listed in Table 5-2 and the three *window* events in Table 5-3. The *document.body* properties are also shown in Figure 5-5. Whenever an event listed in Table 5-3 fires, a script computes and applies the necessary x and y coordinates so each corner image remains, in fact, in the corner.

TABLE 5-2. *document.body* Properties Used by The UFO Corner page.	
Property	**Description**
clientHeight	The interior height of the browser window in pixels.
clientWidth	The interior width of the browser window in pixels.
scrollLeft	The distance between the left edge of the document and the left edge of the browser's view space. Also, the number of document pixels currently scrolled beyond the left margin.
scrollTop	The distance between the top of the document and the top of the browser's view space. Also, the number of document pixels currently scrolled above the top margin.

TABLE 5-3. *window* Events Used by The UFO Corner page.	
Property	**Description**
onLoad	Occurs when the browser initially loads the document.
onResize	Occurs whenever the size of the browser's viewing space changes.
onScroll	Occurs whenever the user (or code) scrolls the document window left or right, up or down.

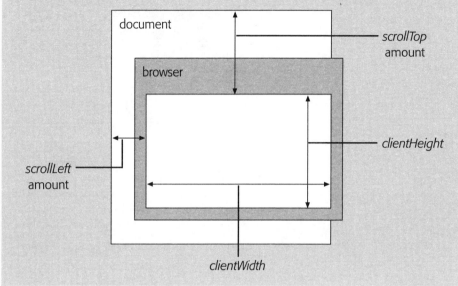

FIGURE 5-5. *The* document.body.clientHeight *and* document.body.clientWidth *properties reflect the current dimensions of the browser's document display area. The* document.body.scrollTop *and* document.body.scrollLeft *properties indicate how much of the document is currently scrolled off the top and left edges.*

The following HTML code adds the four corner images to the Web page:

```
<p><img id="UL" src="../images/corner1.gif"
        style="position: absolute;"
        width="85" height="92">
    <img id="UR" src="../images/corner2.gif"
        style="position: absolute; "
        width="85" height="92">
    <img id="LL" src="../images/corner3.gif"
        style="position: absolute;"
        width="85" height="92">
    <img id="LR" src="../images/corner4.gif"
        style="position: absolute; "
        width="85" height="92"> </p>
```

This is very ordinary code with two exceptions:

- First, each <IMG> tag has an ID= attribute. This gives the image a name we can refer to in JavaScript.

- Second, each <IMG> tag contains a STYLE= attribute that puts absolute CSS Positioning into effect. This lets us move each image around the page at will. Setting an image's *top* property to, say, 100 will position the image 100 pixels from the top of the document. Setting an image's *left* property to 75 will position the image 75 pixels from the document's left edge.

The four images are named UL (upper-left), UR (upper-right), LL (lower-left), and LR (lower-right). Positioning the UL and UR images at the top of the browser window is easy if the window is scrolled to the top of the document: we set UL's and UR's *top* properties to 0. Zero is the top of the document, which we said was also the top of the window.

Now, suppose the user has scrolled the browser window 100 pixels down the document. This means the top 100 pixels of the document are hidden above the browser's visible area. To position the UL and UR images at the top of the browser window, we need to position them 100 pixels from the top of the document. The following JavaScript statements accomplish this:

```
UL.style.top  = document.body.scrollTop ;
UR.style.top  = document.body.scrollTop ;
```

At any given moment, the *document.body.scrollTop* property tells us how much of the document body is scrolled off the top of the window. Setting UL's and UR's *style.top* property to the *document.body.scrollTop* value positions those images at the top of the browser window.

This is all very well and good, you say, but how do we know when to execute these two statements? We need to execute them whenever *document. body.scrollTop* changes, and that would be:

- Whenever the page initially loads.

- Whenever the user operates the scroll bars.

 Tip: Naming is a key programming skill. When assigning names to script variables, Web page objects, or anything else, use short, concise, meaningful names, and avoid special characters.

Fortunately, we can tell the browser to catch these events and run a JavaScript routine whenever they occur. This is something we code on the <BODY> statement as follows:

```
<body onload="SetCorners();" onscroll="SetCorners();">
```

SetCorners() is a JavaScript function defined in the <HEAD> section with code like this (much abbreviated):

```
<script language="JavaScript">
<!--
function SetCorners() {
    UL.style.top  = document.body.scrollTop ;
    UR.style.top  = document.body.scrollTop ;
}
// -->
</script>
```

So now, whenever the page loads or whenever the user scrolls the document, the browser will run the *SetCorners()* function and thereby execute our two positioning statements. Phew, but is that cool or what?

Controlling the *left* properties of the UL (upper-left) and LL (lower-left) corner images turns out to be just as easy. Suppose 75 pixels of the document are scrolled off the left side of the browser window. To position the UL and LL images at the left edge of the browser window, we need to position them 75 pixels from the left edge of the document. We can do this by adding two statements to the *SetCorners()* function:

```
UL.style.left = document.body.scrollLeft;
LL.style.left = document.body.scrollLeft;
```

Similar to *document.body.scrollTop*, the *document.body.scrollLeft* property tells us how many pixels of the document area are currently scrolled beyond the left edge of the browser window. You can do this in your sleep now, right?

Positioning things at the right and bottom edges of the browser window involves only a few extra wrinkles.

Consider the problem of aligning an image to the right edge of the browser window. Horizontal measurements always apply to the left edges of things. So, if the browser window is 600 pixels wide and the image is 85 pixels wide, the left edge of the image needs to be 515 pixels from the left edge of the window. In JavaScript, the calculation looks like this:

```
UR.style.left = document.body.clientWidth
              - UR.width ;
```

The *document.body.clientWidth* property always contains the number of horizontal pixels available for displaying a document, the document's visible width, 600 in the example just above. *UR.width* is the width in pixels of the upper-right image (which we named UR, remember). This was 85 in the example.

There's one remaining problem with the calculation of *UR.style.left*. The *UR.style.left* property isn't measured from the left edge of the window; it's measured from the left edge of the document. Suppose, as before, the browser is 600 pixels wide and the image is 85. Suppose also, though, that 100 pixels of the document are hidden behind the left edge of the window. *UR.style.left* needs to be:

	100	The distance from the left edge of the document to the left edge of the window.
plus	600	The distance from the left edge of the window to the right.
minus	85	The width of the image.
equals	615	The required distance from the left edge of the document to the left edge of the image (required, that is, to align the right edge of the image to the right edge of the window.)

In code, the finished calculation for the upper-right image looks like this:

```
UR.style.left = document.body.scrollLeft
              + document.body.clientWidth
              - UR.width ;
```

Likewise, the calculation to horizontally position the lower-right image is:

```
LR.style.left = document.body.scrollLeft
              + document.body.clientWidth
              - LR.width ;
```

Tip: JavaScript doesn't require a continuation character when statements span more than one line. A semicolon, and not a line break, indicates the end of a statement.

Vertically positioning the LL (lower-left) and LR (lower-right) images involves the same mindset. Take the distance from the top of the document to the top of the window, add the distance from the top of the window to the bottom of the window, and then subtract the height of the image. In code:

```
LL.style.top  = document.body.scrollTop
              + document.body.clientHeight
              - LL.height ;
LR.style.top  = document.body.scrollTop
              + document.body.clientHeight
              - LR.height ;
```

Integrating all these calculations into the *Set Corners()* function produces the following code. There are eight calculations in all: a top and a left calculation for each of the four images:

```
<script language="JavaScript">
<!--
function SetCorners() {
    UL.style.top  = document.body.scrollTop ;
    UL.style.left = document.body.scrollLeft;
    UR.style.top  = document.body.scrollTop ;
    UR.style.left = document.body.scrollLeft
                  + document.body.clientWidth
                  - UR.width ;
    LL.style.top  = document.body.scrollTop
                  + document.body.clientHeight
                  - LL.height ;
    LL.style.left = document.body.scrollLeft;
    LR.style.top  = document.body.scrollTop
                  + document.body.clientHeight
                  - LR.height ;
    LR.style.left = document.body.scrollLeft
                  + document.body.clientWidth
                  - LR.width ; }
// -->
</script>
```

There's one final detail to consider. Earlier, we added ONLOAD= and ONSCROLL= properties to the <BODY> tag so the *SetCorners()* function would run whenever the *document.body.scrollTop* property or the *document.body.scrollLeft* property changed. Unfortunately, this won't pick up cases where the *document.body.clientWidth* or the *document.body.clientHeight* properties change. Fortunately, the fix is easy: we also run the *SetCorners()* function whenever the *onResize* event occurs (that is, whenever the user resizes the browser window). The <BODY> statement now looks like this:

```
<body onload="SetCorners();"
      onresize="SetCorners();"
      onscroll="SetCorners();">
```

We've covered a lot of new ground in this section but we've also achieved a very cool effect with not much code. We've learned a good bit about CSS Positioning, about accessing style properties from JavaScript, about responding to events that occur while the Web page is on display, and about changing a Web page *after* it's displayed. That's not only a lot of material, it's a lot of very useful stuff. Congratulations!

There are three other minor tricks on this page. First, the choices are arranged by means of a three-column table. To make each row an equal height, the first cell in each row displays not only the visible image, but also a transparent GIF file stretched by HTML attributes to 85 pixels high and 1 pixel wide. A *nowrap* attribute in the <TD> tag keeps the second image from wrapping to a second line.

The second minor trick involves keeping the main content away from the corner images. Unlike the situation in ordinary HTML, nothing keeps positioned elements from overlapping each other. Overlapping is fine if that's what you want, but in this case we don't, so it isn't. Fine, that is. The corner images are all 85 pixels wide, so we reserve 85-pixel left and right margins by adding the following style attribute to the <BODY> tag:

```
style="margin-left:85px; margin-right:85px;"
```

Tip: You can reserve margins on any side of the document by coding *margin-left*, *margin-right*, *margin-top*, and *margin-bottom* style properties. To set all four properties simultaneously, code the *margin* property.

The third minor trick creates the gray border lines above and to the left of the choices list. These lines result from the following attribute added to the <TABLE tag>:

```
style="border-left: medium solid; border-top: medium solid; "
```

The properties following *border-left* apply to the table's left border; those following *border-top* apply to the top border. No surprise there. Here's an incredibly brief introduction to the values you can assign:

- *Medium* is a border width keyword; you can also code *thin*, *thick*, or a standard CSS measurement like 3px or 4pt.

- *Solid* is a border style keyword; the list of possibilities includes *none, dotted, dashed, solid, double, groove, ridge, inset,* and *outset.*

- You can also code any valid color as part of a border specification; things like *black, red, #CC00CC, rgb(204,0,204),* yada, yada, yada.

- To assign properties to all four borders at once, assign them to the *border* property.

Complete HTML Listing

OK, that's enough talk; let's take a look at the full HTML listing for The UFO Corner page.

Define style sheet rules for choice list.

```
<html>
<head>
<title>The UFO Corner</title>
<style>
<!--
 .cat { font-family: Arial, sans-serif;
        font-size: 16pt;
        font-weight: bold }
 .des { font-family: Arial, sans-serif; }
-->
</style>
```

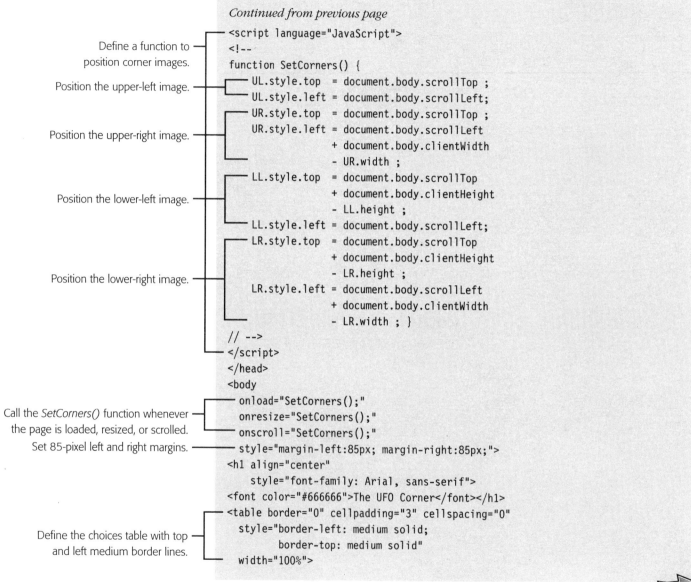

Continued from previous page

```
<script language="JavaScript">
<!--
function SetCorners() {
    UL.style.top  = document.body.scrollTop ;
    UL.style.left = document.body.scrollLeft;
    UR.style.top  = document.body.scrollTop ;
    UR.style.left = document.body.scrollLeft
                        + document.body.clientWidth
                        - UR.width ;
    LL.style.top  = document.body.scrollTop
                        + document.body.clientHeight
                        - LL.height ;
    LL.style.left = document.body.scrollLeft;
    LR.style.top  = document.body.scrollTop
                        + document.body.clientHeight
                        - LR.height ;
    LR.style.left = document.body.scrollLeft
                        + document.body.clientWidth
                        - LR.width ; }
// -->
</script>
</head>
<body
    onload="SetCorners();"
    onresize="SetCorners();"
    onscroll="SetCorners();"
    style="margin-left:85px; margin-right:85px;">
<h1 align="center"
        style="font-family: Arial, sans-serif">
<font color="#666666">The UFO Corner</font></h1>
<table border="0" cellpadding="3" cellspacing="0"
    style="border-left: medium solid;
            border-top: medium solid"
    width="100%">
```

Define a function to position corner images.

Position the upper-left image.

Position the upper-right image.

Position the lower-left image.

Position the lower-right image.

Call the *SetCorners()* function whenever the page is loaded, resized, or scrolled.

Set 85-pixel left and right margins.

Define the choices table with top and left medium border lines.

Continued from previous page

Choice 1: The Spacecraft.

```
<tr>
  <td valign="middle" nowrap>
    <img src="../images/saucer.gif" alt="Spacecraft"
        width="100" height="59">
    <img src="../images/trans5x5.gif"
        width="1" height="85"></td>
  <td class="cat">Spacecraft</td>
  <td width="99%" class="des">Saucers, cigars, balloons,
    and other objects never identified.</td></tr>
```

Choice 2: The Landings.

```
<tr>
  <td valign="middle" nowrap>
    <img src="../images/park2.gif" alt="Landings"
        width="124" height="71">
    <img src="../images/trans5x5.gif"
        width="1" height="85"></td>
  <td class="cat">Landings</td>
  <td class="des">Back yards, farms, parks, wilderness
    areas, and other areas never occupied.</td></tr>
```

Choice 3: The Home Planets.

```
<tr>
  <td valign="middle" nowrap>
    <img src="../images/cosmos.gif" alt="Home Planets"
        width="103" height="85"></td>
  <td class="cat">Home Planets</td>
  <td class="des">How to identify a home planet even if
    you can't identify the flying object.</td></tr>
```

Choice 4: The Meteors.

```
<tr>
  <td valign="middle" nowrap>
    <img src="../images/meteor1.gif" alt="Meteors"
        width="100" height="66">
    <img src="../images/trans5x5.gif"
        width="1" height="85"></td>
  <td class="cat">Meteors</td>
  <td class="des">Guess what's coming for dinner. (Hint:
    It's not vegetables.)</td></tr>
```

Trick 5

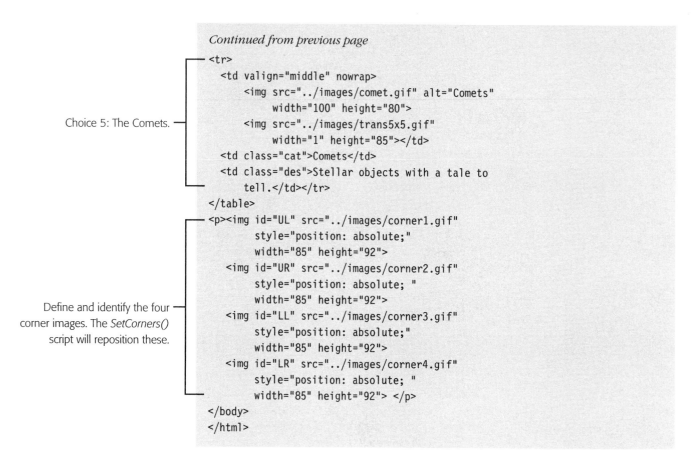

Continued from previous page

Choice 5: The Comets.

```
<tr>
  <td valign="middle" nowrap>
    <img src="../images/comet.gif" alt="Comets"
       width="100" height="80">
    <img src="../images/trans5x5.gif"
       width="1" height="85"></td>
  <td class="cat">Comets</td>
  <td class="des">Stellar objects with a tale to
     tell.</td></tr>
</table>
```

Define and identify the four corner images. The *SetCorners()* script will reposition these.

```
<p><img id="UL" src="../images/corner1.gif"
     style="position: absolute;"
     width="85" height="92">
  <img id="UR" src="../images/corner2.gif"
     style="position: absolute; "
     width="85" height="92">
  <img id="LL" src="../images/corner3.gif"
     style="position: absolute;"
     width="85" height="92">
  <img id="LR" src="../images/corner4.gif"
     style="position: absolute; "
     width="85" height="92"> </p>
</body>
</html>
```

CSS Positioning is a powerful feature but using it can be a frustrating experience, at least at first. Positioning not only permits, but in most cases requires, that you adjust positions on-the-fly based on conditions at the browser. I'm afraid CSS Positioning won't bring much comfort to layout specialists yearning for the good old days of fixed page sizes.

On the other hand, CSS Positioning provides a powerful approach for making your pages more interactive. Now you can hide or reveal items at will, and even move them around the page as the user watches in awe. Not bad, not bad at all.

With version 4, Netscape Navigator introduced *layers*, a proprietary scheme developed before the standards for CSS Positioning were finalized. Layers are the topic of the next trick.

6 Positioning with Layers

A s we've begun to see in the first five tricks, Microsoft Internet Explorer turns HTML authoring into an extreme sport. IE provides almost total flexibility to modify the structure, content, and style of your Web pages in real time, as the remote user watches and interacts in transfixed awe. (Well, that's the objective…) This is the essence of Dynamic HTML.

In version 4.0, Netscape Navigator implemented a more limited approach to Dynamic HTML, which it called *layers*. A layer is a block of HTML content you can move around the page, make visible or invisible, move over and beneath other layers, and so forth. There are two ways to define a layer:

- The Netscape way, using either <LAYER>…</LAYER> or <ILAYER>…</ILAYER> tags.

- The W3C (World Wide Web Consortium) way, using <SPAN>…</SPAN> or <DIV>…</DIV> tags.

Netscape Navigator and Internet Explorer both support the <SPAN> and <DIV> tags, but differently. IE doesn't support <LAYER> tags at all. It's hard to see how this divergence benefits anyone except the aspirin companies, but such is the halting forward march of progress. "That which does not kill us makes us stronger" (Nietzsche).

The first two examples in this trick use the <ILAYER> and <LAYER> tags so, from an IE point of view, they're majorly dysfunctional. These are the kinds of pages you might create if you only care about Netscape Navigator or if you're doing different versions for different browsers. The third example is a miracle of engineering, a single Dynamic HTML page that works in both IE and Netscape. Applause, applause, thank you.

AERO Message Service (NS)

This example shows a Netscape-only page that closely resembles the first example in Trick 5. Remember, the planes...floating banners...all that? The resemblance isn't perfect, as you can see by comparing Figure 6-1 to Figure 5-1, but the results are close. As to which is better, well, there's no accounting for taste.

FIGURE 6-1. *This Netscape-only page closely resembles the first example in Trick 5 (which was IE-only).*

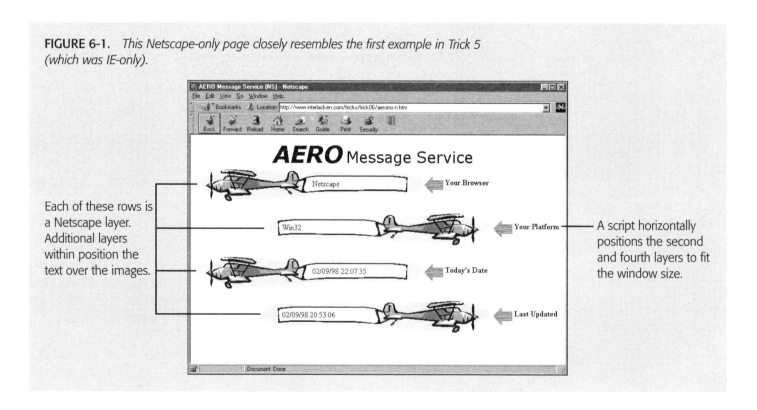

Each of these rows is a Netscape layer. Additional layers within position the text over the images.

A script horizontally positions the second and fourth layers to fit the window size.

Page Layout Details

Wonder of wonder, there are no tables in this version of the AERO Message Service page. Instead, each combination of an airplane, arrow, and title constitutes a layer. In all, there are four layers on this page; go ahead and count 'em if you don't believe me.

You can use either the <LAYER> or the <ILAYER> tag to define a layer. Both tags define the same kind of layer, and both position the layer at the opening tag's natural location in the document (unless overridden by script code or by TOP and LEFT attributes in the HTML).

The difference between the two layer tags lies in the position of whatever comes *after* the layer:

- However large or small a <LAYER>...</LAYER> area might be, it takes up no space on the underlying Web page. The browser positions any content before and after the layer as if the layer didn't exist.

  Also, the TOP and LEFT attributes in a LAYER tag are *absolute*. That is, they're measured from the top left corner of layer's container (which is either another layer or the document itself).

- With the <ILAYER>...</ILAYER> tags, the browser skips over the space beneath the layer before it displays any further content.

  Also, the TOP and LEFT attributes in an <ILAYER> tag are *relative*. They're measured from the <ILAYER> tag's natural position in the document.

Figure 6-2 illustrates these differences.

Tip: The PAGEX and PAGEY attributes always position a layer—even a layer inside another layer—relative to the entire document.

Layers, Transparencies, and Color Cartoons

Did you ever see how cartoons were made before the age of computer graphics? Artists drew the background scene on paper or art board, and then drew the movable elements on clear acetate sheets. To assemble a complete scene, they stacked the acetates over the background.

Layers, Transparencies, and Color Cartoons *(continued)*

This is pretty much how layers work. Everything *not* included in a layer appears on the base Web page. Each layer, including its content, hovers *over* the base Web page. From there:

- You can make the layer visible or invisible.

- You can move the layer (and its contents) around the page.

- If you have several layers, you can stack them in different orders.

By default, content on the base page doesn't flow around a layer; the layer just appears *on top of* any other content. To make the browser reserve a blank space beneath a layer's initial position, define the layer with <ILAYER>...</ILAYER> tags.

FIGURE 6-2. *When you define a layer with <LAYER> tags, the browser reserves no blank space beneath it. Use <ILAYER> tags if you want blank space reserved.*

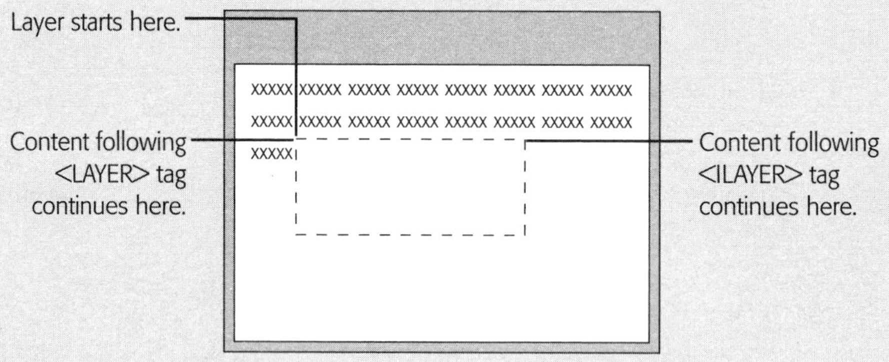

Layer starts here.

Content following <LAYER> tag continues here.

Content following <ILAYER> tag continues here.

The AERO Message Service page uses <ILAYER> tags to define each airplane layer. This prevents the layers from appearing on top of each other. To make sure the layers appear sequentially down the page, a new paragraph contains each one:

Caution: When displaying pages that contain layers or style sheets, Netscape Navigator sometimes deals poorly with changes to the window size. If a page gets jumbled after users resize the window, they'll have to click the Reload button.

 Caution: Because Internet Explorer doesn't support layers, it has no *document.layers* collection. Scripts that use this collection cause IE to complain loudly and display error messages. To see an IE-specific version of the AERO Message Service page, refer to the first example in Trick 5.

```
<p>
<ilayer>
   <!-- Layer content goes here -->
</ilayer>
</p>
```

Scripting Techniques

Because layers aren't part of the base Web page, traditional alignment tags don't apply. We can't simply code ALIGN=RIGHT in the second and fourth layers, for example. Instead, the following JavaScript code aligns the second and fourth layers to the right margin whenever the page loads:

```
function adjust() {
    leftoff = window.innerWidth
           - (16 + document.layers.lay02.document.width);
    document.layers["lay02"].moveTo(leftoff ,document.layers.lay02.top);
    document.layers["lay04"].moveTo(leftoff ,document.layers.lay04.top);
}
```

The property *window.innerWidth* provides the width of the current view space in pixels. From this, the script subtracts a 16-pixel margin plus the width of the second layer. The remainder, stored in a variable named *leftoff*, tells us where layers 2 and 4 need to start, horizontally, so their right edges line up to the right edge of the browser window.

> **What's in a Name? Or an ID?**
>
> When the World Wide Web Consortium introduced Cascading Style Sheets, it recommended using a new attribute, ID, for identifying HTML tags and their associated content. The coding looks like this:
>
> `<SPAN ID=yourName>`
>
> When Netscape designed its LAYER specification, it used the existing NAME attribute for identification. That is:
>
> `<LAYER NAME=yourName>`

Tip: Your code will be easier to read and maintain if you're consistent in its notation and format. Whenever there's a choice of techniques, pick one and stick to it whenever possible.

Tip: When positioning layers, the starting point isn't always what you think it is. For objects within a layer, the starting point is the layer's upper-left corner. For layers not contained in any other layer, it's the upper-left corner of the window.

The next two statements move layers 2 and 4 to their new positions. Note the reference to document.layers["lay02"] rather than document.layers.lay02. Both these notations are equivalent; I only used both forms to show off. One nice feature of the ["bracket"] notation, however, is that you can put a variable name (rather than a constant) between the brackets.

The moveTo method moves a layer to a different location on the page, and it requires both a left and a top value. The left value is the result we saved in leftoff. The top value requires no change in this example, so we simply reinstate the current value (that is, document.layers.lay02.top).

Layers 1 and 2, as before, use <SPAN> tags to lay variable text over the airplane images. Layers 3 and 4 use <LAYER> tags for variety, to show the equivalence of both tag types, and because Emerson says, "A foolish consistency is the hobgoblin of little minds." Here are the two forms:

```
<span style="position: absolute; top:23; left:250">

<layer top=23 left=250>
```

One final comment, and then we'll look at the full HTML listing. You may have noticed that in the IE page, but not on the Netscape page, the arrows always pointed in the same direction as the airplanes:

Internet Explorer Version	Netscape Navigator Version
Plane, Arrow, Your Browser	Plane, Arrow, Your Browser
Your Platform, Arrow, Plane	Plane, Arrow, Your Platform
Plane, Arrow, Today's Date	Plane, Arrow, Today's Date
Last Updated, Arrow, Plane	Plane, Arrow, Last Updated

Hyperlink: This listing uses the Date object. The following sites provide information on the Date object in JavaScript:

Microsoft:
http://www.microsoft.com/Scripting/ JScript/Jslang/jsobjDate.htm

Netscape:
http://developer.netscape.com/docs/ manuals/communicator/jsref/ core3.htm

The problem with putting text in front of the airplanes in layers 2 and 4 is that we don't exactly know how many pixels the text will consume, so we don't know how far to offset the variable text. (Don't forget, the remote user can change font size on us.) More scripting and calculating could probably determine the necessary values at browse time, but to avoid complicating the example I leave this as an exercise to the reader. After all, you paid for the book and you deserve some of the fun.

Complete HTML Listing

Now here's the code:

Set paragraph margin to 0. —

Define script to right-justify layers 2 and 4. —

Run right-justification script as soon as the page loads. —

Display the page heading. —

```html
<html>
<head>
<style>
 P { margin: 0; }
</style>
<script language="JavaScript">
<!--
function adjust() {
  leftoff = window.innerWidth
          - (16 + document.layers.lay02.document.width);
  document.layers["lay02"].moveTo(leftoff ,document.layers.lay02.top);
  document.layers["lay04"].moveTo(leftoff ,document.layers.lay04.top);
}
// -->
</script>
<title>AERO Message Service (NS)</title>
</head>
<body onload="adjust()">
<p align="center" style="font-family: Verdana, sans-serif">
<font size="7"><em><strong>AERO</strong></em></font>
<font size="6">Message Service</font></p>
```

Continued from previous page

Define layer 1.

Define the subordinate layer and script for variable text.

```
<p><ilayer name="lay01">
<img src="../images/airmsg2.gif" align="middle"
        width="481" height="71">
<span style="position: absolute; top:23; left:250">
<script language="JavaScript">
<!--
document.write(navigator.appName);
// -->
</script>
</span>
<img src="../images/arrowlf.gif" align="middle"
      width="41" height="38">
<strong> Your Browser</strong>
</ilayer></p>
```

Define layer 2.

Define the subordinate layer and script for variable text.

```
<p><ilayer name="lay02">
<img src="../images/airmsg1.gif" align="middle"
      width="481" height="71">
<span style="position: absolute; top:23; left:40">
<script language="JavaScript">
<!--
document.write(navigator.platform);
// -->
</script>
</span>
<img src="../images/arrowlf.gif" align="middle"
      width="41" height="38">
<strong> Your Platform</strong>
</ilayer></p>
```

Define layer 3.

```
<p><ilayer name="lay03">
<img src="../images/airmsg2.gif" align="middle"
      width="481" height="71">
```

Continued from previous page

Define the subordinate layer and script for variable text.

```
<layer top=23 left=250>
<script language="JavaScript">
<!--
CurDt = new Date();
LocDt = CurDt.toLocaleString();
document.write(LocDt);
// -->
</script>
</layer>
<img src="../images/arrowlf.gif" align="middle"
     width="41" height="38">
<strong> Today's Date</strong>
</ilayer></p>
```

Define layer 4.

```
<p><ilayer name="lay04">
<img src="../images/airmsg1.gif" align="middle"
     width="481" height="71">
<layer top=23 left=40>
<script language="JavaScript">
<!--
```

Define the subordinate layer and script for variable text.

```
document.write(document.lastModified);
// -->
</script>
</layer>
<img src="../images/arrowlf.gif" align="middle"
     width="41" height="38">
<strong> Last Updated</strong>
</ilayer></p>
</body>
</html>
```

Hyperlink: For an introduction to a working example of moving layers around a Web page, refer to the Swimming Fish Example at:

http://developer.netscape.com/docs/ manuals/communicator/dynhtml/ layers35.htm

Using layers might seem complicated at first, and for many jobs HTML tables provide a simpler solution. However, layers have three capabilities that tables completely lack:

- You can stack layers to superimpose one set of content over another. The AERO Message Service page, for example, superimposes text over a graphic.

- You can move layers around the Web page after it's displayed.

- You can make individual layers visible or invisible while the Web page is on display. The next two examples in this trick, The Flower Scene and Creatures You May Find, illustrate this.

The Flower Scene

The Netscape version of the AERO Message Service page used <ILAYER> tags so the four main layers would advance down the page and not appear on top of each other.

The variable text strings used <LAYER> tags because they weren't supposed to occupy any space of their own. Instead, they were supposed to appear on top of the airplane images. <SPAN> tags with STYLE="position: absolute; " turned out to work the same as <LAYER> tags.

The Flower Scene page shown in Figure 6-3 has five layers positioned exactly on top of each other. No confusion results, though, because only one layer at a time is visible. Clicking on any of the menu choices reveals one layer and hides all the rest. The effect is much like updating one frame in a frameset, except that 1) it's faster and 2) we could show and hide multiple layers with one click.

Scripting Techniques

The code that defines the first layer follows. The NAME attribute gives the layer its name and the VISIBILITY attribute tells the browser to make it, well visible. The other layers are defined with different names, of course, and with VISIBILITY="HIDE" to make them initially invisible:

```
<layer name="lr01" visibility="show">
```

FIGURE 6-3. *The space between the horizontal rules contains five overlapping layers, but only one at a time is visible. The menu choices run scripts that show and hide various layers.*

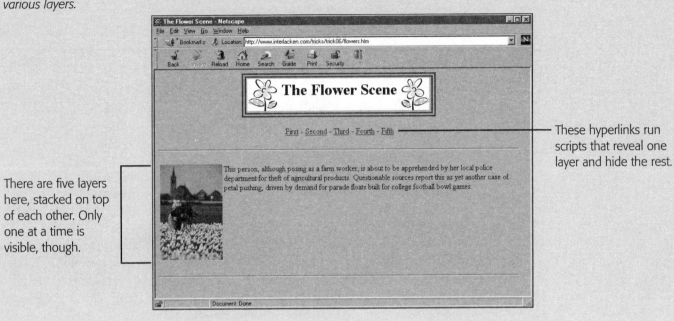

These hyperlinks run scripts that reveal one layer and hide the rest.

There are five layers here, stacked on top of each other. Only one at a time is visible, though.

 Note: Whenever you click a hyperlink, the browser changes the mouse pointer to an hourglass or clock, and then, when it's done following the hyperlink, changes the pointer back to an arrow or hand. Unfortunately, for JavaScript hyperlinks, some versions of Netscape Navigator never reset the pointer. It remains an hourglass or clock until you happen to move the mouse. This is an apparent bug that also affects other kinds of links within the same page.

The menu bar consists of this drill, repeated five times, with feeling:

```
<a href="javascript:reveal(1)">First</a>
```

This creates a hyperlink that, instead of jumping to a Web page, executes some JavaScript code. In this case the code is the function called *reveal(1)*. The *reveal()* function is something we coded in the <HEAD> section, and it does five reps of this:

```
if (num == 1){
    document.layers.lr01.visibility="show";
}else{
    document.layers.lr01.visibility="hide";
}
```

If *num* is 1, the script makes layer 1 visible. If *num* is anything else, it makes layer 1 invisible. We named layer 1 *lr01* a few paragraphs ago. Pay attention. Additional reps test *num* for values of 1, 2, 3, and 4, show the corresponding layer if the values match, and hide it if they don't.

The variable *num* gets its value when the JavaScript hyperlinks invoke the function. The function definition looks like this:

```
function reveal (num) {
}
```

and so, when we call it as:

```
reveal(1)
```

the function runs with 1 as the value of *num*.

There's one last adventure in The Flower Scene, namely drawing the lower horizontal rule. Because all five layers are defined with <LAYER> tags, none of them takes up any space and the second rule would appear right under the first. This is way unacceptable.

Making the fifth layer an ILAYER is one possible solution, but a bad one. All the layers have about the same format, and their tallest object is a left-aligned image 194 pixels high. The browser displays the image first and then wraps the text around it, so the last thing the browser displays is the period at the end of the text. So far so good, but now the browser thinks the layer ends where the text ends. So it draws the horizontal rule just below the text rather than just below the image. Still unacceptable.

I suppose I could have stretched a transparent GIF image to soak up a couple hundred horizontal pixels but, you know, been there, done that, and besides, this trick is about layers. So I skipped over 200 pixels with an empty layer as follows:

```
<ilayer height="200">
</ilayer>
```

Complete HTML Listing

I'm tired of all this talk; how about you? Let's get down and dirty once again with a view of the code shown on the following pages.

Define script to show the layer specified in num and hide the other layers.

```html
<html>
<head>
<title>The Flower Scene</title>
<script language="JavaScript">
<!--
function reveal (num) {
    if (num == 1){
        document.layers.lr01.visibility="show";
    }else{
        document.layers.lr01.visibility="hide";
    }

    if (num == 2){
        document.layers.lr02.visibility="show";
    }else{
        document.layers.lr02.visibility="hide";
    }

    if (num == 3){
        document.layers.lr03.visibility="show";
    }else{
        document.layers.lr03.visibility="hide";
    }

    if (num == 4){
        document.layers.lr04.visibility="show";
    }else{
        document.layers.lr04.visibility="hide";
    }

    if (num == 5){
        document.layers.lr05.visibility="show";
    }else{
        document.layers.lr05.visibility="hide";
    }
}
// -->
</script>
```

Test for layer 1.

Test for layer 2.

Test for layer 3.

Test for layer 4.

Test for layer 5.

Continued from previous page

```
</head>
<body bgcolor="#99CCFF">
<h1 align="center"
    style="background-color: white;
           border: medium double rgb(255,0,0);">
<img src="../images/flower1.gif" alt="Flower" align="middle"
    width="62" height="66">
<font color="#0000FF">The Flower Scene</font>
<img src="../images/flower2.gif" alt="Flower" align="middle"
    width="62" height="66"></h1>
<p align="center">
<a href="javascript:reveal(1)">First</a> -
<a href="javascript:reveal(2)">Second</a> -
<a href="javascript:reveal(3)">Third</a> -
<a href="javascript:reveal(4)">Fourth</a> -
<a href="javascript:reveal(5)">Fifth</a></p>
<hr>
<p>
<layer name="lr01" visibility="show">
<img src="../images/5167.gif" alt="Picking" align="left"
    width="130" height="194">
This person, although posing as a farm worker, is about
to be apprehended by her local police department for theft
of agricultural products. Questionable sources report this
as yet another case of petal pushing, driven by demand for
parade floats built for college football bowl games.
</layer>
<layer name="lr02" visibility="hide">
<img src="../images/5194.gif" alt="Giant"
    align="left" width="130" height="194">
These giant flowers, often growing larger than a two-story
house, were frequently used as cover by soldiers
<img src="../images/armyspy.gif" alt="Spy Flowers"
    align="right" width="70" height="72">
```

Display the page heading. Use STYLE tag to create fancy border.

Create the menu bar. Five hyperlinks each call the same script, but with different values.

Define layer 1.

Define layer 2.

Continued from previous page

```
in the European theater of both world wars. Unfortunately,
enemy forces firing into the large centers released huge
clouds of pollen that forced the hidden troops into
tremendous fits of sneezing, and thus into revealing their
positions.
</layer>
<layer name="lr03" visibility="hide">
<img src="../images/01004.jpg" alt="Oblong Object"
    align="left" width="130" height="194">
For decades scholars have debated the identity of the
object in this photograph. Some believe it to be a flower,
but others maintain strongly that it's a champagne glass.
<img src="../images/telescp.gif" alt="Telescope"
    align="right" width="90" height="91">
Other opinions classify it as <i>haute couture</i> fashion from
the 1952 Christian Dior collection. A respected New Mexico
commune holds that the photo records the engine blast from
an extraterrestrial craft with secret but peaceful intentions.
The inhabitants of the object are quite reclusive and have
never spoken to reporters.
</layer>
<layer name="lr04" visibility="hide">
<img src="../images/sunflowr.jpg" alt="Sunflower)"
    align="left" width="130" height="194">
This is the only known photograph of a being from the planet
Phlour. It was taken at great risk to the photographer, whom
the being, for unknown reasons, covered with three inches of
potting soil and watered for ten days. Presumably this was an offer
of friendship.
</layer>
<layer name="lr05" visibility="hide">
<img src="../images/summer.jpg" alt="Sneak"
    align="left" width="130" height="194">
```

Define layer 3.

Define layer 4.

Define layer 5.

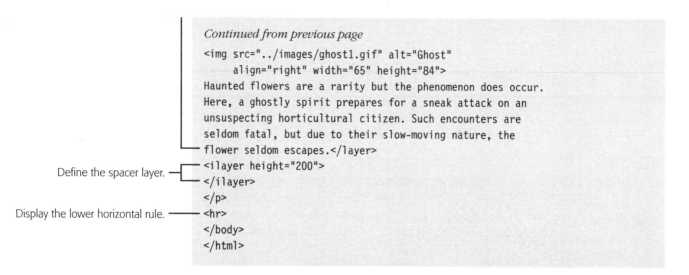

Continued from previous page

```
<img src="../images/ghost1.gif" alt="Ghost"
    align="right" width="65" height="84">
Haunted flowers are a rarity but the phenomenon does occur.
Here, a ghostly spirit prepares for a sneak attack on an
unsuspecting horticultural citizen. Such encounters are
seldom fatal, but due to their slow-moving nature, the
flower seldom escapes.</layer>
<ilayer height="200">
</ilayer>
</p>
<hr>
</body>
</html>
```

Define the spacer layer.

Display the lower horizontal rule.

Netscape layers aren't as flexible as the CSS Positioning features in Internet Explorer, but if you want to position, hide, reveal, or move content around a Web page displayed by Netscape Navigator 4, layers provide the only means.

To provide a level of compatibility with CSS Positioning, Netscape accepts the <DIV> tag, the <SPAN> tag, and some CSS Positioning properties. Internally, however, Netscape still treats these tags, attributes, and properties as layers. The next example will highlight this.

Creatures You May Find

As shown by the AERO Message Service page, Netscape Navigator recognizes layers defined not only with its own <LAYER> and <ILAYER> tags, but also with the <DIV> and <SPAN> tags that Internet Explorer uses. A curious but rational person might easily ask whether, despite other differences in the browsers, a single Web page using <DIV> and <SPAN> can be made to work with both.

Figure 6-4 proves this trick is indeed possible. Each cell in the second table row contains a division that's marked with <DIV> and </DIV> tags. Each of these

FIGURE 6-4. *This Dynamic HTML page works in both Netscape Navigator and IE. Clicking on a Show or Hide link displays or conceals an image immediately below.*

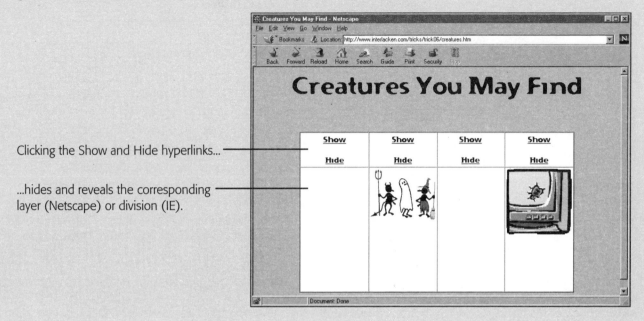

Clicking the Show and Hide hyperlinks...

...hides and reveals the corresponding layer (Netscape) or division (IE).

Tip: To make something invisible in Internet Explorer, set the *visibility* property to *hidden*. In Netscape Navigator, set the *visibility* property to anything beginning with *hid....* Close enough. Unfortunately, to make something visible, IE uses *visibility: show* and Navigator uses *visibility: visible*. Oh well, at least we know.

divisions, in turn, contains an image. Clicking on any Show or Hide anchor shows or hides the division (and therefore the image) beneath that anchor.

Page Layout Details

The four divisions containing the images are supposed to be invisible when the page loads, so we define a style class named *pics* as follows. The *position* property is *relative* so the browser reserves space under the division (that is, so the browser doesn't flow other stuff beneath it):

```
.pics { position: relative; visibility: hidden; }
```

Defining divisions is as simple as this. The content inside the division can be as complex as you like. Me, I go for simple:

```
<div ID="layer1" class=pics>
<p><img src="../images/frnknst2.gif" alt="Frankenstein"
        width="136" height="208"></p>
<p align=center class="clicks">Frankenstein</p>
</div>
```

Tip: You don't have to trigger scripts from hyperlinks if you only care about Internet Explorer compatibility. With IE, almost every element on the page responds to *onClick* events. Here's some typical IE-friendly HTML:

```
<p onclick="showIt('layer1')">Show</p>
```

Here's some typical HTML code for a hyperlink that reveals a division. If the remote user clicks this hyperlink, the browser runs the JavaScript routine named *showit*, passing the value *'layer1'* as an argument. The hyperlinks that hide a division are similar, but they run a script named *hideIt()*:

```
<a href="javascript:showIt('layer1')">Show</a>
```

Scripting Techniques

The JavaScript code for the *showIt()* routine follows. Because the Internet Explorer statement to make something visible is quite a bit different from the Netscape Navigator statement, we test the browser type and execute the corresponding statement:

```
function showIt(layer) {
    if (navigator.appName.substring(0,9) == "Microsoft"){
        document.all[layer].style.visibility="visible";
    }else{
        document.layers[layer].visibility="show";
    }
}
```

Document Object Models

The Creatures You May Find page really highlights how differently Internet Explorer and Netscape Navigator arrange their objects.

• In Internet Explorer, the visibility property of a division named xyz has this path:

```
document.all.xyz.style.visibility
```

Document Object Models *(continued)*

- The *document* object is the current Web page.

- Everything on the Web page belongs to the *all* collection. (Some objects also belong to other collections, but that's not relevant here.)

- Within the *all* collection, we can look for the division (or anything else) by name.

- Within the named division (or other object), we can access all its styles.

- Within the *styles* collection, we can access the *visibility* property.

- For Netscape Navigator, the equivalent drill goes:

```
document.layers.xyz.visibility
```

- The *document* object is the current Web page.

- Netscape accepts the syntax for divisions and spans, but treats them internally as layers. Divisions and spans therefore show up in the *layers* collection.

- Within the *layers* collection, we can address a particular layer by name.

- Given any particular layer, we can access its *visibility* property.

To make matters worse, these overall structures aren't particularly well documented. You can try looking for information on the Microsoft and Netscape Web sites, but the combination of a working example and some trial and error will often produce faster results.

Complete HTML Listing

I'll bet you thought we'd skip the full HTML listing for the Creatures You May Find page, just for a change of pace. Well, you're wrong. Here it is:

Define STYLE classes for clickable text and picture divisions. →

```
<html>
<head>
<style>
<!--
```

Continued from previous page

```
.clicks { font-family: Flexure, sans-serif }
.pics   { position: relative; visibility: hidden; }
 P      { margin:0; padding:3;}
-->
</style>
<script language="JavaScript">
<!--
function hideIt(layer) {
    if (navigator.appName.substring(0,9) == "Microsoft"){
        document.all[layer].style.visibility="hidden";
    }else{
        document.layers[layer].visibility="hide";
    }
}
function showIt(layer) {
    if (navigator.appName.substring(0,9) == "Microsoft"){
        document.all[layer].style.visibility="visible";
    }else{
        document.layers[layer].visibility="show";
    }
}
// -->
</script>
<title>Creatures You May Find</title>
</head>
<body bgcolor="#CCCCCC" link="#000000" vlink="#666666">
<p align="center"
   class="clicks">
<font size="7">Creatures You May Find</font></p>
<table border="1" cellpadding="3" cellspacing="0"
        bordercolor="#000000" bgcolor="#FFFFFF" align=center>
<tr>
<td align="center" class="clicks">
```

Define scripts.

Define script for hiding a picture division.

Define script for showing a picture division.

Display the page heading.

Define the table for displaying clickable text and images.

Start of row 1.

Continued from previous page

Define Show and Hide links for the Frankenstein image.

```html
<p><a href="javascript:showIt('layer1')">Show</a></p>
    <p><a href="javascript:hideIt('layer1')">Hide</a></p>
</td>
<td align="center" class="clicks">
```

Define Show and Hide links for the Goblin image.

```html
    <p><a href="javascript:showIt('layer2')">Show</a></p>
    <p><a href="javascript:hideIt('layer2')">Hide</a></p>
</td>
<td align="center" class="clicks">
```

Define Show and Hide links for the Mummy image.

```html
    <p><a href="javascript:showIt('layer3')">Show</a></p>
    <p><a href="javascript:hideIt('layer3')">Hide</a></p>
</td>
<td align="center" class="clicks">
```

Define Show and Hide links for the Bug image.

```html
    <p><a href="javascript:showIt('layer4')">Show</a><p>
    <p><a href="javascript:hideIt('layer4')">Hide</a></p>
</td>
</tr>
```

Start of row 2

```html
<tr>
<td valign="top">
```

Define division for the Frankenstein image.

```html
    <div ID="layer1" class=pics>
    <p><img src="../images/frknst2.gif" alt="Frankenstein"
            width="136" height="208"></p>
    <p align=center class="clicks">Frankenstein</p>
    </div>
</td>
<td valign="top">
```

Define division for the Goblin image.

```html
    <div ID="layer2" class=pics>
    <p><img src="../images/goblins.gif" alt="Goblins"
            width="136" height="103"></p>
    <p align=center class="clicks">Goblin</p>
    </div>
</td>
```

Continued from previous page

Define division for the Mummy image.

```
<td valign="top">
  <div id="layer3" class=pics>
  <p><img src="../images/mummy.gif" alt="Mummy"
       width="136" height="204"></p>
  <p align=center class="clicks">Mummy</p>
  </div>
</td>
<td valign="top">
  <div ID="layer4" class=pics>
  <p><img src="../images/compbug.gif" alt="Computer Bug"
       width="136" height="133"></p>
  <p align=center class="clicks"> Computer Bug</p>
  </div>
</td>
</tr>
</table>
</body>
</html>
```

Define division for the Bug image.

The combined Netscape Navigator / Internet Explorer page is more complex than a comparable page specific to either browser. The stickier this gets, the more attractive separate pages become. Spooky, eh?

A Word About Browser Compatibility

A lot of people are staunch proponents of the one-page-for-all-browsers school of Web page construction. They pound their fist on the table and declare that, by gum, they're going to insist on absolute browser compatibility from the vendors.

In real life, whoever implements a feature first will, by definition, be releasing something no other browser can do. Then, as Web pages using these features begin to fail on other browsers, the other browsers release new versions that support the new features (plus some added ones nobody else supports yet). This is what competitive marketplaces are all about.

When it comes to Dynamic HTML in Netscape, moving, hiding, revealing, and reordering layers are pretty much the beginning and end of the story. As we saw in the Creatures You May Find example, there *is* a modicum of compatibility between Netscape and Microsoft in this area. You can use this page as a starting point, if you want, and add additional capabilities such as timers, animations, and interactivity.

For the rest of this book, I'm going to be essentially IE-intensive and Netscape-tolerant. Maintaining full IE/Netscape compatibility adds both significant complexity and significant restrictions to every page you create. I'm not going to try and make Netscape do things it can't, and I'm not going to withhold cool tricks just because Netscape can't do them. However, I *will* try to keep pages at least usable under Netscape, and I'll tell you how I did it. And hopefully, someday, Netscape and Microsoft will make this easy by supporting the same, official, World Wide Web Consortium standards. Deal?

Using Timers

The eye and the brain react strongly to motion because it means something around us is changing, and we'd better figure out fast whether to snag it, run away, or talk our way out of it. It's a hard-wired, primitive reflex. That's why most people go for the action, the animation, the things that go poof and surprise us.

Creating motion on a Web page almost always involves timers—objects that wait a certain amount of time and then run a script. The script then changes the Web page in whatever way you programmed it. Timer scripts offer far more control, far more user interaction, and far less download time than video files and animated GIFs. Timers can either fire once and then disappear, or they can fire repeatedly at a fixed interval.

In this trick we'll use timers to create two kinds of animation.

In the first example, we'll display four electronic cue cards one by one, as if on a teleprompter. You can apply the same technique to control any sort of content you want to appear gradually.

In the second example, we'll use CSS Positioning to arrange five objects uniformly across the browser window. Then, we'll have a timer run a script that gradually draws the objects closer together until they overlap pleasantly at the center of the page. Simultaneously, we'll gradually zoom the heading size from almost nothing to 54 points. You can use the same techniques to move or resize almost anything on your Web pages.

Radio Broadcast Test

Our first timer example is a relatively simple page that automatically displays four sentences, one at a time. Aspiring radio announcers are supposed to read the sentences as if from a teleprompter. Yes, I know radio announcers don't look into the camera and no, I don't know why they'd use a teleprompter. Just play along and look at Figure 7-1.

Page Layout Details

HTML tables provide the overall layout for this page; no surprise here. Figure 7-2 displays the tables with borders visible. The upper table has two rows and three columns. The large cell in the center column spans both rows, and a

FIGURE 7-1. *The sentence in the box is one of four in a timed sequence. The remaining three appear progressively lower on the screen, one at a time.*

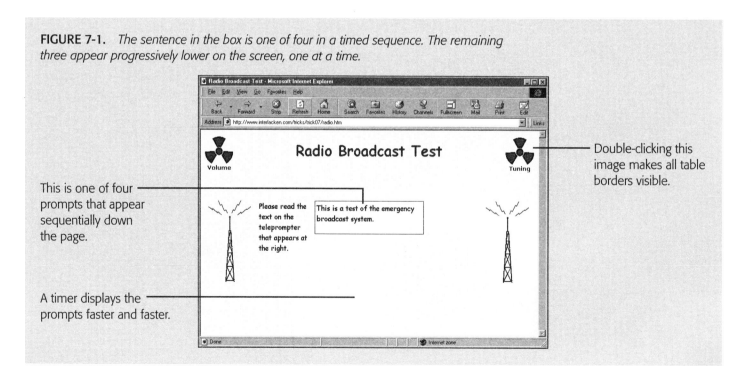

This is one of four prompts that appear sequentially down the page.

A timer displays the prompts faster and faster.

Double-clicking this image makes all table borders visible.

FIGURE 7-2. *Two tables, made visible here, control page layout. The second sentence in the announcer test happens to be visible in this illustration.*

One HTML table organizes the page heading.

Another table organizes everything else on the page.

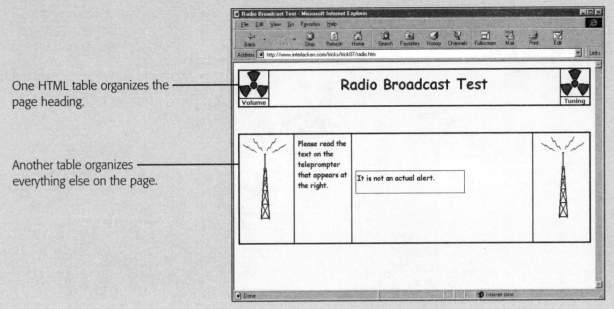

WIDTH=99% attribute maximizes its width. The lower table is a standard one-row, four-column job.

Each sentence in the radio test is an HTML division, coded like this:

```
<div id="box01" class="box">
    <p>This is a test of the emergency
       broadcast system.</p></div>
```

The three remaining divisions have the names *box02, box03,* and *box04,* and of course they each have different text. Coding each of these areas as a <DIV> arranges them progressively down the page, and not on the same line.

Events—Your Back Door to Debugging

If you load the Radio Broadcast Test page into your own copy of Microsoft Internet Explorer—which you really should, so you can see the animation—you can display the table borders yourself by double-clicking the Tuning button. The borders will disappear when you move the pointer off the button. This occurs because of JavaScript routines provided for the image's *onDblClick* and *onMouseOut* events:

```
<img src="../images/radioatv.gif"
     width="65" height="60" alt="Tuning"
     ondblclick="bordOn();"
     onmouseout="bordOff();"></td>
```

Whenever someone double-clicks this image, the browser runs the *bordOn()* function. Users aren't accustomed to double-clicking things on a Web page, so the chances they'll do this by accident are small. And even if a user does succeed in displaying the borders, the borders will disappear as soon as the mouse pointer moves away from the image.

The *bordOn()* function appears as follows: *tab1* and *tab2* are the names of the two tables, assigned by ID tags. The *bordOff* function is very similar, except that it sets the border values to 0. Here's the *bordOn()* function:

```
function bordOn(){
   document.all.tab1.border = "2" ;
   document.all.tab2.border = "2" ;
}
```

Back-door programming like this is often useful for debugging Web pages. If you want, you can remove the code before putting the page on the Web for the public. No great harm usually results from leaving it in, though. The extra download time is usually trivial.

Style Sheet Usage

The following style rule, coded in the <HEAD> section, defines the *box* class. We'll assign his class to each of the four divisions:

Tip: Because IE and Navigator handle divisions and visibility so differently, this example flashes the teleprompter divisions for IE users only. Under Navigator, we'll make all four teleprompter divisions visible when the page loads and we won't start the timers that flash them.

 Tip: Whenever you request a specific font family, always specify a generic font family as well. This gives the browser at least some guidance if the exact font you specify isn't available on the remote user's system. There are five generic font families: *serif, sans-serif, monospace, cursive,* and *fantasy.*

 Caution: When presenting timed content, be sure your visitors have enough time to assimilate it. Time yourself carefully reading any timed text, for example, and then multiply it by 1.5 or 2 (unless you're the world's slowest reader).

```
.box { visibility: hidden;
       width:250; height:50;
       padding: 3;
       border:1px solid rgb(0,0,0);
       font-family: Comic Sans MS, sans-serif; }
```

Visibility: hidden tells Internet Explorer not to display any object coded CLASS=box. At the same time, it tells Netscape Navigator nothing. Netscape seems to ignore the visibility property in style sheets but, because we aren't going to be hiding and revealing the boxes with Netscape, this is a happy accident. Anything coded CLASS=box is initially hidden in IE and visible in Netscape.

The rest of the *box* class properties are pretty ordinary. We give the class a specific height and width so all the boxes are the same size. For readability we ask for three pixels of padding between the division border and anything inside it. We specify a solid black border one-pixel wide; and we specify a couple of fonts, one specific and one generic.

Scripting Techniques

OK, now for the fun stuff: the timers. A <SCRIPT>…</SCRIPT> block in the <HEAD> sections contains two statements that aren't part of any function, and which therefore execute immediately. These are:

```
msgNr = 0;
flashTm = 3000;
```

We'll be using the *msgNr* variable to keep track of which division box is currently visible: 0 for *box01*, 1 for *box02*, and so forth. The *flashTm* variable specifies, in milliseconds, how long each division box will remain visible. The value 3000 means 3 seconds.

When the Radio Broadcast Test finishes loading, an *onLoad* event in its <BODY> tag runs a script called *promptMe()*. Here's the <BODY> tag code that makes this happen:

```
<body onLoad="promptMe ();" >
```

The *promptMe()* function first checks whether the browser is Internet Explorer, and executes nothing more if it isn't. This makes the page static but at least legible under Netscape Navigator. Recall that all four sentences in the test are initially visible for Netscape users; now we know why.

If the browser is IE, the script tests the *msgNr* variable. If *msgNr* is 0, the *promptMe()* function:

- Makes *box04* (which contains the fourth sentence) invisible.

- Makes *box01* (which contains the first sentence) visible.

The code that does this is:

```
if (msgNr == 0) {
    document.all.box04.style.visibility="hidden";
    document.all.box01.style.visibility="visible";
}
```

If *msgNr* is 1, the function hides *box01* and shows *box02*. The madness continues by hiding *box02*, showing *box03*, and so forth on subsequent passes.

The following code appears at the end of the *promptMe()* function:

```
if (msgNr < 3) {
  msgNr = msgNr + 1;
}else{
  msgNr = 0;
  if (flashTm > 100){
    flashTm = flashTm * 0.7;
  }
}
setTimeout("promptMe();",flashTm);
```

 Tip: Milliseconds are the unit of measure for JavaScript time intervals. The value 2500, for example, means 2.5 seconds. In this code, 100 means .1 seconds.

Consider the last statement first, the one beginning with *setTimeout*. This function accepts two arguments: a JavaScript statement and a time interval. Once it executes the *setTimeout* function, the browser waits the specified interval and then runs the JavaScript statement. In this case, the *setTimeout()* function tells the browser to run the *promptMe()* function again.

The first statement in this block of code tests the *msgNr* variable:

- If *msgNr* is less than 3 (that is, if *box01*, *box02*, or *box03* is on display), the routine adds 1 to *msgNr*.

- If *msgNr* is 3 or more, the script resets *msgNr* to 0 and then considers the *flashTm variable*.

We initialized *flashTm* to 3000, so each division box appears for 3 seconds in the first iteration of the test. However, when the *promptMe()* function finds that the fourth and final box is on display (that is, when it finds that *msgNr* is 3), it multiplies *flashTm* by 0.7. This means that the second time through the test, each division box appears for 2.1 seconds instead of 3. The third time through, each box appears for 1.47 seconds and so forth. This continues until *flashTm* is 100 milliseconds or less, when we stop decreasing its value. No one can possibly read that fast. Diabolical.

In any event, we've now updated *msgNr* to indicate the next box the script should display. When the *setTimeout* statement runs the *promptMe()* function again, *promptMe()* will display the next division box in sequence.

Complete HTML Listing

Preliminaries completed, we're now equipped to confront the full HTML listing. Follow me in, soldiers.

Define styles for teleprompter boxes and knobs.

```
<html>
<head>
<title>Radio Broadcast Test</title>
<style>
 .box { visibility: hidden;
        width:250; height:50;
        padding: 3;
        border:1px solid rgb(0,0,0);
        font-family: Comic Sans MS, sans-serif; }
 .knob { font-family: Verdana, sans-serif;
        font-size: 10 pt; font-weight: bold; }
</style>
```

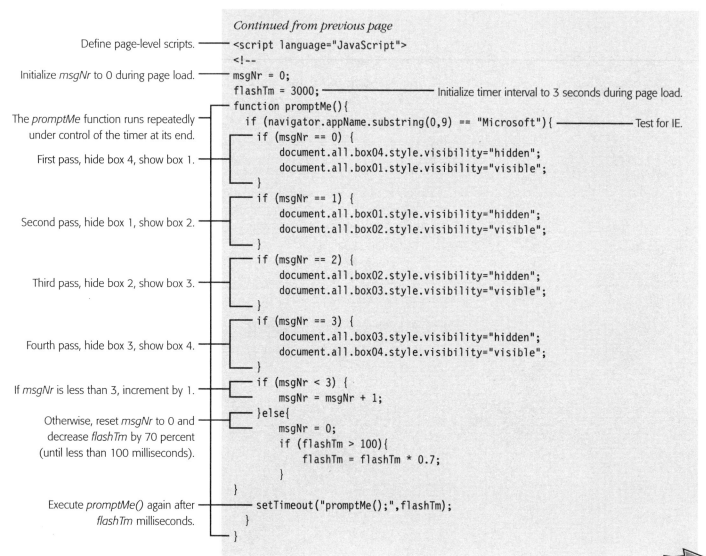

Continued from previous page

Define page-level scripts. ──
```
<script language="JavaScript">
<!--
```

Initialize *msgNr* to 0 during page load. ──
```
msgNr = 0;
flashTm = 3000;
```
────── Initialize timer interval to 3 seconds during page load.

```
function promptMe(){
```

The *promptMe* function runs repeatedly under control of the timer at its end. ──
```
  if (navigator.appName.substring(0,9) == "Microsoft"){
```
────── Test for IE.

First pass, hide box 4, show box 1. ──
```
    if (msgNr == 0) {
        document.all.box04.style.visibility="hidden";
        document.all.box01.style.visibility="visible";
    }
```

Second pass, hide box 1, show box 2. ──
```
    if (msgNr == 1) {
        document.all.box01.style.visibility="hidden";
        document.all.box02.style.visibility="visible";
    }
```

Third pass, hide box 2, show box 3. ──
```
    if (msgNr == 2) {
        document.all.box02.style.visibility="hidden";
        document.all.box03.style.visibility="visible";
    }
```

Fourth pass, hide box 3, show box 4. ──
```
    if (msgNr == 3) {
        document.all.box03.style.visibility="hidden";
        document.all.box04.style.visibility="visible";
    }
```

If *msgNr* is less than 3, increment by 1. ──
```
    if (msgNr < 3) {
        msgNr = msgNr + 1;
```

Otherwise, reset *msgNr* to 0 and decrease *flashTm* by 70 percent (until less than 100 milliseconds). ──
```
    }else{
        msgNr = 0;
        if (flashTm > 100){
            flashTm = flashTm * 0.7;
        }
    }
```

Execute *promptMe()* again after *flashTm* milliseconds. ──
```
    setTimeout("promptMe();",flashTm);
  }
}
```

Continued from previous page

```
function bordOn(){
   document.all.tab1.border = "2" ;
   document.all.tab2.border = "2" ;
}
function bordOff(){
   document.all.tab1.border = "0" ;
   document.all.tab2.border = "0" ;
}
// -->
</script>
</head>
<body onLoad="promptMe();" bgcolor="#FFFFCC">
<table id="tab1" width="100%"
       border="0" cellpadding="0" cellspacing="0"
       bordercolor="#000000">
<tr>
  <td align="center">
     <img src="../images/radioatv.gif"
          width="65" height="60" alt="Volume"></td>
  <td width="99%" rowspan="2">
     <p style="text-align: center;
                font-family: Comic Sans MS, sans-serif;
                font-size: 24pt; font-weight: bold;
                color: rgb(153,0,0)">
     Radio  Broadcast Test</p></td>
  <td align="center">
     <img src="../images/radioatv.gif"
          width="65" height="60" alt="Tuning"
          ondblclick="bordOn();"
          onmouseout="bordOff();"></td>
</tr><tr>
  <td align="center" class="knob">Volume</td>
  <td align="center" class="knob">Tuning</td>
</tr>
```

Make borders visible for tables tab1 and tab2.

Make borders invisible for tables tab1 and tab2.

Run *promptMe* for the first time as soon as the page loads.

Define table for radio knobs and page heading.

Display the Volume knob.

Display page heading.

Display the Tuning knob. The *onDblClick* and *onMouseOut* events run scripts to make table borders visible and invisible.

Display the Volume and Tuning knob labels.

Trick 7

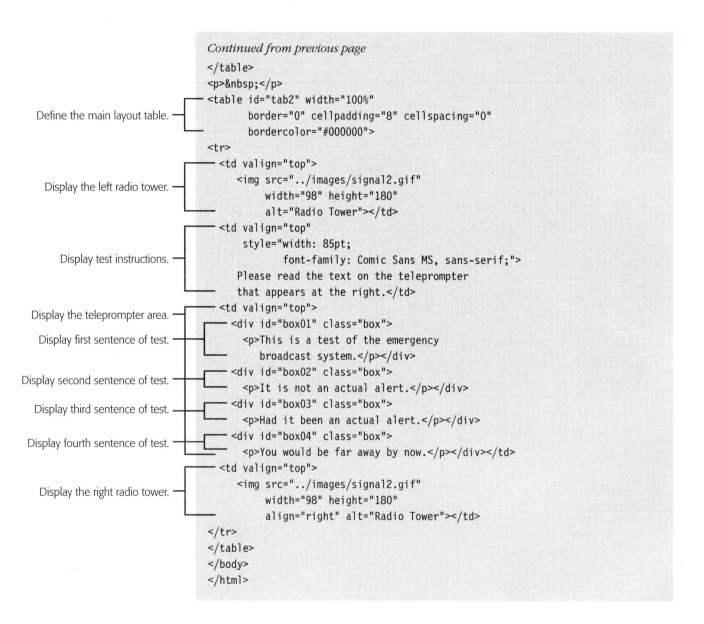

Continued from previous page

```html
</table>
<p> </p>
<table id="tab2" width="100%"
        border="0" cellpadding="8" cellspacing="0"
        bordercolor="#000000">
<tr>
    <td valign="top">
        <img src="../images/signal2.gif"
            width="98" height="180"
            alt="Radio Tower"></td>
    <td valign="top"
        style="width: 85pt;
                font-family: Comic Sans MS, sans-serif;">
        Please read the text on the teleprompter
        that appears at the right.</td>
    <td valign="top">
    <div id="box01" class="box">
        <p>This is a test of the emergency
            broadcast system.</p></div>
    <div id="box02" class="box">
        <p>It is not an actual alert.</p></div>
    <div id="box03" class="box">
        <p>Had it been an actual alert.</p></div>
    <div id="box04" class="box">
        <p>You would be far away by now.</p></div></td>
    <td valign="top">
        <img src="../images/signal2.gif"
            width="98" height="180"
            align="right" alt="Radio Tower"></td>
</tr>
</table>
</body>
</html>
```

Define the main layout table.

Display the left radio tower.

Display test instructions.

Display the teleprompter area.

Display first sentence of test.

Display second sentence of test.

Display third sentence of test.

Display fourth sentence of test.

Display the right radio tower.

Cool, eh? Just make sure you use this page with someone who can read teleprompters.

The Stranger Arranger

Like the Radio Broadcast Test, this example involves a script that runs automatically when the page loads. This time, however:

- The script runs a limited number of times and then quits.

- Instead of showing and hiding divisions, the script first arranges five images uniformly across the available window space, and then moves them closer and closer together toward the center. This provides an animated entry for the page.

- While moving the images, the script also increases the font size used for the page heading. As the heading grows larger, the rest of the page compresses vertically, creating another element of motion.

In total, the animation runs two seconds and results in the Web page shown in Figure 7-3. You should really load this page in your copy of IE4 to understand the animation, though.

Page Layout Details

The flower arrangement consists of five images, not one. Each image is a GIF file that's transparent around the edges, but even so, it's surprising for images on a Web page to overlap. The lower five images have transparent edges, for example, but they certainly don't overlap. Overlapping the flower images involves two tricks:

- Dynamic CSS Positioning overlaps the image areas. Ordinary HTML would never overlap objects this way.

- A CSS property called *z-index* controls which objects overlap others. If you look closely at the flowers in Figure 7-2, you'll notice that flowers 2 and 4 are *behind* flowers 1, 3, and 5, for example.

FIGURE 7-3. *When this page loads, a timer script initially distributes the five flower images uniformly across the page, then gradually centers them closer together. The same script gradually increases the heading's font size.*

A timer script zooms this heading into view by gradually increasing the font size.

Initially, these five images are spread evenly across the entire window. The same timer script gradually moves them closer together.

Absolute positioning permits moving each flower image around the page independently. The *zorder* property controls how they overlap.

Double-clicking here makes all table borders visible.

Page layout involves, once again, two tables. The same sort of code that revealed the table borders in the Radio Broadcast Test works again here, and you can see the results in Figure 7-4.

The main page layout table is five rows by four columns. In row 1, a single large cell spans all four columns. In rows 2 and 4, columns 2 and 3 are combined. Cell background colors create the vertical and horizontal bars in row 2, in column 1, and in column 5. A second table inside row 4, cell 2, arranges the five icons and their titles.

The entire outer table is coded both WIDTH=100% and HEIGHT=100% so it occupies the entire browser window at all times. A script checks the browser

FIGURE 7-4. *This view of The Stranger Arranger page shows the borders of the page layout tables. To see these yourself, double-click the bottom of the right vertical bar.*

This table organizes the major elements of the page. All rows except 3 and 5 have cells spanning multiple columns.

A smaller table organizes these five images and their captions.

type and, if it's IE4, sets the large middle cell in row 4 to HEIGHT=99%. This minimizes the height of rows 1, 2, 3, and 5, and concentrates all vertical white space in row 4. (Netscape Navigator overreacts to coding HEIGHT=99% directly in the HTML; it makes row 4 taller than the entire browser window.)

Scripting Techniques

When The Stranger Arranger page first loads, the five flower images are centered, not overlapping each other at all. Also, the heading font is 54 pixels high. This is the static view Netscape Navigator users will see—the top row diagrammed in Figure 7-5. Each box represents a flower image.

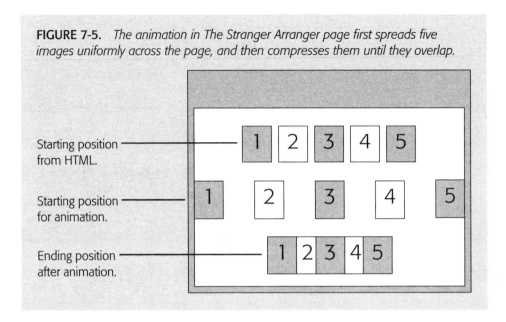

FIGURE 7-5. *The animation in The Stranger Arranger page first spreads five images uniformly across the page, and then compresses them until they overlap.*

Starting position from HTML.

Starting position for animation.

Ending position after animation.

The middle row shows where we want the five images to appear at the start of the animation, and the bottom row shows their desired ending positions. We'll compute the ending positions first:

- To get the total width of the final composition, add the widths of images 1, 3, and 5, plus the margin between images 1 and 3 (35 pixels), plus the margin between images 3 and 5 (also 35 pixels).

- To get the left margin of the final composition, subtract its width from the current window size, then divide by 2. This is also the left offset required for image 1.

- The left offset for image 3 is the left offset for image 1, plus the width of image 1, plus the 35-pixel margin.

- The left offset for image 5 is the left offset for image 3, plus the width of image 3, plus the 35-pixel margin.

The following code makes these calculations:

```
hdrWid = document.all.img1.width + 35
         + document.all.img3.width + 35
         + document.all.img5.width;
lftMar = Math.round((document.body.clientWidth
                         - hdrWid) / 2);
fin1 = lftMar;
fin3 = fin1 + document.all.img1.width + 35;
fin5 = fin3 + document.all.img3.width + 35;
```

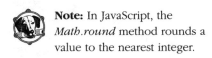

Note: In JavaScript, the *Math.round* method rounds a value to the nearest integer.

For the animation, the left offset for image 1 will be somewhere between 0 (the left margin) and the ending position computed above. For image 5, the left offset will be somewhere between its flush right position (the window size minus the width of image 5) and its ending position.

The easiest way to visualize the animation is by percent complete. We therefore initialize a variable named *pct* to 0 and increase it by 5 for each iteration of the timer routine. Each iteration computes image locations from *pct* as follows:

- The left offset for image 1 increases from 0, at start, to the *fin1* value computed above, at end.

- The left offset for image 5 starts at the window size minus the width of image 5, then decreases to the *fin5* value at end.

- Image 3 remains fixed.

The JavaScript code that performs these calculations is:

```
pos1 = Math.round(fin1 * (pct/100));
pos3 = fin3;
pos5 = fin5 + ((document.body.clientWidth
                - (fin5 + document.all.img5.width))
              * ((100 - pct)/100));
```

Computing the offsets for images 2 and 4 is a simple matter of averaging:

- The left offset for image 2 is always the average of those for images 1 and 3.

- The left offset for image 4 is the average of those for images 3 and 5:

```
pos2 = Math.round((pos1 + pos3)/2);
pos4 = Math.round((pos3 + pos5)/2);
```

Implementing the animation is now just a matter of mechanics. We start the *pct* variable at 0, perform the calculations above, assign the results to the five images, and increase *pct* by 5. If *pct* is 100 or less, we set a timer to execute the routine again in 0.1 second. As *pct* increases, the images get closer and closer until they reach their final positions. We stop looping after we've processed *pct*=100.

The flower images need *z-index* values to make them overlap just the way we want. When two objects on the same Web page overlap, the one with the larger *z-index* is fully visible and the one with the smaller *z-index* is partially obscured.

The default *z-index* is 0. This represents the depth of objects on the base Web page. An object with a larger *z-index* covers anything in the base Web page. An object with a *z-index* of 2 will overlap objects in the base Web page *and* objects with a *z-index* of 1. And so forth. To make objects appear behind the normal Web page (and in front of the background image), make their *z-index* properties negative.

The HTML to assign a *z-index* is quite simple. It looks like:

```
style="z-index: 5; "
```

To create the overlap we want, we assign these *z-index* values:

Image	z-index
1	3
2	1
3	5
4	2
5	4

This puts images 1, 3, and 5 in front and images 2 and 4 in back Assigning *z-index* values 2, 1, 2, 1, and 2 would've produced the same result, but *z-index*es were on sale that day and I just went crazy.

We're going to look at the full HTML listing in a minute, but first we'd better look at the magic expanding title. The code that displays the page heading is:

```
<h1 id="hdr" align="center" style="font-size: 54; ">
```

This identifies the heading as *hdr* and makes it 54 pixels high. The HTML describes the heading's final appearance because this is what Netscape users will see. The zoom effect is only programmable in IE.

The code to change the heading's font size is:

```
document.all.hdr.style.fontSize = hdrSiz * (pct/100);
```

The variable *hdrSiz* contains the font size coded in the HTML; some initialization code retrieves this value and saves it for later user. As *pct* varies from 0 to 100, the font size grows from nothing to its final value.

Oops, one last pesky detail: without any more precautions, the flower arrangement won't stay centered if the user resizes the browser window. More elegant solutions are possible but we'll take the quick fix; we'll run the animation not only when the page loads, but whenever the user resizes the window.

Complete HTML Listing

OK, now read through the entire HTML listing and see if you can recognize all the parts. This oughta be kid stuff by now.

```
<html>
<head>
<title>The Stranger Arranger</title>
<style>
<!--
 P { margin:0; }
 H1 { margin:0; font-family: Bradley Hand ITC, cursive; }
 .event { font-family: Verdana, sans-serif; font-weight }
 .subhd { font-family: Mead Bold, sans-serif;
          font-size: 20pt; color: rgb(102,0,102) }
-->
</style>
<script language="JavaScript">
<!--
```

Specify styles.

Start of page-level scripts.

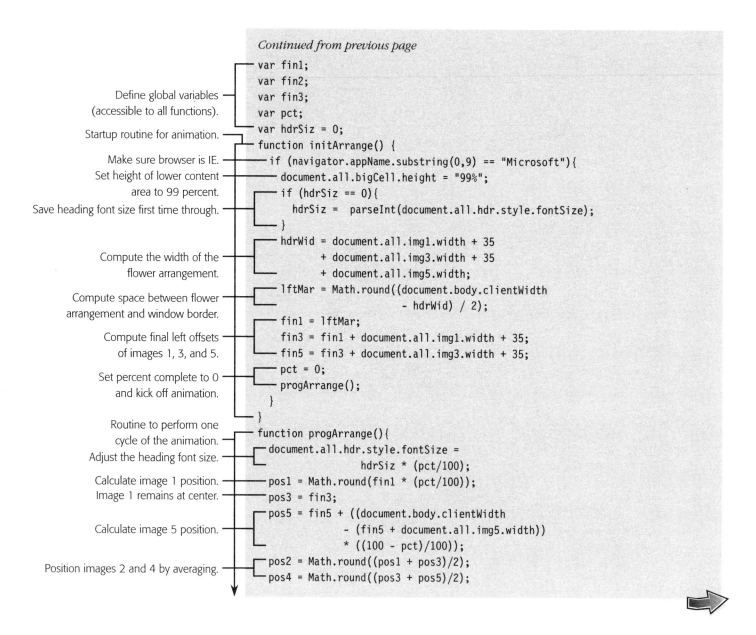

Continued from previous page

Define global variables (accessible to all functions).

Startup routine for animation.

Make sure browser is IE.

Set height of lower content area to 99 percent.

Save heading font size first time through.

Compute the width of the flower arrangement.

Compute space between flower arrangement and window border.

Compute final left offsets of images 1, 3, and 5.

Set percent complete to 0 and kick off animation.

Routine to perform one cycle of the animation.

Adjust the heading font size.

Calculate image 1 position.

Image 1 remains at center.

Calculate image 5 position.

Position images 2 and 4 by averaging.

```javascript
var fin1;
var fin2;
var fin3;
var pct;
var hdrSiz = 0;
function initArrange() {
    if (navigator.appName.substring(0,9) == "Microsoft"){
        document.all.bigCell.height = "99%";
        if (hdrSiz == 0){
            hdrSiz = parseInt(document.all.hdr.style.fontSize);
        }
        hdrWid = document.all.img1.width + 35
                + document.all.img3.width + 35
                + document.all.img5.width;
        lftMar = Math.round((document.body.clientWidth
                            - hdrWid) / 2);
        fin1 = lftMar;
        fin3 = fin1 + document.all.img1.width + 35;
        fin5 = fin3 + document.all.img3.width + 35;
        pct = 0;
        progArrange();
    }
}
function progArrange(){
    document.all.hdr.style.fontSize =
                        hdrSiz * (pct/100);
    pos1 = Math.round(fin1 * (pct/100));
    pos3 = fin3;
    pos5 = fin5 + ((document.body.clientWidth
            - (fin5 + document.all.img5.width))
            * ((100 - pct)/100));
    pos2 = Math.round((pos1 + pos3)/2);
    pos4 = Math.round((pos3 + pos5)/2);
```

Continued from previous page

Apply calculated positions to images.

```
document.all.img1.style.posLeft = pos1;
document.all.img2.style.posLeft = pos2;
document.all.img3.style.posLeft = pos3;
document.all.img4.style.posLeft = pos4;
document.all.img5.style.posLeft = pos5;
```

Increment percent, check if animation is complete, and continue (after timer delay) if not.

```
pct = pct + 5;
if (pct < 101){
    setTimeout("progArrange();",100);
}
}
```

Routine to make the table borders visible.

```
function bordOn(){
    document.all.tab1.border = "2" ;
    document.all.tab2.border = "2" ;
}
```

Routine to hide the table borders.

```
function bordOff(){
    document.all.tab1.border = "0" ;
    document.all.tab2.border = "0" ;
}
// -->
```

End of page-level scripts.

```
</script>
</head>
```

Start animation when page loads or gets resized.

Define page layout table.

```
<body onload="initArrange()" onresize="initArrange()">
<table id="tab1" height="100%" width="100%"
        border="0" cellpadding="0" cellspacing="0"
        bordercolor="#000000">
```

Start row 1 of page layout table.

```
<tr>
    <td align="center" valign="top" colspan="4">
```

Display page heading.

```
        <h1 id="hdr" align="center" style="font-size: 54; ">
            The Stranger Arranger</h1>
```

Display images in flower arrangement.

Reserve 150 vertical pixels for remaining images.

Define flower image 1.

```
        <img src="../images/trans5x5.gif" width="1" height="150">
        <img id="img1" src="../images/roses.gif"
             style="position:absolute; z-index: 3;"
             width="129" height="150">
```

Trick 7

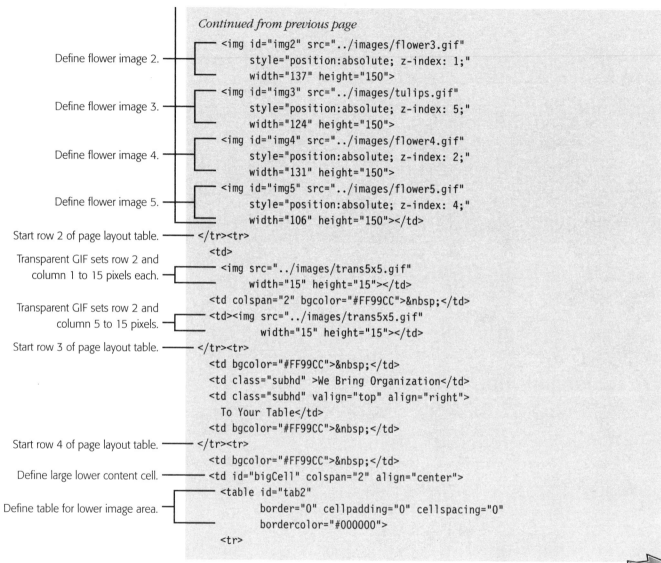

Continued from previous page

Define flower image 2.

```
<img id="img2" src="../images/flower3.gif"
     style="position:absolute; z-index: 1;"
     width="137" height="150">
```

Define flower image 3.

```
<img id="img3" src="../images/tulips.gif"
     style="position:absolute; z-index: 5;"
     width="124" height="150">
```

Define flower image 4.

```
<img id="img4" src="../images/flower4.gif"
     style="position:absolute; z-index: 2;"
     width="131" height="150">
```

Define flower image 5.

```
<img id="img5" src="../images/flower5.gif"
     style="position:absolute; z-index: 4;"
     width="106" height="150"></td>
```

Start row 2 of page layout table.

```
</tr><tr>
  <td>
```

Transparent GIF sets row 2 and column 1 to 15 pixels each.

```
  <img src="../images/trans5x5.gif"
       width="15" height="15"></td>
<td colspan="2" bgcolor="#FF99CC"> </td>
```

Transparent GIF sets row 2 and column 5 to 15 pixels.

```
<td><img src="../images/trans5x5.gif"
         width="15" height="15"></td>
```

Start row 3 of page layout table.

```
</tr><tr>
  <td bgcolor="#FF99CC"> </td>
  <td class="subhd" >We Bring Organization</td>
  <td class="subhd" valign="top" align="right">
  To Your Table</td>
  <td bgcolor="#FF99CC"> </td>
```

Start row 4 of page layout table.

```
</tr><tr>
  <td bgcolor="#FF99CC"> </td>
```

Define large lower content cell.

```
<td id="bigCell" colspan="2" align="center">
```

Define table for lower image area.

```
<table id="tab2"
       border="0" cellpadding="0" cellspacing="0"
       bordercolor="#000000">
  <tr>
```

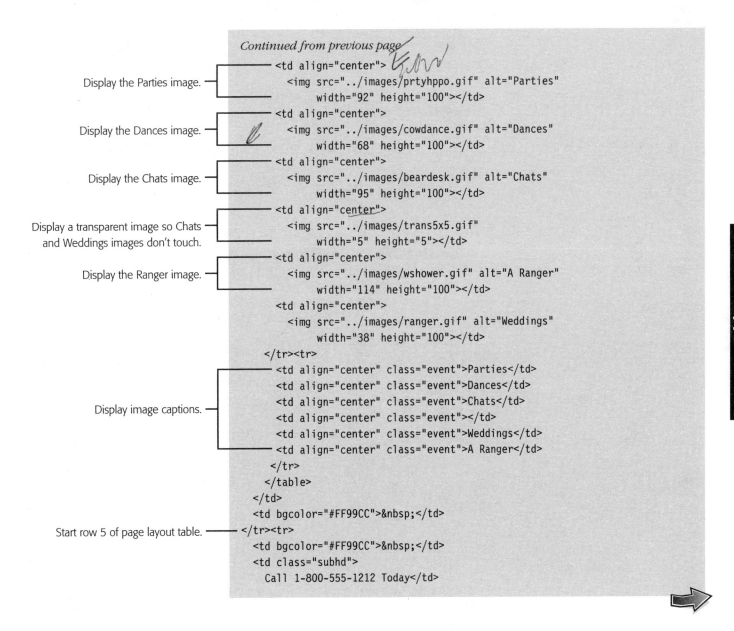

Continued from previous page

Display the Parties image. —

```html
<td align="center">
    <img src="../images/prtyhppo.gif" alt="Parties"
         width="92" height="100"></td>
```

Display the Dances image. —

```html
<td align="center">
    <img src="../images/cowdance.gif" alt="Dances"
         width="68" height="100"></td>
```

Display the Chats image. —

```html
<td align="center">
    <img src="../images/beardesk.gif" alt="Chats"
         width="95" height="100"></td>
```

Display a transparent image so Chats and Weddings images don't touch. —

```html
<td align="center">
    <img src="../images/trans5x5.gif"
         width="5" height="5"></td>
```

Display the Ranger image. —

```html
<td align="center">
    <img src="../images/wshower.gif" alt="A Ranger"
         width="114" height="100"></td>
<td align="center">
    <img src="../images/ranger.gif" alt="Weddings"
         width="38" height="100"></td>
</tr><tr>
```

Display image captions. —

```html
<td align="center" class="event">Parties</td>
<td align="center" class="event">Dances</td>
<td align="center" class="event">Chats</td>
<td align="center" class="event"></td>
<td align="center" class="event">Weddings</td>
<td align="center" class="event">A Ranger</td>
</tr>
</table>
</td>
<td bgcolor="#FF99CC"> </td>
```

Start row 5 of page layout table. —

```html
</tr><tr>
<td bgcolor="#FF99CC"> </td>
<td class="subhd">
    Call 1-800-555-1212 Today</td>
```

Continued from previous page

```
    <td class="subhd" align="right">
    And Get Your Act Together</td>
<td bgcolor="#FF99CC"
            ondblclick="bordOn()"
            onmouseout="bordOff()"> </td>
    </tr>
</table>
</body>
</html>
```

Clicking on lower-right page layout cell shows table borders.

Moving mouse off lower-right page layout cell hides table borders.

Additional Timer Issues

There are two additional timer topics worth talking about:

- Resetting timers—that is, changing your mind about a timer you've already set.

- Interval timers—timers that fire not just once, but over and over again.

Suppose you have a Web page where the user has 10 seconds to make a decision, otherwise something happens automatically. You display the page, and then set a 10-second timer to trigger the default action. The user makes up his or her mind within the allotted time, however, and clicks some button. In cases like this, you need to reset a timer before it fires. This is a two-step process:

Tip: The *alert* function displays a message in the standard message box for the user's operating system.

1. Save the timer's identify number when you define it. The code looks like this:

```
timerID = setTimeout("alert('Timer has fired.');",5000);
```

2. To cancel the timer before it fires, use the following statement:

```
clearTimeout(timerID);
```

Resize events can occur in great bunches as the user drags the window border around. You might want to filter these by waiting for one second of no resize events before starting an animation or some other effect. If you got a second resize

Tip: Some people save the *timerID* from every timer they create, and then cancel it when the document's *onUnload* event occurs. This seems like the kind of cleanup the browser should do automatically, but I guess it never hurts to be tidy.

event while the timer was still running, you would kill the first timer and then start another one.

The second topic pertains to repeating timers. Oh sure, you can repeat a timer loop forever by ending the routine with a *setTimeout* statement that executes it again. The following statement, however, runs the *myThing()* routine every five seconds forever. This might be useful for producing never-ending animations or incessant beeping:

```
intervalID = setInterval("myThing();",5000);
```

Well, it doesn't really run *forever*. It runs until the user unloads the page, or until you execute:

```
clearInterval(intervalID)
```

Timers are indispensable for scripting any sort of repeating behavior or delayed reaction on your Web page. What's more, using them isn't particularly difficult. Is that pure happiness or what?

Redirecting to Another Page

One of the great things about the Web is that if you don't like where you are, it's very easy to go somewhere else. Click an image, click some underlined text, click anything that catches your eye, and off you go. *Bon voyage* and don't forget to send a postcard.

Jumping from one Web page to another is so common and so powerful that you might expect a constant flow of new and better techniques for doing it. And you'd be right; here they are, right in this trick and the next.

We'll start with the most time-honored of all automatic hyperlink mechanisms: the oft-spoken and many-fabled REFRESH <META> tag. This isn't exactly cutting edge HTML, but it's simple, not well-known, and handy for setting up timed sequences of pages. It's also useful for redirecting users to new pages after you've deleted old ones.

Later in the trick we'll look at four ways to automatically deliver a different Web page, depending on the type of browser making the request. As the diversity and complexity of browsers increase (and they will, have no doubt of that), so will the need to deliver customized pages.

There are other reasons to deliver customized pages as well; different pages for different dates, different pages for different database values, different pages for different user profiles, yada, yada, yada. With minor changes, the same code that displays different pages for different browsers can work for these other cases as well. Useful stuff. You there, in the back row, put away those magazines.

Hyperlink: To find out more about <META> tags, refer to the following sources:

Netscape:
http://developer.netscape.com/library/documentation/htmlguid/tags3.htm

W3C:
http://www.w3.org/TR/REC-html40/struct/global.html

Note: When a Web server transmits a page, it precedes the HTML you create with several lines of header information. These contain a status code from processing the page request, information about the Web server, cookie values the browser should echo, and other normally boring stuff.

Please Wait 5 Seconds

For some time, browsers have supported a feature that loads a specified page after a certain number of seconds. All that's required is a single line of code, such as this, in the <HEAD> section of the page:

```
<meta http-equiv="refresh" content="5; url=thanks.htm">
```

In a general sense, a <META> tag provides information *about* a Web page, rather than information that's actually part of it. <META> tags can record information like the editor that created a page, titles and keywords for search engines, and when the page should expire in the user's cache.

A <META> tag that contains an HTTP-EQUIV= attribute simulates data arriving from the Web server as header lines. The value you assign to HTTP-EQUIV

FIGURE 8-1. *This page contains an HTTP-EQUIV <META> tag telling the browser to load a different page after 5 seconds.*

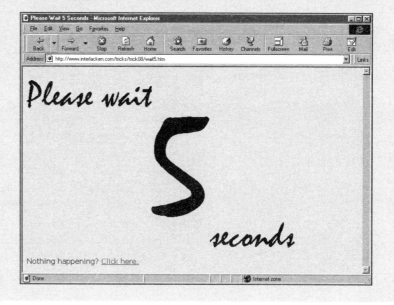

gives the name of the header. Any values associated with that header appear in the content attribute.

An HTTP-EQUIV value of *refresh* tells the browser to reload the page after a specified number of seconds. In the example:

```
<meta http-equiv="refresh" content="5; url=thanks.htm">
```

the browser waits 5 seconds and then loads a Web page named *thanks.htm*. For what it's worth, Figure 8-1 illustrates a page containing the <META> tag we just created, and Figure 8-2 illustrates the results.

A few old browsers don't support the META refresh tag; for users locked into those versions, it's polite to provide a Jump Now or Stop Waiting hyperlink that jumps to the same location as the <META> tag. In this case, we chose the

Note: It's usually good practice to specify a fully qualified URL in the content attribute of a META refresh tag. That is, you should begin the URL with *http://<site name>*. The example uses a relative URL only because, if you load the page off the accompanying CD, there's no way to predict the fully qualified URL on your system.

FIGURE 8-2. *The browser displays this page 5 seconds after the page in Figure 8-1 appears.*

Trick 8

hyperlink title, "Nothing happening? Click here?" OK, *I* chose it; you'll just have to cope.

Complete HTML Listing

The HTML listing for the Please Wait 5 Seconds page follows, relatively short and certainly sweet. There's nothing new here except the META refresh tag.

<META> tag loads *thanks.htm* page 5 seconds after the current page loads.

```
<html>
<head>
<title>Please Wait 5 Seconds</title>
<meta http-equiv="refresh" content="5; url=thanks.htm">
<style>
 td { margin: 0;  font-family: Mistral, fantasy; font-size: 60pt; }
</style>
</head>
<body bgcolor="#FFCCFF">
<table border="0" cellpadding="0" cellspacing="0">
  <tr>
    <td class="fancy" valign="top">Please wait</td>
    <td class="fancy" style="font-size: 250pt">5</td>
    <td class="fancy" valign="bottom" align="right">seconds</td>
  </tr>
  <tr>
    <td class=ss colspan=3>Nothing happening?
        <a href="thanks.htm">Click here.</a></td>
  </tr>
</table></body>
</html>
```

Here's the HTML listing for the *thanks.htm* file as well. There's absolutely nothing tricky about this page: nothing up my sleeve, nothing hidden in my hat. Honest, if you don't believe me, you can search me, especially if you're any sort of warrior princess.

```
<html>
<head>
<title>Thank You For Waiting</title>
<style>
 td { margin: 0;   font-family: Mistral, fantasy; font-size: 60pt; }
</style>
</head>
<body bgcolor="#CCFFCC">
<table border="0" cellpadding="0" cellspacing="0">
  <tr>
    <td valign="top">Thank You</td>
    <td><img src="../images/welcome.gif" alt="Thank You"
            width="120" height="350"></td>
    <td valign="bottom" align="right">for waiting.</td>
  </tr>
</table>
</body>
</html>
```

Additional Details

At one time, sequences of Web pages timed with <META> tags were very cool. Nowadays, dynamic pages like The Stranger Arranger in the previous trick make META refresh sequences look pretty tame. Many Web page authors still use <META> tags in Web pages containing We Have Moved notices, though.

We need to discuss one more facet of using the META refresh tag before moving on, namely the browser's Back button. If the remote user receives a page with a META refresh tag, waits for the tag to fire, and then clicks the browser's Back button, the user will go back to the page containing the META refresh tag. At this point, it's a real nuisance if the timeout value in the content attribute is 0. This makes the browser jump forward immediately, before the user can click the Back button again. For this reason, it's usually best to use timeout values of a few seconds, at least.

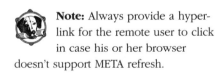 **Note:** Always provide a hyperlink for the remote user to click in case his or her browser doesn't support META refresh.

AERO Message Service (Auto)

Jumping at intervals from one page to another is fine, as far as it goes, but jumping to alternate pages based on logical decisions can be even more useful. It seems patently useful, for example, to display a different page based on the user's browser. Well, there are at least four ways to do just that, and this section presents the first of them: using JavaScript logic to select a new page. The three sections that follow this present the remaining approaches.

Loading a new Web page into the current browser window is quite easy with JavaScript; it requires only a single statement such as the following:

```
window.location.href = "../trick05/aeroms-i.htm";
```

The *window.location.href* property contains the URL of the current page. You can read its value any time to find out where you are, and you can change its value to go elsewhere. The example just shown loads the Microsoft Internet Explorer version of the AERO Message Service page, which last appeared in Figure 5-1.

Well, this little assignment is starting to look easy. All we need to do is test the browser version and jump to a different page depending on the result. Something like this:

Note: There's no illustration for this Web page because it really doesn't display anything permanent or useful. However, you can load it from the menu page *\tricks\default.htm* on the accompanying CD, or directly as *\tricks\trick08\aeroms-a.htm*.

```
if (navigator.appName.substring(0,9) == "Microsoft"){
    window.location.href = "../trick05/aeroms-i.htm";
}else{
    window.location.href = "../trick06/aeroms-n.htm";
}
```

This loads the IE version of the AERO Message page if the browser is IE, and the Netscape Navigator version otherwise. (The Netscape version was shown in Figure 6-1.) It works pretty well, too.

Complete HTML Listing

Here's the code that loads the correct AERO Message Service page—Netscape Navigator or Internet Explorer.

```
<html>
<head>
<title>AERO Message Service (Auto)</title>
<script>
<!--
if (navigator.appName.substring(0,9) == "Microsoft"){
    window.location.href = "../trick05/aeroms-i.htm";
}else{
    window.location.href = "../trick06/aeroms-n.htm";
}
// -->
</script>
</head>
<body>
<h1>AERO Message Service</h1>
<p><a href="../trick05/aeroms-i.htm">
    Internet Explorer Version</a></p>
<p><a href="../trick06/aeroms-n.htm">
    Netscape Navigator Version</a></p>
</body>
</html>
```

Test browser version and jump to different pages depending on the browser version.

Fallback hyperlinks for browsers with JavaScript missing or turned off.

Additional Details

The body of this page could've been completely blank, but I put in some hyperlinks to each of the AERO Message Service pages for display just in case JavaScript isn't enabled on the user's browser.

The catch with this technique—and it's a big one—is that it plays havoc with the browser's Back button. Think about it. A hyperlink on some page jumps to the *aeromsg-a.htm* page. That page jumps in turn to *aeroms-i.htm* or *aeroms-n.htm*. So far, so good. Now, the user clicks the browser's Back button. The browser jumps not, as the user expects, to the starting page, but to *aeroms-a.htm*. And *aeromssg-a.htm* jumps the user right back to *aeroms-i.htm* or *aeroms-n.htm*!

This phenomenon bears several colorful names, none of them complimentary; the point of no return, the Back button black hole effect, that sort of thing. Don't let this happen to you. Treat *aeroms-a.htm* as an interesting mental exercise and an example of what not to do.

What's *window.location.href* Good For?

There's nothing inherently bad in using script logic to choose a hyperlink location; the problem lies in:

- Passing through two Web pages on a journey that, to the remote user, appears to pass through one.

- Jumping out of a Web page so quickly—under program control—that the user has no chance to click the Back button before the jump occurs.

No confusion results, for example, from a hyperlink coded:

```
<a href="javascript:aeroms()">AERO Message Service</a>
```

where the *aeroms()* function consisted of:

```
aeroms(){
   if (navigator.appName.substring(0,9) == "Microsoft"){
       window.location.href = "../trick05/aeroms-i.htm";
   }else{
       window.location.href = "../trick06/aeroms-n.htm";
   }
}
```

The problem with this approach is that you have to include all this code on *every* page that links to the AERO Message Service page. It's avoiding this nuisance that makes creating a single page-switching page so attractive.

AERO Message Service (Framed)

This example involves a self-modifying frameset with exactly one frame. The code that defines this frame isn't hard-coded into the HTML; instead, a script generates the frame code on the fly, as the page loads. The generated frame code displays a different page depending on, surprise, the browser type. Becuase there's only one frame and its borders are 0, the remote user never knows a frameset's being used. And best of all, there's only one URL for any number of page versions.

The frameset code we want should end up looking like this:

```
<frameset rows="100%, *"
          frameborder=0 border=0>
<frame src="../trick05/aeroms-i.htm"
       scrolling=auto>
</frameset>");
```

The first (and only) row of the frameset occupies 100 percent of the horizontal space, and the second (which doesn't exist) occupies the rest (of which there is none—100 percent minus nothing equals everything). The frame borders are 0, making them invisible. Scroll bars appear and disappear automatically, whenever the displayed page is wider or taller than the browser window. In short, this one-frame frameset will be visually indistinguishable from an ordinary window.

JavaScript's *document.write method* adds code to a Web page as it loads. The JavaScript to generate the HTML just shown would be:

```
document.write('<frameset rows="100%, *" ');
document.write(' frameborder=0 border=0>');
document.write("<frame src=");
document.write("../trick05/aeroms-i.htm");
document.write(" scrolling=auto>");
document.write("</frameset>");
```

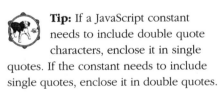 **Tip:** If a JavaScript constant needs to include double quote characters, enclose it in single quotes. If the constant needs to include single quotes, enclose it in double quotes.

Adding an *if-then-else* statement to test the browser version completes the code.

Complete HTML Listing

The complete code for the Web page is:

```html
<html>
<head>
<title>AERO Message Service (Frame)</title>
</head>
<script>
<!--
document.write('<frameset rows="100%, *" ');
document.write(' frameborder=0 border=0>');
document.write("<frame src=");
if (navigator.appName.substring(0,9) == "Microsoft"){
    document.write("../trick05/aeroms-i.htm");
}else{
    document.write("../trick06/aeroms-n.htm");
}
document.write(" scrolling=auto>");
document.write("</frameset>");
//. -->
</script>
<body bgcolor="#ffffff">
<h1>AERO Message Service</h1>
<p><a href="../trick05/aeroms-i.htm">
    Internet Explorer Version</a></p>
<p><a href="../trick06/aeroms-n.htm">
    Netscape Navigator Version</a></p>
</body>
</html>
```

Create HTML for frameset.

Test browser version and display the corresponding page.

Manual-choice HTML for browsers that don't support JavaScript

What This Page Does

Figure 8-3 shows the one-frame frameset in action. The figure is remarkably similar to Figure 5-1, but notice that the URL is that of the frameset and not that of *aeroms-i.htm*. Anyone who bookmarks or links to this page will link to the *frameset aeroms-f.htm* and not to either of the version-specific pages it loads.

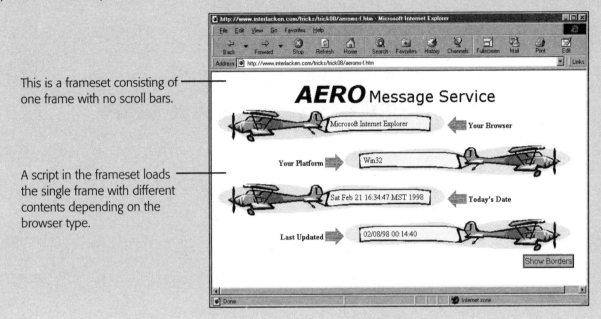

This is a frameset consisting of one frame with no scroll bars.

A script in the frameset loads the single frame with different contents depending on the browser type.

With the one-frame frameset approach, the Back button works just as it should. The user never jumps forward through multiple pages, so backing up one page at a time never presents a problem.

This is so cool, I hear you saying, there must be a catch. Well, you're right. Nothing we've seen so far unloads the frameset when the user clicks on a hyperlink, and this creates two curious problems:

- As the user follows additional hyperlinks, the URL in the browser window remains that of the frameset.

- If your site is chock full of these puppies, the browser can end up with a lot of framesets inside each other, and it'll eventually run out of resources (RAM, most likely).

Tip: To override the frame target set by a <BASE> tag, code the TARGET attribute on individual hyperlinks; for instance, <A HREF= yourpage.htm TARGET="_parent">.

To avoid these problems, add the following line to the <HEAD> section of any page the one-frame frameset displays:

```
<base target="_top">
```

This tells the browser to replace the entire frameset whenever it loads hyperlinks in the current frame. Otherwise, it replaces only the current frame and not the frameset.

AERO Message Service (ASP)

Just as browser scripts can tell the browser to load a new Web page, so can scripts running on the Web server. If your Web server is from Microsoft, an Active Server page script is probably the easiest and most direct approach. This is the topic of the current section. For other Web servers, you'll probably want to use Perl, as described in the next section.

Following the pattern of the previous examples, we'll again choose between delivering IE or Netscape Navigator versions of the AERO Message Service page. The server-side script will be in a Web page named *aeroms.asp*; this is the URL users must submit (probably by hyperlink) to run the script that switches to the appropriate Web page.

What This Page Does

The *aeroms.asp* page determines the user's browser type the same way as the Active Server Browser Menu page did back in Figure 3-5. Please don't tell me you've forgotten this. Oh, all right.

First we create an object containing the properties of the current user's browser, with this statement:

```
Set bc = Server.CreateObject("MSWC.BrowserType")
```

Once the *bc* object exists, its browser property tells us the name of the software: IE, Navigator, or whatever. We could test the major version number too, if we wanted, using the *bc* object's *majorver* property.

Normally, running the *aeroms.asp* page would deliver any HTML included therein, plus any HTML generated by server-side scripts. The following statement, however, instead tells the browser to display a completely different Web page:

```
response.redirect("../../trick05/aeroms-i.htm")
```

This code elicits the following response:

- If the *response.redirect* method specifies a page on the server that's running the script, the server responds with a status code of 302 (which means "This object has moved") plus the content of the alternate page. The 302 status code makes the browser display the redirected URL rather than *aeroms.asp*, the originally requested URL.

- If *response.redirect* specifies a page on a different Web server, the local server still sends out the 302 status code, but it can't, of course, send out the corresponding page content. Instead, it's the browser's job to get the content from the other server.

Complete HTML Listing

This said, here's the complete listing for the *aeroms.asp* page. Ignore the first line for now—I'll explain it in the next section.

Activate Response buffering.
Create the browser type object.
Test the browser type and send the corresponding Web page.

```
<% response.buffer = True %>
<%
Set bc = Server.CreateObject("MSWC.BrowserType")
if (bc.browser = "IE") then
    response.redirect("../../trick05/aeroms-i.htm")
else
    response.redirect("../../trick06/aeroms-n.htm")
end if
%>
<html>
<head>
<title>AERO Message Service (ASP)</title>
```

```
</head>
<body>
<h1>AERO Message Service (ASP)</h1>
<p><a href="../../trick05/aeroms-i.htm">
    Internet Explorer Version</a></p>
<p><a href="../../trick06/aeroms-n.htm">
    Netscape Navigator Version</a></p>
</body>
</html>
```

Dummy content, in case the script fails.

Additional Details

OK, now about that first line of code. It's not really needed for this example, but I'm going to explain it anyway. Am I a great guy or what? Here's the line we're talking about:

```
<% response.buffer = True %>
```

A problem occurs if, for some reason, you have to put a *response.redirect* statement anywhere after the <HTML> tag. There could be some processing down there, a database query, for example, whose results affect the redirection. In such cases, the Web server has already sent some HTML to the browser—and the browser has already started displaying it—before your script issues its redirection. There's no way to withdraw the HTML already sent, so the server has to fail the redirection.

To solve this problem, the Web server can *buffer* outgoing ASP pages until they're complete. That is, instead of transmitting the ASP script's output to the user immediately, the server saves up all the output and doesn't begin transmitting until the entire script finishes. As long as all the output remains in the buffer, the *response.redirect* method can purge it (or add more headers) without failure.

In this example, all the *response.redirect* statements occur before the <HTML> tag so the *response.buffer = True* statement isn't required. It's only there to illustrate the syntax.

Tip: The *response.redirect* statement adds an HTTP header called *Location:* to the front of your Web page—that is, to the information the server sends about itself and the current Web page. Once it sends the <HTML> tag of your Web page, the server can't send any more HTTP headers. That's why, normally, you must put the *response.redirect* statement before the <HEAD> tag.

No Back-button weirdness results from using *response.redirect* in an ASP script. Clicking a link that points to *aeroms.asp* causes either the *aeroms-i.htm* page (and URL) to be displayed, or *aeroms-n.htm* if the browser isn't IE. Clicking the Back button returns the user to the page containing the ASP link, just as the user expects.

Why use an ASP page instead of, say, a single-frame frameset? For one thing, there are fewer variables to account for; your script needs to work on one Web server, not fifty zillion browsers. For another, with a server-side script, the user only sees the results and not the logic that produces them. Finally, page redirection may be a part of other server-side scripting on the same page.

The advantages of single-frame framesets are that no server-side processing or permissions are required, and the browser displays the frameset URL, rather than the browser-specific location. On the downside, you have to deal with fifty zillion browsers and code a <BASE> statement within each page that'll appear within the single frame.

AERO Message Service (Perl)

The final example of this trick solves the same problem once again, this time in Perl. The code to determine the browser version is stolen directly from the page titled Browser Information in Perl, which you undoubtedly remember seeing in Figure 3-7. The code to perform the redirection looks like this:

```
print "Location: ../../trick05/aeroms-i.htm\n";
```

The *Location:* line must appear first in the Perl program's output stream. This performs exactly the same function as the *response-redirect* statement in an ASP page. With the browser name stored in the variable *$Bname*, the complete *if-then-else* statement looks like this:

```
if ($Bname eq "MSIE"){
    print "Location: ../../trick05/aeroms-i.htm\n";
}else{
    print "Location: ../../trick06/aeroms-n.htm\n";
}
```

Strictly speaking, this one line of output followed by a blank line is all that's required. The example also writes a dummy Web page though, just to avoid a blank page if something goes wrong.

Complete Perl Listing

Here's the complete listing:

Start of routine to determine the browser type, as in Trick 3.

```
$browser = $ENV{HTTP_USER_AGENT};
$browser =~ s/Windows /Win/gi;
$browser =~ tr#[]/(;) #        #s;
@brw = split(/ /,$browser);
if ($#brw > 1) {
  $Bname = $brw[0];
  $Bvers = $brw[1];
  $Boper = "";
  for ($pos = 2; $pos <= $#brw; $pos++){
    $inf = $brw[$pos];
    if ($inf eq "MSIE"){
      $Bname = $inf;
      if ($pos+1 < $#brw){
        $Bvers = $brw[$pos+1];
      }
    }
    if ((substr($inf,0,3) eq "Win")
      || (substr($inf,0,3) eq "Mac")
      || (substr($inf,0,3) eq "Web")
      || (substr($inf,0,3) eq "Sun")
      || (substr($inf,0,2) eq "HP")
      || (substr($inf,0,3) eq "AIX")
      || (substr($inf,0,3) eq "BSD")
      || (substr($inf,0,7) eq "FreeBSD")
      || (substr($inf,0,3) eq "OSF")
      || (substr($inf,0,4) eq "IRIX")
      || (substr($inf,0,5) eq "Linux")
      || (substr($inf,0,4) eq "OS/2")){
```

Continued from previous page

```
        $Boper = $inf;
    }
  }
}
$Bmaj = int($Bvers);
if ($Bname eq "MSIE"){
    print "Location: ../../trick05/aeroms-i.htm\n";
}else{
    print "Location: ../../trick06/aeroms-n.htm\n";
}
print "Content-type: text/html\n";
print "\n";
print "<HTML>\n";
print "<HEAD>\n";
print "<TITLE>AERO Message Service</TITLE>";
print "</HEAD>\n";
print "<BODY>\n";
print "</BODY>\n";
print "</HTML>\n";
```

End of routine to determine the browser type.

Determine the browser version and redirect to the corresponding Web page.

Create a dummy Web page (actually superfluous).

The advantages and disadvantages of using a Perl script are pretty much the same as those for using an Active Server Page. Choosing between ASP and Perl is easy on a non-Microsoft Web server, because ASP won't be available.

On a Microsoft server, ASP is an integral part of the server, not an add-on (albeit free) product like Perl. ASP is also a bit less cryptic and a more concise than Perl. But if other parts of your application are already written in Perl, you'll probably want to use Perl for redirection as well.

Well, now you can redirect users to Web pages all over the universe using HTML, JavaScript, ASP, and Perl. If only redirecting those pesky telemarketers were so easy!

Interacting with Form Elements

P oint-and-click is all well and good, but a complete graphical user interface (GUI) involves much more. Whether entering data, displaying long lists in limited space, or providing interest through variety, interfaces built only with hyperlinks come up short. Users expect familiar user interface objects like drop-down lists, scrolling lists, text boxes, check boxes, radio buttons, and push buttons.

Centuries ago (Internet centuries, that is), GUI objects like push buttons, radio buttons, and drop-down lists were always part of an HTML form—a section of Web page marked by <FORM> and </FORM> tags. Clicking a Submit button sent the form data to some sort of program on the server—an Active Server Page, a Perl program, whatever. The server-side program did its thing, sent a new Web page to the remote user, and life went on.

Nowadays, you can process form elements with browser-side scripts as well. You can write scripts for fancy hyperlinking, for validating data before a user submits a form, or for producing complete applications. And no, I don't know how many dog years make an Internet century.

This trick delivers three examples that illustrate how scripts interact with form elements. One is easy, one is stylish, and one goes nuts.

The easy one contains one form element—a push button. Clicking the button jumps to another Web page. This page introduces some important topics but it's not the sort of thing that'll get you appointed to the Academy of Science.

The stylish one uses drop-down lists and radio buttons to select a new Web page. As is, these techniques offer your visitors lots of hyperlink choices without

205

requiring a lot of real estate on your Web page. Additionally, though, they show how JavaScript can interact with more kinds of form objects.

The page that goes nuts not only reads the contents of form elements; it also updates them. First, it modifies one drop-down list based on selections made in another. Second, it calculates and displays item prices as the Web visitor enters an order. Finally, it computes the total price for the order before the user even submits the page. Yes, that's right; the Academy of Science is a real possibility here.

The Jump Start Page

As promised, the first example of this trick is an easy one. (I love it when a plan comes together.) The Jump Start Page appears in Figure 9-1.

FIGURE 9-1. *This simple page consists of one active element—the push button.*

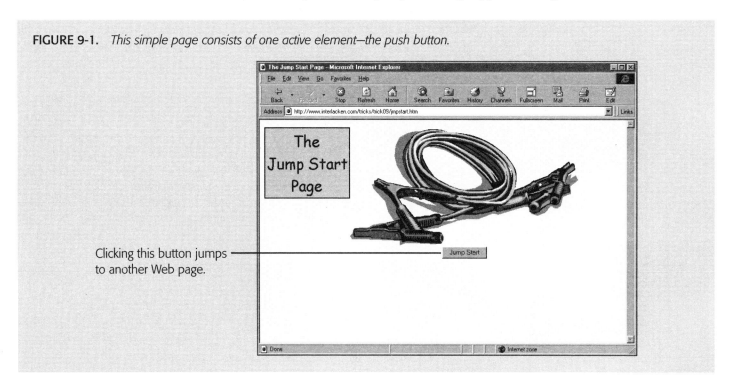

Clicking this button jumps to another Web page.

The push button jumps to the page shown in Figure 9-2. That's it; the Jump Start Page has no other features. I told you this was a simple page.

There's nothing very fancy about page layout, either. The heading square is a one-cell by one-cell table with a background color and a 1-pixel-wide black border. A 2 × 2 table controls the rest of the page layout; the cells in row one contain the heading table and the large graphic. The second row contains a blank cell and one containing the push button. Is that simple or what?

FIGURE 9-2 *Clicking the push button in Figure 9-1 jumps to this page—no rocket science required.*

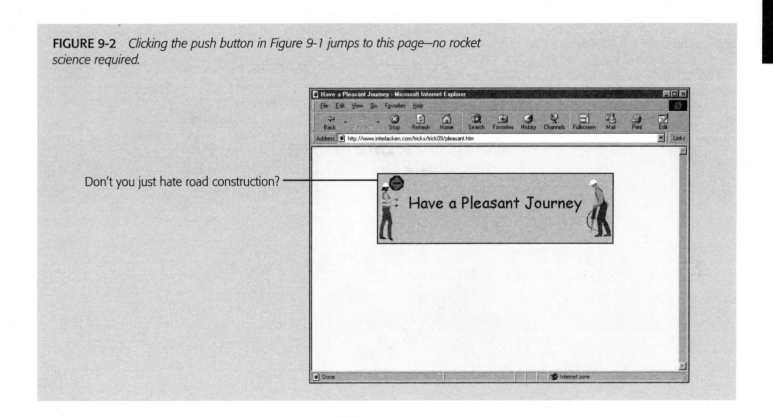

Don't you just hate road construction?

Tip: Because *onClick* is an HTML attribute, its spelling isn't case sensitive.

Caution: Netscape ignores form elements, like push buttons, that aren't part of a form.

Tip: Don't put more than one or two JavaScript statements directly inside an *onClick* or other event attribute. This clutters up your HTML and makes it hard to work with. Instead, define lengthy code as a function in the <HEAD> section.

Scripting Techniques

The HTML/JavaScript for the push button looks like this.

```
<form>
  <p><input type="button" value="Jump Start"
  onclick="window.location.href ='pleasant.htm'"></p>
</form>
```

Microsoft Internet Explorer doesn't require the <FORM> and </FORM> tags for jobs like this, but Netscape Navigator does. The <INPUT TYPE="button"> tag defines a push button, and the VALUE= attribute controls the caption on the button's face.

The *onClick* attribute is the interesting feature of this example. When the remote user clicks the button, the browser interprets the value of the *onClick* attribute as JavaScript and executes it. In this case, the JavaScript code tells the browser to display the *pleasant.htm* page. It's as simple as that.

Complete HTML Listing

The HTML for these two very simple pages should hold no surprises:

```
<head>
<title>The Jump Start Page</title>
</head>
<body bgcolor="#FFFFCC">
<table>
<tr>
  <td valign="top">
    <table border="1" cellpadding="3" cellspacing="0"
          bordercolor="#000000"  bgcolor="#FFCC99">
    <tr>
      <td align="center"
          style="font-family: Comic Sans MS, sans-serif;
                 font-size: 24pt;">
        The<br>Jump Start<br>Page</td></tr>
</table></td>
```

Start of page layout table.

Heading table and heading.

```
Continued from previous page
    <td><img src="../images/jmprcbl.gif" alt="Jumper Cables"
             width="481" height="243"></td>
</tr><tr>
    <td align="left"></td>
    <td align="center">
      <form>
       <p><input type="button" value="Jump Start"
              onclick="window.location.href ='pleasant.htm'"></p>
      </form></td></tr>
</table>
</body>
</html>
```

Define an HTML form that contains an input button with the *onClick* attribute.

End of page layout table.

The following page is nothing more than a place for the Jump Start Page to land.

```
<html>
<head>
<title>Have a Pleasant Journey</title>
</head>
<body bgcolor="#FFFFCC">
<p align="center"> </p>
<table align="center"
        border="1" cellpadding="3" cellspacing="0"
        bgcolor="#FFCC99" bordercolor="#000000">
<tr>
    <td style="font-family: Comic Sans MS, sans-serif;
              font-size: 24pt;">
      <img src="../images/flagger.gif" alt="Flagger"
          align="middle" width="51" height="134">
      Have a Pleasant Journey
      <img src="../images/jackhmr.gif" alt="Jack Hammer"
          align="middle" width="51" height="118"></td>
```

Start of a one-cell table for heading.

Heading content.

Continued from previous page

```
</tr>
</table>
</body>
</html>
```

End of one-cell table for heading. ─── </table>

Additional Details—Events and Event Handlers

Different browsers, different browser versions, and different form elements support different events. Table 9-1 lists the most common and useful events. In general, the newer the browser, the more events it supports. Version 4 of IE supports just about any event that makes sense for any object. Netscape Navigator 4 generally supports fewer events, and only for anchor tags and form elements.

TABLE 9-1. Common Browser Events.	
Event	**How to Trigger**
onClick	Press and release the mouse.
onDblClick	Double-click the mouse button.
onMouseDown	Depress (but don't release) the mouse button.
onMouseUp	Release the mouse button.
onMouseOver	Move the mouse pointer over an object.
onMouseMove	Move the mouse pointer.
onMouseOut	Move the mouse pointer off an object.
onKeyPress	Type a character.
onKeyDown	Depress a key.
onKeyUp	Release a key
onDragStart	Depress the mouse button and, before releasing it, move the mouse.
onSelectStart	Begin selecting an area of the Web page.

TABLE 9-1. Common Browser Events. *(continued)*	
Event	**How to Trigger**
onSelect	Continue selecting an area of the Web page.
onScroll	Scroll up or down, right or left.
onFocus	Use the Tab key or mouse to select a form element for input.
onBlur	Use the Tab key or mouse to deselect a form element for input.
onHelp	Press the system-defined Help key (F1).

The best way to see these events in action is to code a simple yet highly visible response, such as the following:

```
onclick="alert('Stuff Happens.')"
```

If nothing happens, the browser doesn't support the event (*onClick*, in this case) for that type of object.

For some events, the fact that they've occurred is all your JavaScript routine needs to know. For others, you'll need additional information. In the case of the *onKeyPress* event, for example, there's an outside chance you'd like to know *which* key was pressed. These values appear by magic, attached to a built-in gizmo called the *event* object. The ASCII value of a keystroke appears in *event.keyCode*, for example.

Table 9-2 lists some commonly used properties of the event object. Again, not all browsers and versions support all properties for all objects. A few seconds of testing is the best determinant.

TABLE 9-2. Common *event* Object Properties.	
Property	**Description**
keyCode	The ASCII value of a keystroke.
shiftKey	True if the Shift key is down, otherwise False.
altKey	True if the Alt key is down, otherwise False.

TABLE 9-2. Common *event* Object Properties. *(continued)*	
Property	**Description**
ctrlKey	True if the Ctrl key is down, otherwise False.
button	The combination of mouse buttons pressed. Add: 0 = none, 1 = left, 2 = right, 4 = middle.
clientX, clientY	The mouse coordinates, measured in pixels from the browser window's top left corner.
offsetX, offsetY	The mouse coordinates measured in pixels from the top left corner of the current object's container.
screenX, screenY	The mouse coordinates relative to the entire screen.
srcElement	The element that first received an event.
cancelBubble	If set to True, stops events from bubbling up. (What the heck is bubbling, you ask? Please refer to the sidebar.)
returnValue	Accepts values that modify the browser's built-in responses.

Tip: You can modify some, but not all, event object properties. You can change typed characters, for example, by modifying *event.keyCode*. This can be quite handy if you'd like to, say, convince people they need typing lessons. To cancel a keystroke, set *event.keyCode* to 0.

Who Turned On the Bubble Machine?

Suppose you have an image that's inside a table cell, and the cell is inside a table row, which is inside a table. You click the image. Which object receives the *onClick* event?

Actually, all of them do, starting from the image and continuing upward all the way through the document and window objects. This is called *bubbling*, and it happens automatically. To stop an event from bubbling upward, set the *event.cancelBubble* property to True in the event routine for the highest level you want to see the event.

Events and event handlers are a very powerful facility. With them, you can write code to handle almost anything that happens while your page is on display. You write and identify the code, and the browser runs it at the necessary moment; this is what The Jump Start Page did for a very simple case. Now, let's move on to something more interesting.

Note: The Ahab's Anchor Asylum page assumes the user won't enlarge fonts or narrow the window so much that the heading text occupies more than 100 pixels. When using absolute positioning, you'll almost always have to make assumptions like this. As long as some page elements are self-adjusting and some not, there's no completely reliable compromise.

Ahab's Anchor Asylum

This example, as promised, is a bit more stylish than the last. The page layout uses three overlapping divisions, as seen in Figure 9-3. Each division is 35 percent as wide as the document area, and the left edges of the second and third divisions are at 33 percent and 65 percent horizontal offsets.

Page Layout Details

All three divisions use absolute positioning, so their vertical positions are measured from the top left corner of the window. The graphic in the heading is 100

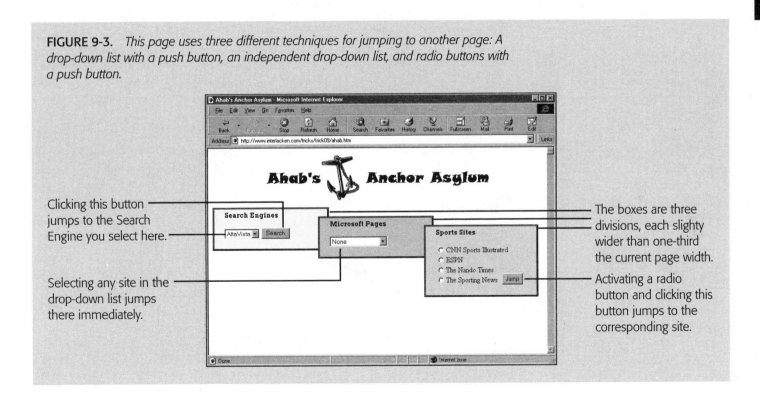

FIGURE 9-3. *This page uses three different techniques for jumping to another page: A drop-down list with a push button, an independent drop-down list, and radio buttons with a push button.*

Clicking this button jumps to the Search Engine you select here.

Selecting any site in the drop-down list jumps there immediately.

The boxes are three divisions, each slighty wider than one-third the current page width.

Activating a radio button and clicking this button jumps to the corresponding site.

Tip: What Windows calls a drop-down list, HTML calls a selection list with the size attribute set to 1. What Windows calls a scrolling list box, HTML calls a selection list with the size attribute set to greater than 1.

Tip: It's always a good idea to give HTML forms a name. This involves simply adding a NAME= attribute to the <FORM> tag.

Tip: If you prefer scrolling list boxes rather than drop-down boxes, set to the size attribute to greater than 1.

pixels high, and the three divisions are positioned 130, 150, and 170 pixels from the top, respectively. We apply background colors, fonts, and border effects using CSS properties.

Each box contains its own HTML form. The box on the far left provides a drop-down list of three popular Internet search engines: Alta Vista, Lycos, and Yahoo. Clicking the Search button jumps to the currently selected site.

Scripting Techniques

If life were perfect (that is, if Netscape Navigator and Internet Explorer worked the same), we could code each of the drop-down options like this:

```
<form name="schform">
<select name="schdest" size="1">
<option value="http://www.altavista.digital.com/">AltaVista</option>
<option value="http://www.lycos.com/">Lycos</option>
<option value="http://www.yahoo.com/">Yahoo </option>
```

and the push button could simply say:

```
onclick="window.location.href=document.all.box1.schdest.value"
```

The value property, after all, is the value transmitted to server-side processes by the browser. You'd think that browsers would make this property available to browser-side scripts, and in fact Internet Explorer does just that. Unfortunately, Netscape Navigator doesn't. An integer property called *selectedIndex* is the only way both browsers uniformly read list box selections. This property is 0 if the first item is selected, 1 if the second is, and so forth.

Using *selectedIndex* to read the list box makes the value clauses in our perfect life scenario rather superfluous; in other words, we can remove them. The coding for the push button's *onClick* event becomes:

```
onclick="jmpSearch(schform.schdest.selectedIndex)"
```

where *jmpSearch* is a script in the <HEAD> section, *schform* is the name of the form, and *schdest* is the name of the drop-down list. The *jmpSearch* function receives the *schform.schdest.selectedIndex* value as an argument called *site*, and interprets it with code like this:

```
if (site == 0) {
  window.location.href = "http://www.altavista.digital.com/"
}
```

The middle box contains a drop-down list with no push button. Instead of a push button's *onClick* event, this box reacts to an *onChange* event coded directly into the drop-down list. Otherwise, it works exactly like the first box.

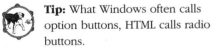

Tip: What Windows often calls option buttons, HTML calls radio buttons.

The first choice in the middle box is None, a selection that does nothing. This provides an escape for people who open the list to see what's there, and then decide against using any of the choices. Without this, the user has no choice but to take one of the jumps. Very rude. Always provide users with an escape option.

The third and rightmost box (or form...or division...) uses radio buttons. Reading values from radio buttons is even more of a nuisance than reading them from list boxes, because all the radio buttons in the same group have the same name. It's kind of like, "Hi, my name is Cletus. This is my brother Cletus and that's my other brother Cletus." Duplicate naming serves an important purpose, however: it associates radio buttons into a group. Clicking one button deselects all others in the same group (that is, with the same name).

There are ways around the problem of duplicate names. You can assign unique ID attributes, in addition to the duplicate NAME= values, but life is too short to mess with them here. Instead, we:

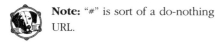

Note: "#" is sort of a do-nothing URL.

- Initialize a variable named *sportUrl* to "#" when the page loads.

- Use each radio button's *onClick* event to update *sportUrl* whenever the user clicks that button.

- Code a push button's *onClick* event to jump to the current *sportUrl* value.

Complete HTML Listing

OK, that wasn't too bad. If you made it this far, you're ready for the full, unabridged HTML listing in all its glory. Let's go. Quiz: How many thingies discussed above can *you* recognize?

Set repeating styles for box formats and box titles.

Initialize the *sportUrl* value for radio box set.

The *onClick* event handler for the Search push button.

```html
<html>
<head>
<title>Ahab's Anchor Asylum</title>
<style>
<!--
.box { width:35%; border: outset #996600; padding: 3 3% 3 3%; }
.title { font-family: Rockwell, serif; font-weight: bold  }
-->
</style>
<script language="JavaScript">
var sportUrl ="#";
function jmpSearch(site) {
  if (site == 0) {
    window.location.href = "http://www.altavista.digital.com/"
  }
  if (site == 1) {
    window.location.href = "http://www.lycos.com/"
  }
  if (site == 2) {
    window.location.href = "http://www.yahoo.com/"
  }
}
```

Continued from previous page

```
function jmpMS(site){
  if (site == 0) {
    return;
  }
  if (site == 1) {
    window.location.href = "http://www.microsoft.com/"
  }
  if (site == 2) {
    window.location.href = "http://mspress.microsoft.com/"
  }
  if (site == 3) {
    window.location.href = "http://www.msnbc.com/"
  }
  if (site == 4) {
    window.location.href = "http://www.msn.com/"
  }
  if (site == 5) {
    window.location.href = "http://www.slate.com/"
  }
}
</script>
</head>
<body bgcolor="#FFFFFF">
<h1 id="hdr" align="center"
    style="font-family: Snap ITC, fantasy">
  Ahab's<img src="../images/anchor1.gif"
            alt="Anchor" align="absmiddle"
            width="87" height="100">
  Anchor Asylum</h1>
<div id="box1" class="box"
    style="position: absolute; top:130;
    background-color: #ffffcc; ">
  <p class="title">Search Engines</p>
  <form name="schform"><p>
```

The *onChange* event handler for the Microsoft Pages selection list.

Set up the page heading.

Define division for box on far left.

Box title.

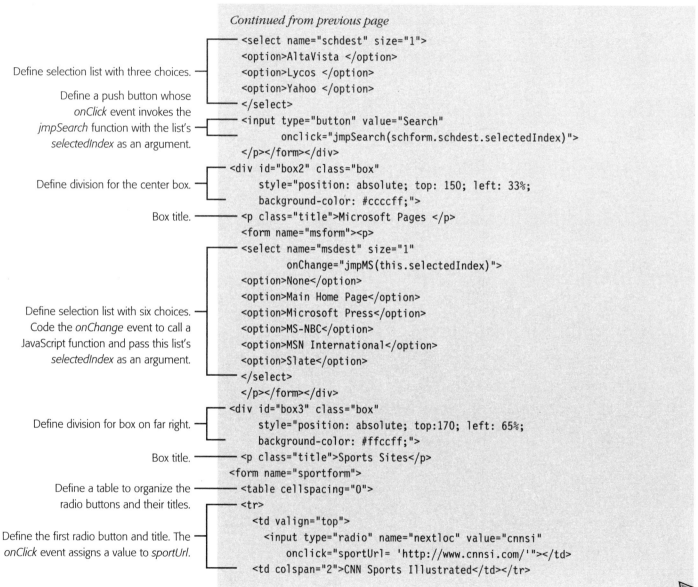

Continued from previous page

Define selection list with three choices.

```
<select name="schdest" size="1">
<option>AltaVista </option>
<option>Lycos </option>
<option>Yahoo </option>
</select>
```

Define a push button whose *onClick* event invokes the *jmpSearch* function with the list's *selectedIndex* as an argument.

```
<input type="button" value="Search"
       onclick="jmpSearch(schform.schdest.selectedIndex)">
</p></form></div>
```

Define division for the center box.

```
<div id="box2" class="box"
     style="position: absolute; top: 150; left: 33%;
     background-color: #ccccff;">
```

Box title.

```
<p class="title">Microsoft Pages </p>
<form name="msform"><p>
```

Define selection list with six choices. Code the *onChange* event to call a JavaScript function and pass this list's *selectedIndex* as an argument.

```
<select name="msdest" size="1"
        onChange="jmpMS(this.selectedIndex)">
<option>None</option>
<option>Main Home Page</option>
<option>Microsoft Press</option>
<option>MS-NBC</option>
<option>MSN International</option>
<option>Slate</option>
</select>
</p></form></div>
```

Define division for box on far right.

```
<div id="box3" class="box"
     style="position: absolute; top:170; left: 65%;
     background-color: #ffccff;">
```

Box title.

```
<p class="title">Sports Sites</p>
<form name="sportform">
```

Define a table to organize the radio buttons and their titles.

```
<table cellspacing="0">
<tr>
```

Define the first radio button and title. The *onClick* event assigns a value to *sportUrl*.

```
  <td valign="top">
    <input type="radio" name="nextloc" value="cnnsi"
           onclick="sportUrl= 'http://www.cnnsi.com/'"></td>
  <td colspan="2">CNN Sports Illustrated</td></tr>
```

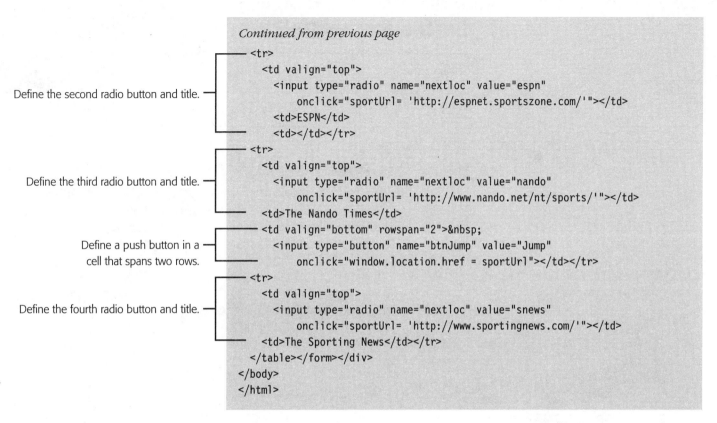

Continued from previous page

Define the second radio button and title.

```
<tr>
  <td valign="top">
    <input type="radio" name="nextloc" value="espn"
        onclick="sportUrl= 'http://espnet.sportszone.com/'"></td>
    <td>ESPN</td>
    <td></td></tr>
```

Define the third radio button and title.

```
<tr>
  <td valign="top">
    <input type="radio" name="nextloc" value="nando"
        onclick="sportUrl= 'http://www.nando.net/nt/sports/'"></td>
  <td>The Nando Times</td>
```

Define a push button in a cell that spans two rows.

```
  <td valign="bottom" rowspan="2"> 
    <input type="button" name="btnJump" value="Jump"
        onclick="window.location.href = sportUrl"></td></tr>
```

Define the fourth radio button and title.

```
<tr>
  <td valign="top">
    <input type="radio" name="nextloc" value="snews"
        onclick="sportUrl= 'http://www.sportingnews.com/'"></td>
  <td>The Sporting News</td></tr>
</table></form></div>
</body>
</html>
```

Trick 9

This example provides much more than a fancy way of jumping to a dozen hyperlink locations. It demonstrates another use of CSS positioning, and more kinds of interaction between form elements and JavaScript code.

Don't overlook the usefulness of hyperlinking via form elements, though, particularly using drop-down lists. You can provide more links in less screen space by this method than almost any other.

Coffee Break Deli

The previous two examples involved fairly limited interaction; the user put values into the form elements, then a script read them and did its thing. Very short, very sweet, let's all pat ourselves on the back. But really, those examples are no more interactive than a vending machine. What about something even more interactive, something that requires multiple interactions to complete, something like placing an order at a restaurant?

What This Page Does

OK, you asked for it. (We'll disregard my tiny bit of prompting.) The Coffee Break Deli page, pictured in Figure 9-4, not only accepts user input from multiple form elements, but it also modifies itself as the transaction proceeds.

FIGURE 9-4. *This Web page modifies its own display, providing visual feedback as the user enters an order.*

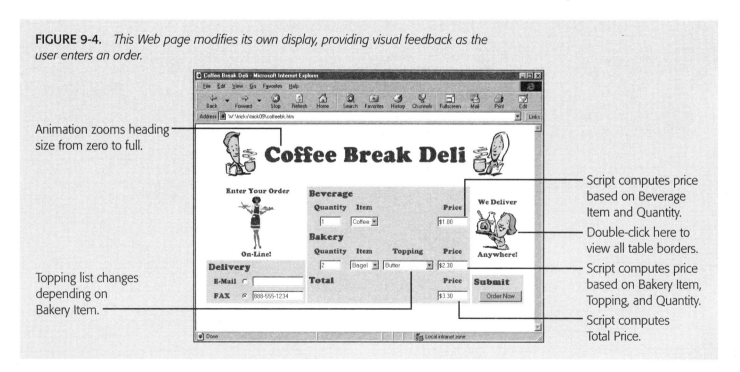

Animation zooms heading size from zero to full.

Topping list changes depending on Bakery Item.

Script computes price based on Beverage Item and Quantity.

Double-click here to view all table borders.

Script computes price based on Bakery Item, Topping, and Quantity.

Script computes Total Price.

Specifically, the form modifies itself in these ways:

- Whenever the user selects a Beverage Item, the script looks up the corresponding price, multiplies it by the Beverage Quantity, and puts the result in the Beverage Price box.

- Another script function recalculates the Beverage Price field whenever the user changes the Beverage Quantity. This is based, of course, on the unit price for the current Beverage Item.

- The Bakery portion works pretty much the same, with Topping as the, ahem, icing on the cake. As the user selects different Bakery Items, a script modifies the Topping list to contain a different selection of toppings. Each topping has a different price. The Bakery Price is therefore Bakery Item Price plus Topping Price, multiplied by Bakery Quantity.

- The functions that calculate Beverage Price and Bakery Price also add the two together, resulting in Total Price.

- The Delivery box doesn't do anything; it's just there for show. You'll also notice there's no way for the user to pay. We'll figure out how to get paid after devising a way to fax the coffee and bagels.

- The Submit button is also a dummy; it simply displays a dialog stating this page is a demo.

In real life, clicking the Submit button would pack up all the form values and transmit them to the Web server for processing by, perhaps, an Active Server Page, a Perl program, or some other gizmo. We could also juice up data entry routines by rejecting keystrokes other than numbers in the quantity fields, by performing completeness checks when the user clicks the Submit button, by accepting a credit card number or account ID, and so forth. But this is an example for a book, not real life, so let's keep it relatively simple.

 See Also: For examples of HTML forms passing data to server-side programs, refer to Trick 15, "Enhancing Your Forms".

Page Layout Details

Page layout consists of the heading plus four tables. When the browser is Internet Explorer, the heading zooms in as it did on The Stranger Arranger page in Trick 7; a timer event gradually increases the heading font size from 0 percent to 100

Tip: Remember, the *setTimeout()* function expects two arguments: A JavaScript statement to execute, and a time delay (in milliseconds) to wait before doing so.

percent of its original size. Netscape Navigator can't do this, so for that browser the script doesn't even try.

The main layout table has three columns and two rows:

- Column 1 has the Enter Your Order Online arrangement in its upper cell and the delivery box in its lower cell.

- Column 2, with its upper and lower cells merged, contains the large Beverage/Bakery/Total box.

- Column 3 contains the We Deliver Anywhere layout and the Submit box in its upper and lower cells, respectively.

The three shaded boxes are the three remaining tables. If their arrangement isn't obvious, load the page into Internet Explorer and double-click the We Deliver Anywhere graphic.

<FORM> and </FORM> tags surround the outermost page layout table, consolidating all its contents into a single HTML form. The HTML for the Beverage Quantity field looks like this:

```
<input type="text" name="bevQty" size="5"
       onChange="bevPrice();" value="1">
```

The TYPE= attribute makes this a text box. The NAME= attribute identifies the field for both browser-side and server-side processing. SIZE= controls the field's width, and VALUE= provides the box's initial contents.

An Incredibly Brief Introduction to HTML Form Elements

HTML provides a variety of standard user interface elements for getting input from users. A single tag, <INPUT>, defines seven of these widgets; the element displayed depends on a TYPE= attribute. Table 9-3 (page 224) lists the possibilities.

List boxes, both drop-down and scrollable, have their own tag: <SELECT>. The HTML begins with a <SELECT> tag, continues with a <OPTION> tag for each possible selection, and concludes with </SELECT>.

An Incredibly Brief Introduction to HTML Form Elements *(continued)*

Here's an example:

```
<SELECT NAME="rating">
<OPTION>Limber
<OPTION>Lame
<OPTION>Off-net
</SELECT>
```

If the <SELECT> tag includes a SIZE= attribute, it controls how many list items are normally visible. SIZE=1, the default, creates a drop-down list while SIZE=2 or more creates a scrolling list.

Every <SELECT> list has a value that's transmitted to the server when the user submits the form. This value depends on the currently selected <OPTION>. If the <OPTION> tag for the current selection contains a VALUE= attribute, that's the <SELECT> list's value. If no such attribute is present, the value is the text that follows the <OPTION> tag. The SELECTED attribute, if present in an <OPTION> tag, controls which option is selected when the form loads.

The <TEXTAREA> tag creates a multiline text entry field, and requires a closing </TEXTAREA> tag. Any text that appears between these tags becomes the default value. The COLS= and ROWS= attributes control horizontal and vertical dimensions:

```
<TEXTAREA NAME="question1" COLS=50 ROWS=4>
Please enter any comments here.
</TEXTAREA>
```

The attributes listed in Table 9-4 further modify the way various form elements work. Include them as necessary within the tag that defines the element.

<FORM> and </FORM> tags surround each distinct collection of form elements in a Web page:

- If you're using the form to submit data to a Web server, the form will normally contain an <INPUT TYPE=SUBMIT> element. This creates a push button that, if pressed, submits the form. Submitting the form means transmitting all non-blank element values from that form to a destination on the server—that is, to a URL that runs a server-side program. An ACTION= attribute coded inside the <FORM> tag specifies that URL, as well as the transmission method it expects (GET or POST).

Hyperlink: For more detailed information about HTML forms, consult:

Microsoft:
http://www.microsoft.com/workshop/author/newhtml/htmlr014.htm

Netscape:
http://developer.netscape.com/docs/manuals/htmlguid/tags10.htm

W3C:
http://www.w3.org/TR/WD-html40-970708/interact/forms.html

An Incredibly Brief Introduction to HTML Form Elements *(continued)*

- If you're using the form to gather data for a script, the <INPUT TYPE=SUBMIT> button is optional. If you decide to include it, specify a URL like:

  ```
  javascript:yourFunction()
  ```

  replacing *yourFunction* with any JavaScript function defined within the page.

  Form elements respond to all the events listed in the earlier Table 9-1 (subject, of course, to the usual variations among browser types and versions). This explains why the <INPUT TYPE=SUBMIT> button is optional for forms used only by JavaScript; JavaScript can respond to all those other events.

  Regardless of the application, you should always give <FORM>, <INPUT>, <SELECT>, and <TEXTAREA> tags a name by coding a NAME= attribute within them. Naming forms and form elements is by far the easiest (and sometimes the only) way of identifying data to scripts and server-side programs.

TABLE 9-3. HTML Form <INPUT TYPE=> Options.

TYPE=	Description
TEXT	A text entry box. This is the default type.
PASSWORD	A text entry box in which typed characters appear as asterisks.
CHECKBOX	A single element that can only be ON or OFF.
RADIO	One of a group of buttons, only one of which can be ON at the same time. All buttons with the same NAME are in the same group.
SUBMIT	A button that assembles the current form data into a query URL and sends it to an HTTP server.
RESET	A button that resets the elements in the form to their default values.
HIDDEN	An input field with a NAME and VALUE but no visible display.

TABLE 9-4. HTML Form <INPUT> Attributes.

Attribute	Description
NAME	The internal (not displayed) name of the input field. This is mandatory for all types but SUBMIT and RESET.
VALUE	For a text or password entry field, this specifies the default contents of the field.
	For a check box or a radio button, this specifies the button's value when checked; the default is ON. Unchecked check boxes don't appear on submitted queries.
	For types SUBMIT and RESET, VALUE overrides the default button label.
CHECKED	Specifies that a check box or radio button is checked by default.
SIZE	Specifies the field's display size in characters. This is only appropriate for TEXT and PASSWORD fields. The default is 20.
MAXLENGTH	Limits the maximum number of characters accepted as input. This is only valid for single-line text entry fields; the default is Unlimited.

Computing the Beverage Price

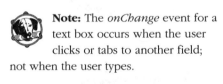

Note: The *onChange* event for a text box occurs when the user clicks or tabs to another field; not when the user types.

We'll need to compute the Beverage Price whenever the user changes either the Beverage Quantity or Beverage Item. Coding the *onChange* attribute within the tags for these elements executes a JavaScript function whenever their values change. The function we choose to run is called *bevPrice()*, and it consists of these statements:

```
bevPrice(){
  bevgPrc = bevArPrc[document.order.bevItm.selectedIndex];
  quan = parseInt(document.order.bevQty.value);
  if (quan < 0){
    document.order.bevQty.value = 0;
  }
  document.order.bevQty.value = quan;
  document.order.bevPrc.value = fmtMoney(bevgPrc * quan);
  totPrice();
}
```

The first statement looks up the price for the currently selected Beverage Item. The *bevArPrc* array has six elements, defined as:

```
bevArPrc = new Array(0,1.00,1.00,1.15,1.00,1.50);
```

The expression *document.order.bevItm.selectedIndex* is an integer that tells the script which Beverage Item is currently selected. The prices in the *bevArPrc* array are synchronized with the items in the Beverage drop-down list so that using the list's *selectedIndex* property as a subscript returns the correct price. The first item, None, has a price of zero; the next two items, Coffee and Cola, are each one dollar; and so forth.

The next few lines do their best to interpret the quantity value as an integer, replace any negative quantities with 0, and update the displayed value with the resulting interpretation. The next-to-last statement multiplies quantity by price and puts the result in the Total box; the last statement kicks off a function that adds the Beverage and Bakery Prices and displays the result in the Total Price box.

Note: The Coffee Break Deli page uses text boxes to display results only because Netscape Navigator can't do this any other way. Netscape Navigator can't display our results by replacing the ordinary text in a table cell, for example, at least not through version 4.x.

Hey Buddy, Can You Spare Me $0. 0999999999999997?

JavaScript treats any non-integer number as floating point. As a result, amounts like $1.50 show up as 1.5 and calculations like 3 x 1.15 give answers like 3.4499999999999997. The mathematics people can give us all the excuses they want, but this still isn't how most people expect to see monetary amounts.

Unfortunately, JavaScript lacks built-in functions for numeric formatting as well. This makes formatting dollars and cents a vigorous exercise in string manipulation. The Coffee Break Deli page uses the following function for currency formatting:

```
function fmtMoney(amt){
  cents = Math.round(amt * 100);
  if (cents < 10){
    cents = "$00" + cents;
  }else{
    if (cents < 100){
      cents="$0" + cents;
```

Updating the Topping List

Tip: Long names like *document. order.bkrTop.options.length* result from the browser's *document object model*. Each period represents a transition from some object to another object it contains.

The drill for handling bakery items greatly resembles what we did for beverages, except that we need to update the Topping list whenever the user chooses a different bakery item. This involves a fairly long, fairly repetitious function called *setTopping*, which you can find in the full HTML listing. Briefly, though, *setTopping* first erases any existing list items with these statements:

```
while (document.order.bkrTop.options.length > 1 ){
   document.order.bkrTop.options[1] = null;
   }
```

The expression *document.order.bkrTop.options.length* tells us how many options are in the select list named *bkrTop* (yup, that's the one we want) in the form named *order* (the name that appears on our one and only <FORM> tag). The *while* loop continues executing the second statement, which removes the second item in the list, until the first item in the list is all that remains. Frowning? OK, removing *document.order.bkrTop.options[1]* removes the *second* list item because the first item is subscripted [0]. And we never bother removing the first item, because it's always None.

Adding items works like this: first, the following statement stores the list position of the current Bakery Item into a variable named *bake*.

```
bake = document.order.bkrItm.selectedIndex;
```

Sequences like the following then add the appropriate list items for each Bakery Item. Bakery Item 3 is doughnuts. The two arguments are, first, the text that appears in the list box, and second, the value that gets transmitted to the server (if this page ever gets out of demo mode, that is).

```
if (bake == 3){
    addTopping("Chocolate","chocolate");
    addTopping("Glazed","glazed");
    addTopping("Jelly","jelly");
    addTopping("Peanut","peanut");
}
```

This is still no explanation, you say, because the *addTopping* function remains a mystery. Good thinking, so here it is:

```
function addTopping(txt, val){
    pos = document.order.bkrTop.options.length;
    var opt = new Option (txt, val);
    document.order.bkrTop.options[pos] = opt;
}
```

 Tip: The statement *"var a = b"* makes *a* an exact copy of *b*. The statement *"var a = new b()"* makes *a* a new *object* with all the methods and attributes of class *b*.

The first statement (after the function declaration) determines where in the list the new option should appear. If the list contains one item, it will be numbered 0, and the new item should be numbered 1. If the list contains four items, the last one will be number 3 and the new one following that will be number 4. Honest, I'm not making this up.

The next statement creates a new Option object named *opt*. Option objects have two properties, *text* and *value*, and we assign these as part of creating the object. The values are those passed as arguments to the *addTopping* function.

The third statement adds the new option *opt* to the list named *bkrTop*, in the form named *order*, at position *pos*. What could be simpler than that?

Computing the Total Bakery Price

Remember the *bevPrice* routine above? Seems like a thousand years ago, right? Well, there's a *bakePrice* routine that's pretty similar except that it takes the Topping selection into account. There are five Bakery Items (counting None) and up to seven toppings (again counting None), so the table of topping prices has 35 entries. The entry for any particular topping combination is located at (7 times the Bakery Item index) plus (the Topping Item index). The array gets defined like this:

```
topArPrc = new Array(0,0.00,0.00,0.00,0.00,0.00,0.00,
                     0,0.15,0.10,0.25,0.13,0.10,0.00,
                     0,0.10,0.10,0.10,0.10,0.10,0.10,
                     0,0.15,0.10,0.10,0.15,0.00,0.00,
                     0,0.15,0.10,0.25,0.10,0.13,0.00);
```

and gets accessed with the following code:

```
bakePrc = bakePrc
        + topArPrc[(7 * document.order.bkrItm.selectedIndex)
                     + document.order.bkrTop.selectedIndex];
```

Computing the Total Price

Take heart, there's only one more script function to examine before looking at the full HTML listing. This is the *totPrice* function, which adds the computed beverage and bakery prices to get an order total.

```
function totPrice(){
  bevVal = document.order.bevPrc.value;
  if (bevVal.substring(0,1) == "$"){
    bevVal = bevVal.substring(1,bevVal.length);
  }
```

Continued from previous page

```
bkrVal = document.order.bkrPrc.value;
if (bkrVal.substring(0,1) == "$"){
  bkrVal = bkrVal.substring(1,bkrVal.length);
}
document.order.totPrc.value
  fmtMoney(parseFloat(bevVal) + parseFloat(bkrVal));
}
```

Adding two numbers to get a total might at first seem a simple task, but there are two complications. Oh goodie. First, the values in the Beverage Total and Bakery Total boxes are strings, not numbers. And second, the *parseFloat* function, which converts strings to decimal numbers, won't accept a string that begins with a dollar sign. The *totPrice* function therefore copies each list box value to a temporary variable, tests for the presence of a dollar sign, removes the dollar sign if present, and then adds the two results (converting the strings to floating point *en route*). The result is run through the *fmtMoney* function on its way to the output (Total Price) text box.

Complete HTML Listing

OK, so this example isn't as straightforward as the first two. Well, I did warn you, and think of all the cool stuff we discovered along the way. No pain, no gain; speaking of which here's the full HTML listing. Gain, that is.

```
<html>
<head>
<title>Coffee Break Deli</title>
<style>
<!--
```
Define style for the page heading.
```
H1 { font-family: Cooper Black, serif;
     color: rgb(102,51,0); margin:0; }
```
Define style for the box titles.
```
H3 { font-family: Cooper Black, serif; font-size: 125%;
     color: rgb(102,51,0);  margin:0;}
```

Continued from previous page

Define style for form element descriptions.

```
.desc { font-family: Cooper Black, serif;
        color: rgb(102,51,0); }
-->
</style>
<script language="JavaScript">
<!--
```

Define variables for initial zoom animation.

```
var pct;
var hdrSiz;
```

Define price tables for Beverages, Bakery Items, and Bakery Toppings.

```
bevArPrc = new Array(0,1.00,1.00,1.15,1.00,1.50);
bkrArPrc = new Array(0,1.00,0.75,0.60,0.50);
topArPrc = new Array(0,0.00,0.00,0.00,0.00,0.00,0.00,
                     0,0.15,0.10,0.25,0.13,0.10,0.00,
                     0,0.10,0.10,0.10,0.10,0.10,0.10,
                     0,0.15,0.10,0.10,0.15,0.00,0.00,
                     0,0.15,0.10,0.25,0.10,0.13,0.00);
```

Check for Internet Explorer. If found, kick off zoom animation.

```
function startZoom(){
  if (navigator.appName.substring(0,9) != "Microsoft"){
    return;
  }
  pct = 0;
  runZoom();
}
```

Animate zoom-in heading. As the *setTimeout()* statement repeatedly calls *runZoom()*, the variable *pct* increases from 0 to 100 in increments of 5. With each iteration, the function multiplies the heading font size by *pct*/100.

```
function runZoom(){
  document.all.hdr.style.fontSize = hdrSiz * (pct/100);
  if (pct < 96){
    pct = pct + 5;
    setTimeout("runZoom()",100);
  }
}
```

Select Beverage Price from table, based on *selectedIndex*. Validate the quantity, compute the extended price, and then compute the total price for the order.

```
function bevPrice(){
  bevgPrc = bevArPrc[document.order.bevItm.selectedIndex];
  quan = parseInt(document.order.bevQty.value);
```

Continued from previous page

```
  if (quan < 0){
    quan = 0
  }
  document.order.bevQty.value = quan;
  document.order.bevPrc.value = fmtMoney(bevgPrc * quan);
  totPrice();
}
```

Start of function to update the Topping list. ———

```
function setTopping(){
```

Delete all but first item from the Topping list. ———

```
  while (document.order.bkrTop.options.length > 1 ){
    document.order.bkrTop.options[1] = null;
  }
  bake = document.order.bkrItm.selectedIndex;
  if ((bake == 1) || (bake == 4)){
```

Add toppings for bagels and toast. ———

```
    addTopping("Butter","butter");
    addTopping("Margerine","marg");
    addTopping("Cream Cheese","creamch");
    addTopping("Honey","honey");
    addTopping("Jelly","jelly");
  }
  if (bake == 2){
```

Add toppings for Danish. ———

```
    addTopping("Apricot","apricot");
    addTopping("Almond","almond");
    addTopping("Cheese","cheese");
    addTopping("Cherry","cherry");
    addTopping("Lemon","lemon");
    addTopping("Prune","prune");
  }
  if (bake == 3){
```

Add toppings for doughnuts. ———

```
    addTopping("Chocolate","chocolate");
    addTopping("Glazed","glazed");
    addTopping("Jelly","jelly");
    addTopping("Peanut","peanut");
  }
```

Position the list to the first item. ———

```
  document.order.bkrTop.selectedIndex = 0;
```

Continued from previous page

Refresh page display if browser is Netscape.
```
if (navigator.appName=="Netscape"){
    history.go(0);
}
```

Recompute total order price.
```
bakePrice();
```

End of function to update Topping list.
```
}
```

```
function addTopping(txt, val){
    pos = document.order.bkrTop.options.length;
    var opt = new Option (txt, val);
    document.order.bkrTop.options[pos] = opt;
}
```
Add a selection (text and value) to the Topping list.

```
function bakePrice(){
```

Compute total price for Bakery.
```
    bakePrc = bkrArPrc[document.order.bkrItm.selectedIndex];
```

Get price for currently selected Bakery Item.
```
    bakePrc = bakePrc
```

Add price for Bakery Topping.
```
            + topArPrc[(7 * document.order.bkrItm.selectedIndex)
                            + document.order.bkrTop.selectedIndex];
```

Convert quantity to an integer, change negative values to zero, and make any changes visible on screen.
```
    quan = parseInt(document.order.bkrQty.value);
    if (quan < 0){
        quan = 0;
    }
    document.order.bkrQty.value = quan;
```

Multiply price by quantity, display as currency.
```
    document.order.bkrPrc.value = fmtMoney(bakePrc * quan);
```

Recompute the total order price.
```
    totPrice();
}
```

```
function totPrice(){
```

Compute the total order price.
```
    bevVal = document.order.bevPrc.value;
```

Copy the Beverage Price to a temporary variable, and remove dollar sign if found.
```
    if (bevVal.substring(0,1) == "$"){
        bevVal = bevVal.substring(1,bevVal.length);
    }
```

Copy the Bakery Price to a temporary variable, and remove dollar sign if found.
```
    bkrVal = document.order.bkrPrc.value;
    if (bkrVal.substring(0,1) == "$"){
        bkrVal = bkrVal.substring(1,bkrVal.length);
    }
```

Convert Beverage and Bakery Prices to floating point, add, and display as currency.
```
    document.order.totPrc.value
        = fmtMoney(parseFloat(bevVal) + parseFloat(bkrVal));
}
```

Continued from previous page

Format a numeric dollar value as currency (dollar sign and two decimals).

Convert a fractional dollar amount to whole cents.

Make value at least three digits and add leading dollar sign.

Insert a decimal point.

Return edited value as the function result.

Supply dummy function for the Submit button.

Make borders visible for tables *tab1* through *tab4*.

Make borders invisible for tables *tab1* through *tab4*.

```javascript
function fmtMoney(amt){
    cents = Math.round(amt * 100);
    if (cents < 10){
        cents = "$00" + cents;
    }else{
        if (cents < 100){
            cents="$0" + cents;
        }else{
            cents="$" + cents;
        }
    }
    bucks = cents.substring(0,cents.length - 2)
            + "." + cents.substring(cents.length - 2, cents.length);
    return bucks;
}
function submitOrder(){
    alert("Sorry, this demo cannot submit orders.");
}
function bordOn(){
    document.all.tab1.border = "2" ;
    document.all.tab2.border = "2" ;
    document.all.tab3.border = "2" ;
    document.all.tab4.border = "2" ;
}
function bordOff(){
    document.all.tab1.border = "0" ;
    document.all.tab2.border = "0" ;
    document.all.tab3.border = "0" ;
    document.all.tab4.border = "0" ;
}
// -->
</script>
</head>
```

Continued from previous page

Start heading animation when the page loads.

Display the page heading.

If browser is Internet Explorer, save the heading's original font size and then reduce it to zero.

Start of the HTML form and page layout table.

Display Enter Your Order On-Line! layout.

Start of the main order table.

Order table row 1: Beverage title.

```html
<body onLoad="startZoom();">
<h1 id="hdr" align="center" style="font-size: 50;">
<img src="../images/cofeebr2.gif" align="absmiddle"
     width="86" height="100" alt="Coffee Break">
Coffee Break Deli
<img src="../images/cofeebr3.gif" align="absmiddle"
     width="84" height="100" alt="Coffee Break"></h1>
<script language="JavaScript">
<!--
if (navigator.appName.substring(0,9) == "Microsoft"){
  hdrSiz = parseInt(document.all.hdr.style.fontSize);
  document.all.hdr.style.fontSize = 0;
}
// -->
</script>
<form name="order">
<table id="tab1" border="0" align="center"
       bordercolor="#990000">
<tr>
  <td class="desc" align="center" valign="top">
    <img src="../images/trans5x5.gif"
         width="5" height="5">
    Enter Your Order<br>
    <img src="../images/server.gif" alt="Server"
         width="83" height="120"><br>
  On-Line!</td>
  <td valign="top" rowspan="2">
    <table id="tab2" border="0" height="100%"
           cellpadding="4" cellspacing="0"
           bgcolor="#FFCC99" bordercolor="#000099">
    <tr>
      <td colspan="5"><h3>Beverage</h3></td>
```

Continued from previous page

Order table row 2: Beverage item labels.

```
</tr><tr>
  <td><img src="../images/trans5x5.gif"
          width="5" height="5"></td>
  <td align="center" class="desc">Quantity</td>
  <td align="center" class="desc">Item</td>
  <td>  </td>
  <td align="center" class="desc">Price</td>
```

Order table row 3: Beverage form elements. Note *onChange* properties on quantity and item elements.

```
</tr><tr>
  <td>  </td>
  <td align="center">
    <input type="text" name="bevQty" size="5"
          onChange="bevPrice();" value="1"></td>
  <td align="center">
    <select name="bevItm" size="1"
          onChange="bevPrice();">
    <option selected value="none">None</option>
    <option value="coffee">Coffee</option>
    <option value="cola">Cola</option>
    <option value="milk">Milk</option>
    <option value="tea">Tea</option>
    <option value="water">Water</option>
    </select></td>
  <td>  </td>
  <td align="center">
    <input type="text" name="bevPrc" size="8"
          readonly="1" value="$0.00"></td>
```

Order table row 4: Bakery title.

```
</tr><tr>
  <td colspan="5"><h3>Bakery</h3></td>
```

Order table row 5: Bakery item labels.

```
</tr><tr>
  <td>  </td>
  <td class="desc" align="center">Quantity</td>
  <td class="desc" align="center">Item</td>
  <td class="desc" align="center">Topping</td>
  <td class="desc" align="center">Price</td>
```

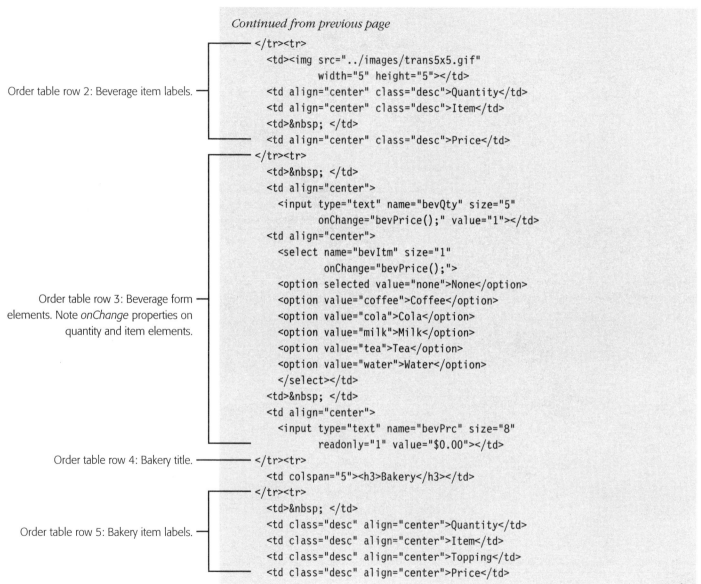

Continued from previous page

```
</tr><tr>
    <td>  </td>
    <td align="center">
        <input type="text" name="bkrQty" size="5"
                onChange="bakePrice();" value="1"></td>
    <td align="center">
        <select name="bkrItm" size="1"
                onChange="setTopping();">
        <option value="none">None</option>
        <option value="bagel">Bagel</option>
        <option value="danish">Danish</option>
        <option value="donut">Donut</option>
        <option value="toast">Toast</option>
        </select></td>
    <td align="center">
        <select name="bkrTop" size="1"
                onChange="bakePrice();">
        <option value="none">None</option>
        </select></td>
    <td align="center">
        <input type="text" name="bkrPrc" size="8"
                readonly="1" value="$0.00"></td>
</tr><tr>
    <td colspan="4"><h3>Total</h3></td>
    <td class="desc" align="center">Price</td>
</tr><tr>
<td>  </td>
<td>  </td>
<td>  </td>
<td>  </td>
<td align="center">
    <input type="text" name="totPrc" size="8"
            value="$0.00" readonly="1"></td></tr>
```

Order table row 6: Bakery form elements. Note *onChange* properties on quantity, item, and topping elements.

Order table row 7: Total heading and labels.

Order table row 8: Total form elements.

Continued from previous page

End of the main order table. ⎯

```
    </table></td>
<td align="center" class="desc" valign="bottom">
    We Deliver<br>
    <img src="../images/milkhony.gif" alt="We Deliver"
        width="100" height="96"
        ondblclick="bordOn()"
        onmouseout="bordOff()"><br>
    Anywhere!</td>
</tr><tr>
    <td class="desc" align="center" valign="bottom">
    <table id="tab3" border="0"
            cellpadding="4" cellspacing="0"
            bgcolor="#FFCC99"  bordercolor="#009900">
    <tr>
        <td colspan="4"><h3>Delivery</h3></td>
    </tr><tr>
        <td class="desc">
          <img src="../images/trans5x5.gif"
               width="5" height="5"></td>
        <td class="desc">E-Mail</td>
        <td>
          <input type="radio" name="delivery"
                 value="dlvEmail"></td>
        <td>
          <input type="text" name="eMail" size="15"></td>
    </tr><tr>
        <td class="desc">  </td>
        <td class="desc">FAX</td>
        <td>
          <input type="radio" name="delivery"
                 value="dlvFax"></td>
        <td>
          <input type="text" name="faxNr" size="15"></td></tr>
        </table></td>
```

Display the We Deliver Anywhere! layout. ⎯

Display the Delivery box. ⎯

Continued from previous page

```
<td valign="bottom">
  <table id="tab4" border="0"
          cellpadding="4" cellspacing="0"
          bgcolor="#FFCC99" bordercolor="#009900">
  <tr>
    <td colspan="2"><h3>Submit</h3></td>
  </tr><tr>
    <td><img src="../images/trans5x5.gif"
            width="5" height="5"></td>
    <td align="right">
      <input type="button" value="Order Now"
            name="orderBtn"
            onclick="submitOrder();"></td></tr>
  </table></td></tr>
</table>
</form>
</body>
</html>
```

Display the Submit box.

End of the page layout table and HTML form.

It might at first appear that, for an ordinary HTML form, The Coffee Break Deli page involves an unusual amount of JavaScript code. I would agree except that this is no ordinary form; it animates its heading; it prices and extends item selections; it modifies one drop-down list based on selections in another, and it computes total price. Each of these functions adds interactivity and interest to the page, but of course each adds code as well. There's no such thing as a free lunch—or, for that matter, a free coffee break.

For additional techniques related to The Coffee Break Deli Page, please refer to:

- Trick 10, "Hover Images," where the Polar Industries Annual Review page provides another example of form elements interacting with JavaScript code.

- Trick 14, "Interacting with Tables," where the Clothes On Line page progressively adds items to a multiline order. As the order grows, script code adds rows to an HTML table already on display.

- Trick 15, "Enhancing Your Forms," where the Mountain O' Mail, Inc., page uses enhanced form controls, validates input fields, submits data to a Web server, and gets a response.

Hover Images

Pointing and clicking is so easy and so pervasive that it's hard to imagine anything easier. There's at least one technique, however, that eliminates fully half the work of point and click: hover images react to the mere presence of the mouse pointer, no clicking required. They're as easy as pie or fried eggs (hover easy, that is).

This trick is basically a variation on two others we've already seen: responding to events and modifying a page already on display. However, in this trick we'll modify displayed pages in a way that even Netscape Navigator 3 and Microsoft Internet Explorer 3 can deal with.

When the mouse passes over a specially coded image, the image will change to a different one. When the mouse moves to a different part of the page, the original image returns. This entices users to look around the page some more, searching for more flashing images but also absorbing more of your message.

Besides increasing overall interest, hover images draw particular attention (without hypnotism or subliminal messages) to those parts of a page you most want visitors to notice. This can increase both message retention and the rate of visitor response. Applause, applause; thank you, thank you very much.

Netscape Navigator can't detect as many events as Internet Explorer, nor can it dynamically change a Web page in as many ways. I suppose by now you're tired of hearing that, but it accounts for doing the first two examples more or less the hard way—that is, by confining the hover action to replacement of one image with another of the same size. The third example will illustrate the easy, IE-specific way—modifying Cascading Style Sheet properties—for part of what it does. If we used CSS for the entire third example, though, it wouldn't work at all in Netscape Navigator.

The Helper Elf

The Web page shown in Figure 10-1 illustrates the basic idea of hover images. The page actually contains two hover images the same size, touching each other, on the same line. The left image initially displays an elf bitmap; the right image is initially a transparent one.

When a user moves the mouse over the left area, a script replaces the elf image on the left with a transparent image, and the transparent image on the right with an elf image. When the user moves the mouse off the left area, a script restores the page to its original appearance. In effect, whenever the user tries to move the mouse over the elf, the elf jumps out of the way. Diabolical.

FIGURE 10-1. *The elf image appears to jump right or left to avoid the mouse.*

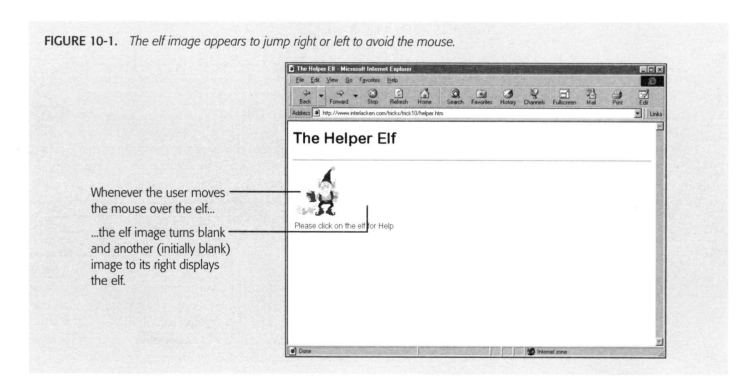

Whenever the user moves the mouse over the elf...

...the elf image turns blank and another (initially blank) image to its right displays the elf.

Scripting Techniques

The two hover images are quite ordinary; the HTML code that displays them looks like this:

```
<img name="elf" src="../images/elflist.gif"
    alt="Helper Elf" border="0"
    width="96" height="104">
<img name="elf2" src="../images/elftrans.gif"
    alt="Helper Elf" border="0"
    width="96" height="104">
```

The NAME attribute gives each image tag a name we can refer to in scripts. The SRC attribute specifies the initial image each tag will display. For each image, ALT specifies a text string to display if images are turned off in the user's browser; the BORDER setting suppresses any visible borders; and the WIDTH and HEIGHT gizmos state the image's size.

Somewhere, we need to put *onMouseOver* and *onMouseOut* tags that will trigger scripts when the user moves the mouse on and off the first image. There are two possibilities:

- Within the <IMG> tag for the first image.

- Within the <A> tag of an <A>...</A> (anchor) pair that encloses the first image.

The first option works for Internet Explorer only, while the second works for both IE and Netscape Navigator. Call me obsessively multiplatformed, if you must, but I choose the second option. So now we have:

```
<a href="javascript:nothing();"
  onmouseover="flip('elf','elftrans.src');
                flip('elf2','elflist.src');"
  onmouseout= "flip('elf','elflist.src');
                flip('elf2','elftrans.src');">
<img name="elf" src="../images/elflist.gif"
    alt="Helper Elf" border="0"
    width="96" height="104"></a>
<img name="elf2" src="../images/elftrans.gif"
    alt="Helper Elf" border="0"
    width="96" height="104">
```

 Tip: If you don't specify the height and width for an image, the browser will obtain them from the image itself. It's usually a good idea to supply dimensions in the HTML, though. That way, the browser can continue formatting the page even if it hasn't received enough of the image file to determine its screen dimensions.

Tip: Despite this example, don't conclude that anchor tags with event attributes can't specify normal HREF values. They can.

 Tip: If the browser can display images, it sets the *document. images* property to *true*. If the browser lacks imaging capability, or if the user has turned it off, the *document. images* property is *false*.

 Tip: Always use the *eval()* function when copying bitmaps from memory to image tags. Otherwise, the browser tries copying the text string into the image tag, with unfortunate results.

All anchor tags need an HREF attribute. For this simple page we don't need the HREF attribute to *do* anything, so we give it a JavaScript function to run, a function that does nothing. To wit:

```
function nothing(){
}
```

The *onMouseOver* and *onMouseOut* events each execute two JavaScript statements, one for the <IMG> tag named *elf* and one for the <IMG> tag named *elf2*. The *flip* routine sits up in the <BODY> section, and it looks like this:

```
function flip(imgName,imgVar) {
  if (document.images)
    document[imgName].src = eval(imgVar);
  return true;
}
```

With this function definition, executing *flip ('elf,' elftrans.src')* is tantamount to executing:

```
document['elf'].src = eval('elftrans.src');
```

For the <IMG> tag named *elf*, this statement modifies the SRC attribute so it contains the value in *elftrans.src*. Once again, solving the mystery has only revealed another: "What could *elftrans.src* possibly be?" Enquiring minds want to know. Well, the following lines of code define it:

```
var elflist = new Image();
elflist.src = "../images/elflist.gif";
```

The first statement creates an image object named *elflist*, and the second gives the value *"../images/elflist.gif"* to its *src* property. Together, these two statements load an image into memory without displaying it on the Web page.

Because we're going to load and reload images as the user moves the mouse around—and without requiring any clicks—we want the images to be available very quickly. If we wait until the images are needed before getting them from the server, the user could easily trigger the *onMouseOut* event long before the *onMouseOver* function can complete its job. The whole effect (and all our work) could be tragically lost. The entire drill, then, consists of this:

1. In the <HEAD> section, preload all hover images into memory with *var <object> = new Image()* and *<object>.src=* statements for each one.

2. Also in the <HEAD> section, define one or more script functions that copy the preloaded images from memory to the Web page. Design these functions to minimize the amount of code needed in step 5 (we'll see that technique in just a moment).

3. Add an <IMG> tag with a NAME= attribute in the <BODY> section.

4. If you want the effect to work in Netscape Navigator, enclose the <IMG> tag between <A>...</A> anchor tags.

5. Code *onMouseOver* and *onMouseOut* attributes within the <A> tag added in step 4 or, if Netscape Navigator operation isn't a concern, within the <IMG> tag coded in step 3. The code in these attributes will execute the script(s) defined in step 2.

Complete HTML Listing

Got it? Let's see. Try to identify each of the five steps just listed in the following HTML listing. And please, enjoy.

```
<html>
<head>
<script LANGUAGE="JavaScript">
<!--
if (document.images) {
   var elflist = new Image()  ; elflist.src = "../images/elflist.gif"
   var elftrans = new Image() ; elftrans.src = "../images/elftrans.gif"
}
function flip(imgName,imgVar) {
   if (document.images)
     document[imgName].src = eval(imgVar);
   return true;
}
```

Preload the images used in the hover effects (provided the browser supports images).

If the browser supports images, load the document object named *imgName* with the image held in memory as *imgVar*.

Continued from previous page

```
function nothing(){
}
// -->
</script>
<style>
<!--
  H1,TD { font-family: sans-serif }
-->
</style>
<title>The Helper Elf</title>
</head>
<body>
<h1>The Helper Elf</h1>
<hr>
<table border="0">
<tr>
  <td>
    <a href="javascript:nothing();"
    onmouseover="flip('elf','elftrans.src');
                 flip('elf2','elflist.src');"
    onmouseout= "flip('elf','elflist.src');
                 flip('elf2','elftrans.src');">
    <img name="elf" src="../images/elflist.gif"
         alt="Helper Elf" border="0"
         width="96" height="104"></a>
    <img name="elf2" src="../images/elftrans.gif"
         alt="Helper Elf" border="0"
         width="96" height="104"> </td>
</tr><tr>
    <td>Please click on the elf for Help</td>
</tr>
</table>
</body>
</html>
```

Define a placeholder function that does nothing.

Set all applicable text styles to sans-serif.

Start the page layout table.

Start row 1 (two images).

Define the first image area, with mouse events and a do-nothing hyperlink.

Define the second image area.

Start row 2 (caption).

End the page layout table.

Widespread browser support has made hover images a popular feature on the Web. The advantages are increased visitor interest and interactivity, but there are downsides as well. Using hover images frequently involves replacing simple text with images—and pairs of images, at that—requiring much longer download times. As always, don't overuse a good thing.

Polar Industries Annual Review

The next example combines on-the-fly image replacement, as described in the previous example, with the form interaction described in Trick 9, "Interacting with Form Elements." It displays two different sets of images depending on which radio button a user selects. For a glance at the page that performs this marvel, see Figure 10-2.

FIGURE 10-2. *Different Reward images appear depending on the Good/Bad choice. Clicking a Reward image in either set enters the correct description.*

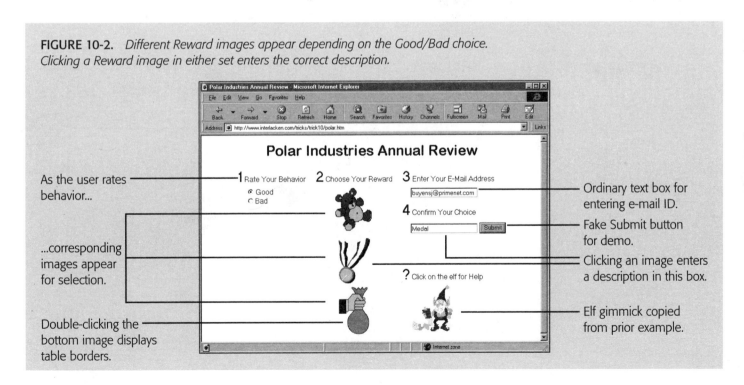

As the user rates behavior...

...corresponding images appear for selection.

Double-clicking the bottom image displays table borders.

Ordinary text box for entering e-mail ID.

Fake Submit button for demo.

Clicking an image enters a description in this box.

Elf gimmick copied from prior example.

Page Layout Details

Double-clicking the third Reward image makes the page layout tables visible, as shown in Figure 10-3. What appear to be three large columns are actually seven:

- The main content areas are columns 1 and 2 (merged), column 4, and columns 6 and 7 (merged). Not merging columns 1 and 6 in certain rows provides a left indent.

- Columns 3 and 5 provide spacing between the main content areas.

  Within each of the first five columns, the cells in rows 2, 3, and 4 are merged.

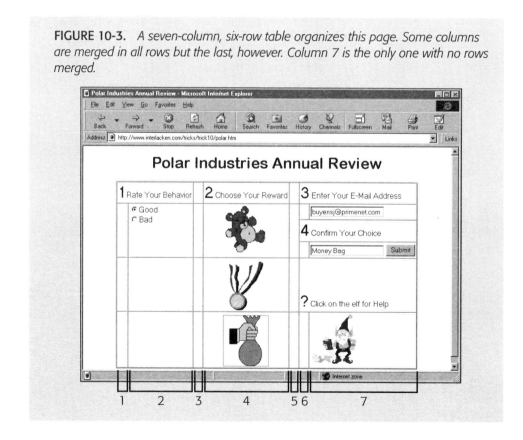

FIGURE 10-3. *A seven-column, six-row table organizes this page. Some columns are merged in all rows but the last, however. Column 7 is the only one with no rows merged.*

See Also: A detailed description of the Ahab's Anchor Asylum page appears in Trick 9, "Interacting with Form Elements."

See Also: A detailed description of The Coffee Break Deli page appears in Trick 9, "Interacting with Form Elements."

Tip: A script can change the alternate text for an image by changing its ALT property. However, this has no effect in Netscape Navigator.

See Also: To see an HTML form sending data to a process on the Web server, refer to the Mountain O' Mail, Inc., example in Trick 15, "Enhancing Your Forms."

What This Page Does

This page doesn't have any radically new ideas; it's more of a concept page that combines several known techniques in a new way. Making a Good or Bad behavior choice triggers an *onClick event*, as in Ahab's Anchor Asylum. Instead of displaying a different page, however, clicking the Good or Bad radio buttons:

- Loads three images—either a teddy bear, medal, and money bag; or a coal pile, trash can, and broom—into the Reward column. This uses the same image replacement technique as The Helper Elf page, shown earlier in this trick.

- Stores corresponding text descriptions in a three-entry table, somewhat like the price tables in The Coffee Break Deli page.

- Updates the alternate text for three Reward images, to agree with the text in the three-entry table.

Clicking any Reward image fires a script that copies the corresponding description into the Confirm Your Choice box. Step 3, Enter Your E-Mail Address, is a text box I included just for show, and to fill out the page. It doesn't actually do anything. The Submit button doesn't do anything either, except to display a message that it doesn't do anything. (Don't worry about this too much for now; you'll just get a headache.)

There was still some space left at the bottom of the page, so I included the Helper Elf gimmick. Elves are supposed to be mischievous and the elaborate but supremely unhelpful Help feature appeals to my sense of the absurd.

Complete HTML Listing

Since all the techniques on the Polar Industries page are repeated from elsewhere in the book, I won't describe them in any further detail. They should bonk you right in the face as you carefully review the complete Polar Industries HTML listing:

```
<html>
<head>
<script language="JavaScript">
<!—
```

Trick 10

Continued from previous page

Initialize array of Reward text descriptions. —

```javascript
var choices = new Array("","","");
if (document.images) {
```

Preload two elf images and six Reward images into memory (unless images are turned off in the user's browser). —

```javascript
    var elflist  = new Image() ; elflist.src  = "../images/elflist.gif"
    var elftrans = new Image() ; elftrans.src = "../images/elftrans.gif"
    var tedbear1 = new Image() ; tedbear1.src = "../images/tedbear1.gif"
    var medal1   = new Image() ; medal1.src   = "../images/medal1.gif"
    var moneybag = new Image() ; moneybag.src = "../images/moneybag.gif"
    var coal     = new Image() ; coal.src     = "../images/coal.gif"
    var broom    = new Image() ; broom.src    = "../images/broom.gif"
    var trashcan = new Image() ; trashcan.src = "../images/trashcan.gif"
}
```

Define the function to flip elf images. —

```javascript
function flip(imgName,imgVar) {
    if (document.images)
        document[imgName].src = eval(imgVar);
    return true;
}
```

Define the function to display Good images. —

```javascript
function wasGood(){
```

Display teddy bear, medal, and money bag images. —

```javascript
    if (document.images){
        document.gift1.src = eval("tedbear1.src");
        document.gift2.src = eval("medal1.src");
        document.gift3.src = eval("moneybag.src");
    }
```

Load table of text descriptions. —

```javascript
    choices[0] = "Teddy Bear";
    choices[1] = "Medal";
    choices[2] = "Money Bag";
```

Update alternative text for each Reward image. —

```javascript
    document.gift1.alt = choices[0];
    document.gift2.alt = choices[1];
    document.gift3.alt = choices[2];
```

Erase any previous entry in the Confirm Your Choice box. —

```javascript
    document.reward.choice.value = "";
    return true;
}
```

Continued from previous page

Define the function to display Bad images. ——

Display coal, trash can, and broom images. ——

```
function wasBad(){
  if (document.images) {
    document.gift1.src = eval("coal.src");
    document.gift2.src = eval("trashcan.src");
    document.gift3.src = eval("broom.src");
  }
```

Load table of text descriptions. ——

```
  choices[0] = "Coal";
  choices[1] = "Trash";
  choices[2] = "Broom";
```

Update alternative text for each Reward image. ——

```
  document.gift1.alt = choices[0];
  document.gift2.alt = choices[1];
  document.gift3.alt = choices[2];
```

Erase any previous entry in the Confirm Your Choice box. ——

```
  document.reward.choice.value = "";
  return true;
}
```

Define a function to copy entries from the table of text descriptions to the Confirm Your Choice text box. ——

```
function choice1(nr){
  document.reward.choice.value = choices[nr];
}
```

Tell the user he or she missed the elf. ——

```
function errMsg(){
  alert("No, No, No! Click on the elf, not on the blank space!");
}
// -->
</script>
```

Set all text styles to generic sans-serif. ——

```
<style>
<!--
  H1,TD { font-family: sans-serif }
-->
</style>
<title>Polar Industries Annual Review</title>
</head>
<body>
<h1 align="center">Polar Industries Annual Review</h1>
```

Trick 10

Hover Images **251**

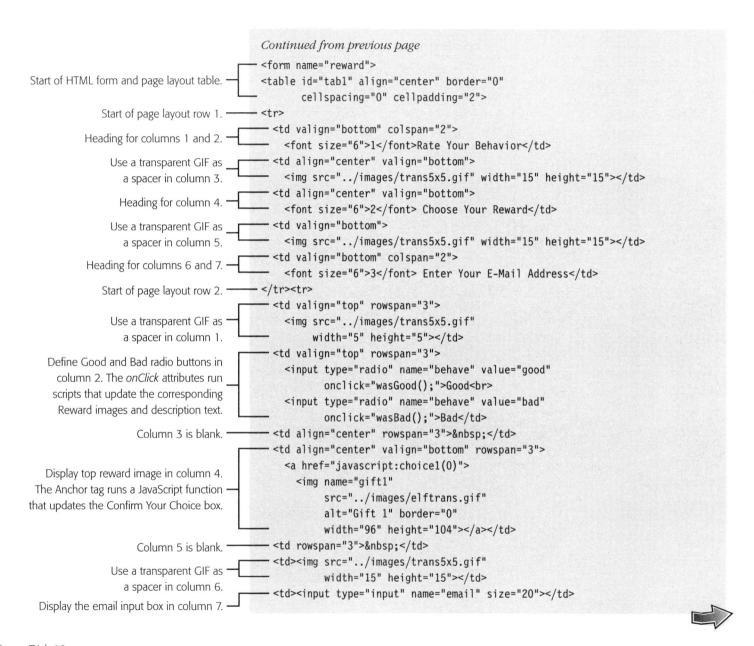

Continued from previous page

Annotation	Code

Start of HTML form and page layout table.	`<form name="reward">`
	`<table id="tab1" align="center" border="0"`
	`        cellspacing="0" cellpadding="2">`

Start of page layout row 1.	`<tr>`
Heading for columns 1 and 2.	`<td valign="bottom" colspan="2">` `    <font size="6">1</font>Rate Your Behavior</td>`
Use a transparent GIF as a spacer in column 3.	`<td align="center" valign="bottom">` `    <img src="../images/trans5x5.gif" width="15" height="15"></td>`
Heading for column 4.	`<td align="center" valign="bottom">` `    <font size="6">2</font> Choose Your Reward</td>`
Use a transparent GIF as a spacer in column 5.	`<td valign="bottom">` `    <img src="../images/trans5x5.gif" width="15" height="15"></td>`
Heading for columns 6 and 7.	`<td valign="bottom" colspan="2">` `    <font size="6">3</font> Enter Your E-Mail Address</td>`
Start of page layout row 2.	`</tr><tr>`

Use a transparent GIF as a spacer in column 1.	`<td valign="top" rowspan="3">`
	`    <img src="../images/trans5x5.gif"`
	`        width="5" height="5"></td>`

Define Good and Bad radio buttons in column 2. The *onClick* attributes run scripts that update the corresponding Reward images and description text.	`<td valign="top" rowspan="3">` `    <input type="radio" name="behave" value="good"` `        onclick="wasGood();">Good ` `    <input type="radio" name="behave" value="bad"` `        onclick="wasBad();">Bad</td>`
Column 3 is blank.	`<td align="center" rowspan="3"> </td>`

Display top reward image in column 4. The Anchor tag runs a JavaScript function that updates the Confirm Your Choice box.	`<td align="center" valign="bottom" rowspan="3">`
	`    <a href="javascript:choice1(0)">`
	`        <img name="gift1"`
	`            src="../images/elftrans.gif"`
	`            alt="Gift 1" border="0"`
	`            width="96" height="104"></a></td>`

Column 5 is blank.	`<td rowspan="3"> </td>`
Use a transparent GIF as a spacer in column 6.	`<td><img src="../images/trans5x5.gif"` `        width="15" height="15"></td>`
Display the email input box in column 7.	`<td><input type="input" name="email" size="20"></td>`

Continued from previous page

Start of page layout row 3.

Display the Confirm Your Choice heading in columns 6 and 7. (Columns 1 through 5 are spanned from row 2.)

```
</tr><tr>
  <td colspan="2">
    <font size="6">4</font> Confirm Your Choice</td>
```

Start of page layout row 4.

Column 6 is blank. (Columns 1 through 5 are spanned from row 2.)

Display the Confirm Your Choice text box and the Submit button in column 7. The button's *onClick* attribute displays a message.

```
</tr><tr>
  <td> </td>
  <td valign="bottom">
    <input type="text" name="choice" size="20" readonly="1">
    <input type="button" name="btnSub" value="Submit"
        onclick="alert
        ('Sorry, Submit not supported in this demo.');"></td>
```

Start of page layout row 5.

Columns 1 through 3 are blank.

```
</tr><tr>
  <td> </td>
  <td> </td>
  <td> </td>
```

Display the middle reward image in column 4. The Anchor tag runs a JavaScript function that updates the Confirm Your Choice box.

```
  <td align="center" valign="bottom">
    <a href="javascript:choice1(1)">
      <img name="gift2"
          src="../images/elftrans.gif"
          alt="Gift 2" border="0"
          width="96" height="104"></a></td>
```

Column 5 is blank.

```
  <td> </td>
```

Columns 6 and 7 contain the elf click teaser.

```
  <td valign="bottom" colspan="2">
    <font size="6">?</font> Click on the elf for Help</td>
```

Start of page layout row 6.

Columns 1 and 3 are blank.

```
</tr><tr>
  <td> </td>
  <td> </td>
  <td> </td>
```

Display the bottom reward image in column 4. The Anchor tag runs a JavaScript function that updates the Confirm Your Choice box.

```
  <td align="center" valign="bottom">
    <a href="javascript:choice1(2)">
      <img name="gift3"
          src="../images/elftrans.gif"
          alt="Gift 3" border="0"
          width="96" height="104"
```

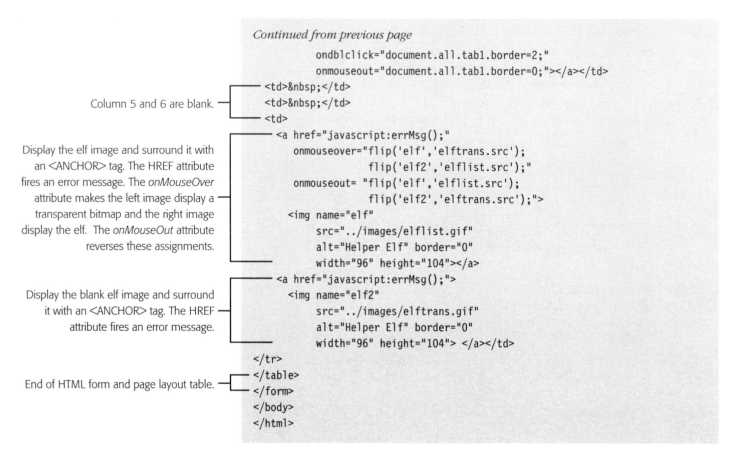

Continued from previous page

Column 5 and 6 are blank.

Display the elf image and surround it with an <ANCHOR> tag. The HREF attribute fires an error message. The *onMouseOver* attribute makes the left image display a transparent bitmap and the right image display the elf. The *onMouseOut* attribute reverses these assignments.

Display the blank elf image and surround it with an <ANCHOR> tag. The HREF attribute fires an error message.

End of HTML form and page layout table.

```
                        ondblclick="document.all.tab1.border=2;"
                        onmouseout="document.all.tab1.border=0;"></a></td>
        <td> </td>
        <td> </td>
        <td>
          <a href="javascript:errMsg();"
             onmouseover="flip('elf','elftrans.src');
                          flip('elf2','elflist.src');"
             onmouseout= "flip('elf','elflist.src');
                          flip('elf2','elftrans.src');">
          <img name="elf"
               src="../images/elflist.gif"
               alt="Helper Elf" border="0"
               width="96" height="104"></a>
          <a href="javascript:errMsg();">
          <img name="elf2"
               src="../images/elftrans.gif"
               alt="Helper Elf" border="0"
               width="96" height="104"> </a></td>
      </tr>
    </table>
  </form>
</body>
</html>
```

The Polar Industries page should start you thinking about how dynamic HTML techniques can transform your boring data entry screens into interesting, interactive experiences. (I know, I know, you text-only junkies probably condemn this as just another stupid trick.)

Fuzzy's School of Business

The previous two examples notwithstanding, the most common use of hover images is for hover buttons. The hovering aspect refers to parts of a Web page "lighting up" as the visitor passes the mouse over them. The button aspect means that clicking a lit image causes some action—usually jumping to a hyperlink.

Properly constructed hover buttons work under the 3.0 and later versions of both Netscape Navigator and Internet Explorer. Such widespread support is undoubtedly a big reason for their popularity.

To create a hover button, you basically:

1. Pick an image to be your button face.

2. Use an image editor to add the button text.

3. Save the results.

4. Modify one or more colors (usually the button text).

5. Save the image again, this time under a new name.

This provides two versions of the same button—one normal and one "activated." In your HTML code, an *onMouseOver* script displays the activated version and an *onMouseOut* script displays the normal one. This passes for high-tech genius in Web design.

What This Page Does

Figure 10-4 shows a typical (OK, way above average, in my humble opinion) Web page that uses hover buttons. These are the buttons labeled Accounting, Communicating, Planning, Reporting, and Scheduling. The five buttons are each GIF files, each with black lettering. A second version of each GIF file has red lettering. The HTML loads the version with black lettering, an *onMouseOver* event loads the version with red lettering, and an *onMouseOut* event brings back the black-lettered version. The entire five-button effect requires creating 10 images, not counting the original button face.

I'm sure this takes your breath away but wait, there's more. The area just right of the buttons—where kindly Mr. Rhinoceros is standing—also changes as the mouse passes over the five buttons. This provides additional interest and visual feedback for the user. Making it fun to see all the pictures might even encourage the user to consider all the associated options.

FIGURE 10-4. *The button captions on this page change from black to red as the mouse passes over them.*

These buttons are actually pairs of images, one with black lettering and one with red. Scripts load the proper image as the mouse passes over each button.

A different image appears here depending on which button is red.

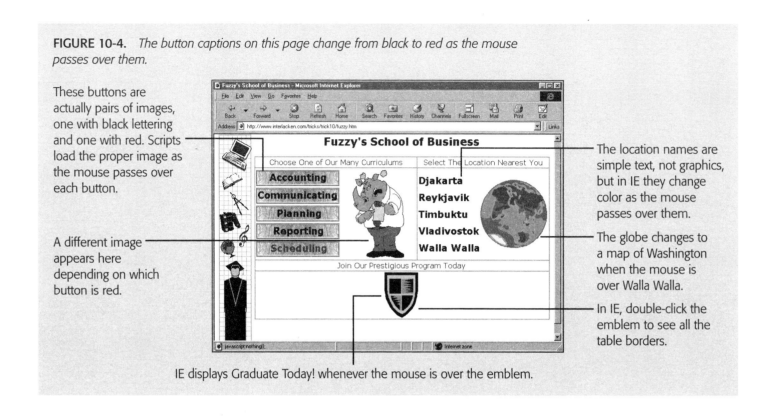

The location names are simple text, not graphics, but in IE they change color as the mouse passes over them.

The globe changes to a map of Washington when the mouse is over Walla Walla.

In IE, double-click the emblem to see all the table borders.

IE displays Graduate Today! whenever the mouse is over the emblem.

Scripting Techniques

The 10 button images and the 5 accompanying plate images make 15 images in all to preload. Anchor tags enclose each image area, so Netscape Navigator can pick up the *onMouseOver* and *onMouseOut* events for each button, 5 buttons, 10 events in all. The coding for each event looks about like this:

```
onmouseover="flipBtn('btnAcc','btnacct2','finance')"
```

The function *flipBtn* expects three arguments: the name of the image tag, the base name of the activated image, and the base name of the accompanying plate image. The code that defines the *flipBtn* function is in the <HEAD> section of the Web page, and looks like this:

```
function flipBtn(btnName, imgBtn, imgPlate) {
  if (document.images){
    document[btnName].src = eval(imgBtn + ".src");
    document.plate.src = eval(imgPlate + ".src");
  }
  return true;
}
```

In essence, invoking the *flipBtn* functions like this:

```
flipBtn('btnAcc','btnacct2','finance')"
```

and runs these two statements:

```
document["btnAcc"].src = eval("btnacct2.src");
document.plate.src = eval("finance.src");
```

I hard-coded the ".src" filename extension into the *flipBtn* routine for three reasons. First, I wanted to show that such a thing is possible. Second, I wanted to show off. Third, the lines containing the *onMouse* events are pretty heavily indented in the HTML listing, and I wanted the *flipBtn* calls to be short enough so the whole line would appear in this book as, you know, one line.

Hover Text with CSS

Well, that pretty much describes this page except for four other features. First, the five location choices work very much like the five hover buttons but require no image preparation and no image preloading at all. Instead, each choice is coded like this:

```
<h3 onmouseover="this.style.color='red';"
    onmouseout="this.style.color='black';">Djakarta</h3>
```

This is utterly shocking in its simplicity and purity of function, wouldn't you agree? Whenever the mouse passes over the area between the <H3> and </H3> tags, all enclosed text turns red. Whenever the mouse passes out of this area, the enclosed text turns black. We didn't even have to give the text area a name; we just referred to it as *this*, meaning the object defined by the current tag.

What about changing other images on the page, as we did with the hover buttons? That's just as easy and it looks like this:

```
<h3 onmouseover="this.style.color='red';
    locn.src='../images/washingt.gif'"
    onmouseout="this.style.color='black';
    locn.src='../images/earth3.gif'">Walla Walla</h3>
```

The name *locn* refers to the other image area we want to change; that image was defined:

```
<img id="locn" ...
```

and so forth. Actually I cheated a bit here; simply changing an image's SRC property requests the image from the server at the time of the *onMouseOver* event, and not in advance. This risks a time delay while the browser requests the image and waits for it to arrive. But if the time delay is small and delivery is fast, the user may not notice. And if the time delay is large, well, these images are only eye candy.

I also cheated by providing a unique location image only for Walla Walla. But this provides enough of an example to illustrate the technique.

This technique doesn't work at all in Netscape Navigator, by the way. Netscape Navigator can't detect *onMouse* events on images, and it can't change text colors once a page is on display. You can add these kinds of features for your Internet Explorer visitors, though, without degrading what Netscape Navigator visitors would see.

Paragraph Margins with CSS

The next feature pertains to the style sheet for the location choices. The default spacing between locations (<H3> tags) was too wide and left more white space than I wanted. The *margin* style sheet property is supposed to control this, but Internet Explorer and Netscape Navigator interpret this property differently. To produce the same results, IE requires top and bottom margin settings of 12, while Netscape Navigator requires the same values to be 0.

 Note: Internet Explorer interprets the *margin* CSS properties as total margins; specifying *margin-bottom: 12*, for example, results in a bottom margin of 12 pixels. Netscape Navigator, however, interprets the margin properties as increments to the default margins; specifying *margin-bottom: 12* results in the standard bottom margin plus 12 pixels.

To accommodate this difference, I coded the <H3> style selector twice: first within normal <STYLE> tags, and then within some <STYLE> tags flagged *disabled*. The results (omitting some other nearby statements) were:

```
<style>
 H3 { margin-top:12; margin-bottom:12; }
</style>
<style disabled>
 H3 { margin-top:0; margin-bottom:0; }
</style>
```

At the style sheet level, the setting *disabled* is supposed to make the browser disregard the whole sheet. Netscape Navigator doesn't understand the disabled setting, though, and discards it. So, by happy accident, a disabled style sheet applies only to Netscape Navigator, and not to IE. You can support both browsers by defining IE styles first and then, in a disabled style sheet, specifying any Netscape Navigator overrides. Scary, but it works.

Text Replacement with Dynamic HTML

The second to last feature is some hover text—a curious concept indeed. After Loading the Fuzzy's School of Business page in Internet Explorer, passing the mouse over the emblem shield at the bottom of the page will display the text "Graduate Today!" just left and just right of the emblem. This works because I defined the <IMG> tag for the emblem like this (I've omitted some unrelated attributes for clarity):

```
<img src="../images/emblem.gif"
    onmouseover="grad1.innerText='Graduate Today!';
                 grad2.innerText='Graduate Today!';"
    onmouseout= "grad1.innerText='';
                 grad2.innerText='';">
```

The names *grad1* and *grad2* refer to two spans defined just before and just after the image. In condensed form, the structure looks like this:

```
<span id="grad1"></span><img … ><span id="grad2"></span>
```

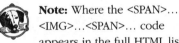

See Also: For another way of overriding IE styles when the browser is Netscape Navigator, see "JavaScript Accessible Style Sheets— Another Approach, Another Syntax," in Trick 15, "Enhancing Your Forms."

Note: Where the <SPAN>… <IMG>…<SPAN>… code appears in the full HTML listing, you'll notice that the <IMG> tag's closing angle bracket and the second <SPAN>'s opening angle bracket appear somewhat unnaturally on the same line. This was necessary to avoid displaying some white space between the two tags. The white space caused the emblem portion of the text-emblem-text arrangement to recenter itself slightly.

Initially the <SPAN> tags contain nothing, but the emblem's *onMouseOver* event inserts the string "Graduate Today!" Similarly, the emblem's *onMouseOut* event changes both <SPAN> tags back to empty. And no, Netscape Navigator can't do this, at least through version 4. Images don't respond to clicks, and the *innerText* property isn't supported. Oh well.

See Also: For more examples using the InnerHTML property, see the "AERO Message Service (IE)" page and "The Brickbat Page," both in Trick 5.

Tired of the Same Old HTML?

Internet Explorer provides four properties that can read and modify a page's HTML code *after* it's on display:

- The *innerText* property refers to everything between an element's opening and closing tags, but excludes any HTML tags.

- The *outerText* property includes everything from the start of an element's opening tag to the end of its closing tag, with all HTML removed.

Reading a tag's *innerText* and *outerText* properties will always produce the same result, because the opening and closing tags are HTML. When you replace a tag's *outerText* property, however, you obliterate the tag. For example, clicking on the display from this HTML line:

```
<h1 onclick="this.innerText='There we go.';">Here we come.</h1>
```

simply replaces the displayed text. If we changed this code from *this.innerText* to *this.outerText,* clicking the displayed text would replace not only the text, but also the <H1> and </H1> tags in their entirety. Visually, the text would lose whatever formatting the <H1> tag imparted. By contrast:

- The *innerHTML* property refers to everything between a pair of opening and closing tags, including any HTML tags.

- The *outerHTML* property includes everything from the start of an element's opening tag to the end of its closing tag, including all HTML tags.

Reading a tag's *innerHTML* and *outerHTML* properties will produce different results. Unlike the *innerHTML* property, the *outerHTML* property contains the HTML that defines the tag itself.

Viewing Borders Temporarily

OK, in case you're counting backwards, there's just one more feature to describe. There are four tables on the Fuzzy's School of Business page, only one of which has visible borders. Double-clicking the emblem image reveals the other three table borders as well. Moving the mouse off the emblem hides the same borders. This is ho-hum stuff; we're just changing border widths from 0 to 2 and back again. Been there, done that, got the T-shirt.

Complete HTML Listing

Now, on to the good stuff—the HTML listing:

```
<html>
<head>
<title>Fuzzy's School of Business</title>
<style>
```

Continued from previous page

Define the font style for all text elements. —
Define the style for H3 elements (cities). —

Override the H3 style if the browser is Netscape Navigator. (Only IE honors *disabled* property) —

Preload images for the hover buttons and plates. —

Define a function to process the hover button during *onMouseOver* and *onMouseOut* events. —

Replace image in *btnName* with bitmap from *imgBtn.src*. —

Replace plate image with bitmap from *imgPlate.src*. —

```
P,TD,H2 { font-family: Verdana, sans-serif }
H3 { font-size: 16pt; font-weight: bold;
     margin-top:12; margin-bottom:12;}
</style>
<style disabled>
  H3 { font-size: 16pt; font-weight: bold;
       margin-top:0; margin-bottom:0}
</style>
<script language="JavaScript">
<!--
if (document.images) {
    var blank196 = new Image() ; blank196.src = "../images/blank196.gif";
    var planning = new Image() ; planning.src = "../images/planning.gif";
    var bearnews = new Image() ; bearnews.src = "../images/bearnews.gif";
    var finance  = new Image() ; finance.src  = "../images/finance.gif";
    var report   = new Image() ; report.src   = "../images/report.gif";
    var schedule = new Image() ; schedule.src = "../images/schedule.gif";
    var btnacct1 = new Image() ; btnacct1.src = "../images/btnacct1.gif";
    var btnacct2 = new Image() ; btnacct2.src = "../images/btnacct2.gif";
    var btncomm1 = new Image() ; btncomm1.src = "../images/btncomm1.gif";
    var btncomm2 = new Image() ; btncomm2.src = "../images/btncomm2.gif";
    var btnplan1 = new Image() ; btnplan1.src = "../images/btnplan1.gif";
    var btnplan2 = new Image() ; btnplan2.src = "../images/btnplan2.gif";
    var btnrept1 = new Image() ; btnrept1.src = "../images/btnrept1.gif";
    var btnrept2 = new Image() ; btnrept2.src = "../images/btnrept2.gif";
    var btnschd1 = new Image() ; btnschd1.src = "../images/btnschd1.gif";
    var btnschd2 = new Image() ; btnschd2.src = "../images/btnschd2.gif";
}
function flipBtn(btnName, imgBtn, imgPlate) {
    if (document.images){
       document[btnName].src = eval(imgBtn + ".src");
       document.plate.src = eval(imgPlate + ".src");
    }
    return true;
}
```

Continued from previous page

Define do-nothing function for anchor tags with no links.

```
function nothing(){
}
function bordOn(){
```

Reveal borders for tables 1, 3, and 4.

```
   document.all.tab1.border = "2" ;
   document.all.tab3.border = "2" ;
   document.all.tab4.border = "2" ;
}
function bordOff(){
```

Hide borders for tables 1, 3, and 4.

```
   document.all.tab1.border = "0" ;
   document.all.tab3.border = "0" ;
   document.all.tab4.border = "0" ;
}
// -->
</script>
</head>
<body>
```

Define overall page layout table.

```
<table id="tab1" border="0" bordercolor="#cc0000"
       cellpadding="0" cellspacing="0" width="100%">
<tr>
```

Column 1 of page layout table contains the graph paper image.

```
 <td>
   <img src="../images/graduate.gif" alt="Graduation"
        width="75" height="459">  </td>
```

Column 2 of page layout table contains everything else.

```
 <td valign="top">
   <h2 align="center">Fuzzy's School of Business</h2>
```

Segment the main page area using a table with visible borders.

```
   <table id="tab2" border="1" bordercolor="#66CCCC"
          cellpadding="2" cellspacing="0" >
   <tr>
```

Curriculum title.

```
    <td align="center">Choose One Of Our Many Curriculums</td>
```

Location title.

```
    <td align="center">Select The Location Nearest You</td>
   </tr><tr>
    <td>
```

Define a table to organize hover buttons and plate images.

```
     <table id="tab3" border="0"  bordercolor="#cc0000"
            cellpadding="0" cellspacing="0">
```

Continued from previous page

Define anchor, events, and image tag for first hover button.

Define the image tag for plate image.

Define anchor, events, and image tag for second hover button.

Define anchor, events, and image tag for third hover button.

Define anchor, events, and image tag for fourth hover button.

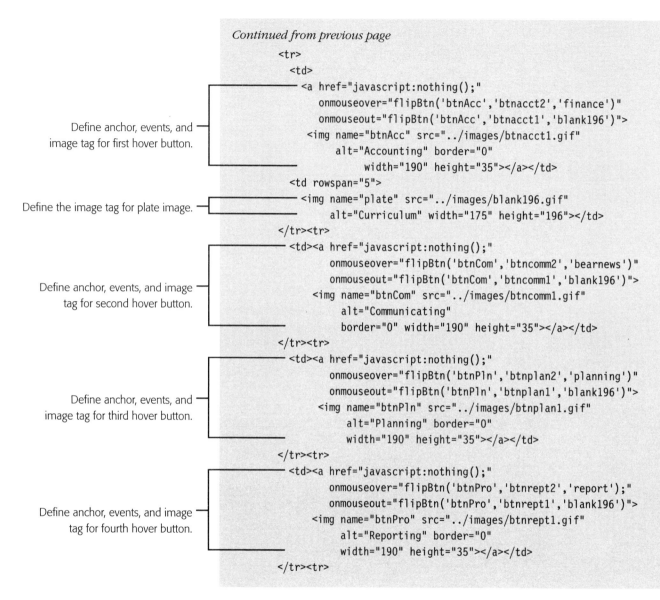

```html
<tr>
 <td>
  <a href="javascript:nothing();"
     onmouseover="flipBtn('btnAcc','btnacct2','finance')"
     onmouseout="flipBtn('btnAcc','btnacct1','blank196')">
    <img name="btnAcc" src="../images/btnacct1.gif"
         alt="Accounting" border="0"
            width="190" height="35"></a></td>
   <td rowspan="5">
    <img name="plate" src="../images/blank196.gif"
         alt="Curriculum" width="175" height="196"></td>
  </tr><tr>
    <td><a href="javascript:nothing();"
        onmouseover="flipBtn('btnCom','btncomm2','bearnews')"
        onmouseout="flipBtn('btnCom','btncomm1','blank196')">
     <img name="btnCom" src="../images/btncomm1.gif"
          alt="Communicating"
          border="0" width="190" height="35"></a></td>
   </tr><tr>
     <td><a href="javascript:nothing();"
        onmouseover="flipBtn('btnPln','btnplan2','planning')"
        onmouseout="flipBtn('btnPln','btnplan1','blank196')">
      <img name="btnPln" src="../images/btnplan1.gif"
           alt="Planning" border="0"
           width="190" height="35"></a></td>
    </tr><tr>
      <td><a href="javascript:nothing();"
        onmouseover="flipBtn('btnPro','btnrept2','report');"
        onmouseout="flipBtn('btnPro','btnrept1','blank196')">
       <img name="btnPro" src="../images/btnrept1.gif"
            alt="Reporting" border="0"
            width="190" height="35"></a></td>
     </tr><tr>
```

Continued from previous page

Define anchor, events, and image
tag for fifth hover button.

```
<td><a href="javascript:nothing();"
    onmouseover="flipBtn('btnSch','btnschd2','schedule')"
    onmouseout="flipBtn('btnSch','btnschd1','blank196')">
  <img name="btnSch" src="../images/btnschd1.gif"
      alt="Scheduling" border="0"
      width="190" height="35"></a></td>
</tr>
```

End of curriculum title.

```
</table></td>
<td valign="top" width="99%">
```

Define a table to organize
location names and images.

```
<table id="tab4" border="0" bordercolor="#CC0000"
    width="100%" cellpadding="0" cellspacing="0">
<tr>
  <td>
```

Put each city in its own H3 tag. Note
onMouse events to change location
colors and, in the case of Walla Walla,
the location image.

```
    <h3 onmouseover="this.style.color='red';"
        onmouseout="this.style.color='black';">Djakarta</h3>
    <h3 onmouseover="this.style.color='red';"
        onmouseout="this.style.color='black';">Reykjavik</h3>
    <h3 onmouseover="this.style.color='red';"
        onmouseout="this.style.color='black';">Timbuktu</h3>
    <h3 onmouseover="this.style.color='red';"
        onmouseout="this.style.color='black';">Vladivostok</h3>
    <h3 onmouseover="this.style.color='red';
        locn.src='../images/washingt.gif'"
        onmouseout="this.style.color='black';
        locn.src='../images/earth3.gif'">Walla Walla</h3>
  </td>
<td align="center" width="100%">
```

Display the location image.

```
  <img id="locn" src="../images/earth3.gif" alt="Earth"
      width="150" height="150"></td></tr>
```

End of location table.

```
</table></td>
</tr><tr>
```

Footing title.

```
<td colspan="2" align="center">
  Join Our Prestigious Program Today</td>
```

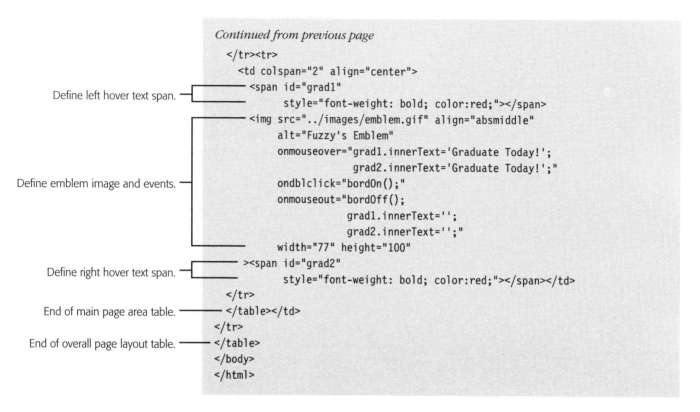

```
Continued from previous page
  </tr><tr>
    <td colspan="2" align="center">
      <span id="grad1"
            style="font-weight: bold; color:red;"></span>
      <img src="../images/emblem.gif" align="absmiddle"
           alt="Fuzzy's Emblem"
           onmouseover="grad1.innerText='Graduate Today!';
                        grad2.innerText='Graduate Today!';"
           ondblclick="bordOn();"
           onmouseout="bordOff();
                       grad1.innerText='';
                       grad2.innerText='';"
           width="77" height="100"
      ><span id="grad2"
             style="font-weight: bold; color:red;"></span></td>
  </tr>
</table></td>
</tr>
</table>
</body>
</html>
```

Define left hover text span.

Define emblem image and events.

Define right hover text span.

End of main page area table.

End of overall page layout table.

Using hover images as menu buttons is an extremely popular technique, especially if the same buttons appear on Web pages throughout your site. (Reusing images of any kind, not just hover images, makes use of the browser's local cache to reduce download time.) Don't overlook modifying CSS properties to achieve nearly the same results, though, especially as more browsers support full dynamic HTML.

Ad Rotators

Pursuing our relentless search for new arenas of Web conquest, we come upon the exciting and vitally important world of advertising. If you don't think advertising is exciting, consider that the world runs on commerce and commerce can't occur unless customers know that products exist. Additionally, putting ads on your site puts checks in your mailbox, an event most people rate highly on a 0 to 10 scale.

Most Web advertising consists of hyperlinked images, often called banner ads and usually sized 60 by 468 pixels. The advertiser supplies the image and the URL it should link to; the site operator displays the image and provides the hyperlinks in various Web pages. It's as simple as that, except that most sites sell fractions of the same space to multiple advertisers. The ad space on a given page might display five different ads, for example, chosen randomly or according to some pattern. The accepted term for the choosing part is *ad rotation*, and in this trick we'll look at four variations:

- Randomly choosing an ad with a browser script each time a user loads the page.

- Randomly choosing one ad when the page loads, and then displaying a series of different ads while the page remains on display. Again, this uses a browser-side script.

- Sequentially choosing different ads at the server, using Active Server Pages.

- Randomly choosing different ads at the server, using Perl.

The use of ad rotators isn't limited to advertising, of course; that would be boring and mundane. You can also use them to display any sort of variable content: tips, jokes, insults, or Uncle Cletus' 1963 vacation pictures from Zanzibar.

Sam's House of Worthwhile Content

Let's get one thing straight right away; this Web page is a candidate for the Worst of the Web award. It's supposed to be so bad, it's funny. Downright stupid, in fact. In the spirit of hating junk mail, junk phone calls, junk faxes, and spam (the mail, not the meat), I started with the idea of putting advertising on a page that promotes the abolition of intrusive and unwanted Web content. From there, things just got out of hand and the result appears, with regrets, in Figure 11-1.

Most of the Sam's House of Worthwhile Content page is just filler. There are three page layout tables: a 3×3 table to organize the bottom half of the page, a 1×1 table to provide the visible border around the four bullet points, and a 4×2

FIGURE 11-1. *The ad banner on this abominable Web page appears between the two pointing hands.*

A different ad appears randomly when the page loads.

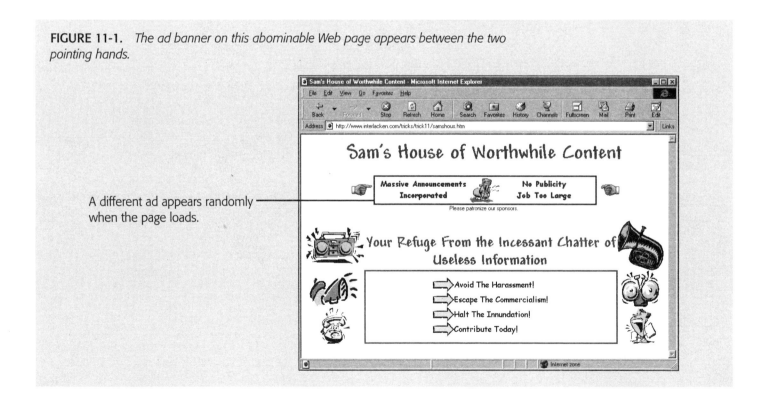

table to organize the bullet points. Double-clicking the screamer in the lower-right corner makes all these tables visible.

The topic at hand, of course, is the ad rotator that appears between the pointing hands. Repeatedly reloading the page displays three different ads at random. Table 11-1 shows the business names, image file names, and hyperlink locations for all three.

TABLE 11-1. Rotating Ads.		
Business Name	**Image**	**Hyperlink**
Massive Announcements Incorporated	massive.gif	massive.htm
Preston's Palace of Produce	prestons.gif	prestons.htm
Sloopy's Super Soup 'n Sandwich	sloopys.gif	sloopys.htm

Scripting Techniques

Note: Although the URLs in these examples are short relative ones, fully qualified URLs (beginning with *http://…*) are just as valid and, in real life, more common.

As ordinary HTML code, the ad would appear like this:

```
<a href="massive.htm">
<img src="../images/massive.gif"
     alt="Massive Announcements Incorporated"
     align=middle border=0 width=468 height=60></a>
```

To make the HREF, SRC, and ALT values changeable, we need to place them under control of a script, and the easiest way to do that is with *document.write* statements. The following code will produce the aforesaid HTML every time the page loads. The first three lines store the ad's hyperlink location, image name, and text equivalent into variables, and the remaining lines send HTML into the browser. Why store these three values into variables? We're psychic.

```
adHref = "massive.htm";
adImag = "massive.gif";
adText = "Massive Announcements Incorporated";
document.write('<a href="');
document.write(adHref);
document.write('"><img src="../images/');
```

Trick 11

Ad Rotators **269**

Tip: If you need to use a single quote mark inside a JavaScript expression, enclose the expression in double quotes. To include a double quote as part of the expression, enclose the expression in single quotes.

Note: Computer-generated random numbers aren't really random; they're produced by mathematical formulas. The same formula will always produce the same series of results unless given a different starting point, or *seed*. The most common seeds are portions of the current time of day.

Continued from previous page

```
document.write(adImag);
document.write('" alt="');
document.write(adText);
document.write('" align=middle border=0 width=468 height=60></a>');
```

OK, now we're getting close; all we need is a way to select an ad at random. JavaScript has a method called *Math.random* that returns a random number between 0 and 1. The *Math.floor* method returns the integer portion of a decimal number without rounding; *Math.floor(2.999997),* for example, returns 2. Picking a random number from 0 to 2 therefore requires this code:

```
choice = Math.floor(Math.random() * 3);
```

Why multiply by 3 to get a random number between 0 and 2? Well, the Math.random method generates a random number between 0 and 1, but never equal to those extremes. This means

```
Math.random() * 3
```

actually returns values between about 0.00000001 and 2.99999997.

```
Math.floor(Math.random() * 3 )
```

therefore returns values between 0 and 2.

Unfortunately, the *Math.random* method lives under a bit of a dark cloud. Somehow Netscape omitted it from all Navigator 2 versions except UNIX, and the seeding procedure isn't well defined. The seconds portion of the current time of day is relatively random and relatively easy to obtain, though, so that's what we'll use. The following code first creates a Date object named *curDate,* initialized (by default) to the current date and time. Then, it obtains the current second from that object, storing it in a variable named *curSec.* Finally, it divides the current second by the number of ads we're rotating and saves the remainder in a variable named *banner:*

```
curDate = new Date();
curSec = curDate.getSeconds();
banner = curSec % 3;
```

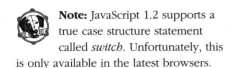

Note: JavaScript 1.2 supports a true case structure statement called *switch*. Unfortunately, this is only available in the latest browsers.

The *banner* value will be 0, 1, or 2: perfect for choosing one of three ads. We could test *banner* with a series of *if-else* statements, but this becomes awkward for more than a few choices. Instead, we use a rather unusual case structure:

```
while (true){
  if (banner == 0){
    <statements>
    break;
  }
  if (banner == 1){
    <statements>
    break;
  }
  <statements>
  break;
}
```

Caution: Always make sure that every image in the same rotation is the same size. The most common size on the Web is 468 pixels wide by 60 pixels high.

The *while (true)* loop is endless unless terminated by a *break* statement. The processing for each possibility—*banner* equaling 0, 1, and other—therefore terminates in a *break* statement. To rotate among more ads, we'd divide *curSec* by the new number of ads and add more *if* statements to test for the additional remainder values in *banner*.

Complete HTML Listing

OK, ready? Here's the full HTML listing:

Play annoying music while the page is on display. ——

Define style rules for type H1 (page heading), type H3 (subheading), and class item (bullet points).

```
<html>
<head>
<title>Sam's House of Worthwhile Content</title>
<bgsound src="../images/mcitest.mid" loop="-1">
<style>
<!--
H1 { font-family: Mead Bold, sans-serif;
     font-size: 32pt; color: rgb(102,51,153); }
```

Continued from previous page

```
H3 { font-family: Mead Bold, sans-serif;
    font-size: 24pt; color: rgb(102,51,153);
    margin:0; }
.item { font-family: Comic Sans MS, sans-serif; }
-->
</style>
<script language="JavaScript">
<!--
function bordOn(){
  document.all.tab1.border = "2" ;
  document.all.tab3.border = "2" ;
}
function bordOff(){
  document.all.tab1.border = "0" ;
  document.all.tab3.border = "0" ;
}
// -->
</script>
</head>
<body>
<h1 align="center">Sam's House of Worthwhile Content</h1>
<p align="center"
    style="font-family: sans-serif; font-size: 8pt">
  <img src="../images/finger1f.gif" alt="Finger"
      align="middle" width="49" height="23">
<script language="JavaScript">
<!--
curDate = new Date();
curSec = curDate.getSeconds();
banner = curSec % 3;
```

Define functions to reveal and hide table borders.

Display the page heading.

Center the ad banner, set paragraph font style for the ad banner caption, and display the first pointing hand.

Start of the ad banner script.

Get the seconds value of the current time, divide by the number of ads, save the remainder (in variable *banner*) as the chosen banner number.

Continued from previous page

Assign ad banner values based on the chosen banner number.

```
while (true) {
  if (banner == 0) {
    adHref = "massive.htm";
    adImag = "massive.gif";
    adText = "Massive Announcements Incorporated";
    break;
  }
  if (banner == 1) {
    adHref = "prestons.htm";
    adImag = "prestons.gif";
    adText = "Preston's Palace of Produce";
    break;
  }
  adHref = "sloopys.htm";
  adImag = "sloopys.gif";
  adText = "Sloopy's Super Soup 'n Sandwich";
  break;
}
```

Emit HTML for ad banner image and hyperlink.

```
document.write('<a href="');
document.write(adHref);
document.write('"><img src="../images/');
document.write(adImag);
document.write('" alt="');
document.write(adText);
document.write('" align=middle border=0 width=468 height=60></a>');
// -->
```

End of the ad banner script.

```
</script>
```

Display the second pointing hand and ad banner caption.

```
<img src="../images/fingerrt.gif" alt="Finger"
     align="middle" width="44" height="23"><br>
Please patronize our sponsors.</p>
```

Start the main layout table.

```
<table id="tab1" width="100%" cellpadding="0" cellspacing="0"
        bordercolor="#FF0000" border="0">
<tr>
```

Trick 11

Continued from previous page

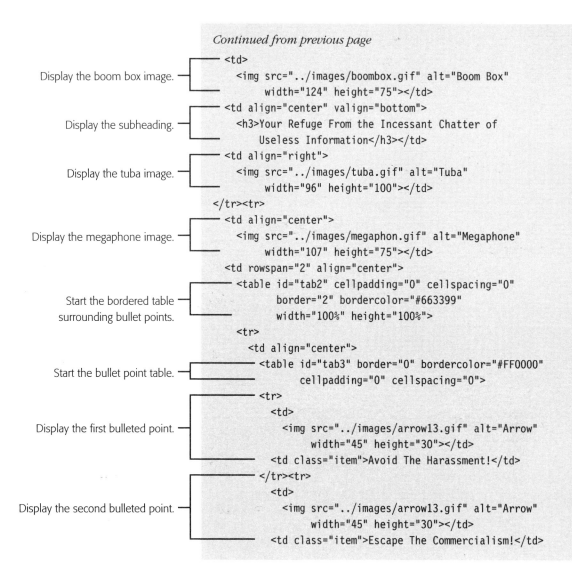

Display the boom box image.

```
<td>
    <img src="../images/boombox.gif" alt="Boom Box"
        width="124" height="75"></td>
```

Display the subheading.

```
<td align="center" valign="bottom">
    <h3>Your Refuge From the Incessant Chatter of
        Useless Information</h3></td>
```

Display the tuba image.

```
<td align="right">
    <img src="../images/tuba.gif" alt="Tuba"
        width="96" height="100"></td>
</tr><tr>
```

Display the megaphone image.

```
<td align="center">
    <img src="../images/megaphon.gif" alt="Megaphone"
        width="107" height="75"></td>
<td rowspan="2" align="center">
```

Start the bordered table surrounding bullet points.

```
<table id="tab2" cellpadding="0" cellspacing="0"
        border="2" bordercolor="#663399"
        width="100%" height="100%">
<tr>
    <td align="center">
```

Start the bullet point table.

```
<table id="tab3" border="0" bordercolor="#FF0000"
        cellpadding="0" cellspacing="0">
```

Display the first bulleted point.

```
<tr>
    <td>
        <img src="../images/arrow13.gif" alt="Arrow"
            width="45" height="30"></td>
    <td class="item">Avoid The Harassment!</td>
```

Display the second bulleted point.

```
</tr><tr>
    <td>
        <img src="../images/arrow13.gif" alt="Arrow"
            width="45" height="30"></td>
    <td class="item">Escape The Commercialism!</td>
```

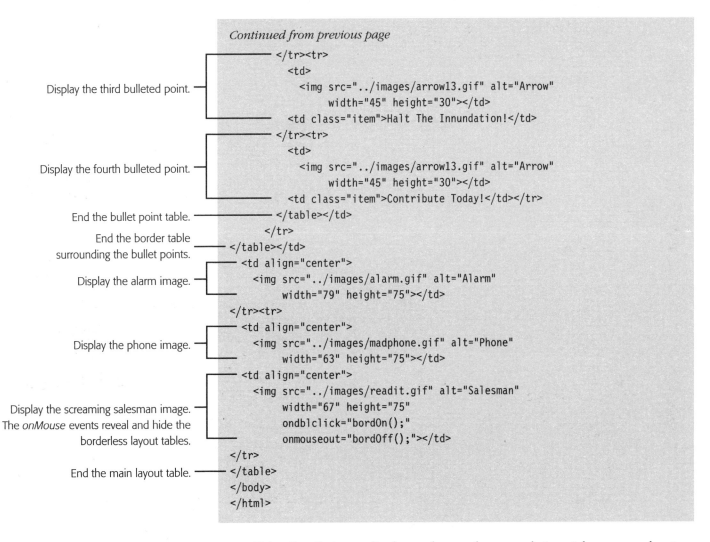

Continued from previous page

Display the third bulleted point.
```
            </tr><tr>
              <td>
                <img src="../images/arrow13.gif" alt="Arrow"
                     width="45" height="30"></td>
              <td class="item">Halt The Innundation!</td>
```

Display the fourth bulleted point.
```
            </tr><tr>
              <td>
                <img src="../images/arrow13.gif" alt="Arrow"
                     width="45" height="30"></td>
              <td class="item">Contribute Today!</td></tr>
```

End the bullet point table.
```
          </table></td>
```

End the border table surrounding the bullet points.
```
        </tr>
      </table></td>
```

Display the alarm image.
```
      <td align="center">
        <img src="../images/alarm.gif" alt="Alarm"
             width="79" height="75"></td>
```

```
    </tr><tr>
```

Display the phone image.
```
      <td align="center">
        <img src="../images/madphone.gif" alt="Phone"
             width="63" height="75"></td>
```

Display the screaming salesman image. The *onMouse* events reveal and hide the borderless layout tables.
```
      <td align="center">
        <img src="../images/readit.gif" alt="Salesman"
             width="67" height="75"
             ondblclick="bordOn();"
             onmouseout="bordOff();"></td>
```

End the main layout table.
```
    </tr>
  </table>
  </body>
</html>
```

Using JavaScript to display and rotate banner ads is quick, easy, and potentially profitable. Furthermore, it's universal: nothing special is required on the browser, nothing special on the server.

Unfortunately, the quick and easy code shown in this example becomes error-prone and unmanageable if you need to rotate a lot of ads. The remaining examples in this Trick provide solutions to this problem along with other enhancements.

Automatic Advertising Incorporated

The Sam's House of Worthwhile Content page displayed different ads each time the page loaded, but the first ad continued to appear until the user refreshed the page. In this example, the ad will change every five seconds. The script that changes the ad is the real story here, not the Web page itself, but the page nevertheless appears in Figure 11-2. Enjoy.

FIGURE 11-2. *The advertising image and associated hyperlink change every five seconds.*

Not only do different ads appear when this page loads, but they keep changing every five seconds.

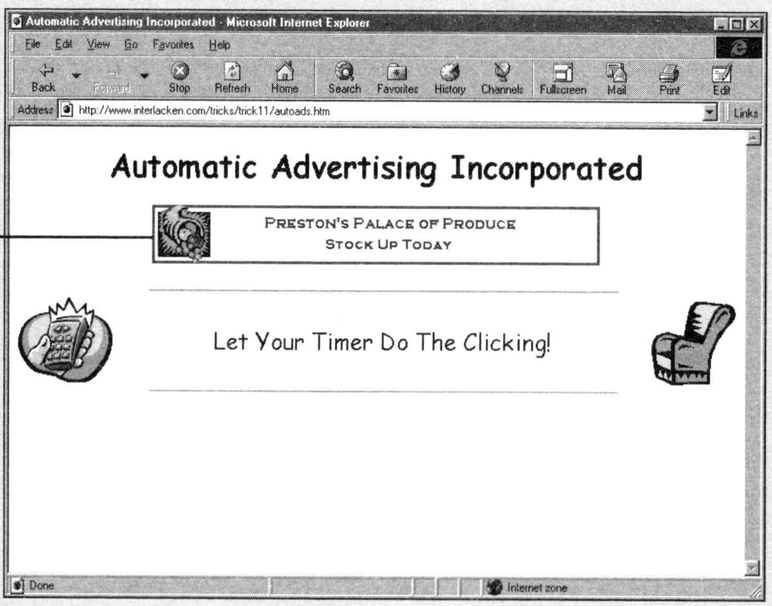

Scripting Techniques

The following HTML code defines the ad image and a hyperlink to surround it. The <IMG> tag's NAME= attribute assigns the name *adDsp*, and the <A> tag's HREF= property runs the JavaScript function *adJumper()*. Note that the initial ad is a completely transparent GIF image. We'll change this as soon as the page loads:

```
<p align="center">
  <a href="javascript:adJumper()">
  <img name="adDsp" src="../images/transad.gif"
        border="0" width="468" height="60"></a></p>
```

Up in the <HEAD> section, the following code defines a table of image locations. The name of the table is *adImg*, and it contains three entries:

```
adImg = new Array("../images/massive.gif",
                  "../images/prestons.gif",
                  "../images/sloopys.gif");
```

The following script, also defined in the <HEAD> section, changes the ad image every five seconds. An *onLoad* attribute in the <BODY> tag gets the *rotate()* function running the first time:

```
function rotate(){
  adNr = adNr + 1;
  if (adNr >= adImg.length) {
    adNr = 0;
    }
  document.adDsp.src = adImg[adNr];
  adTimer = setTimeout("rotate()",5000);
}
```

The variable *adNr* tell us which image from the *adImg* array to display. The *rotate()* function first increments *adNr* by 1, and then checks to see if *adNr* now points beyond the end of the array. If it does, the script sets *adNr* back to 0.

Either way, the script now knows which image to display, so it pulls that URL out of the *adImg* table and assigns it to the *src* property of the *adDsp* image. This tells the browser to display and retrieve the new image.

Caution: It's not customary to preload all the banner images in a rotation. For one thing, there are usually too many of them. For another, their size makes the time to preload an entire set impractical.

Caution: Image download time is an important consideration when setting ad rotation time. For modem-connected Internet users, a five-second delay (which I used to keep this example moving) is likely to replace images faster than they can appear.

Fortunately, Netscape Navigator can accept new values for the *document.<image name>.src* property and it responds by retrieving and displaying the new image. Unfortunately, it can't accept new values for the *href* or *alt* properties of an anchor tag. We can decide to bag the *alt* tag and just leave it blank. When it comes to the *href* property, though, we can't skip it and we can't change it. Woe is us.

Fortunately, the *adNr* variable is still lying about and telling us which image is on display. A script triggered by the anchor tag can use *adNr* to select a URL from a table, assign it to *window.location.href*, and make the browser jump to that location. You see, there *is* joy in Muddville and this is how it looks:

```
function adJumper(){
  clearTimeout(adTimer);
  window.location.href = adUrl[adNr];
}
```

If you look back a page or two you'll see that the *rotate()* function saves the rotation timer's identity in a variable called *adTimer*. The first statement in the *adJumper()* routine clears that timer so the value of *adNr* won't change unexpectedly. The second statement jumps to a location taken from the *adUrl* table, which we defined as follows:

```
adUrl = new Array("../trick11/massive.htm",
                  "../trick11/prestons.htm",
                  "../trick11/sloopys.htm");
```

Um, let's see, anything left to talk about? Oh yeah, how does *adNr* get initialized? The code that follows does a credible job. As in the first example, it gets the current second, divides it by the number of ads (the length of the *adImg* table, in this case), and keeps the integer remainder:

```
curDate = new Date();
curSec = curDate.getSeconds();
adNr = curSec % adImg.length;
```

Caution: If you decide to try this trick at home, kids, be sure to keep the entries in *adImg* and *adUrl* synchronized. Both tables should always have the same number of entries, and the *n*th image in *adImg* should correspond to the *n*th URL in *adUrl*. (Sorry about the lispth; that's what I get for trying to blow bubbles with gummi bears.)

Complete HTML Listing

OK, that should do it; you're fully prepared for exposure to the full, unadulterated HTML listing. Watch for the hidden prize.

Define the array of ad images.

Define the array of ad URLs.

Initialize *adNr* based on the current second.

Initialize timer ID.

Define a function to increment *adNr*, display the next ad, and set the timer for next iteration.

Define a function that jumps to a hyperlink corresponding to the current image.

```html
<html>
<head>
<title>Automatic Advertising Incorporated</title>
<script language="JavaScript">
<!--
adImg = new Array("../images/massive.gif",
                  "../images/prestons.gif",
                  "../images/sloopys.gif");
adUrl = new Array("../trick11/massive.htm",
                  "../trick11/prestons.htm",
                  "../trick11/sloopys.htm");
curDate = new Date();
curSec = curDate.getSeconds();
adNr = curSec % adImg.length;
adTimer = 0;
function rotate(){
  adNr = adNr + 1;
  if (adNr >= adImg.length) {
    adNr = 0;
    }
  document.adDsp.src = adImg[adNr];
  adTimer = setTimeout("rotate()",5000);
}
function adJumper(){
  clearTimeout(adTimer);
  window.location.href = adUrl[adNr];
}
// -->
</script>
```

Continued from previous page

Define text styles.

```
<style>
<!--
 H1, TD { font-family: Comic Sans MS, sans-serif }
 TD { font-size: 150%; }
-->
</style>
</head>
```

Initiate ad rotation when page first loads.

```
<body onload="rotate();">
```

Display the page heading.

```
<h1 align="center">Automatic Advertising Incorporated</h1>
```

Define the initial ad image, surround the image with a hyperlink, and surround the hyperlink with a centering paragraph.

```
<p align="center">
  <a href="javascript:adJumper()">
  <img name="adDsp" src="../images/transad.gif"
      border="0" width="468" height="60"></a></p>
```

Begin the page layout table.

```
<table width="100%" border="0"
        cellpadding="0" cellspacing="0">
<tr>
```

Contents of row 1 of page layout table.

```
  <td></td>
  <td align="center"><hr noshade color="#CC99CC"></td>
  <td align="right"></td>
</tr><tr>
```

Contents of row 2 of page layout table.

```
  <td>
    <img src="../images/clicker.gif" alt="Clicker"
        width="100" height="86"></td>
  <td align="center">
    Let Your Timer Do The Clicking!</td>
  <td align="right">
    <img src="../images/recliner.gif" alt="Recliner"
        width="88" height="86"></td>
</tr><tr>
```

Contents of row 3 of page layout table.

```
  <td><!-- Please buy yourself a nice dinner from me. --></td>
  <td align="center"><hr noshade color="#CC99CC"></td>
  <td align="right"></td>
</tr>
```

End the page layout table.

```
</table>
</body>
</html>
```

This example really introduces two new techniques: (1) using a timer to change images, and (2) using tables to hold the lists of hyperlinks and images. Both are valuable, but the table idea is perhaps more so: managing any more than a few ads is much easier with tables than with *if-then* logic. Oh, and in case you didn't find the prize, it's in the seventh line of code from the bottom. Bon appetite!

The Amazing Rotating Advertising Executive

Internet Information Server, Microsoft's premier Web server, has a very slick built-in feature for managing ad rotators. If your Web server's operating system is Microsoft Windows NT Server—or could be—this is an option worth considering. Unlike the first two examples, server-based rotation doesn't transmit all your code to the browser whenever a user loads the page. This conserves bandwidth but it also—perhaps more importantly—stops anyone who understands their browser's View Source command from looking at your list of advertisers.

In terms of appearance, there's nothing unusual about The Amazing Rotating Advertising Executive page. It appears in Figure 11-3 on the following page. A table organizes everything except the ad banner, as if this would be a surprise. Double-clicking the geeky guy with the glasses and the hoops reveals the table borders.

ASP Ad Rotation—An Overview

There are three steps in supporting ad rotation using Active Server Pages. Later sections explain each step in detail, but the overall approach is this:

- **ASP Redirection Script.** Place a special, one-line ASP page in an executable location somewhere on the Web server. There can be a single copy of this file, provided by the Webmaster, or each user can have his or her own.

- **ASP Redirection File.** Create a simple text file on the server that lists the rotating ad images, associated URLs, and other related information. Stay with me here, this will all be explained in a moment.

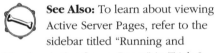

Caution: To display correctly on your browser, Active Server Pages have to be processed and delivered by a Microsoft Web server. As with Perl programs, you can't just open them as files (for instance, from the accompanying CD).

See Also: To learn about viewing Active Server Pages, refer to the sidebar titled "Running and Viewing Active Server Pages" in Trick 2.

FIGURE 11-3. *An Active Server Page component rotates the ads on this page.*

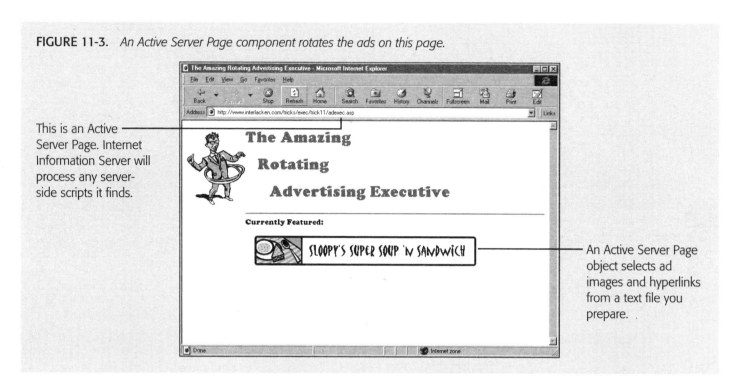

This is an Active Server Page. Internet Information Server will process any server-side scripts it finds.

An Active Server Page object selects ad images and hyperlinks from a text file you prepare.

- **Adrotator Object.** Add two lines to your Web page where you want the ad to appear. Change the Web page's filename extension to .asp and place the file in an executable directory on the Web server.

ASP Redirection Script

Here's the complete HTML listing for the one-line ASP page:

```
<% response.redirect (request.QueryString("url")) %>
```

You might remember the *response.redirect* method from The AERO Message Service page, ASP version, in Trick 8. It sends an instruction to the browser, telling it to jump to another page. In this case, it tells the browser to jump to the URL in *request.QueryString("url")*, as if you knew what that was. If you don't, please read the following sidebar titled "An Incredibly Brief Introduction to Query Strings."

An Incredibly Brief Introduction to Query Strings

A query string is a way to transmit named values from a browser to a program that runs on the Web server. A normal URL specifies the name of the server-side program, and then the query string begins with a question mark and continues with one or many *name=value* pairs, each separated by ampersands.

The following URL contains a query string:

```
http://www.yourserver.com/exec/thing.asp?user=Jim&ans=Yes
```

The identifiers *user* and *ans* are field names (usually form fields named with NAME= attributes), and in this case the corresponding values are *Jim* and *Yes*.

There are two ways of building query strings:

- The browser builds them automatically whenever it submits a form that has TYPE=GET (or no TYPE= attribute at all) in its <FORM> tag. The browser appends a *name=value* pair for each non-blank element in the form.

- You can build them yourself by appending a question mark and the *name=value* pairs to any URL that invokes a server-side program.

As in other parts of a URL, a percent sign followed by two hex digits can represent any character. This is the only way to transmit certain reserved characters such as a question mark, ampersand, plus sign, equal sign, and percent sign. To transmit a space, replace it either with %20 or a plus sign. To transmit a plus sign (other than one indicating a space) replace it with %2B. The name for this entire scheme is *URLencoding*. Encoding is automatic when the browser submits an HTML form, but it's your responsibility if you build a query string URL by hand.

An ASP page can retrieve query string values with statements such as these. *URLdecoding* is automatic:

```
value1 = request.QueryString("user")
value2 = request.QueryString("ans")
```

Perl programs and most other server-side programs generally need to retrieve query strings from an environment variable and decode them with application code. The last example in this Trick, "Counting Ad Hits in Perl," provides more information and a working example.

Caution: The *adredir.asp* file in your server, if it exists, will probably have a different path. The path */exec/* is only an example. Contact your Webmaster, system administrator, or Internet service provider to find out (1) if your Web server supports Active Server Pages, (2) if there's a central copy of the *adredir.asp* file you can use, and (3) if not, where you can put one. Both *adredir.asp* and any Web pages that use it need to be in folders that have permission to execute Active Server Pages.

 Note: If you want to collect more information about people who click on ads, you can just add additional statements to *adredir.asp*. Each time *adredir.asp* runs, for example, you could write a data record with the date, time, requesting IP address, and requested URL.

 See Also: For an example of ASP performing file I/O on the server, refer to the Vicksville Varmints Season Results example in Trick 13, "Reading Data from a File."

Stay with me; this'll get even more interesting and useful shortly. You see, the ASP ad rotator doesn't generate hyperlinks like:

```
http://www.ads.com/heads.htm
```

Instead, it generates links such as the following:

```
http://www.yours.com/exec/adredir.asp?url=http://www.ads.com/heads.htm
```

Instead of just telling the user's browser where to jump, this URL tells it to run the *adredir.asp* page so that *adredir.asp* can tell the browser where to jump. So what, you ask? Well, this must be the more interesting and more useful part. By counting hits to *adredir.asp*, we can tell how many people are clicking ad images. Phew.

ASP Redirection File

So much for the one-line ASP file; now let's talk about the text file that specifies the names of the ad images and certain other pesky details. The first four lines (the listing of the text file follows) are identified by keywords; they specify the path to the one-line redirection file and the width, height, and border width for the ad images. A line containing an asterisk comes next, and then groups of five statements as follows:

- The relative URL of an ad image (relative to the current ASP page).
- The URL that clicking the ad will follow.
- The text equivalent for the ad. (This appears as the hyperlink's *alt* attribute.)
- A relative frequency.
- A blank line.

The relative frequencies work like this: If all the ads described in the same file have the same frequency values—such as 20—they appear equally often. If, however, one of the ads has a frequency value of 10, it appears half as often as those with 20. An ad with a frequency of 40 would appear twice as often as one with a value of 20. The actual values are immaterial; we could use 1, 2, and 4 as easily as 10, 20, and 40, and achieve identical results.

Here's the complete file for this example. Its name is *adrot.txt*.

Specify the location of the one-line ASP file for redirection.
Specify the width for all ad images.
Specify the height for all ad images.
Specify the border width for all ad images.

```
redirect adredir.asp
width 468
height 60
border 0
*
```

Specify the image name, jump location, alternate text, and frequency for the first ad in the rotation.

```
../../images/massive.gif
../../trick11/massive.htm
Massive Announcements Incorporated
20
```

Specify the same attributes for the second ad in the rotation.

```
../../images/prestons.gif
../../trick11/prestons.htm
Preston's Palace of Produce
20
```

Specify the same attributes for the third ad in the rotation.

```
../../images/sloopys.gif
../../trick11/sloopys.htm
Sloopy's Super Soup 'n Sandwich
20
```

Adrotator Object

Now that we know everything about the one-line, redirection ASP file (*adredir.asp*) and about the rotation list file (*adrot.txt*), we're finally prepared to look at the two lines that actually display the ad. They are:

```
<% Set Ad = Server.CreateObject("MSWC.Adrotator")
   Response.Write(Ad.GetAdvertisement("adrot.txt")) %>
```

This code does a lot. Specifically:

- The first line creates an *Adrotator* object called *Ad*.

- The second statement tells the *Ad* object to generate ad rotation HTML based on the settings and the ad list in the *adrot.txt* file.

Caution: In this example, the Web page that displays the ads, the *adrot.txt* file, and the *adredir.asp* file all reside in the same folder. This accounts for the lack of server names and path names in the URLs. If your situation differs, so might the need for server and path names in your URLs.

- Acting on the generated HTML, the browser sends clicks on any ad to *adredir.asp* (or whatever page *adrot.txt* specified).

- The *adredir.asp* page tells the browser where to jump.

- We can tell how many people are clicking ads by counting hits to *adredir.asp*.

  That's not so bad, is it?

Complete HTML Listing

Other than the two lines just shown, the HTML for the Amazing Rotating Advertising Executive page is quite unremarkable. Here, see for yourself:

```html
<html>
<head>
<title>The Amazing Rotating Advertising Executive</title>
<style>
<!--
H1, TD { font-family: Cooper Black, sans-serif; color: #996633; }
TD {color: black; }
-->
</style>
</head>
<body>
<table id="tab1"  border="0" bordercolor="#6666FF"
       width="100%" cellpadding="0" cellspacing="0" >
<tr>
  <td rowspan="3">
    <img src="../../images/adexec.gif" alt="Ad Executive"
         width="123" height="148"
         ondblclick="document.all.tab1.border=2;"
         onmouseout="document.all.tab1.border=0;"></td>
  <td colspan="3">
    <h1>The Amazing</h1></td>
```

Define style rules for text. ⎯

Define the heading layout table. ⎯

Start heading layout row 1. ⎯

Reveal table borders when the user double-clicks the ad executive. ⎯

Hide table borders when the mouse moves off the ad executive. ⎯

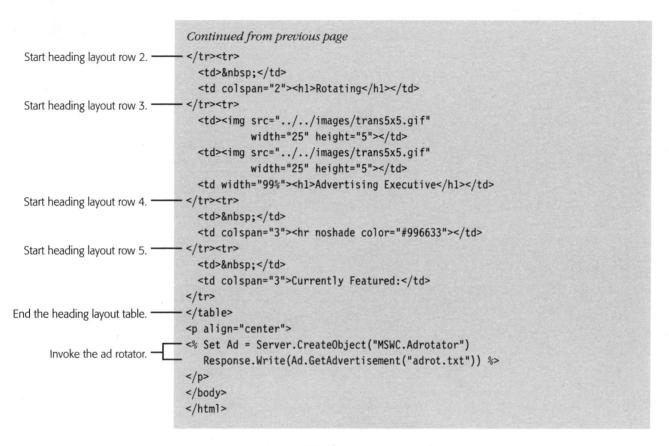

Continued from previous page

Start heading layout row 2. →
```
</tr><tr>
  <td> </td>
  <td colspan="2"><h1>Rotating</h1></td>
```

Start heading layout row 3. →
```
</tr><tr>
  <td><img src="../../images/trans5x5.gif"
        width="25" height="5"></td>
  <td><img src="../../images/trans5x5.gif"
        width="25" height="5"></td>
  <td width="99%"><h1>Advertising Executive</h1></td>
```

Start heading layout row 4. →
```
</tr><tr>
  <td> </td>
  <td colspan="3"><hr noshade color="#996633"></td>
```

Start heading layout row 5. →
```
</tr><tr>
  <td> </td>
  <td colspan="3">Currently Featured:</td>
</tr>
```

End the heading layout table. →
```
</table>
<p align="center">
```

Invoke the ad rotator. →
```
<% Set Ad = Server.CreateObject("MSWC.Adrotator")
  Response.Write(Ad.GetAdvertisement("adrot.txt")) %>
</p>
</body>
</html>
```

Using ASP's *Adrotator* object really isn't difficult: it requires only three lines of code (two of which never change) and a text file that lists the ad images and corresponding hyperlinks. Understanding it does involve a lot of new concepts, though, and running it requires a Windows NT Server running Internet Information Server.

Defining the list of ads in a text file is actually a very good policy. It means that someone who doesn't know HTML—your client, for example—can keep the list up-to-date.

See Also: The On-Track Messenger Service example in Trick 13, "Reading Data from a File," provides another example (using Perl) of ad rotation lists maintained as text files.

New Spin Promotions and Associates

If you want to control ad rotation on the server but can't use Active Server Pages, Perl provides a ready alternative. A Perl program generates the Web page shown in Figure 11-4, complete with a randomly chosen ad.

Scripting Techniques

The HTML for the ad image and its hyperlink are very simple; the trick lies in randomly choosing the ad image and accompanying URL. Here's the HTML:

```
<a href="../../trick11/massive.htm">
<img src="massive.gif" height=60 width=468 border=0></a>
```

FIGURE 11-4. *A Perl program randomly chooses the ad in this Web page.*

A Perl program that runs on the Web server creates this page.

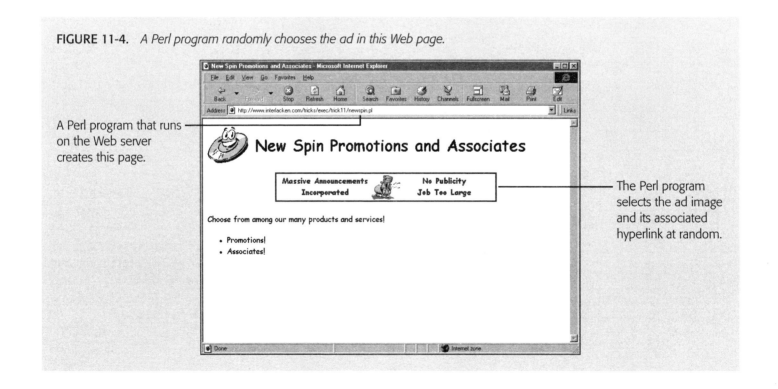

The Perl program selects the ad image and its associated hyperlink at random.

Perl has a random number function called *rand()*. Calling *rand()* without an argument produces a result between 0 and 1; calling it *with* an argument produces a result between 0 and the argument.

The list of ad images is going to be in a table named *@imgs* and defined in the following code;

```
@imgs = ("massive.gif",
         "prestons.gif",
         "sloopys.gif");
```

We could select a random subscript by coding:

```
$choice = int(rand(3));
```

Note: The *rand()* function in Perl, like most random number generators, never returns a maximum value. The result of *rand(3)*, for example, will always be less than 3.

but this complicates ongoing maintenance; every time we add or remove entries from the ad image table, we must remember to update the *rand(3)* expression as well. This is the sort of thing I, for one, tend to forget, so I prefer to code:

```
$choice = int(rand($#imgs+1));
```

The expression $#*imgs* returns the highest subscript in the array *@imgs*. In our example this is 2. Adding 1 produces the result 3, which is what we need. Adding or removing table elements will automatically modify the range of choices.

Like virtually all random number generators, the *rand()* function produces the same series of random numbers every time it starts. This means we'd always choose the same ad to display. Bummer. The *srand()* function *seeds* the *rand()* function: that is, it gives it a random starting point. This is why, in the complete program listing, you'll see these two statements together:

```
srand;
$choice = int(rand($#imgs+1));
```

As in the Amazing Rotating page, New Spin uses a table of URLs corresponding to each ad image. Here's the code that defines this table:

```
@urls = ("../../trick11/massive.htm",
         "../../trick11/prestons.htm",
         "../../trick11/sloopys.htm");
```

The expressions to select an image and a URL based on this subscript are then:

```
$imgs[$choice]
$urls[$choice]
```

Giant Strings in Perl

We'll look at the complete Perl program in a minute, but there's one more topic to discuss first. A common complaint when using Perl to generate HTML is the nuisance of making each line of HTML into a *print* statement. It's *so boring* to put a *print* statement and quote mark in front of each line of HTML, a quote mark and semicolon at the end, and backslashes in front of each quote mark that's actually in the HTML. Well, you can avoid this nuisance by using << to define a giant string that contains your HTML. In combination with the *print* statement, the << operator works like this:

```
print <<"EOP";
<html>
<head>
    <!--Your stuff goes here -->
</head>
<body>
    <!--Your stuff goes here -->
</body>
</html>
EOP
```

Perl makes one *giant string* out of everything between the line following <<*"EOP"* and the line preceding *EOP*, and then the *print* statement prints it (sends it as HTML to the remote user). This is much easier than making every line of HTML into a literal.

The characters << indicate that a giant string begins on the next line. Then:

- If you don't specify a delimiter string after the << (or put a space after <<), the first blank line ends the string.

Hint: There's nothing special about using the characters *EOP* to mark the end of a giant string in Perl. You can use any ordinary characters you want, as long as they're the same at the start and the end of the giant string.

- If you specify the delimiter within quotes, as above, any variable names (like *$choice*) are converted to their values.

- If you specify the delimiter without quotes, no variable substitution occurs.

Complete Perl Listing

OK, now we're ready. Here's the full Perl listing for the New Spin Promotions and Associates page, ad rotator and all.

Define the path prefix for images.

Define an array of ad image locations.

Define an array of ad URLs.

Seed the random number generator.

Choose a random subscript for the ad tables.

Begin copying the giant string to standard output.

Content-type header and blank line (required).

Define text styles.

Display the page heading.

```perl
$imgDir = "../../images/";
@imgs = ("massive.gif",
         "prestons.gif",
         "sloopys.gif");
@urls = ("../../trick11/massive.htm",
         "../../trick11/prestons.htm",
         "../../trick11/sloopys.htm");
srand;
$choice = int(rand($#imgs+1));
print <<"EOP";
Content-type: text/html

<html>
<head>
<title>New Spin Promotions and Associates</title>
<style>
<!--
  h1, p, li { font-family: Comic Sans MS, sans-serif }
-->
</style>
</head>
<body>
<h1><img src="../../images/cdrom.gif"
     width="86" height="75"
     alt="New Spin" align="absmiddle">
  New Spin Promotions and Associates</h1>
```

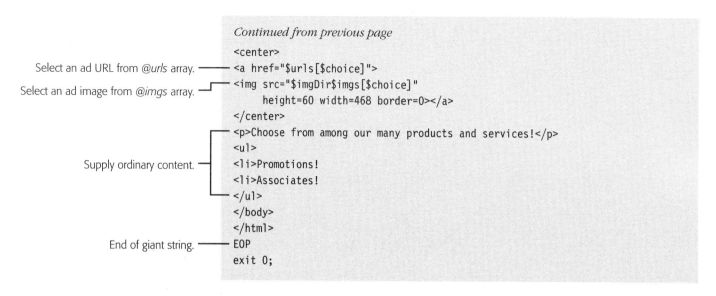

Continued from previous page

```
<center>
<a href="$urls[$choice]">
<img src="$imgDir$imgs[$choice]"
    height=60 width=468 border=0></a>
</center>
<p>Choose from among our many products and services!</p>
<ul>
<li>Promotions!
<li>Associates!
</ul>
</body>
</html>
EOP
exit 0;
```

Select an ad URL from *@urls* array.

Select an ad image from *@imgs* array.

Supply ordinary content.

End of giant string.

The last line in this program uses the *exit* command to, uh, exit the program. The value *0* following *exit* supplies a return code; by convention, *0* means normal end. This is superfluous, in a way, because falling through the bottom of a Perl program exits the program with code 0. Even so, it's good practice to use an *exit* statement so that anyone working with your code later (including you) knows that exiting is what you *meant* to do. Speaking of exiting, let's. An exciting new section awaits.

Counting Ad Hits in Perl

For certain boring and mundane processes—such as, um, billing—you might want to know how many people are clicking on your ad rotator images. Or, you might want to know how many people were happily gallivanting through your site until they fell for some cheap ad and went elsewhere. Either way, the only way to count ad clicks is to process them on your Web server. You can't collect statistics on ad clicks the user's browser handles remotely.

The Amazing Rotating Advertising Executive example discussed this problem and explained how the ad rotator built into Active Server Pages solves it. In

See Also: To review what's necessary to run a Perl script for the Web, refer to the "Running Perl Programs via CGI" sidebar in Trick 2.

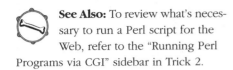

Caution: It's best to specify a fully qualified URL as the url value—that is, a URL beginning with *http://* and a site name.

See Also: For information on query strings, refer to the sidebar titled, "An Incredibly Brief Introduction to Query Strings," in The Amazing Rotating Advertising Executive example of this Trick.

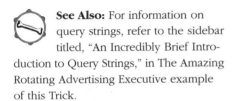

Hint: Analyzing Web server logs is the most common way to count Web hits for an entire site. Contact your Webmaster, system administrator, or Internet service provider to find out what logs and analysis tools are available on your site.

Hint: You can save yourself a lot of grief by using only lowercase letters, numbers, hyphens, and periods in site, folder, and file names.

case you forgot (or weren't paying attention), the ASP ad rotator passes all ad clicks through an ASP script on your server, and the ASP script redirects the user to the advertiser's site.

This is fine if your Web server is Microsoft Internet Information Server, but not so fine if it's not. In that case, you'll need something like the Perl script presented right here in this example. I called it *adredir.pl*.

To use *adredir.pl*, you first need to put it in an executable directory on your Web server. Suppose that directory is */scripts*. You would then change all your ad rotator hyperlinks (or at least the ones you care about) to look like this:

```
href="/scripts/adredir.pl?url=http://www.adsite.com/"
```

This runs the *adredir.pl* program, telling it to redirect the user to the URL specified in the query string: *http://www.adsite.com*. Counting hits on *adredir.pl* then counts how many people left your site by clicking on an ad.

Query Strings in Perl

The value, so to speak, of query strings lies in passing data from a Web page on the browser to a program on the server. Before starting such a program, the Web server copies the query string into an environment variable called, um, *QUERY_STRING*. Remember environment variables from DOS? Yup, these are them.

Our Perl program needs to receive a query string like:

```
url=http://www.adsite.com/
```

but that's actually a rather simple, boring case. A more comprehensive example would be:

```
url=http://www.adsite.com/&author=Jim+Buyens&score=100%25
```

The first step in decoding this string is to split out each of the three *name=value* pairs. Perl is good at this sort of thing; it has all sorts of fancy string handling functions. The following statement obtains the environment variable named *QUERY_STRING*, splits it apart based on ampersands, and stores the results in a table named *@flds*:

```
@flds = split(/&/,$ENV{"QUERY_STRING"});
```

In the case of the second (more comprehensive) preceding example, the *@flds* table would have these three entries:

```
url=http://www.adsite.com/
author=Jim+Buyens
score=100%25
```

Next, we use the *foreach* construct to run a block of statements once for each entry. It is:

```
foreach $fld (@flds) {
    ($fkey, $fval) = split(/=/,$fld);
    $fval =~ tr/+/ /;
    $fval =~ s/%([a-fA-F0-9][a-fA-F0-9])/pack("C", hex($1))/eg;
    $fkey =~ tr/+/ /;
    $fkey =~ s/%([a-fA-F0-9][a-fA-F0-9])/pack("C", hex($1))/eg;
    $in{$fkey} = $fval;
}
```

The first statement within the block splits the name and value parts of each entry into variables named *$fkey* and *$fval*. The second statement translates any plus signs in *$fval* to spaces. The third statement searches for any pattern of three characters consisting of a percent sign, one of the characters a–f, A–F, 0–9, and again one of the the characters a–f, A–F, 0–9. If found, any such combinations are converted from hex to the ASCII character equivalent. The three query string characters *%25*, for example, become hex 25, which is decimal 37, the percent sign character.

The fourth and fifth statements inside the *foreach* block perform the same two transformations on the *$fkey* value, and the last statement stores the name and value in an associative array named *$in*. When the *foreach* loop stops executing, *$in* contains:

```
url      http://www.adsite.com/
author   Jim Buyens
score    100%
```

Note: A Perl associative array is subscripted by character values rather than numeric subscripts.

See Also: For another example of redirection using the *Location:* header, review the Perl version of the AERO Message Service page in Trick 8.

Scripting Techniques

Having decoded the query string, our Perl program checks to see if it received a value for *url*. If so, it emits a *Location:* header to send the browser there. If not, it displays a simple error message page.

Complete Perl Listing

There's nothing else fancy about the *adredir.pl* program. Here it is:

Split query string *name=value* pairs into *@flds* array.

Split each *@flds* entry into separate name and value fields, decode them, and add them to *@in* associative array.

Return an error page if no *url* value is received.

Redirect to a *url* value if present.

```perl
@flds = split(/&/,$ENV{"QUERY_STRING"});
foreach $fld (@flds) {
    ($fkey, $fval) = split(/=/,$fld);
    $fval =~ tr/+/ /;
    $fval =~ s/%([a-fA-F0-9][a-fA-F0-9])/pack("C", hex($1))/eg;
    $fkey =~ tr/+/ /;
    $fkey =~ s/%([a-fA-F0-9][a-fA-F0-9])/pack("C", hex($1))/eg;
    $in{$fkey} = $fval;
}
if ($in{"url"} eq ""){
    print "Content-type: text/html\n";
    print "\n";
    print "<HTML>\n";
    print "<HEAD>\n";
    print "<TITLE>Error</TITLE>";
    print "</HEAD>\n";
    print "<BODY>\n";
    print "<H1>Error</H1>";
    print "<P>No URL supplied for redirection</P><P>";
    for $key (sort keys %in) {
        print "$key=$in{$key}<BR>\n";
    }
    print "</P></BODY>\n";
    print "</HTML>\n";
}else{
    print "Location: " .$in{"url"} . "\n\n";
}
```

Caution: Security is a major concern for server-side programs (such as Active Server pages and Perl programs) that write or append files on the Web server. Contact your Webmaster, system administrator, or Internet service provider to discuss file locations, permissions, and local requirements.

Hint: Perl uses the backslash as an escape character (that is, a character that adds special meaning to character that follows it). The expression \n, for example, means *new line character* and not a backslash followed by an *n*. The Perl expression that means one backslash character is two backslashes: \\.

Custom Logging in Perl

Inspecting your Web server logs (assuming you have access to them) will reveal how often the *adredir.pl* program runs, but it won't tell you which ad the user clicked on. To gather that information, add the following lines just after the *print "Location: "* statement:

```
if (open (LOG, ">>\\iislogs\\adredir\\adredir.log")){
    print LOG ("\"$ENV{REMOTE_HOST}\",");
    print LOG ("\"$ENV{HTTP_REFERER}\",");
    print LOG ("\"$in{url}\"\n");
}
```

The first statement tries to open the file named within the quotes. The two greater than signs aren't part of the actual file name; they indicate we're appending to the named file. The double backslashes are present because I tested this code on a Windows NT server, where backslashes separate directory names, and because backslash is a reserved character in Perl. You'll almost certainly have to modify this file name to accommodate conventions and permissions on your server.

If the *open* statement succeeds, the three *print* statements add a single data record to the open file. Each record contains three fields, enclosed in quotation marks and separated by commas:

- The host name or IP address of the remote user (which you get depends on the configuration of your Web server).

- The name of the page that invoked *adredir.pl*. This field will be blank if the user invokes *adredir.pl* from the browser's Address or Location line.

- The *url* value supplied in the query string.

What you make of such a file is totally up to you. You'll probably want to have a scheduled command copy the file to another location and delete the original once a day. Then, you could import each day's file into a program like Microsoft Access or Microsoft Excel for analysis. The world is your oyster.

This little example, by the way, isn't limited to working with Perl-based ad rotators. Assuming that you've satisfied all other requirements for running Perl programs on your server, you can easily use *adredir.pl* with pages like Sam's House of Worthwhile Content and Automatic Advertising Incorporated; just code the hyperlinks for each ad as

```
/path/adredir.pl?url=ad-site/
```

where *path* points to the location of the *adredir.pl* program (on the Web server) and *ad-site* is the ad's actual URL.

Time-Sensitive Content

To predict is to err, especially regarding the future. But I predict that most of your Web pages will never be finished; updating them with the latest and greatest content will be a constant chore. Yech.

If you have some Web pages that change routinely or on some sort of schedule, this is the trick for you. It shows how to program Web pages so they display different content depending on the current date. You can set up your pages to change on schedule for periods of days, months, or years in the future, limited only by your ability to predict what the content should be. Back to predicting; I knew that was gonna happen.

There are two examples in this Trick. Petunia's Palace of Pets is a simple page on which New and Updated icons appear for up to 14 days, and then individually and automatically disappear.

Bernie's Bargain Bazaar is a more complex page that changes its contents and appearance based on the current month, the day of the month, and the day of the week. It also introduces the concept of browser-side databases. (All this in one example is quite a bargain, wouldn't you say?)

Your time-sensitive pages will probably differ from these in all the incidentals, but the same basic techniques will apply.

Petunia's Palace of Pets

The first example of time-sensitive content appears in Figure 12-1. The little New! and Upd! icons appear for 14 days after you insert them, and then they disappear.

FIGURE 12-1. *The New! and Upd! icons in this Web page disappear 14 days after you insert them.*

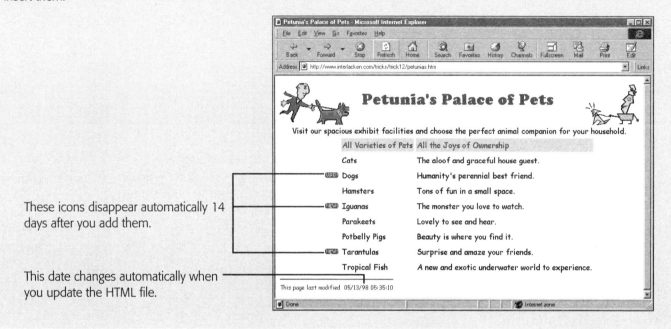

These icons disappear automatically 14 days after you add them.

This date changes automatically when you update the HTML file.

Scripting Techniques

If you look at the HTML for this page, you won't find <IMG> tags where the New! and Upd! icons appear. Instead, you'll find a block of JavaScript code such as the following:

Caution: If you copy this code directly into your Web page, be sure to insert the current date.

```
<script language="JavaScript">
<!--
dateIcon("Jun 12, 1998", "u");
// -->
</script>
```

The important part, of course, is the call to the *dateIcon()* function. The call passes two arguments, first the date you added the icon—the block of script, actually—and then *u* for an Upd! icon and anything else for a New! icon. The code for the *dateIcon()* function looks like this:

```
function dateIcon(effDate, act) {
  curDate = new Date();
  modDate = new Date(effDate);
  days = Math.round((curDate.getTime() - modDate.getTime())
                    / (24 * 60 * 60 * 1000));
  if (days < 14){
    document.write("<IMG SRC=../images/");
    if (act == "u"){
        document.write("upd.gif");
    } else {
        document.write("new.gif");
    }
    document.write(" height=11 width=28 border=0>");
  }
  return 0;
}
```

To do date arithmetic in JavaScript, you first need to create date objects for each date involved in the calculation. The statements that do this in the *dateIcon()* function are:

```
modDate = new Date(effDate);
curDate = new Date();
```

Because no date is specified in its declaration, the *curDate* object receives the value of the current date. The *modDate* object takes on the value of the *effDate* variable, which is the value assigned in the JavaScript code that invoked the *dateIcon()* function.

As it turns out, JavaScript stores dates as milliseconds since January 1, 1970. Subtracting the *modDate* object from the *curDate* object therefore tells us how many milliseconds separate the current date and the effective date we coded on the icon. If this is less than 14 days, we display the icon; otherwise, we don't.

 Note: In the full HTML listing, you'll see *curDate* defined a second time with a fixed date of June 15, 1998. This is only so you'll see the icons when you view the example with your browser. If you decide to copy the *dateIcon()* routine into your own Web pages, you'll need to remove the second definition.

To convert the difference in milliseconds to a difference in days, we divide by the number of milliseconds in a day. To get that divisor, we multiply 24 hours by 60 minutes by 60 seconds by 1000 milliseconds. Phew. Finally, we round the result. Behold.

```
days = Math.round((curDate.getTime() - modDate.getTime())
                  / (24 * 60 * 60 * 1000));
```

The *dateIcon* function writes the HTML for an icon whenever the calculation of days produces a result less than 14. Three *document.write* statements produce the tag in pieces:

```
<IMG SRC=../images/
upd.gif
height=11 width=28 border=0>
```

An *if* statement switches the middle portion between upd.gif and new.gif, depending on whether the second function argument is a *u* or not.

Note: *Document.write* statements don't automatically write carriage returns or line feeds. Thus, even if you use multiple statements to write some HTML, the browser receives it all as one continuous line. If you *want* a line break, use the *document.writeln* method or include \n inside the string you write. The *document.writeln* method works just like *document.write*, except that it adds a line break to the end of whatever it writes.

An Incredibly Brief Introduction to JavaScript Date Methods

Once something is a JavaScript date object, you can get information about the date using a variety of methods. Some of the most useful ones are:

- *getTime()* returns the number of milliseconds since midnight on January 1, 1970. (Midnight, January 1, 1970 is a common starting point for computer dates stored as 32-bit numbers. This was a decision made by the early inventors of UNIX.)

- *getYear()* returns the year portion of a date. This is a two-digit value.

- *getMonth()* returns the month as a number from 1 (January) to 12 (December).

- *getDate()* returns the day of the month. This will be an integer between 1 and 31.

- *getHours()* returns the hour, from 0 to 23.

- *get Minutes()* returns the minute, from 0 to 59.

- *getSeconds()* returns the second, from 0 to 59.

Each *get()* method has a corresponding *set()* method that modifies the object's corresponding property.

- *getDay()* returns the date's day of the week, 0-6, beginning with Sunday.

- *getTimezoneOffset()* returns the number of minutes between local time and Greenwich Mean Time (that is, the time at the Greenwich Observatory at 0 degrees longitude in England).

- *toGMTString()* returns the date in standard character format; that is: Day, DD Mon YYYY HH:MM:SS GMT (Tue, 02 Mar 1998 23:59:59 GMT).

- *toLocalString()* returns the date in character format, using conventions on the local system.

- *UTC(year, month, day, hours, minutes, seconds)* returns the number of seconds between the given date and time and midnight, January 1, 1970.

To invoke any of these methods, append a period, the method name, and the parentheses to any date object; for instance:

curDate.getDay()

Note: All modern Web servers send the *document.lastModified* property with every Web page they deliver. Browsers then remember this property for every page or file they cache, and use it to avoid downloading information that hasn't changed.

That's about all there is to say about the Petunia's Palace of Pets page. Other than the time-sensitive icons, the page consists of ordinary content we've already seen several times. OK, there's one small wrinkle: at the bottom of the page you can see the date and time someone last changed the Web page. This is the date and time you'd see if you ran a *dir* or *ls* command on the Web server. To write this date into a Web page, use this statement:

```
document.write(document.lastModified);
```

Complete HTML Listing

OK, now that's *really* all there is to say about the Petunia's Palace of Pets page. The whole shebang starts on the next page.

```html
<html>
<head>
<script language="JavaScript">
<!--
function dateIcon(effDate, act) {
    modDate = new Date(effDate);
    curDate = new Date();
    curDate = new Date("Jun 15, 1998");
    days =  Math.round((curDate.getTime() - modDate.getTime())
                        / (24 * 60 * 60 * 1000));
    if (days < 14){
        document.write("<img src=../images/");
        if (act == "u"){
            document.write("upd.gif");
        } else {
            document.write("new.gif");
        }
        document.write(" height=11 width=28 border=0>");
    }
    return 0;
}
// -->
</script>
<title>Petunia's Palace of Pets</title>
<style>
<!--
 H1 { font-family: Cooper Black, serif; color: rgb(153,51,0) }
 TD { font-family: Comic Sans MS, sans-serif }
 .hdr {color: rgb(153,51,0);}
-->
</style>
</head>
<body>
<table border="0" cellpadding="0" cellspacing="0" width="100%">
<tr>
```

Start of *dateIcon()* function.

Create date objects for effective date, current date.

Override the current date for the demo.

Calculate the difference in days between effective date and current date.

If the difference is less than 14 days, write an <IMG> tag for the New! or Upd! icon.

End of *dateIcon* function.

Define text styles.

Start of layout table for the page heading.

Continued from previous page

```
                               <td>
Display the left image. ———————    <img src="../images/mandog.gif" alt="Petunia's"
                                       width="148" height="85"></td>
                               <td align="center">
Display the heading caption. ——————   <h1>Petunia's Palace of Pets</h1></td>
                               <td align="right">
Display the right image. ————————    <img src="../images/dogwalk.gif" alt="Petunia's"
                                       width="148" height="85"></td>
                               </tr><tr>
Create a subhead that ————————   <td colspan="3" align="center">
spans all three columns.            Visit our spacious exhibit facilities and choose
                                    the perfect animal companion for your household.</td>
                               </tr>
End of layout table for the page heading. ——— </table>
Start of layout table for the pet listing. ——— <table align="center" border="0" cellpadding="2" cellspacing="4">
                               <tr>
                                 <td></td>
Row 1 contains headings. ————————  <td bgcolor="#FFCC99" class="hdr">All Varieties of Pets</td>
                                 <td bgcolor="#FFCC99" class="hdr">
                                   All the Joys of Ownership</td>
                               </tr><tr>
                                 <td></td>
Display row 2, Cats. ——————————    <td>Cats</td>
                                 <td>The aloof and graceful house guest.</td>
                               </tr><tr>
                                 <td>
                                   <script language="JavaScript">
                                   <!--
Display row 3, Dogs. Note script to specify —   dateIcon("Jun 12, 1998", "u");
effective date and icon type.                   // -->
                                   </script></td>
                                 <td>Dogs</td>
                                 <td>Humanity's perennial  best friend.</td>
```

Continued from previous page

Display row 4, Hamsters.

```
</tr><tr>
    <td></td>
    <td>Hamsters</td>
    <td>Tons of fun in a small space.</td>
```

Display row 5, Iguanas. Note script to specify effective date and icon type.

```
</tr><tr>
    <td>
      <script language="JavaScript">
      <!--
      dateIcon("Jun 12, 1998", "a");
      // -->
      </script></td>
    <td>Iguanas</td>
    <td>The monster you love to watch.</td>
```

Display row 6, Parakeets.

```
</tr><tr>
    <td></td>
    <td>Parakeets</td>
    <td>Lovely to see and hear.</td>
```

Display row 7, Potbelly Pigs.

```
</tr><tr>
    <td></td>
    <td>Potbelly Pigs</td>
    <td>Beauty is where you find it.</td>
```

Display row 8, Tarantulas. Note script to specify effective date and icon type.

```
</tr><tr>
    <td>
      <script language="JavaScript">
      <!--
      dateIcon("Jun 12, 1998", "a");
      // -->
      </script></td>
    <td>Tarantulas</td>
    <td>Surprise and amaze your friends.</td>
```

Display row 9, Tropical Fish.

```
</tr><tr>
    <td></td>
    <td>Tropical Fish</td>
    <td>A new and exotic underwater world to experience.</td>
```

End of layout table for the pet listing.

Start of layout table for
Last Modified message.

Horizontal rule in the first row will only be
as large as the text in the second row .

The second row contains caption text and
a script to display Last Modified date.

End of layout table for
Last Modified message.

```
Continued from previous page
</tr>
</table>
<table border="0" cellpadding="0" cellspacing="0">
<tr>
  <td><hr noshade color="#993300"></td>
</tr><tr>
  <td style="font-size: 75%">
    This page last modified 
    <script language="JavaScript">
    <!--
    document.write(document.lastModified);
    // -->
    </script>
  </td>
</tr>
</table>
</body>
</html>
```

This example shows two simple yet extremely common uses of date-sensitive content: showing icons or other indicators that disappear after a certain time, and displaying the date someone last updated a page. Useful as these techniques are, you may have been expecting more beef. If so, read on.

Bernie's Bargain Bazaar

The next example looks simple enough, but there's a lot going on in the background. The hypothetical client (Bernie) wanted his page to look fresh and different every day, without the muss and fuss of actually having to change it that often. Timed content provides the solution. For a great deal, check out Figure 12-2 and buy now.

FIGURE 12-2. *Either the text or the position of nearly everything on this page changes automatically over time.*

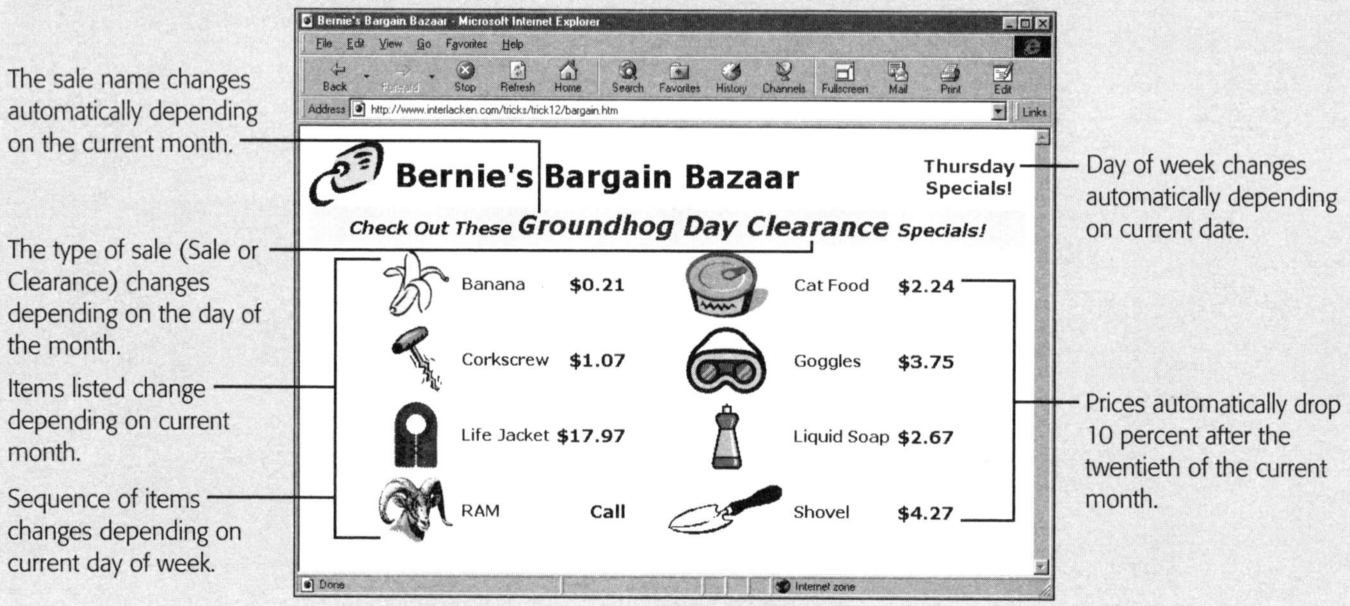

The sale name changes automatically depending on the current month.

The type of sale (Sale or Clearance) changes depending on the day of the month.

Items listed change depending on current month.

Sequence of items changes depending on current day of week.

Day of week changes automatically depending on current date.

Prices automatically drop 10 percent after the twentieth of the current month.

Bernie's Bargain Bazaar - Microsoft Internet Explorer

File Edit View Go Favorites Help

Address http://www.interlacken.com/tricks/trick12/bargain.htm

Bernie's Bargain Bazaar

Thursday Specials!

Check Out These **Groundhog Day Clearance** *Specials!*

Banana	$0.21	Cat Food	$2.24
Corkscrew	$1.07	Goggles	$3.75
Life Jacket	$17.97	Liquid Soap	$2.67
RAM	**Call**	Shovel	$4.27

What This Page Does

Here's the list of ongoing changes Bernie wanted the Bargain Bazaar's Web page to have:

- The day of the week in the upper-right corner changes automatically, depending on the current date.

- The name of the sale changes depending on the current month: New Year's for January, Groundhog Day for February, and so forth.

- The type of sale changes depending on the day of the month. From the first through the twentieth, it's just a sale. From the twenty-first onward, it's a clearance, and everything gets discounted an extra 10 percent. The heading and the listed prices reflect this automatically.

- On Sunday and Monday, the items appear in reading order (left-to-right, top-to-bottom) by image width (narrowest to widest). On Tuesday, Wednesday, and Thursday, they appear in order by description. On Friday and Saturday, they're in order by price.

- Bernie can designate that certain items appear on sale only during certain months.

Converting Dates to Words

The process of converting date subfields to words should be relatively obvious if you read the sidebar about JavaScript date methods in the previous example. The *getMonth()* method gives us the month number (1 through 12) of any date. The *getDate()* method give us the day of the month, and the *getDay()* method returns the day of the week (0 is Sunday and 6 is Saturday). The following code creates a new *Date* object named *curDate*, initialized by default to the current date, and obtains these three properties:

```
curDate = new Date();
curMo = curDate.getMonth();
curDt = curDate.getDate();
curDay = curDate.getDay();
```

The variables *curMo*, *CurDt*, and *curDay* are all numeric and therefore perfect for subscripting an array of phrases. I bet you've already got the whole script written in your head, so please check the following and see if I made any mistakes.

First, here are the phrase tables, which get defined in the <HEAD> section. The *events* table gives the name of the same for each month, and the *weekDay* table gives us the name of each weekday (minus the last three letters, which are constant).

```
events = new Array("New Year's","Groundhog",
                   "Spring","Easter",
                   "Memorial Day","Flag Day",
                   "Independence Day","Labor Day",
                   "Back To School","Fall",
                   "Thanksgiving","Holiday");
weekDay = new Array("Sun","Mon","Tues","Wednes","Thurs","Fri","Satur");
```

Tip: The most common use for the *getMonth()*, *getDate()*, and *getDay()* methods is to get subscripts for table lookups.

The following expressions, located within <SCRIPT> tags in the <BODY> section, display the sale name and the day of the week. Notice how we use *curMo* and *curDay* as subscripts.

```
document.write(events[curMo]);
document.write(weekDay[curDay] + "day");
```

A simple *if* statement is sufficient to display the word *Clearance* after the twentieth of the month and *Sale* before. The leading space separates the name of the same from the words *Clearance* or *Sale*, as in *Spring Clearance*.

```
if (curDt > 20){
  document.write(" Clearance");
}else{
  document.write(" Sale");
}
```

Is that stunning or what? Well, this sort of thing works for the page heading but it doesn't explain how to change the sequence of sale items, select different items for different months, and discount prices after the twentieth. I saved those topics for the next few sections.

Building Browser-Side Databases

Displaying the sale items in different sequences provides some unique challenges. The information about each item consists of multiple fields, and there are too many combinations to hand-code separate HTML in advance.

On a server, we'd probably sort and select the information using a database system of some kind. For this example, however, we'll assume no such facility is available; that is, we'll assume browser-side scripting is as good as it gets.

JavaScript on the browser has no true database facilities, but JavaScript tables have some very powerful features we really haven't touched upon yet. It turns out that you're not limited to tables of strings or integers or whatever; you can also have tables of *objects*. This means each table entry can have multiple *properties*, which we access by putting a period and a property name after the subscript. To wit:

```
items[5].price = 1.29;
items[7].descr = "Bean Bag";
```

Tip: You can use the techniques in this example to display almost any kind of time-variable content: time-of-day greetings, messages of the day, seasonal content, whatever.

Such a structure is perfect for Bernie's list of sale items. Each item gets one table entry, and each entry contains all properties we need to construct its HTML: description, price, image file name, image height and width. We'll add one additional field that indicates which months an item should appear; this will be a 12-character field with each character indicating whether an item is on sale for the corresponding month. If position 3 is blank, for example, the item shouldn't appear in March. Otherwise, it should.

Creating custom objects in JavaScript (and that's what we're doing here) requires a *constructor function*. For this example, the constructor function looks like this:

```
function sku(flg,prc,pic,wid,hgt,dsc){
  this.flg = flg;
  this.prc = prc;
  this.pic = pic;
  this.wid = wid;
  this.hgt = hgt
  this.dsc = dsc;
}
```

Note: In many inventory systems a *sku* is a stock keeping unit: an item.

The function name *sku* also becomes the name of the object type. That is, when some code wants to create a new object of this type, it'll create a new *sku*. The six arguments *flg*, *prc*, *pic*, *wid*, *hgt*, and *dsc* provide a way to initialize the new object's properties. No doubt, an example will make this clearer. Consider:

```
items = new Array();
items[0] = new sku("123456789abc",4.17,"goggles.gif",85,68,"Goggles");
```

This statement creates a new *sku* object as the first entry in the *items* table. It does so by running the *sku* constructor function, which puts the value "123456789abc" in *this.flg* (that is, in *items[0].flg*). Next, it'll put 4.17 in *this.prc* (that is, in *items[0].prc*). You can guess the rest. The keyword *this* means *items[0]* because we coded *items[0] = new sku(...)*.

There are 10 records (OK, objects) in Bernie's database, and I could have created the objects directly as *items[0]*, *items[1]*, and so forth. That seemed rather mundane, though, and error-prone as well. It would have been easy for me (or

Bernie) to forget a subscript or use one twice. Therefore, I wrote a function called *addItem()* that always creates *sku* objects at the end of the *items* table. Here it is:

```
function addItem(flg,prc,pic,wid,hgt,dsc){
  items[items.length] = new sku(flg,prc,pic,wid,hgt,dsc);
  }
```

Subscripts, remember, are zero-based. If the items table has 4 entries, their subscripts will be 0, 1, 2, and 3. The next entry should be subscript 4. What an amazing coincidence: the current length of the table gives us the subscript of the next entry we should create. Well, I'm impressed, anyway.

Here's the complete code to load Bernie's 10 items into an object array. Note that it calls the *addItem()* function we just discussed, and that *addItem()* uses the *sku()* constructor we discussed before that. I love it when a plan comes together.

```
items = new Array();
addItem("1 3 5 7 9 b ",2.13,"plunger1.gif",69,68,"Plunger");
addItem(" 2 4 6 8 a c",4.74,"grdntrl1.gif",124,68,"Shovel");
addItem("123456789abc",2.49,"foodcan.gif",88,68,"Cat Food");
addItem("123456789abc",4.17,"goggles.gif",85,68,"Goggles");
addItem("123456789abc",0.23,"banana1.gif",69,68,"Banana");
addItem("123456789abc",0,"ram1.gif",78,68,"RAM");
addItem("123456789abc",2.97,"soapbttl.gif",32,68,"Liquid Soap");
addItem("123456789abc",1.19,"corkscrw.gif",52,68,"Corkscrew");
addItem("  34  78  bc",13.57,"coinprs1.gif",77,68,"Purse");
6addItem("12  56  9a ",19.97,"lifevest.gif",45,68,"Life Jacket");
```

One note about the *flg* property: all that matters is blank or non-blank for each of the 12 positions. Using strings like "123456789abc" just makes it easier to find the character for month 9 than if the string were something like "xxxxxxxxxxxx".

Sorting Browser-Side Databases

JavaScript arrays have a built-in method for sorting; you just code:

```
array.sort();
```

where *array* is the name of the table, and JavaScript puts all the entries in ascending sequence. This is simple enough for, uh, simple tables but complications arise for tables of objects. Which object property should the method sort on?

To resolve such issues, the *sort()* method can accept the name of a function that examines two values and returns:

1   If the first is greater than the second
0   If the values are equal
−1   If the first is less than the second

The *sort()* method calls this function every time it needs to compare two table entries, and uses the results to correctly order the table.

Bernie wanted the table sorted on image width, description, or price, depending on the day of the week. The first task when sorting the *items* table is therefore to figure out what sequence we're using today. Here's the code to do so:

```
if (curDay < 2){
  srtFld = "wid";
}else{
  if (curDay < 5){
    srtFld = "dsc"
  }else{
    srtFld = "prc"
  }
}
```

The variable *curDay*, you may remember, came from the expression *curDate.getDay()*, where *curDate* was a date object containing today's date. If *curDay* is 0 or 1 (Sunday or Monday), we'll sort on *wid*, the image width property. If it's 2, 3, or 4, we'll sort on *dsc* (description) and otherwise on *prc* (price).

The statement that actually sorts the *items* table follows. To make sure we sort the table before displaying it, the code appears in the <HEAD> section:

```
items.sort(seqItems);
```

and the code for *seqItems()* function is:

```
function seqItems(a,b){
  if (a[srtFld] > b[srtFld]) return 1;
  if (a[srtFld] < b[srtFld]) return -1;
  if (a.dsc > b.dsc) return 1;
  if (a.dsc < b.dsc) return -1;
  return 0;
}
```

The arguments *a* and *b* are any two table entries the *sort()* method wants to compare. The variable *srtFld* will contain "wid", "dsc", or "prc". Substituting a value for *srtFld*, if *a["wid"]* is greater than *b["wid"]* (that is, if *a.wid* is greater than *b.wid*), we return 1. If *a["wid"]* is less than *b["wid"]*, we return –1.

If these comparisons fail to produce a winner (that is, if the values are equal), we compare the *dsc* properties. In essence, this provides a secondary sort field. If the two descriptions are equal as well, we tell the sort methods these two objects are well and truly equal; that's right, we return 0.

Scanning Browser-Side Databases

Reading through the entire database (all 10 records) involves nothing more than a simple *for* loop. Here it is:

```
for (pos = 0; pos < items.length; pos++){
  if (items[pos].flg.slice(curMo,curMo+1) != " "){
    displayItem(pos);
  }
}
```

The *for* statement initializes the variable *pos* to 0, continues looping as long as *pos* is less than the length of the *items* table, and increments *pos* by 1 after each iteration through the loop.

The expression *items[pos].flg* gives us the 12-character field containing an indicator for each month. The *slice* method picks off the character corresponding to the current month (stored previously in *curMo*). If the indicator isn't a space, the *displayItem()* function writes the HTML to display the item.

Tip: The *slice* method extracts part of a string using two arguments, both zero-based. The first argument indicates the first character position to extract, and the second indicates the first character position *not* to extract. Suppose, for example, a variable named *str* contains "abcdefg". The expression *str.slice(2,4)* returns "cd".

Tip: To find a table entry containing any desired value, loop through the table and compare each entry.

Displaying Items from a Database

OK, we're close to the end. All that remains is the *displayItem()* function. We'll use a 7-column HTML table to organize the items on sale:

- Columns 1, 2, and 3 will display the first item's image, description, and price, respectively.

- Column 4 will provide some white space.

- Columns 5, 6, and 7 will display the second item's image, description, and price.

- The third item will display columns 1, 2, and 3 of the next row, the fourth item columns 5, 6, and 7 of the same row, and so forth.

If this still seems confusing, perhaps a diagram and another explanation will help. In the following tag summary, each sequence of bold <TD></TD> tags represents one sale item: the three table cells contain the image, the description, and the price, respectively.

```
<TABLE>
<TR> <TD></TD><TD></TD><TD></TD> <TD></TD> <TD></TD><TD></TD><TD></TD> </TR>
<TR> <TD></TD><TD></TD><TD></TD> <TD></TD> <TD></TD><TD></TD><TD></TD> </TR>
<TR> <TD></TD><TD></TD><TD></TD> <TD></TD> <TD></TD><TD></TD><TD></TD> </TR>
<TR> <TD></TD><TD></TD><TD></TD> <TD></TD> <TD></TD><TD></TD><TD></TD> </TR>
</TABLE>
```

- The opening <TABLE> and <TR> are hard-coded in the <BODY> section: we don't have to create them with script code.

- There's nothing left to write before we write the first bold <TD></TD> sequence (that is, the first item).

- Before writing the second item's <TD></TD> sequence, we need to reserve some white space by writing the center pair of <TD> and </TD> tags. Furthermore, we need to display a transparent GIF file between those tags, to establish the width of the blank column.

- Before writing the third item's <TD></TD> sequence, we need to write a </TR><TR> tag pair to start a new row.

- Before writing the fourth item's <TD></TD> sequence, we need to write a <TD></TD> tag pair to skip the blank column.

- The pattern of the two previous bullets repeats until there are no more items to display.

- The closing </TR> and </TABLE> tags are hard-coded in the <BODY> section: we don't have to create them with script code.

The normal HTML to display an item would look like this (note the three <TD></TD> tag pairs):

```
<td align=center>
    <img src="../images/plunger1.gif"
        alt="Plunger" width=69 height=68></td>
<td>"Plunger"</td>
<td align=right class=price>$2.13</td>
```

The variable portions are the image name (plunger.gif), the alternate text (Plunger), the image width and height (69 and 68), the description (again, Plunger), and the price ($2.13).

To repeat this pattern we'll write it out using *document.write* statements, inserting variables where the changeable content should appear. For ease in coding, we won't combine variables and constants in the same statement. Here's the result:

```
document.write("<td align=center><img src='../images/");
document.write(items[pos].pic);
document.write("' alt='");
document.write(items[pos].dsc);
document.write("' width=");
document.write(items[pos].wid);
document.write(" height=");
document.write(items[pos].hgt);
document.write("></td><td>");
document.write(items[pos].dsc);
document.write("</td><td align=right class=price>");
document.write(items[prc]);
document.write("</td>");
```

Tip: Remember, to include a single-quote character in a string, enclose the string in double-quotes. To include a double-quote character in a string, enclose the string in single quotes. In *document.write* statements, however, the path of least complexity is usually to avoid HTML quote marks whenever possible.

This is close to what we need except for two pesky details. The first detail occurs in the second line from the bottom, which displays the item price. We've neglected three requirements:

- We haven't taken the extra 10 percent discount Bernie wants after the twentieth of each month.
- We haven't formatted the price with a dollar sign.
- We haven't replaced zero prices with the word *Call*. (This ruins the Ram gag. Despicable.)

To correct these omissions, replace the second line from the bottom (in the previous code) with this:

```
if (items[pos].prc == 0){
  document.write("Call");
}else{
  price = items[pos].prc;
  if (curDt > 20){
    price = price * 0.9;
  }
  document.write(fmtMoney(price));
}
```

If the item price is 0, we write the word *Call*. Otherwise, we temporarily store the price in a variable called *price,* and then test the date. If *curDt* (where we previously stored the day of the month) is greater than 20, we multiply *price* by 0.9. Finally, we use the *fmtMoney()* function (from The Coffee Break Deli page in Trick 9) to round the price to two decimal places and display it with a dollar sign and decimal point.

The very last pesky detail (in this trick, anyway) lies in arranging the *document.write* output into a cohesive HTML table. Here's what we need to do:

- Assume the regular HTML already contains the <TABLE> tag and the first <TR> tag. (This is pretty safe because we're doing the job ourselves.)
- If no other items have been displayed yet, display the new item by writing its three <TD> tags and their content.

- If one item has already been displayed, precede the second item with a <TD></TD> pair enclosing the HTML for a transparent GIF file. This guarantees white space between columns 1, 2, and 3 and columns 5, 6, and 7.

- If 2, 4, or some other even number of items have already been displayed, precede the new item with a </TR><TR> tag pair (so the new item starts a new row).

- If 3, 5, or some other odd number of items have already been displayed, precede the new item with a <TD></TD> tag pair for the white space column.

- Assume the regular HTML contains the closing </TR> and </TABLE> tags. (Believe me, it does.)

The code to implement this logic follows, and a wonderful piece of code it is. The variable *dspCnt*, by the way, counts how many items the *displayItem()* functions have already displayed. The % operator divides two numbers and returns the remainder; the expression *(dspCnt % 2)* is therefore 0 if an even number of items have already been displayed and 1 otherwise.

```
if (dspCnt > 0){
  if (dspCnt == 1){
    document.write("<td><img src='../images/trans5x5.gif'");
    document.write(" width=30 height=5></td>");
  }else{
    if ((dspCnt % 2) == 1){
      document.write("<td></td>");
    }else{
      document.write("<tr></tr>");
    }
  }
}
dspCnt = dspCnt + 1;
```

Complete HTML Listing

If you've been wondering how all this date manipulation, database building, database sorting, and HTML writing can possibly fit together, this is definitely your lucky day. Feast yourself to the full HTML listing.

Define style rules for text.

Create a Date object named *curDate* equal to the current date. Obtain the current month, current day of month, and current day of week from that object.

Define a table of monthly sale names.

Define a table of weekday names.

Intialize count of sale items displayed.

Define an empty table for the *items* database.

Add 10 records to the *items* database.

```html
<html>
<head>
<title>Bernie's Bargain Bazaar</title>
<style>
<!--
 H1 { font-family: Verdana, sans-serif; margin:0;}
 H3 { font-family: Verdana, sans-serif; font-style: italic;
      margin:0 0 7 0; }
 TD { font-family: Verdana, sans-serif; font-weight: bold; }
 .price { font-size: 110%; }
 .day   { color: #900; font-size: 110%; }
-->
</style>
<script language="JavaScript">
<!--
curDate = new Date();
curMo = curDate.getMonth();
curDt = curDate.getDate();
curDay = curDate.getDay();
events = new Array("New Year's","Groundhog Day",
                   "Spring","Easter",
                   "Memorial Day","Flag Day",
                   "Independence Day","Labor Day",
                   "Back To School","Fall",
                   "Thanksgiving","Holiday");
weekDay = new Array("Sun","Mon","Tues","Wednes","Thurs","Fri","Satur");
dspCnt = 0;
items = new Array();
addItem("1 3 5 7 9 b ",2.13,"plunger1.gif",69,68,"Plunger");
addItem(" 2 4 6 8 a c",4.74,"grdntrl1.gif",124,68,"Shovel");
addItem("123456789abc",2.49,"foodcan.gif",88,68,"Cat Food");
addItem("123456789abc",4.17,"goggles.gif",85,68,"Goggles");
addItem("123456789abc",0.23,"banana1.gif",69,68,"Banana");
addItem("123456789abc",0,"ram1.gif",78,68,"RAM");
```

Continued from previous page

```
addItem("123456789abc",2.97,"soapbttl.gif",32,68,"Liquid Soap");
addItem("123456789abc",1.19,"corkscrw.gif",52,68,"Corkscrew");
addItem("  34  78  bc",13.57,"coinprs1.gif",77,68,"Purse");
addItem("12  56  9a  ",19.97,"lifevest.gif",45,68,"Life Jacket");
```

Choose sort field based on the current day of the week.

```
if (curDay < 2){
   srtFld = "wid";
}else{
   if (curDay < 5){
     srtFld = "dsc"
   }else{
     srtFld = "prc"
   }
}
```

Sort *items* database using *seqItems* function to determine sequence.

```
items.sort(seqItems);
```

Add a new *sku* object to the end of the *items* database.

```
function addItem(flg,prc,pic,wid,hgt,dsc){
   items[items.length] = new sku(flg,prc,pic,wid,hgt,dsc);
}
```

Create a Constructor function to create new *sku* objects

```
function sku(flg,prc,pic,wid,hgt,dsc){
   this.flg = flg;
   this.prc = prc;
   this.pic = pic;
   this.wid = wid;
   this.hgt = hgt
   this.dsc = dsc;
}
```

Define function to compare two *sku* objects in *items* database.

```
function seqItems(a,b){
   if (a[srtFld] > b[srtFld]) return 1;
   if (a[srtFld] < b[srtFld]) return -1;
   if (a.dsc > b.dsc) return 1;
   if (a.dsc < b.dsc) return -1;
   return 0;
}
```

Start of function to display one item from *items* database.

If no previous items have been displayed, drop through.

```
function displayItem(pos){
   if (dspCnt > 0){
```

If one previous item has been displayed, write HTML for a table cell containing a transparent GIF file.

```
if (dspCnt == 1){
    document.write("<td><img src='../images/trans5x5.gif'");
    document.write(" width=30 height=5></td>");
}else{
```

If an odd number of items has already been displayed, write HTML for an empty table cell.

```
    if ((dspCnt % 2) == 1){
        document.write("<td></td>");
    }else{
```

If an even number of items has already been displayed, write HTML to end one row and begin another.

```
        document.write("<tr></tr>");
    }
}
```

Increment the number of items already displayed.

```
dspCnt = dspCnt + 1;
document.write("<td align=center><img src='../images/");
```

Write file name of image as HTML.

```
document.write(items[pos].pic);
document.write("' alt='");
```

Write alternate text (item description) as HTML.

```
document.write(items[pos].dsc);
document.write("' width=");
```

Write width of image as HTML.

```
document.write(items[pos].wid);
document.write(" height=");
```

Write height of image as HTML.

```
document.write(items[pos].hgt);
document.write("></td><td>");
```

Write item description as HTML.

```
document.write(items[pos].dsc);
document.write("</td><td align=right class=price>");
```

If price is zero, display "Call".

```
if (items[pos].prc == 0){
    document.write("Call");
}else{
```

Store item price in *price* variable

```
    price = items[pos].prc;
```

After the twentieth of the month, reduce *price* by 10 percent.

```
    if (curDt > 20){
        price = price * 0.9;
    }
```

Format *price* as money and write as HTML.

```
    document.write(fmtMoney(price));
}
document.write("</td>");
```

End of function to display one item from the *items* database.

```
}
```

Trick 12

Continued from previous page

Start of function to format a number as currency (dollar sign and two decimals).

Convert fractional dollar amount to whole cents.

Make value at least three digits and add leading dollar sign.

Insert a decimal point.

Return edited value as the function result.

End of function to format a number as currency.

Start of title layout.

Display name of the day of the week.

```javascript
function fmtMoney(amt){
  cents = Math.round(amt * 100);
  if (cents < 10){
    cents = "$00" + cents;
  }else{
    if (cents < 100){
      cents="$0" + cents;
    }else{
      cents="$" + cents;
    }
  }
  bucks = cents.substring(0,cents.length - 2)
        + "." + cents.substring(cents.length - 2, cents.length);
  return bucks;
}
// -->
</script>
</head>
<body>
<table border="0" cellpadding="0" cellspacing="0" width="100%">
<tr>
  <td>
    <h1><img src="../images/tag.gif"
             alt="Bernie's Bargain Bazaar"
             align="absmiddle" width="78" height="68">
    Bernie's Bargain Bazaar</h1>
  </td>
  <td class="day" align="center">
    <script language="JavaScript">
      <!--
      document.write(weekDay[curDay] + "day");
      // -->
    </script>
    <br>Specials!</td>
```

Continued from previous page

```
</tr><tr>
  <td align="center" bgcolor="#FFFF99" colspan=2>
    <h3>Check Out These
    <span style="font-size: 150%; color:#900;">
    <script language="JavaScript">
    <!--
    document.write(events[curMo]);
    if (curDt > 20){
       document.write(" Clearance");
    }else{
       document.write(" Sale");
    }
    // -->
    </script>
    </span>
    Specials!</h3>
  </td>
</tr>
</table>
<table align=center
        border="0" cellpadding="4" cellspacing="0">
<tr>
<script language="JavaScript">
<!--
for (pos = 0; pos < items.length; pos++){
  if (items[pos].flg.slice(curMo,curMo+1) != " "){
    displayItem(pos);
  }
}
// -->
</script>
</tr>
</table>
</body>
</html>
```

Display name of the current sale, based on the current month.

Display "Clearance" or "Sale" depending on the day of the month.

End of title layout.
Start of item display.

Iterate through each item in the database.

Check flag for space in position corresponding to current month.

Display database item *pos* if its flag isn't a space.

End of item display.

Technically, what I've been calling a browser-side database is really a JavaScript array of user-defined objects. What you call them isn't nearly as important as what they can do, however, and that's organizing collections of related values so you can sort, select, search, and display them with relatively simple code.

Don't overlook the true purpose of this example, though, namely to illustrate date-sensitive content. Whether your application is simple or complex, don't ignore the usefulness of coding content that changes automatically based on the calendar. It sure beats changing Web pages on schedule in the middle of the night.

Reading Data from a File

Many kinds of data are easier to maintain as text files than as Web pages. These includes price lists, departmental rosters, best sellers, hyperlink collections, bottle cap collections, almost anything! Unfortunately, text files are a lousy way to *present* data. What you need is a doohickey that reads text files and displays them as Web pages. Bingo, here you are, exactly at the right place.

Unfortunately, browser scripts aren't capable of reading files, either locally, from the user's hard disk, or remotely, from a Web server. This is probably related to security, even though the browser reads all kinds of files from the server anyway. In any event, since browser-side scripting can't do the job, both of this trick's examples are server-based—one ASP and one Perl.

Vicksville Varmints Season Results is an Active Server Page that reads data from a file, displays records dated prior to the current date in one table column, and displays records dated later in a different column. This lets you present current information based on the date. Remember, though, that the point of this example is reading data from a file, and not time-sensitive content (which we've already covered in Trick 12).

On-Track Messenger Service is a Perl program with an ad rotator much like that of the New Spin Promotions and Associates page in Trick 11. However, the data for the rotating ads comes from an ASCII file rather than tables defined within the program, and each record in that file has a start and stop date. Again, the emphasis is on reading the file, and not on ad rotation or date sensitivity.

Despite that fact that both of these examples are time-sensitive, this is hardly a requirement. You can read, filter, format, and display content based on any criteria you want. Just don't let the text files get too long. Repeatedly opening and scanning long files will eventually bog down the server and provide slow response to the remote user. Files up to a few hundred lines shouldn't be a problem, though. Reading small files and pushing data out the network port is mostly what Web servers do anyway.

One final reminder: this book isn't a complete reference guide for Active Server Pages, nor for Perl. For detailed explanations on syntax, related functions, and debugging, you'll have to consult another source, such as those cited in the Introduction.

Vicksville Varmints Season Results

As you can see in Figure 13-1, the Vicksville Varmints Season Results page shows two columns of scheduled games; those already played and those remaining. A score appears for games already played but not, of course, for games in the future.

What This Page Does

Updating this Web page after every game would be a tedious chore, and perhaps not something the team scorekeeper is comfortable doing. Updating a simple text file—the one listed below, for example—would be much easier. The columns contain the game date, location, Varmints' score, opponent's score, and opponent name:

```
04/01/98 Away 02 00 Gainless
04/09/98 Home 05 05 Whooping Gulch
04/21/98 Home 01 02 Ashville
05/05/98 Away 03 04 Whooping Gulch
05/07/98 Home 02 01 Chaos City
05/12/98 Away 07 04 River Ridge
05/14/98 Home 01 03 Juniper Junction
06/03/98 Home 04 05 River Ridge
06/21/98 Away 00 00 Chaos City
```

 See Also: To learn about viewing Active Server Pages, refer to the sidebar titled "Running and Viewing Active Server Pages" in Trick 2, "Generating Tables Dynamically."

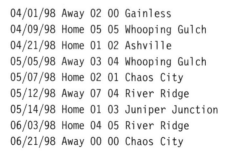 **Note:** For this entire example, assume the current date is June 15, 1998.

```
06/27/98 Away 00 00 Ashville
07/04/98 Away 00 00 Gainless
07/15/98 Home 00 00 Juniper Junction
08/03/98 Away 00 00 River Ridge
08/15/98 Away 00 00 Ashville
08/26/98 Home 00 00 Chaos City
08/31/98 Home 00 00 Gainless
09/17/98 Away 00 00 Juniper Junction
09/22/98 Home 00 00 Whooping Gulch
```

FIGURE 13-1. *Games played prior to the current date appear in the left column, and those remaining appear on the right. Games automatically move to the left column as the current date increases.*

The data on this Web page comes from a text file on the server.

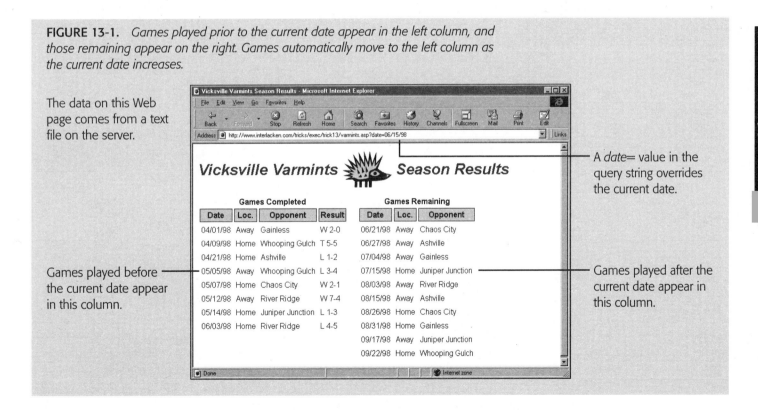

A *date=* value in the query string overrides the current date.

Games played before the current date appear in this column.

Games played after the current date appear in this column.

Opening and Reading a Text File

 See Also: The next example in this Trick shows you how to read and process server-based files using Perl.

Because JavaScript can't open such a file across the network, we'll develop a script that runs on the Web server, using Active Server Pages and Microsoft Visual Basic. ASP scripts *can* read files located on the server, and in addition, a server-based process saves bandwidth by not transmitting all its code and data to the remote user.

Reading a file from within an ASP page requires three special methods and one special property. The three methods are:

- **Server.CreateObject("Scripting.FileSystemObject")** creates an object containing methods to read and write simple text files.

- **OpenTextFile()** opens a text file for processing.

- **ReadLine** obtains data from an open text file one line at a time.

The special property is *AtEndOfStream*, a property of the file object that *OpenTextFile()* creates. When the *AtEndOfStream* property is true, the file contains no more records to read.

The statement to create the file system object is quite standard; the only part you can change is the name of the new object. The statement looks like this:

```
set fileSys = Server.CreateObject("Scripting.FileSystemObject")
```

The *OpenTextFile* method belongs to the *fileSys* object just created. That is, opening the file requires this statement:

```
set schFile = fileSys.OpenTextFile(fileName)
```

This *OpenTextFile* method opens the file named within the parentheses, creating a file object called, in this case, *schFile*.

The filename argument, by the way, needs to contain a path in the server's file system and *not* a URL path. On my server, for example, the file with URL *http://www.interlacken.com/tricks/exec/trick13/varmints.asp* actually resides at *h:\inetpub\wwwroot\tricks\exec\trick13\varmints.asp*, and it's the latter form that the *OpenTextFile()* method requires. I could hard-code the path *h:\inetpub* and so forth in the ASP page, but that would require adjusting the code to make it work on any other server (such as yours).

Fortunately, there's an ASP method called *Server.MapPath* that can translate a URL path to a file system path. A period, you may recall, always indicates the current directory. The following expression therefore provides the server path name to the directory where the ASP page resides (that is, to *h:\inetpub*, yada, yada, yada, or the equivalent on your server):

```
Server.MapPath (".")
```

The data file listed earlier is named *varmints.txt*, and I put it in the same directory as the ASP page. The *Server.MapPath(".")* method therefore gives us the path to the varmints.txt file. The following code fragment should now make sense:

```
fileName = Server.MapPath(".") & "\varmints.txt"
set fileSys = Server.CreateObject("Scripting.FileSystemObject")
set schFile = fileSys.OpenTextFile(fileName)
do until schFile.AtEndOfStream
    game = schFile.ReadLine
'   <code to process game record goes here>
    loop
```

Trick 13

Tip: The *&* operator in Visual Basic always joins two strings. The + operator adds two values if they're numeric, but it joins them alphabetically if either is a string.

Let's review. First we get a fully qualified file name for the varmints.*txt* file, then create a file system object, then open the file. Then, until the file is out of records, we read them and process them one at a time. Now, that wasn't so bad, was it?

Selecting Fields from Records

Built-in Visual Basic functions can easily select the individual fields from each record. Getting the date field, for example, is a simple matter of taking the leftmost eight characters in each record, like this:

```
gmDate = left(game,8)
```

The statement to get points scored by Vicksville uses three built-in Visual Basic functions: *mid* to select two characters starting at position 15, *trim* to eliminate any leading or training blanks, and *int* to make the result an integer:

```
gmVpts = int(trim(mid(game,15,2)))
```

The same three functions extract the rest of the data fields as well, although of course we don't use *int* on the alphabetic fields because, silly rabbit, *int* is for integers. And on the team name field, we don't tell the *mid* function how many characters to take; this tells *mid* to take everything out to the end of the record. The following makes perfect sense now, right?

```
gmDate = left(game,8)
gmLocn = trim(mid(game,10,4))
gmVpts = int(trim(mid(game,15,2)))
gmOpts = int(trim(mid(game,18,2)))
gmTeam = trim(mid(game,21))
```

Now, as to formatting the output, our job is much easier if we can write the entire Games Completed column before starting on the Games Remaining column. Otherwise we'd have to write the first Games Completed entry, the first Games Remaining entry, the second Games Completed entry, and so forth, alternating between the two columns. Ugly. So instead, we create three tables: one for overall page layout, one to contain the Games Completed entries, and one to contain the Games Remaining entries. Hopefully, all this will become marvelously clear after you check out Figure 13-2.

Selecting Data Records by Date

OK, so now here we are, trucking along, reading records from the varmints.txt file, splitting out the individual fields, and putting HTML around them to make rows in the Games Completed table. Life is good. Somehow, though, we need to check the date on each record, compare it to the current date, and switch to the Games Remaining table at the necessary moment. Simple. Visual Basic has a built-in *DateValue* function that converts text dates, like those in the varmints.txt file, to days since December 30, 1899. Remember, we saved the date from the varmints.txt record in a variable named *gmDate*, so the expression *DateValue(gmDate)* gives us the date value for the current record. Congratulate ourselves.

Getting the current date in Visual Basic is usually easy; there's a function called *now* that provides it. The problem comes with testing. If we always use the *now*

Tip: No conflict arises from using server-side and browser-side scripts on the same page. The server-side stuff runs on the server and the browser side stuff runs on the browser. Cool, eh?

FIGURE 13-2. *There are three HTML tables in this Web page: one for Games Completed, one for Games Remaining, and one that surrounds them both.*

Double-clicking the varmint makes the table borders visible.

The outer table (shown in gray) organizes two inner tables (shown in black) side by side.

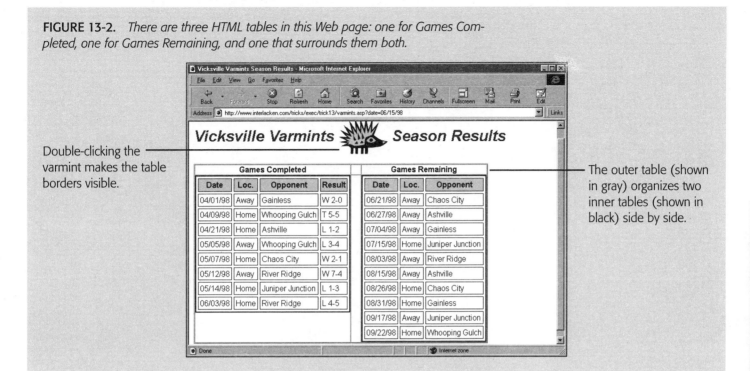

Vicksville Varmints Season Results - Microsoft Internet Explorer

File   Edit   View   Go   Favorites   Help

Back   Forward   Stop   Refresh   Home   Search   Favorites   History   Channels   Fullscreen   Mail   Print   Edit

Address http://www.interlacken.com/tricks/exec/trick13/varmints.asp?date=06/15/98   Links

Vicksville Varmints   Season Results

Games Completed

Date	Loc.	Opponent	Result
04/01/98	Away	Gainless	W 2-0
04/09/98	Home	Whooping Gulch	T 5-5
04/21/98	Home	Ashville	L 1-2
05/05/98	Away	Whooping Gulch	L 3-4
05/07/98	Home	Chaos City	W 2-1
05/12/98	Away	River Ridge	W 7-4
05/14/98	Home	Juniper Junction	L 1-3
06/03/98	Home	River Ridge	L 4-5

Games Remaining

Date	Loc.	Opponent
06/21/98	Away	Chaos City
06/27/98	Away	Ashville
07/04/98	Away	Gainless
07/15/98	Home	Juniper Junction
08/03/98	Away	River Ridge
08/15/98	Away	Ashville
08/26/98	Home	Chaos City
08/31/98	Home	Gainless
09/17/98	Away	Juniper Junction
09/22/98	Home	Whooping Gulch

Done   Internet zone

Tip: To see the Vicksville Varmints table borders in your browser, double-click the varmint.

function, how can we tell if the page will work correctly in the future, when the users will be visiting? Will the script blow up after the end of the season, when no games remain and the left column will be empty? Inquiring minds want to know. Well, remember that *request.querystring* thingie we used in Trick 11, "Ad Rotators"? We coded *?user=Jim&ans=Yes* at the end of the URL for an ASP page, and the ASP page retrieved the values *Jim* and *Yes* with these expressions:

```
request.QueryString("user")
request.QueryString("ans")
```

OK, so you forgot. Take my word for it, this works, and we can use it for dates too. If we code *?date=03/15/98* at the end of the URL that runs *varmints.asp*, the following code sets *today* to the date value for 03/15/98. If we don't use *?date=* or if we supply an invalid date, the code uses the integer portion of the current date:

```
if IsDate(request.querystring("date")) then
    today = DateValue(request.querystring("date"))
else
    today = int(now())
end if
```

An Incredibly Brief Introduction to Visual Basic Dates

Visual Basic represents dates as days since December 30, 1899. For example, here's how Visual Basic internally represents some typical dates:

December 30, 1899	0
December 31, 1899	1
June 15, 1998	35596
January 1, 2000	36526
June 15, 2001	37057

VBScript automatically converts date values to text whenever you display them, but knowing the internal format is handy when you're comparing two dates or doing date arithmetic. For example, the following code displays the day after April Fool's Day, 1998:

```
<% = #April 1, 1998# + 1 %>
```

and this code displays the day after tomorrow:

```
<% = date() + 2 %>
```

- To code a date literal, surround the date with pound signs, as done above for April 1.

- The *date()* function returns the current date.

- Times are fractions of 1. Midnight is 0, 6:00 A.M. is 0.25, Noon is 0.5, and so forth. The date value for 6:00 A.M., June 12, 1949, for example, is 17330.25.

- The *time()* function returns the current time, and the *now()* function returns both combined.

Take heart, we're getting close to the end. Back in simpler times, before all this started, I initialized a variable named *future* to *false*. As long as *future* is *false*, the script checks each record to see if *DateValue(gmDate)* is greater than *today*. The first time this occurs, the script does two things:

- It sets future to true.

- It runs a Visual Basic subroutine called *FlipToFuture* that:

- Terminates the Games Completed table.

  - Terminates row 2, cell 1 of the large page layout table.

  - Displays row 2, cell 2 of the large table.

  - Begins row 2, cell 3 of the large table.

  - Begins the Games Remaining table.

  I made FlipToFuture a subroutine for two reasons:

- First, I wanted to avoid clutter within the main code.

- Second, there's another situation where the same code needs to run. If we get to AtEndOfStream without having run the FlipToFuture routine (that is, without having found a game scheduled for the future), we must force it to run. Otherwise, the HTML for the Games Completed table will be incomplete and that for the Games Remaining table totally missing. The Games Remaining heading just dangles over nothing and the page looks incomplete. Making the code in FlipToFuture a subroutine facilitates running it under two different situations.

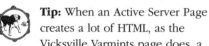 **Tip:** When an Active Server Page creates a lot of HTML, as the Vicksville Varmints page does, a lack of line endings can make the results very hard to read (if, for example, you check your work by using the browser's View Source command). To avoid such problems, use the expression *chr(13)* wherever you'd like a carriage return to appear. The *chr()* function converts a decimal value (like 13) to an ASCII character (like carriage return).

Complete HTML Listing

There are a two more gimmicks in this Web page. One determines a Won, Lost, or Tied code (W, L, or T) based on the score. The other involves two statements near the end of the page that close the *schFile* file and *fileSys* objects. I'll handle them in passing as we motor through the full HTML listing. Sit tight, this is gonna be fun. Trust me on this.

```
<html>
<head>
<title>Vicksville Varmints Season Results</title>
<style>
<!--
 H1, TD, TH { font-family: Arial, sans-serif }
 H1 { font-style: italic; color: rgb(102,0,153) }
 TH { font-weight: bold }
 .box { background-color: rgb(204,204,255); border: 1 solid rgb(0,0,0) }
-->
</style>
<script language="JavaScript">
function bordOn(){
  document.all.tab1.border = "2" ;
  document.all.tab2.border = "2" ;
  document.all.tab3.border = "2" ;
}
function bordOff(){
  document.all.tab1.border = "0" ;
  document.all.tab2.border = "0" ;
  document.all.tab3.border = "0" ;
}
// -->
</script>
</head>
<body>
<h1>Vicksville Varmints
    <img src="../../images/varmint.gif"
        alt="Varmint" align="absmiddle"
        width="103" height="75"
        ondblclick="bordOn()"
        onmouseout="bordOff()">
    Season Results</h1>
<table id="tab1" border="0"
        cellpadding="0" cellspacing="0">
```

Define style rules for text.

Define scripts to show and hide table borders.

Display page heading.

Start of main layout table.

Continued from previous page

Continued from previous page

Row 1 of the main layout table contains two main column headings and a spacer GIF.

```html
<tr>
  <th align="center">Games Completed</th>
  <th><img src="../../images/trans5x5.gif"
          width="20" height="5"></th>
  <th>Games Remaining</th>
```

Row 2 of the main layout table contains the Games Completed and Games Remaining tables.

```html
</tr><tr>
  <td valign="top">
```

Start of the Games Completed table.

```html
    <table id="tab2" border="0" bordercolor="#000000"
          cellpadding="3" cellspacing="4">
```

Display Games Completed column headings.

Start of the server-side ASP script.

Begin *FlipToFuture* subroutine to switch from Games Completed to Games Remaining.

```html
    <tr>
      <th class="box">Date</th>
      <th class="box">Loc.</th>
      <th class="box">Opponent</th>
      <th class="box">Result</th>
    </tr>
<%
sub FlipToFuture()
```

End of the Games Completed table.
End of row 2, cell 1 of main layout table.
Display row 2, cell 2 of main layout table.
Start row 2, cell 3 of main layout table.

```asp
response.write("</table>" & chr(13))
response.write("</td>" & chr(13))
response.write("<td> </td>" & chr(13))
response.write("<td valign=top>" & chr(13))
```

Start the Games Remaining table.

```asp
response.write("<table id=tab3 border=0 bordercolor=#000000")
response.write(" cellpadding=3 cellspacing=4>" & chr(13))
```

Display Games Remaining column headings.

```asp
response.write("<tr>" & chr(13))
response.write("<th class=box>Date</th>" & chr(13))
response.write("<th class=box>Loc.</th>" & chr(13))
response.write("<th class=box>Opponent</th>" & chr(13))
response.write("</tr>" & chr(13))
```

End of the *FlipToFuture* subroutine.
Check for a valid date in query string.
If found, use the valid date as current date.

Otherwise, use the real current date.

```asp
end sub
if IsDate(request.querystring("date")) then
  today = DateValue(request.querystring("date"))
else
  today = int(now())
end if
```

Indicate no future games found as yet.	`future = false`
Build a local path to the schedule file.	`fileName = Server.MapPath(".") & "\varmints.txt"`
Load the file system object.	`set fileSys = Server.CreateObject("Scripting.FileSystemObject")`
Open the schedule file.	`set schFile = fileSys.OpenTextFile(fileName)`
Loop until the end of the schedule file.	`do until schFile.AtEndOfStream`
Read one record from the schedule file.	`    game = schFile.ReadLine`

```
        gmDate = left(game,8)
        gmLocn = trim(mid(game,10,4))
        gmVpts = int(trim(mid(game,15,2)))
        gmOpts = int(trim(mid(game,18,2)))
        gmTeam = trim(mid(game,21))
```

Split schedule records into subfields.

```
        if (not future) then
          if IsDate(gmDate) then
            if (DateValue(gmDate) > today) then
              future = true
              FlipToFuture
            end if
          end if
        end if
```

Check to see if this is the first record for a future game. If so, set indicator and run the *FlipToFuture* subroutine.

```
        response.write("<tr>")
        response.write("<td>" & gmDate & "</td>")
        response.write("<td>" & gmLocn & "</td>")
        response.write("<td>" & gmTeam & "</td>")
```

Write the data fields as table cells.

```
        if (not future) then
          if (gmVpts > gmOpts) then
            gmRslt = "W"
          else
            if (gmVpts < gmOpts) then
              gmRslt = "L"
            else
              gmRslt = "T"
            end if
          end if
```

Only display the Results column for Games Completed.

Check game score to determine Win, Loss, or Tie.

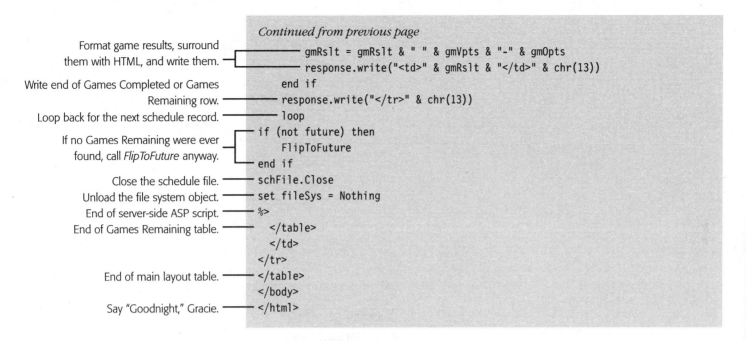

Format game results, surround them with HTML, and write them.

```
        gmRslt = gmRslt & " " & gmVpts & "-" & gmOpts
        response.write("<td>" & gmRslt & "</td>" & chr(13))
```

Write end of Games Completed or Games Remaining row.

```
   end if
```

Loop back for the next schedule record.

```
   response.write("</tr>" & chr(13))
   loop
```

If no Games Remaining were ever found, call *FlipToFuture* anyway.

```
if (not future) then
   FlipToFuture
end if
```

Close the schedule file.

```
schFile.Close
```

Unload the file system object.

```
set fileSys = Nothing
```

End of server-side ASP script.

```
%>
```

End of Games Remaining table.

```
   </table>
   </td>
```

```
</tr>
```

End of main layout table.

```
</table>
</body>
```

Say "Goodnight," Gracie.

```
</html>
```

While reading files with Active Server Pages isn't terribly difficult, the techniques are admittedly somewhat afield of normal HTML. That's why I chose a relatively simple application to illustrate it.

Think about that date we passed the ASP page as an argument, though. With a little work, you could submit that date and execute the ASP page with an HTML form. Such a form could also submit a part number, and a similar ASP page could search for matching inventory records. Just as easily, you could submit a Student ID and search for matching classes. You could submit an employee name and look up a phone number. All the while, someone else (or some other process) could be keeping the data up to date. And you thought *Godzilla* was big…

On-Track Messenger Service

This example is a Perl program that enhances (that is, rips off) the New Spin Promotions and Associates page in Trick 11. The New Spin page, you may remember, featured an ad rotator that randomly selected ads and corresponding hyperlinks from a pair of tables coded within the program. The On-Track Messenger Service page adds two enhancements:

- It loads the ad image and corresponding hyperlink tables from records in a text file.

- In addition to an image name and hyperlink location, each record in the text file contains a start date and a stop date. The program verifies that the current date falls between these two dates before accepting the ad.

As in the Vicksville Varmints page, the real trick here is reading data records from a file. This makes the On-Track page much more than an ad rotator; it's a page your client, your secretary, your boss, or anyone else can keep up-to-date without knowing a whit about HTML.

The On Track page itself isn't very interesting in a visual sense; it's the data file *behind* the ad rotation that bears our attention. Just to be consistent, though, a screen shot appears in Figure 13-3. Brace yourself.

Handling Dates in Perl

Like JavaScript, Perl internally stores dates as milliseconds since midnight, GMT, January 1, 1970. The standard Perl subroutine library includes a function called *&timelocal()* that converts dates and times to millisecond format, but it requires splitting out the month, day, and year and passing them as separate arguments. For this application, it's much easier to just consider dates as eight-digit values consisting of four digits for the year, two for the month, and two for the day. For example, June 15, 1998, works out to 19980615. This is the format we'll use for dates in our text file.

Perl provides a built-in function called *time* that returns the current date and time as milliseconds since January 1, 1970. A second function called *localtime* translates this to an array of nine values: second, minute, hour, day of month, month, year, day of week, day of year, and a daylight savings time indicator. Remember this for the test. Our code receives these values as follows:

```
($sec,$min,$hour,$mday,$mon,$year,$wday,$yday,$isdst) = localtime(time);
```

See Also: To review what's necessary to run a Perl script for the Web, refer to the "Running Perl Programs via CGI" sidebar in Trick 2, "Generating Tables Dynamically."

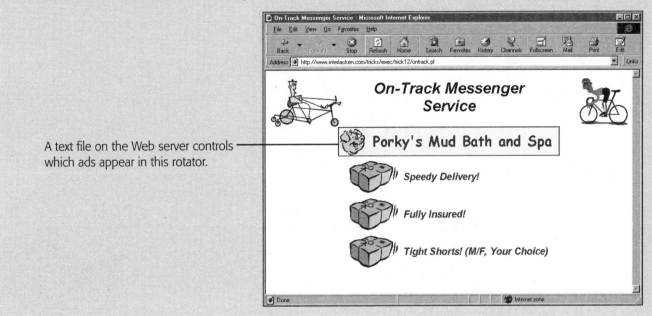

A text file on the Web server controls which ads appear in this rotator.

The year value is only two digits, so we have to guess which century it's in. If the two-digit year is 00 through 96, we add 2000; if it's 97 or more we add 1900. Then, we perform the following calculation to get a single, eight-digit date:

	Year	×	10000	=	19980000
+	Month	×	100	=	0600
+	Day of Month			=	15
					19980615

In code, the same procedure looks like this:

```
($sec,$min,$hour,$mday,$mon,$year,$wday,$yday,$isdst)
      = localtime(time);
   if ($year < 97){
       $year = $year + 2000;
   }else{
       $year = $year + 1900;
   }
$today = (10000 * $year) + (100 * ($mon+1)) + $mday;
```

File Processing in Perl

The data file, *ontrack.txt*, has seven records:.

```
19980201,19980228,coffeebk.gif,../../trick09/coffeebk.htm
19980101,19980131,fuzzyad.gif,../../trick10/fuzzy.htm
19980131,19981231,massive.gif,../../trick11/massive.htm
19980131,19981231,prestons.gif,../../trick11/prestons.htm
19980131,19981231,sloopys.gif,../../trick11/sloopys.htm
19980401,19980431,shadesad.gif,../..//trick04/shades.htm
19980101,20011231,porkys.gif,../../trick12/porkys.htm
```

To open this file requires that we find the directory where it resides. The handiest directory to find, at least if you're using Microsoft Internet Information Server, is the directory where the Perl program resides. IIS provides the Perl program's full path and filename in an environment variable called *PATH_TRANSLATED*. Here's a typical value:

```
h:\inetpub\wwwroot\tricks\exec\trick13\ontrack.pl
```

Dealing with backslashes in Perl is a mess, so translating all backslashes to slashes is an excellent first move. (Remember, Perl considers the backslash a special character.) The next step is discarding everything past the last slash (to lop off the file name so we're left with a directory)—something we can do by repeatedly chopping off the last character until we find a slash. Here's the code that does all this:

Tip: The *tr* function is normally easy to read: *tr/a/b/* translates each *a* in a string to *b*, for example. To translate backslashes to slashes, though, you have to code \\ where you mean one backslash and \/ where you mean one slash. The result is *tr/\\\/\//*.

Note: A *handle* is a pointer to something: an identity code. In the case of a file, Perl assigns a handle when it opens a file, tells us the handle's value, and expects us to specify that value for all future operations on that file.

Note: Perl for Microsoft Windows NT, in case you're wondering, handles slashes in file names as if they were backslashes. This provides compatibility for Perl programs developed under UNIX.

```
$path = $ENV{PATH_TRANSLATED};
$path =~ tr/\\/\//;
while (($path ne "") &&
       (substr($path,length($path)-1,1) ne "/")) {
   chop($path);
}
```

The Perl statement to open the file looks like this:

```
open(ADS, $path . "ontrack.txt");
```

This opens the file *h:/inetpub/wwwroot/tricks/exec/trick13/ontrack.txt* for input with handle ADS. The following code then reads the file and stores the data:

```
while(!eof(ADS)){
   $ads = <ADS>;
   $ads =~ tr/\x0a\x0d//d;
   ($beg,$end,$img,$url) = split(/,/,$ads);
   if (($beg <= $today) && ($end >= $today)){
       @imgs[$cnt] = $img;
       @urls[$cnt] = $url;
       $cnt = $cnt + 1;
   }
}
```

The *while* statement keeps the loop going as long as the ADS file isn't at the end of the file. The statement *$ads=<ADS>* reads a line from the file and stores it in the variable *$ads*. The third line removes any line feeds (hex 0A) and carriage returns (hex 0C) by translating them to null strings.

The four fields in each record, you may have noticed, are separated by commas. The statement

```
($beg,$end,$img,$url) = split(/,/,$ads);
```

splits the line into four fields: *$beg*, *$end*, *$img*, and *$url*.

The fifth line checks to see if the current date is included within the record's starting and ending date. If so, we add the image name and URL to a couple of tables named *@imgs* and *@urls*, and then increment the subscript *$cnt* in readiness for the next entry.

It's possible, of course, that the input file may be empty, or that no records are active for the current date. The following statements, executed before opening the ontrack.txt file, accommodate this possibility:

```
$cnt = 0;
@imgs[0] = "transad.gif";
@urls[0] = "#";
```

This code first sets the ad subscript to 0, and then stores default entries in the corresponding *@imgs* and *@urls* entries. The transad.gif image is completely transparent, and the URL *"#"* means the top of the current Web page. The first ad loaded from the ontrack.*txt* file, if any, will overlay these values.

The code that chooses the rotating ad is lifted directly from the New Spin Promotions and Associates page in Trick 11. As you may recall:

- The *srand* function seeds the random number generator.

- The expression *$#imgs* gives the number of entries in the *@imgs* array.

- The function *rand ($#imgs)*chooses a random number between 0 and *$#imgs*.

- The function *int* selects the integer portion of that random number:

```
srand;
$choice = int(rand($#imgs+1));
```

The HTML code for the On-Track Web page appears as a giant string, which the Perl program simply copies to standard output (and thus to the remote user). The following expressions, appearing within the giant string, insert the randomly selected ad image and URL:

```
$urls[$choice]
$imgs[$choice]
```

We're almost done except for one tiny detail. As with the Vicksville Varmints page, we need a way to override the current date for testing. To do this, we first steal the query string decoder code from the *adredir.pl* program in Trick 11, and then check for an eight-character value named *date*. If found, we use that value as the current date; otherwise, we get the system date as previously described.

Complete Perl Listing

OK, that's it, we're done, *am ende, finito, rigor mortis, sayonara*. Here's the complete program listing, and a marvelous thing it is.

Split query string name=value pairs into @*flds* array.

Split each @*flds* entry into separate name and value fields, decode, and add to @*in* associative array.

If the query string contains an eight-character value named *date*, use it as the current date.

Otherwise, get and decode the system date and time.

Convert a two-digit year to four digits.

Combine the year, month, and day into one value.

Get system file name for the URL pointing to the Perl program.

Translate backslashes to slashes.

Keep chopping off the last character of *$path* until the last character is a slash.

```perl
@flds = split(/&/,$ENV{"QUERY_STRING"});
foreach $fld (@flds) {
    ($fkey, $fval) = split(/=/,$fld);
    $fval =~ tr/+/ /;
    $fval =~ s/%([a-fA-F0-9][a-fA-F0-9])/pack("C", hex($1))/eg;
    $fkey =~ tr/+/ /;
    $fkey =~ s/%([a-fA-F0-9][a-fA-F0-9])/pack("C", hex($1))/eg;
    $in{$fkey} = $fval;
}
if (length($in{"date"}) == 8){
    $today = $in{"date"};
}else{
    ($sec,$min,$hour,$mday,$mon,$year,$wday,$yday,$isdst)
        = localtime(time);
    if ($year < 97){
        $year = $year + 2000;
    }else{
        $year = $year + 1900;
    }
    $today = (10000 * $year) + (100 * ($mon+1)) + $mday;
}
$path = $ENV{PATH_TRANSLATED};
$path =~ tr/\\/\//;
while (($path ne "") &&
        (substr($path,length($path)-1,1) ne "/")) {
    chop($path);
}
```

Continued from previous page

Initialize the ad rotator subscript to 0.

Initialize default ad rotator table entries.

Open the ontrack.txt file.

Define the loop that reads all records until the end of file.

Read one record from the ontrack.txt file.

Split apart the current record as comma-delimited.

Remove any linefeeds and carriage returns from the current record.

Determine if the current date is within the current record's beginning and ending date.

If so, store the image and URL, and then increment the subscript for next time.

Define the path prefix for images.
Seed the random number generator.

Choose a random subscript for the ad tables.

Begin copying the giant string to standard output.

Provide a Content-type header and blank line (required).

Define text styles.

```perl
$cnt = 0;
@imgs[0] = "transad.gif";
@urls[0] = "#";
open(ADS, $path . "ontrack.txt");
while(!eof(ADS)){
    $ads = <ADS>;
    $ads =~ tr/\x0a\x0d//d;
    ($beg,$end,$img,$url) = split(/,/,$ads);
    if (($beg <= $today) && ($end >= $today)){
        @imgs[$cnt] = $img;
        @urls[$cnt] = $url;
        $cnt = $cnt + 1;
    }
}
$imgDir = "../../images/";
srand;
$choice = int(rand($#imgs+1));
print <<"EOP";
Content-type: text/html

<html>
<head>
<title>On-Track Messenger Service</title>
<style>
<!--
TD { font-family: Arial, sans-serif; font-size: 125%;
     font-weight: bold; font-style: italic ; color: #906;}
H1 {color: black}
-->
</style>
</head>
<body bgcolor="#FFFFFF">
```

Continued from previous page

Display the page heading.

```html
<table border="0" cellpadding="0" cellspacing="0" width="100%">
  <tr>
    <td>
      <img src="../../images/biker2.gif" alt="On-Track"
          width="156" height="100"></td>
    <td align="center">
       <h1>On-Track Messenger Service</h1></td>
    <td align="right">
      <img src="../../images/biker1.gif" alt="On-Track"
          width="156" height="100"></td>
  </tr>
</table>
<center>
```

Select an ad URL from *@urls* array.

```html
<a href="$urls[$choice]">
```

Select an ad image from *@imgs* array.

```html
<img src="$imgDir$imgs[$choice]"
    height=60 width=468 border=0></a>
</center>
<center>
```

Start the packages table.

```html
<table border="0" cellpadding="6" cellspacing="0">
```

Display row 1 of the packages table.

```html
  <tr>
    <td>
      <img src="../../images/package.gif" alt="Package"
          width="101" height="64"></td>
    <td>Speedy Delivery!</td>
  </tr>
```

Display row 2 of the packages table.

```html
  <tr>
    <td>
      <img src="../../images/package.gif" alt="Package"
          width="101" height="64"></td>
    <td>Fully Insured!</td>
  </tr>
```

Trick 13

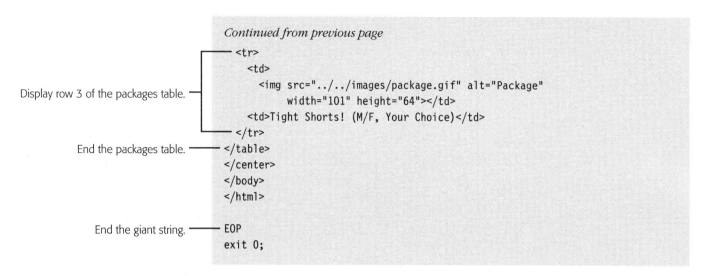

Continued from previous page

Display row 3 of the packages table.

End the packages table.

End the giant string.

```
<tr>
  <td>
    <img src="../../images/package.gif" alt="Package"
         width="101" height="64"></td>
  <td>Tight Shorts! (M/F, Your Choice)</td>
</tr>
</table>
</center>
</body>
</html>

EOP
exit 0;
```

Again, ad rotation isn't the real point of this example. It is a Web process you can turn over to your client, user, or coworker for maintenance even if they don't understand HTML. That's a lot of value for a hundred lines of code.

Interacting with Tables

Trick 2, "Generating Tables Dynamically," showed how to generate variable-sized tables, first using code that runs when the page loads, and then using code that runs on the server. This Trick expands on that concept by showing how to change the size of tables after a Web page is on display. It does so using two examples.

The Downsizing Game shows how to delete rows from a table. The page displays a table with five rows, each containing the name and picture of one employee. One employee is designated for retention. Your mission is to fire the other four employees (by clicking on their table row) without clicking on the protected employee's row. Clicking on an employee, of course, deletes his or her row from the table.

Clothes on Line shows how to add rows to a table. Web visitors see a list of items they can order, and as they select items, the Web page builds a multiline order (an ever-expanding HTML table) that displays the entire order and a subtotal. This provides a faster, smoother, and more interactive shopping experience than sending each item individually to a shopping cart application on the Web server.

Along the way, you'll also see how to modify the contents and properties of table cells. And be forewarned, this is full-bore Dynamic HTML stuff that Netscape Navigator doesn't support at all, at least not through version 4. To support Netscape users, you'll have to code your application a second time and route users to the correct page for their browser. Trick 8 explains how to do this.

Why would you develop the same application twice? This depends on how state-of-the art you want your site to be. If working with the greatest number of browsers (that is, with the oldest ones) is important, and if complex, interactive content isn't, design low and aim for Netscape Navigator 2. To get the most advanced, high-tech impact each current browser can deliver, you'll need separate pages optimized for each. Or, you can walk the line and develop hybrid pages that, even though not completely optimized for either browser, do take advantage of some of the newest features. The trade-offs depend entirely on your application's requirements.

Who Put the D in HTML?

In case you haven't noticed by now, there are three distinct approaches to self-modifying Web pages:

- A Web page sends input to an ASP page or program on the Web server, and that process sends the browser a customized version of the page.

- JavaScript uses the *document.write* method to customize HTML as the page loads.

- JavaScript modifies a page after it's loaded—typically in response to timer events or event handlers you code into the HTML.

The third approach is the one in which Microsoft Internet Explorer most differs from Netscape Navigator. Once a page is loaded, Netscape only lets you change the contents of images (with no resizing), modify the contents of form fields, and change the visibility and position of layers. Internet Explorer lets you twiddle with almost anything on the page. If you change the size of something, add elements, or remove them, Internet Explorer adjusts the rest of the page accordingly. This is that Dynamic HTML thing you've all been hearing about (and which I've been craftily introducing throughout the book).

The Downsizing Game

Rows in HTML tables are like most things in life; it's easier to destroy them than create them. Our first example deals with the simpler case: mass destruction of table rows. Figure 14-1 illustrates the demolition site.

FIGURE 14-1. *Only one of the five employees listed at the right, chosen at random, is going to be retained. Clicking the others deletes their row from the table.*

Double-click this image to reveal all table borders.

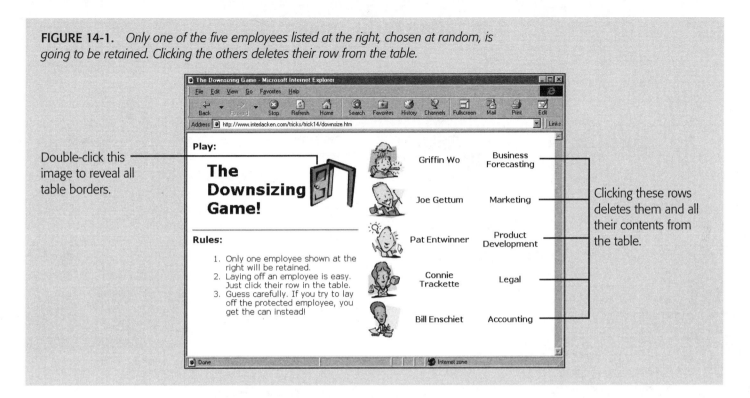

Clicking these rows deletes them and all their contents from the table.

This Web page asks you to "downsize" four employees (substitute the euphemism of your choice) but not a specially chosen fifth; choose that one and *you* get the boot. As you click vulnerable employees, a script deletes their rows from the table. If you click the protected employee, a dialog box tells you you're fired. If you correctly fire all four vulnerable employees, a dialog box promotes you to Vice President, Human Resources.

There are three tables: one to organize the page heading and rules, one to list the five employees, and a three-column job that arranges the other two side by side with some white space between them. To see the table borders, load the page in Internet Explorer and double-click the open door.

Scripting Techniques

When the page loads, some JavaScript code divides the current second by 5 and takes the remainder as a random number between 0 and 4. This identifies the one employee being protected.

Clicking on the row for any employee normally removes that row from the table. The one exception is clicking the protected employee's row, which loses the game. The user wins the game by reducing the number of table rows to one without clicking on the protected employee. After the game is won or lost, clicking on any row simply repeats the won or lost message. Thank you, thank you, you can buy tokens at the cashier.

The table listing the five employees is called *emps*. OK, if you don't believe me, check the full HTML listing. There it is, ID="emps", right there inside the <TABLE> tag. Deleting a row from this table is as simple as running the following statement:

```
emps.deleteRow(nr);
```

You already know how to pick up mouse clicks, right? Sure you do, it's the *onclick* HTML attribute. (Weren't you paying attention? I showed you this in Trick 9!) The HTML that begins each row of the *emps* table looks like this:

```
<tr onclick="layOff(this.rowIndex)">
```

This says, "Whenever somebody clicks on this table row, run the *layOff()* function and pass the current row number as an argument." The *rowIndex* property supplies the current row number (the first row equals 0), and using *this* within an HTML tag, as you surely recall, always refers to the element created by that tag.

Why not just code, say, *layOff(4)* for the last row? Well, after deleting some other row—row 2, for example—the last row won't be row 4 anymore; it'll be row 3! So using *this.rowIndex* always gets the current number of a row, not its number when the page was loaded. Amazing.

The following statements run every time the Web page loads. They're located within the page's <HEAD> section, but outside any function definition:

```
now = new Date();
prot = (now.getSeconds() % 5);
rslt = "";
```

Caution: Netscape Navigator doesn't support the *deleteRow* method, at least not through version 4.

See Also: If you've forgotten about *this,* please refer to the sidebar in Trick 9 titled (what else), "What's This?"

The first statement is hopefully familiar by now; it creates a new Date object named *now* with the value of the current date and time. The second statement gets the current second from the *now* date, divides it by 5, and saves the remainder as *prot*. Statement three initializes the result of playing the game; eventually, this will be *W* for a win and *L* for a loss.

The *layOff()* function works like this—if the game result is still an empty string, *layOff()* runs the following block of code:

```
if (nr == prot){
   rslt = "L";
}else{
   emps.deleteRow(nr);
   if (nr < prot){
     prot = prot - 1;
   }
   if (emps.rows.length == 1){
     rslt = "W";
   }
}
```

The variable *nr* is the row number passed by the calling statement, which is the value the *onClick* event got from *this.rowIndex*. If this equals *prot*, the row number of the protected employee, we declare the game a loss by setting *rslt* to *L*. Otherwise, we delete the row, using the *deleteRow* method we just discussed. (Well, *I* discussed it, anyway.)

There are two more tasks to complete whenever we delete a row. First, we need to see if the deleted row fell earlier in the table than the protected employee's row. Suppose, if you will, that Connie Trackette is the protected employee and she's in row 3. Now delete row 1. Connie's entry is now row 2. So whenever we delete a row with a number less than *prot*, we need to decrease *prot* by *1*.

Finally, after you delete a row, you need to check how many rows are left. If it's only one, our crafty user has deleted everyone but the protected employee and thereby won the game. We celebrate by setting *rslt* to *W*. Oh, and huzzah.

Tip: You can define table cells using <TD> tags, <TH> tags, or a mixture. By intent, <TH> tags are for table headings and <TD> are for table data, but the only difference between them is the appearance of any text they contain; by default, text in <TH> cells is normally bold. <TH> cells gain new significance under CSS, though, because assigning different CSS properties to the types TD and TH is so easy.

Once the game is won or lost, the following code displays a message to inform the user. Obviously, no further employee rows can be deleted now; the user continues to get the same won or lost message:

```
if (rslt == "W"){
  alert("Congratulations, you win.\n" +
        "Your new job is VP of Human Resources.");
}
if (rslt == "L"){
    alert("Sorry, you clicked the protected employee.\n" +
          "You get the can.");
}
```

Two details remain. First, I found it unsightly that the *emps* table got narrower as it got shorter. This was just Internet Explorer doing its job, trying to optimize overall table appearance, but I found it annoying nevertheless. I tried various solutions, and the one that worked the best was to put a transparent GIF file at the bottom of the table and set its width to half the browser window.

That's why, whenever the Web page loads or gets resized, it runs a function called *spaceEmp()*. Initially, *spaceEmp()* checks whether the browser is Internet Explorer 4 or later, and issues a warning message to the user if it's not. Then, with the following statement, it sets the width of an image named *empSpace* to half the total width of the document area:

```
document.all.empSpace.width = (document.body.clientWidth / 2);
```

The very last detail consists of the *bordOn()* function, the *bordOff()* function, and a pair of event attributes on the open door image. As in several prior examples, these show and hide the table borders, just in case you have trouble visualizing them while invisible (the borders, not you).

Complete HTML Listing

And now, the main event you've all been waiting for: here's the complete HTML listing. Are you ready to rumble?

Caution: Netscape Navigator doesn't support the *document. body.clientWidth* property, at least not through version 4.

Caution: Netscape Navigator 4 can't resize images already on display.

```
<html>
<head>
<title>The Downsizing Game</title>
<style>
<!--
 TD { font-family: Verdana, sans-serif; }
-->
</style>
<script language="JavaScript">
now = new Date();
prot = (now.getSeconds() % 5);
rslt = "";
function layOff(nr){
  if (rslt == ""){
    if (nr == prot){
      rslt = "L";
    }else{
      emps.deleteRow(nr);
      if (nr < prot){
        prot = prot - 1;
      }
      if (emps.rows.length == 1){
        rslt = "W";
      }
    }
  }
  if (rslt == "W"){
    alert("Congratulations, you win.\n" +
        "Your new job is VP of Human Resources.");
  }
}
if (rslt == "L"){
    alert("Sorry, you clicked the protected employee.\n" +
        "You get the can.");
}
```

Define text styles.

Get the current date and time.

Divide the current second by 5 and save the remainder.

Initialize the game result.

Define the function to delete employees.

Determine whether the game is still in progress

Determine if the employee is protected.

If so, user loses the game.

If not, delete the row from the table.

If the deleted row was ahead of the row with the protected employee, adjust *prot* variable accordingly.

If only one employee remains, indicate the user has won.

Congratulate the winner.

Inform the losing player.

Continued from previous page

This function runs whenever the page loads or gets resized.

Get the browser name and version.

Display a warning if not Internet Explorer 4 or later.

Size column by setting the width of a transparent GIF.

Reveal table borders.

Hide table borders.

Run the *spaceEmp()* function whenever the page loads or gets resized.

Start of the main layout table.

Start of heading and instructions table.

Insert heading kicker.

```
function spaceEmp(){
    browser = navigator.appName.substring(0,9);
    version = parseInt(navigator.appVersion);
    if ((browser != "Microsoft") || (version < 4)){
        alert("Warning!\n" +
                "This page requries Internet Explorer 4.")
    }else{
        document.all.empSpace.width = (document.body.clientWidth / 2);
    }
}
function bordOn(){
    document.all.tab1.border = "2" ;
    document.all.tab2.border = "2" ;
    document.all.emps.border = "2" ;
}
function bordOff(){
    document.all.tab1.border = "0" ;
    document.all.tab2.border = "0" ;
    document.all.emps.border = "0" ;
}
// -->
</script>
</head>
<body onLoad="spaceEmp();" onResize="spaceEmp();">
<table id="tab1" cellpadding="0" cellspacing="1"
        border="0" bordercolor="#009900">
<tr>
  <td valign="top">
    <table id="tab2" cellpadding="0" cellspacing="0"
            border="0" bordercolor="#000000">
      <tr>
        <td colspan="2">
            <h3>Play:</h3></td>
        <td rowspan="2">
```

Continued from previous page

Display the open door image. Note *onDblClick* and *onMouseOut* events to reveal and hide table borders.

```
<img src="../images/dooropen.gif" alt="Open Door"
        width="97" height="100"
        ondblclick="bordOn();"
        onmouseout="bordOff();"></td>
</tr><tr>
  <td>
```

Transparent GIF spacer.

```
<img src="../images/trans5x5.gif"
        width="30" height="15">
<td>
```

Main heading text.

```
<h1>The<br>Downsizing<br>Game!</h1></td>
</tr><tr>
  <td colspan="3">
    <hr noshade></td>
</tr><tr>
  <td colspan="3">
    <h3>Rules:</h3></td>
</tr><tr>
  <td></td>
  <td colspan="2">
```

Print ordinal (numbered) list of rules.

```
<ol>
  <li>Only one employee shown at the right will
      be retained.</li>
  <li>Laying off an employee is easy. Just click
      their row in the table.</li>
  <li>Guess carefully. If you try to lay off the
      protected employee, you get the can instead!</li>
</ol></td></tr>
```

End of heading and instructions table.

```
</table></td>
<td></td>
<td valign="top">
```

Start of the employee table.

```
<table id="emps" cellpadding="3" cellspacing="0"
        border="0" bordercolor="#000000">
```

Trick 14

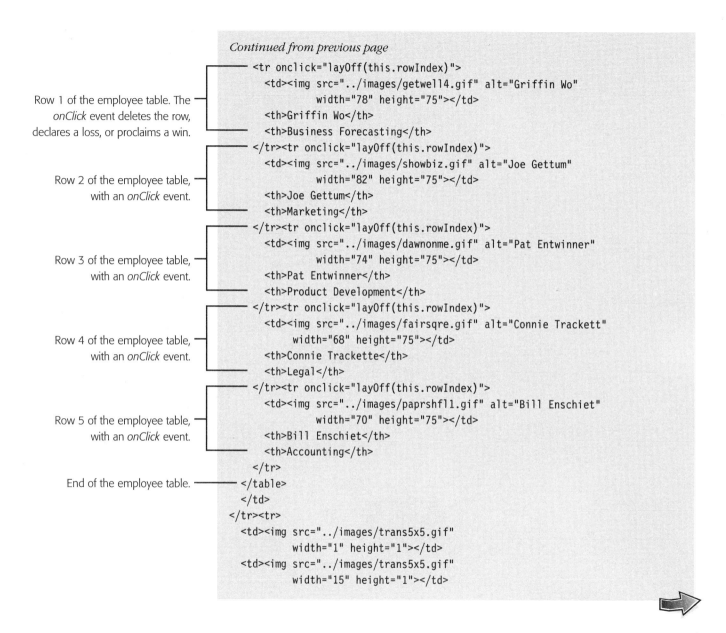

Continued from previous page

Row 1 of the employee table. The *onClick* event deletes the row, declares a loss, or proclaims a win.

Row 2 of the employee table, with an *onClick* event.

Row 3 of the employee table, with an *onClick* event.

Row 4 of the employee table, with an *onClick* event.

Row 5 of the employee table, with an *onClick* event.

End of the employee table.

```html
<tr onclick="layOff(this.rowIndex)">
  <td><img src="../images/getwell4.gif" alt="Griffin Wo"
       width="78" height="75"></td>
  <th>Griffin Wo</th>
  <th>Business Forecasting</th>
</tr><tr onclick="layOff(this.rowIndex)">
  <td><img src="../images/showbiz.gif" alt="Joe Gettum"
       width="82" height="75"></td>
  <th>Joe Gettum</th>
  <th>Marketing</th>
</tr><tr onclick="layOff(this.rowIndex)">
  <td><img src="../images/dawnonme.gif" alt="Pat Entwinner"
       width="74" height="75"></td>
  <th>Pat Entwinner</th>
  <th>Product Development</th>
</tr><tr onclick="layOff(this.rowIndex)">
  <td><img src="../images/fairsqre.gif" alt="Connie Trackett"
      width="68" height="75"></td>
  <th>Connie Trackette</th>
  <th>Legal</th>
</tr><tr onclick="layOff(this.rowIndex)">
  <td><img src="../images/paprshfl1.gif" alt="Bill Enschiet"
       width="70" height="75"></td>
  <th>Bill Enschiet</th>
  <th>Accounting</th>
</tr>
</table>
</td>
</tr><tr>
  <td><img src="../images/trans5x5.gif"
       width="1" height="1"></td>
  <td><img src="../images/trans5x5.gif"
       width="15" height="1"></td>
```

Continued from previous page

```
        <td><img id="empSpace"
                 src="../images/trans5x5.gif"
                 width="1" height="1"></td>
    </tr>
  </table>
  </body>
</html>
```

Transparent GIF to preserve width of employee table.

End of main page layout table.

Sending table rows (or other employees) to oblivion is all well and interesting, but also a bit one-sided. Without a way to add table rows as well, you soon run out of rows to delete. Well, fear not, adding rows (and cells) is the subject of the next example.

Clothes on Line

No matter what kind of data a table displays, someone will occasionally need to update it. If it's an order, someone can modify line items. If it's a schedule, someone can add or remove events. If it's a class, someone can add students. If it's a student, someone can add classes.

Until now, a typical way of handling such requirements would involve (1) displaying a Web page with the existing data in an HTML table, (2) providing an Add button that jumped to a data entry form, (3) asking the user to complete the form, (4) submitting the completed form to the server, and (5) having the server retransmit the page displaying the existing data (now with updates). Such an approach is well-known and time-tested, but it's not terribly fast or interactive. To be so, the whole process should occur within one Web page, and entirely on the browser.

This example doesn't implement a complete table editing application; that would be too lengthy and too complex for a book such as this. However, as previously promised, it does add rows and cells to a table and, also as promised, it's a bit more complicated than The Downsizing Game. The Web page and the table we'll extend both appear in Figure 14-2.

Trick 14

FIGURE 14-2. *Clicking the Order button adds a row to the Your Order table.*

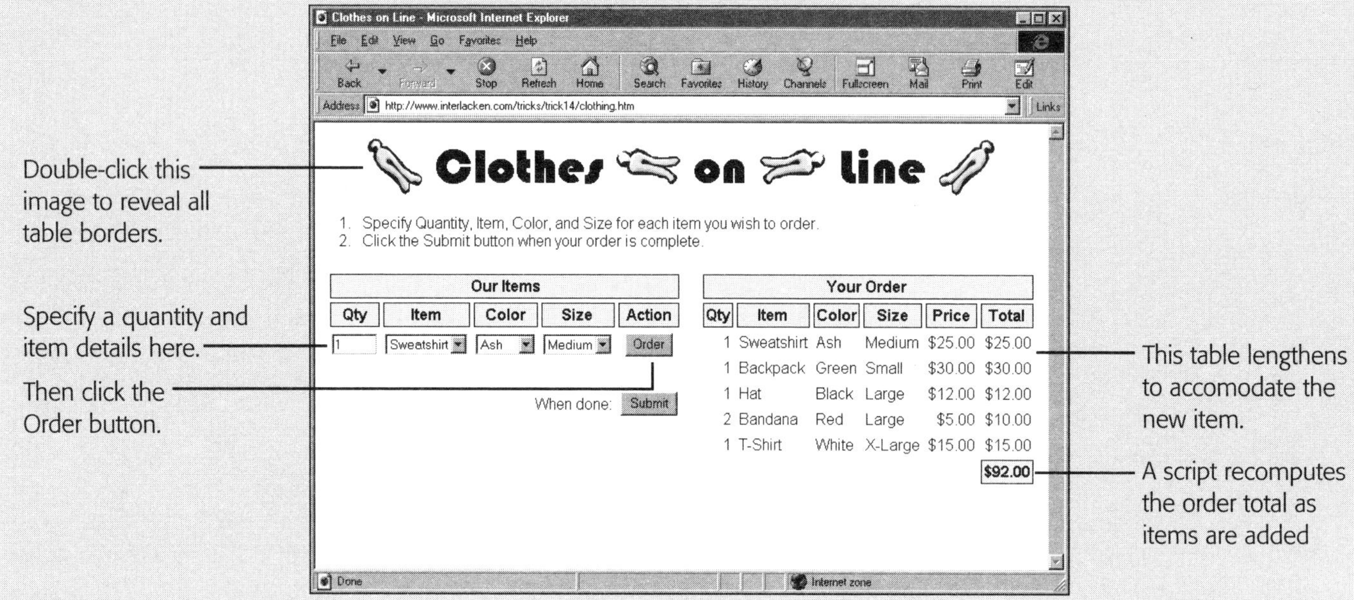

Double-click this image to reveal all table borders.

Specify a quantity and item details here.

Then click the Order button.

This table lengthens to accomodate the new item.

A script recomputes the order total as items are added

There are three tables in the Clothes on Line page: one titled Our Items, one titled Your Order, and a two-celled table with the sole purpose of making the other two appear side by side. We'll enlarge the Your Order table.

The statement to insert a new row is relatively straightforward. Here's an example:

```
newRow = document.all.ordTb.insertRow(2);
```

The *insertRow()* method creates a new row with, in this case, *rowIndex=2*. If the table already contains a row in this position, the existing row gets pushed down and becomes *rowIndex=3*. The *newRow* variable receives a pointer to the new row, but as we'll see shortly, it's not the new row's *rowIndex*. As to *ordTb*, that's the table's name, assigned with an ID attribute in the <TABLE> tag.

The following expression retrieves the *rowIndex* property of the new row:

```
rowNr = newRow.rowIndex;
```

Creating a new row doesn't create any cells. That would be too easy. If you want cells (and who doesn't), you have to use the *insertCell* method. To wit:.

```
newCell = document.all.ordTb.rows[rowNr].insertCell(1);
```

The expression *[rowNr]* indicates the row in which the new cell should appear, and the argument *(1)* indicates the new cell's position.

Once the cell exists, you can refer to it using either of these expressions:

```
document.all.ordTb.rows[rowNr].cells[1]
newCell
```

The *insertCell* method doesn't *require* a receiving variable such as *newCell;* if you want, you can code:

```
document.all.ordTb.rows[rowNr].insertCell(1);
```

instead of:

```
newCell = document.all.ordTb.rows[rowNr].insertCell(1);
```

A variable like *newCell* just provides a shorthand reference for accessing the new cell.

You can modify the cell's default properties from code just as you'd modify the properties of a cell defined with ordinary HTML tags. The following sidebar, "Accessing Element Properties from Code," explains more about this, and the HTML listing for this example will show the technique in use.

Tip: Remember that in JavaScript, [square brackets] indicate sub-scripting and (parentheses) indicate either function arguments or expression grouping.

Accessing Element Properties from Code

When reading or modifying Web page object properties from code, the naming scheme follows Cascading Style Sheet—rather than HTML—conventions. The syntax is:

```
identifier.style.property = value
```

Trick 14

Hyperlinks: For more information about the *outerHTML* property, select it from the list at:

http://www.microsoft.com/msdn/sdk/ inetsdk/help/dhtml/references/ properties/properties.htm

Hyperlinks: For more information about the insertAdjacent HTML method, select it from the list at:

http://www.microsoft.com/msdn/sdk/ inetsdk/help/dhtml/references/ methods/methods.htm

Hyperlinks: The TextRange object is an extremely powerful and difficult way to modify HTML already on display. For more information, select it from the list at:

http://www.microsoft.com/msdn/sdk/ inetsdk/help/dhtml/references/objects/ objects.htm

Accessing Element Properties from Code *(continued)*

- For elements defined in HTML, the most common *identifier* is *document.all.id*, where *id* is a value you assign to the ID attribute of the tag that defines the element. This includes HTML you create with *document.write* statements.

  For example, you code this HTML

  ```
  <TD ID="enos" BGCOLOR="#FFFFCC">Whatever</TD>
  ```

  and later want to change the background color from JavaScript. Code:

  ```
  document.all.enos.style.backgroundColor = "#FFCCCC";
  ```

- If your code creates elements by dynamically adding HTML to the currently displayed Web page, that HTML can also assign *id* values by specifying ID attributes within tags. There are three ways to add such HTML:

  - By adding it to an *outerHTML* property.

  - By using the insertAdjacentHTML method. (Without jumping into all the gory details, insertAdjacentHTML adds HTML to a Web page just before or just after an element's opening or closing tags.)

  - By modifying the TextRange object. (This is a very advanced technique whereby you can insert or remove HTML from any part of a Web page.)

  Once defined, you can use these id properties just as if they appeared in the original HTML.

- For elements created directly in memory, such as table rows and cells, there appears to be no way of assigning id values. The id property is both blank and read-only. Fortunately, however, the methods that create such elements can also create references and store them in variable names for you. Such elements may also be accessible in other ways, such as:

  - The rows collection of a table (accessible by row number).

  - The cells collection of a row (accessible by cell number).

Accessing Element Properties from Code *(continued)*

- The valid property identifiers are generally the same as Cascading Style Sheet properties, subject to these conversions:

  - Express the entire property name in lowercase.

  - Change each letter following a hyphen to uppercase.

  - Remove all the hyphens.

  For example, the border-style CSS property would appear in code as borderStyle.

- The acceptable values are whatever you'd use in CSS style sheets.

See Also: For more information about the *innerText* and *innerHTML* properties, refer to the "Tired of the Same Old HTML" sidebar in Trick 10. For another example of its use, see the AERO Message Service (IE) page in Trick 5.

To modify the cell's content, use the *innerText* or *innerHTML* properties. All together then, the code to create a row, add a cell to that row, make the cell right-justified, and add some content follows immediately. For all the complexity of explaining it, I'd say it looks pretty simple just sitting there, wouldn't you?

```
newRow = document.all.ordTb.insertRow(2);
rowNr = newRow.rowIndex;
document.all.ordTb.rows[rowNr].insertCell(0);
document.all.ordTb.rows[rowNr].cells[0].style.textAlign = "right";
document.all.ordTb.rows[rowNr].cells[0].innerText = qty;
```

The following code is both shorter and equivalent, albeit slightly less direct:

```
newRow = document.all.ordTb.insertRow(2);
rowNr = newRow.rowIndex;
newCell = document.all.ordTb.rows[rowNr].insertCell(0);
newCell.textAlign = "right";
newCell.innerText = qty;
```

The rest of the Clothes on Line page should be pretty familiar if you understood the Coffee Break Deli page in Trick 9. The data entry form contains an ordinary text box for the *Qty* field and three drop-down lists for Item, Color, and Size. We sell only five items: Backpack, Bandana, Hat, Sweatshirt, and T-Shirt.

Trick 14

All five items are available in the same six colors and the same four sizes. This isn't a book about merchandising.

There's so much Internet Explorer–specific code on this page that we might as well read values from the drop-down lists the easy way—with a technique that Netscape Navigator doesn't support. Getting the selected descriptions for Item, Color, and Size follows this pattern:

```
sel = document.ordFm.ddItm.selectedIndex;
itm = document.ordFm.ddItm.options(sel).text;
```

The *selectedIndex* property tells us which item is selected. The name of the Item drop-down is *ddItm* and the name of the data entry form is *ordFm*. The variable *sel* thus receives the currently selected item number. The *options* collection of a drop-down list box contains the properties of each option. An option's *text* property contains the text the user sees. See how easy that was?

The customer price varies by item but not by size or color. It's convenient to store the price in the list box's *value* property, which changes automatically as the user selects different items in the list. The following statement reads the *value* value and stores it in the variable *prc*:

```
prc = document.ordFm.ddItm.value;
```

The full HTML listing (page 364) shows how to assign values to each option in the *ddItm* list box.

Multiplying price by quantity requires no special explanation. The routine *fmtMoney* formats a numeric variable as currency (that is, with a dollar sign and decimal point). This is the same routine we used on the Coffee Break Deli page; please refer back to Trick 9 if that memory has sadly faded.

The routine that computes the total price of the order is worth a look because, if for no other reason, it shows how to access table cells that have no *id* properties. Here's the routine:

```
rows = document.all.ordTb.rows.length;
tot = 0;
for (rw=2; rw < rows-1; ++rw){
  rwPrc = document.all.ordTb.rows[rw].cells[5].innerText;
```

Caution: The *options* collection of a drop-down list isn't accessible in Netscape Navigator, at least not through version 4.

Tip: When you define a selection list (for instance, a drop-down list), you define text and values for each option. However:

- The user sees the text, not the value.
- Submitting the form transmits the current value but not the text.
- Netscape Navigator provides no access to the text and value properties from JavaScript. Only the *selectedIndex* property is accessible.
- Internet Explorer does provides access to the text and value properties, and to the *selectedIndex* property as well.

```
if (rwPrc.substring(0,1) == "$"){
    rwPrc = rwPrc.substring(1,rwPrc.length);
}
tot = tot + parseFloat(rwPrc);
}
document.all.ordTb.rows[rows-1].cells[5].innerText
    = fmtMoney(tot);
```

The first line of code gets the length of the order table's *rows* collection—that is, the number of rows in the table—and stores it in *rows*. The second line initializes a variable called *tot* that'll accumulate the total price for the order.

Line 3 initiates a *for* loop. The three expressions inside the parentheses have these meanings:

- The first expression, *rw=2*, runs once when the loop begins executing. It sets a variable named *rw* to 2. Rows 0 and 1 contain headings, so the first row with a value counting toward the total order price is row 2.

- The second expression, *rw < rows-1*, is a condition that's tested just before each iteration of the loop. The loop stops executing as soon as the condition is false.

  Note that if the table contains six rows, they're numbered 0 through 5. Furthermore, row 5 is the total line and not an order detail. Row 4 is therefore the last row that counts toward the total. The value 4 is less than 6 minus 1, so the loop processes row 4. On the next iteration, *rw* is 5 and that *isn't* less than 6 minus 1; the loop therefore stops.

- The third expression, *++rw*, is a statement that's executed at the end of each pass through the loop. The ++ operator adds one to the variable that follows it—*rw*, in this case.

In line 4, the following expression retrieves any characters contained in cell 5 of row *rw*:

```
document.all.ordTb.rows[rw].cells[5].innerText
```

Nifty, eh? The next couple of lines remove the leading dollar sign (if any), convert what's left to floating point, and add that to the running total. The last

Tip: Hexadecimal color values in CSS can be either 3 or 6 digits, representing either 16 or 256 color levels for each primary color: red, green, and blue. The following color values are therefore equivalent:

background-color: #F00 and
background-color: #FF0000,

background-color: #C0C and
background-color: #CC00CC,

background-color: #009 and
background-color: #000099.

Be warned, however, that three-digit color values aren't valid in ordinary HTML. Coding BGCOLOR="#F00" isn't valid and won't produce bright red, for example.

statement converts the *tot* value to dollars and cents, and then stores it in cell 5 of the last row in the table.

The *bordOn()* and *bordOff()* functions reveal and hide all the table borders; the usual *onDblClick* and *onMouseOut* events are coded on the clothespin that precedes the page title.

Complete HTML Listing

I've run out of things to say so please talk amongst yourselves. I'll give you a topic. It's the full HTML listing.

```
<html>
<head>
<style>
<!--
LI { font-family: Arial, sans-serif; color: #009;}
H1 { font-family: Bauhaus 93, sans-serif ; font-size: 50px;}
TD { font-family: Arial, sans-serif; color: #009;}
TH { font-family: Arial, sans-serif; background-color: #cff;
     border: 1 solid black }
-->
</style>
<script language="JavaScript">
<!--
function ckBrowser(){
   browser = navigator.appName.substring(0,9);
   version = parseInt(navigator.appVersion);
   if ((browser != "Microsoft") || (version < 4)){
     alert("Warning!\n" +
           "This page requries Internet Explorer 4.0.")
   }
}
function addItm(){
```

Define text styles.

Check the browser and display an error message if not Internet Explorer 4 or later.

Start of the routine to add an order row.

Continued from previous page

Get quantity from the list box. If it's less than 1 or not a number, exit with an error message.

```
qty = document.ordFm.txtQty.value;
if ((qty < 1) || isNaN(qty)){
   alert("Please specify a valid quantity.");
   return;
}
```

Get index of selected item, and then the corresponding text.

```
sel = document.ordFm.ddItm.selectedIndex;
itm = document.ordFm.ddItm.options(sel).text;
```

Item list's *value* property contains a price.

```
prc = document.ordFm.ddItm.value;
```

Get index of selected color, and then the corresponding text.

```
sel = document.ordFm.ddClr.selectedIndex;
clr = document.ordFm.ddClr.options(sel).text;
```

Get index of selected size, and then the corresponding text.

```
sel = document.ordFm.ddSiz.selectedIndex;
siz = document.ordFm.ddSiz.options(sel).text;
```

Create a new order row.

```
newRow = document.all.ordTb.insertRow(2);
```

Get the row number of the new row.

```
rowNr = newRow.rowIndex;
```

Insert cell 0, set alignment to right, and display quantity as text.

```
document.all.ordTb.rows[rowNr].insertCell(0);
document.all.ordTb.rows[rowNr].cells[0].style.textAlign
    = "right";
document.all.ordTb.rows[rowNr].cells[0].innerText = qty;
```

Insert cell 1 and display item as text.

```
document.all.ordTb.rows[rowNr].insertCell(1);
document.all.ordTb.rows[rowNr].cells[1].innerText = itm;
```

Insert cell 2 and display color as text.

```
document.all.ordTb.rows[rowNr].insertCell(2);
document.all.ordTb.rows[rowNr].cells[2].innerText = clr;
```

Insert cell 3 and display size as text.

```
document.all.ordTb.rows[rowNr].insertCell(3);
document.all.ordTb.rows[rowNr].cells[3].innerText = siz;
```

Insert cell 4, set alignment to right, and display formatted price as text.

```
document.all.ordTb.rows[rowNr].insertCell(4);
document.all.ordTb.rows[rowNr].cells[4].style.textAlign
    = "right";
document.all.ordTb.rows[rowNr].cells[4].innerText
    = fmtMoney(prc);
```

Insert cell 5, set alignment to right, and display formatted extended price as text.

```
document.all.ordTb.rows[rowNr].insertCell(5);
document.all.ordTb.rows[rowNr].cells[5].style.textAlign
    = "right";
document.all.ordTb.rows[rowNr].cells[5].innerText
    = fmtMoney(qty * prc);
```

Trick 14

Continued from previous page

Get current number of rows in the table.	`rows = document.all.ordTb.rows.length;`
Initialize total order price.	`tot = 0;`
Start loop to examine rows 2 through the last row of the table, minus one.	`for (rw=2; rw < rows-1; ++rw){`
Get extended price for row.	`    rwPrc = document.all.ordTb.rows[rw].cells[5].innerText;`
Remove dollar sign, if present.	`    if (rwPrc.substring(0,1) == "$"){`
	`        rwPrc = rwPrc.substring(1,rwPrc.length);`
Convert extended price for row to floating point, and then add to *tot*.	`    }`
	`    tot = tot + parseFloat(rwPrc);`
End of loop.	`}`
Display total order price in cell 5 of last row.	`document.all.ordTb.rows[rows-1].cells[5].innerText`
	`    = fmtMoney(tot);`
End of routine to add an order row.	`}`
Format a numeric dollar value as currency (dollar sign and two decimals).	`function fmtMoney(amt){`
Convert a fractional dollar amount to whole cents.	`cents = Math.round(amt * 100);`
	`if (cents < 10){`
	`  cents = "$00" + cents;`
	`}else{`
Make value at least three digits and add leading dollar sign.	`  if (cents < 100){`
	`    cents="$0" + cents;`
	`  }else{`
	`    cents="$" + cents;`
	`  }`
	`}`
Insert a decimal point.	`bucks = cents.substring(0,cents.length - 2) + "."`
	`      + cents.substring(cents.length - 2, cents.length);`
Return edited value as the function result.	`return bucks;`
	`}`
	`function bordOn(){`
Make table borders visible.	`  document.all.tab1.border = "2" ;`
	`  document.all.tab2.border = "2" ;`
	`  document.all.ordTb.border = "2" ;`
	`}`

Continued from previous page

```
function bordOff(){
    document.all.tab1.border = "0" ;
    document.all.tab2.border = "0" ;
    document.all.ordTb.border = "0" ;
}
// -->
</script>
<title>Clothes on Line</title>
</head>
<body onload="ckBrowser();">
<h1 align="center">
    <img src="../images/cpin3.gif" alt="Clothes on Line"
        align="absmiddle" width="58" height="59"
        ondblclick="bordOn();"
        onmouseout="bordOff();">
    Clothes
    <img src="../images/cpin1.gif" alt="Clothes on Line"
        align="absmiddle" width="68" height="59">
    on
    <img src="../images/cpin4.gif" alt="Clothes on Line"
        align="absmiddle" width="68" height="59">
    Line
    <img src="../images/cpin2.gif" alt="Clothes on Line"
    align="absmiddle" width="58" height="59"></h1>
<ol>
    <li>Specify Quantity, Item, Color, and Size for each
        item you wish to order.</li>
    <li>Click the Submit button when your order is complete.</li>
</ol>
<table id="tab1" cellpadding="2" cellspacing="0"
            border="0" bordercolor="#009900" >
<tr>
    <td valign="top">
```

Make table borders invisible.

Run the *ckBrowser()* function when the page loads.

Start of page heading.

Run *bordOn()* function, making table borders visible, when the *onDblClick* event occurs.

Run *bordOff()* function, making table borders invisible, when the *onMouseOut* event occurs.

End of page heading.

Display instructions.

Start of overall page layout table.

Continued from previous page

Start of data entry form. ——— `<form name="ordFm">`

Start of data entry layout table. ———
```
<table id="tab2" cellspacing="4" cellpadding="2"
       border="0" bordercolor="#000000">
```

Order entry heading row 1. ———
```
<tr>
  <th colspan="5">Our Items</th>
  <td><img src="../images/trans5x5.gif"
           width="5" height="5"></td>
```

Order entry heading row 2. ———
```
</tr><tr>
  <th>Qty</th>
  <th>Item</th>
  <th>Color</th>
  <th>Size</th>
  <th align="center">Action</th>
  <td> </td>
```

Start of data entry row. ———
```
</tr><tr>
  <td>
```

Quantity box. ———
```
    <input type="text" name="txtQty"
           size="5" value="1"></td>
  <td>
```

Item drop-down list. Value is price, text is description. ———
```
    <select name="ddItm" size="1">
      <option value="30">Backpack</option>
      <option value="5">Bandana</option>
      <option value="12">Hat</option>
      <option value="25">Sweatshirt</option>
      <option value="15">T-Shirt</option>
    </select></td>
  <td>
```

Color drop-down list. ———
```
    <select name="ddClr" size="1">
      <option value="Ash">Ash</option>
      <option value="Black">Black</option>
      <option value="Blue">Blue</option>
      <option value="Green">Green</option>
      <option value="Red">Red</option>
      <option value="White">White</option>
    </select></td>
```

Continued from previous page

Size drop-down list.

```html
<td>
  <select name="ddSiz" size="1">
    <option value="Small">Small</option>
    <option value="Medium">Medium</option>
    <option value="Large">Large</option>
    <option value="X-Large">X-Large</option>
  </select></td>
<td align="center">
```

Order button runs *addItm* script.

```html
  <input type="button" value="Order" name="ordBtn"
         onclick="addItm()"></td>
<td> </td>
```

End of data entry row.

```html
</tr><tr>
<td> </td>
<td> </td>
<td> </td>
<td> </td>
```

Display transparent GIF as spacer for Submit button.

```html
<td><img src="../images/trans5x5.gif"
         width="5" height="20"></td>
<td> </td>
</tr><tr>
```

Display dummy Submit button.

```html
<td> </td>
<td colspan="3" align="right">When done:</td>
<td valign="top" align="center">
  <input type="button" value="Submit" name="subBtn"
         onclick="alert('Sorry, this is just a demo. '
                        + 'Try the mall.');"></td>
<td> </td>
```

End of data entry layout table.

```html
</tr></table>
```

End of data entry form.

```html
</form></td>
```

Start of order table.

```html
<td valign="top">
<table id="ordTb" cellpadding="2" cellspacing="4"
       border="0" bordercolor="#000000">
```

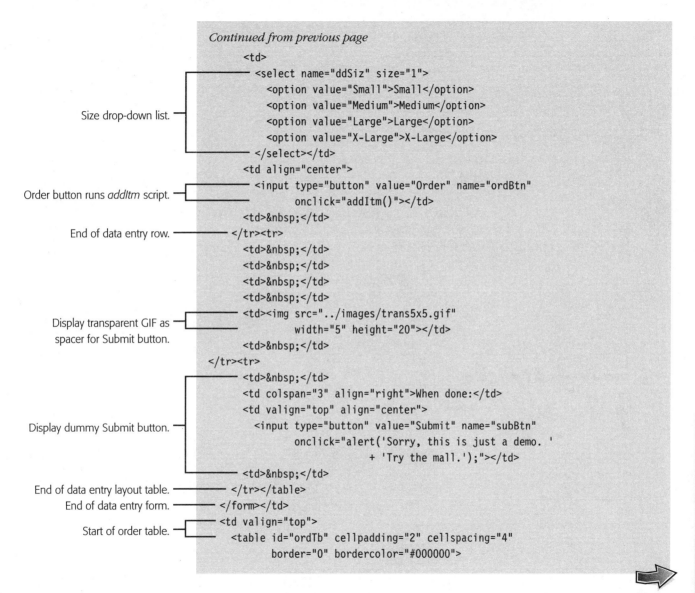

Trick 14

Interacting with Tables   **369**

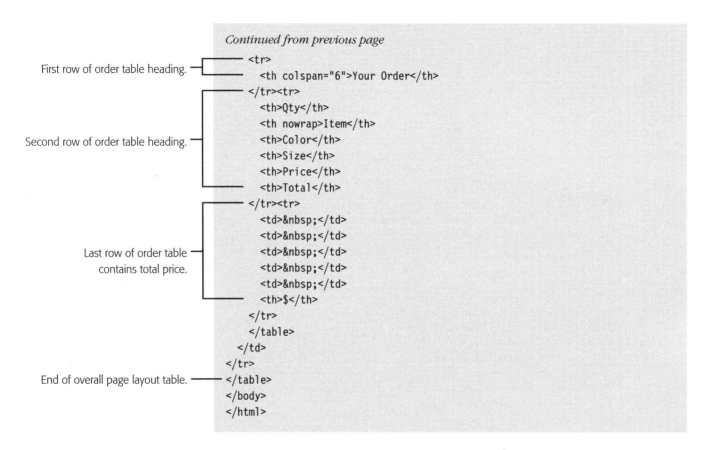

Continued from previous page

First row of order table heading.

Second row of order table heading.

Last row of order table contains total price.

End of overall page layout table.

```
    <tr>
      <th colspan="6">Your Order</th>
    </tr><tr>
      <th>Qty</th>
      <th nowrap>Item</th>
      <th>Color</th>
      <th>Size</th>
      <th>Price</th>
      <th>Total</th>
    </tr><tr>
      <td> </td>
      <td> </td>
      <td> </td>
      <td> </td>
      <td> </td>
      <th>$</th>
    </tr>
    </table>
  </td>
</tr>
</table>
</body>
</html>
```

Very briefly, here are a couple of techniques you'll eventually need if you start mucking around with pages like Clothes on Line. The first pertains to receiving mouse clicks on the table as a whole and then figuring out what row and column were clicked. The following function does this job nicely, and a wonderful thing it is:

```
function ordClick(){
    row = -1;
    col = -1;
```

```
      if ((event.srcElement.tagName == "TD") ||
          (event.srcElement.tagName == "TH")){
          col = event.srcElement.cellIndex;
          row = event.srcElement.parentElement.rowIndex;
      }
      if (event.srcElement.tagName == "TR"){
          row = event.srcElement.rowIndex;
      }
      alert(row + " " + col);
  }
```

You would call this function from an *onClick* attribute in your <TABLE> tag, somewhat like this:

```
<table onclick="ordClick();">
```

When the *ordClick()* function runs, it first initializes the *row* and *col* variables to –1. If these values are still –1 when the routine ends, it'll mean we couldn't figure out the row or the column number, respectively. If the values are 0 or a positive value, it'll mean we discovered good values for them.

Then, we test a property called *event.srcElement.tagName* to see what the user managed to click. Here's how this works:

See Also: To learn more about information the *event* object can provide, refer to Table 9-2, "Common *event* Object Properties."

- The *event* object is a general purpose thingie that gets initialized whenever a browser event occurs. Whenever we're processing something like an *onClick*, for example, it can tell us details about that event.

- The *srcElement* object is a pointer to the object that received the event. For an *onClick* event, it points to the object the user clicked.

- The *tagName* property tells us what kind of HTML tag defined an object. For an *onClick* event associated with a table, the only tag names that seem to come up are <TABLE>, <TD>, and <TH>. I put in code to handle the <TR> tag anyway, though.

If the user clicks a cell—either the <TD> or <TH> type—we can get the cell's position within its row directly, by asking for its *cellIndex* property. A cell doesn't

Hyperlink: For more information about the *event* object, browse:

http://www.microsoft.com/msdn/sdk/ inetsdk/help/dhtml/references/objects/ obj_event.htm

Caution: A table's *cellspacing* property tells the browser to insert blank pixels between adjacent cells. Clicking on these pixels is considered clicking on the table background and not on any particular row or cell. To avoid confusion, try to code *cellspacing=0* in any table where the user will select rows or columns by clicking on cells.

See Also: For an example showing an HTML form and a server-side process actually working together, please refer to the examples in Trick 15, "Enhancing Your Form."

have a *rowIndex* property, though; only its parent, the row element, has that property. That's why the code finds a cell's row number using:

```
event.srcElement.parentElement.rowIndex
```

rather than just:

```
event.srcElement.rowIndex
```

If the user manages to click within a row but not within a cell—and who's to say that's impossible—the code obviously can't get a cell number. It can and does get the row number, however.

The second little nuisance with pages like Clothes on Line is that table contents don't get transmitted to the Web server when the user clicks the Submit button. Here's a brief overview of what you'll need to do:

1. Make sure the <FORM> tag contains a valid ACTION= attribute. This should be a URL that names the ASP page, Perl program, or other server-based program that will process the form submission.

2. If possible, make sure the <FORM> tag contains a METHOD="POST" attribute as well. Transmitting an entire table can involve a lot of data: more data than the GET method can cope with. Only code METHOD="GET" if the server-side program can't accept anything else.

3. Don't include a normal Submit button in the form. Nothing like this, for example:

```
<input type="submit" value="Submit">
```

4. Do include a button that runs a script, such as the following:

```
<input type="button" value="Submit" onclick="submitMe()">
```

5. In the script, copy all the table values to hidden form fields. A hidden field is invisible to the user, of course, but gets transmitted to the server just the same. This HTML creates a hidden form field named *tabData:*

```
<input type="hidden" name=" tabData" value="secret">
```

You can use one form field for the entire table or one form field per cell. Here's what the *submitMe()* function looks like if one hidden form field named *tabData* transmits the entire table *tb01:*

```
function submitMe(){
  val = "";
  for (row = 0; row < document.all.tb01.rows.length; row++){
    for (col = 0; col < document.all.tb01.rows[row].cells.length; col++){
      cellid = "r" + row + "c" + col;
      celltx = document.all.tb01.rows[row].cells[col].innerText;
      val = val + cellid + "=" + celltx  + ",";
    }
  }
  document.all.tabData.value=val;
  document.fm01.submit()
}
```

The first statement initializes a variable named *val* to nothing; this will receive all the values in the table. Statements 2 and 3 loop through all the row and cell numbers in the table. Statement four builds an identifier for the cell (of the form *r1c2* for row 1, column 2). The fifth statement copies the value of the current cell into a variable named *celltx*, and the sixth appends *"cellid=celltx"* to the *val* string. The last two statements copy the entire *val* string to the hidden form field *tabData* and then submit the form.

Alternatively, you can create a new form field for each table cell. Here's another version of the *submitMe()* function that does this:

```
function submitMe(){
for (row = 0; row < document.all.tb01.rows.length; row++){
    for (col = 0; col < document.all.tb01.rows[row].cells.length; col++){
      cellid = "r" + row + "c" + col;
      celltx = document.all.tb01.rows[row].cells[col].innerText;
      document.all.pg01.insertAdjacentHTML("beforeEnd",
        "<input type=hidden name=" + cellid + " value='" + celltx + "'>");
      }
  }
  document.fm01.submit()
}
```

The three statements that define, extend, and store the variable *val* are missing from this version; in their place is a rather lengthy statement that uses the *insertAdjacentHTML* method to create hidden form fields on the fly. The name *pg01* is the id of a paragraph inside the HTML form, a paragraph defined like this:

```
<P ID="pg01"> </P>
```

The *insertAdjacentHTML* method takes two arguments: a position and some HTML. Specifying *"beforeEnd"* for the first argument means the new HTML will go just in front of *pg01*'s closing tag: that is, just before </P>. The second argument supplies HTML like this:

```
<input type=hidden name=cellid value='celltx'>
```

Well, that's all there is to it. All you need now is to start your own apparel business.

Enhancing Your Forms

It's inevitable, you know. Every release of every browser contains a few new tags that are useful, attractive, not exactly standard, but at least harmless to browsers that don't support them. True to its class, Microsoft Internet Explorer 4.0 introduced a number of these tags, and this, being a book of tricks, just can't pass them up. So there. Here's a list of what we'll cover, and a wonderful list it is:

- **Access Keys**—This feature provides a way to associate Alt plus *key* combinations with a given field on a form. Pressing that key combination jumps to that form field.

- **Advisory Text**—Modern user interfaces like Microsoft Windows invariably describe interface elements by displaying tool tips, help balloons, or other little bits of text when the mouse hovers over them. Browsers do this too, but until now, only for images. The advisory text feature provides tool tip messages for any element on a Web page.

- **Button Element**—Ordinary Web push buttons are boring. If you want anything more than simple text on the button face, you're out of luck. IE's new button element can display anything you can describe with HTML—formatted text, images, lists, tables, animations, anything!

- **Disabling Controls**—It often happens that the value of one form field controls whether a user should enter data in another field. Turning on a field's *disabled* property supports this by dimming the field's display and inhibiting input. Turning it off does the opposite.

- **Fieldset Element**—Until now, HTML hasn't provided a way to draw those boxes that usually surround groups of related elements—groups of radio buttons, check boxes, related fields, whatever. Well, the advent of the fieldset element changes all that.

- **Graphic Bullets**—This isn't a form enhancement and it's an official CSS feature, but it's cool nevertheless. Basically, you can define images, rather than text characters, as the bullets in an ordinary unnumbered list.

- **Labels**—In most user interfaces, clicking on a field's label is the same as clicking on the field itself. Clicking on a radio button's description activates the radio button, for example. IE's new <LABEL> tag associates a field's descriptive text with the field itself in just this way.

If these exciting new features don't take your breath away, try this: I've constructed a single Web page that incorporates them all. Not only that, but it's legible and it actually works—even in Netscape Navigator, albeit lacking the features Netscape doesn't support. Yeah, I know, applause, applause. Thank you, thank you, you really needn't. Well, OK.

Mountain O' Mail, Inc.

Aren't you just panting to see this marvel of advanced trickery with your very own eyes? Sure you are. The best approach is probably to load up the *trick15/mountain.htm* file in your browser, but a reasonable facsimile appears in Figure 15-1.

The *graphic bullets*, of course, are the four little envelope icons that appear along the left margin. There are four *fieldsets*, identified by the legends Sign Up Here, Type of Mail, Your Status, and Your Net Worth. The text next to each check box, radio button, and text box is designated a *label* of its corresponding form element, so clicking on the text is the same as clicking on the element.

As indicated by the underlined E in Email Address, this field has an access key: Alt-E. Pressing this key combination instantly gives focus to the Email Address field. The pop-up text "Click here if you're a geek" is *advisory text* that appears for a few seconds whenever the mouse comes to rest over the Programmer label. The text box just below the Over $100,000 label is *enabled*—capable

Tip: Having focus means that a form field is currently selected, contains the active cursor, will receive any keystrokes, yada, yada, yada. Only one field at a time can have the focus. Fields get the focus when the user clicks on them, tabs to them, or types their associated access key. To set focus on a field from code, use the *setFocus* method on that field.

FIGURE 15-1. *This page makes use of CSS graphic bullets plus several IE4 enhancements related to HTML forms.*

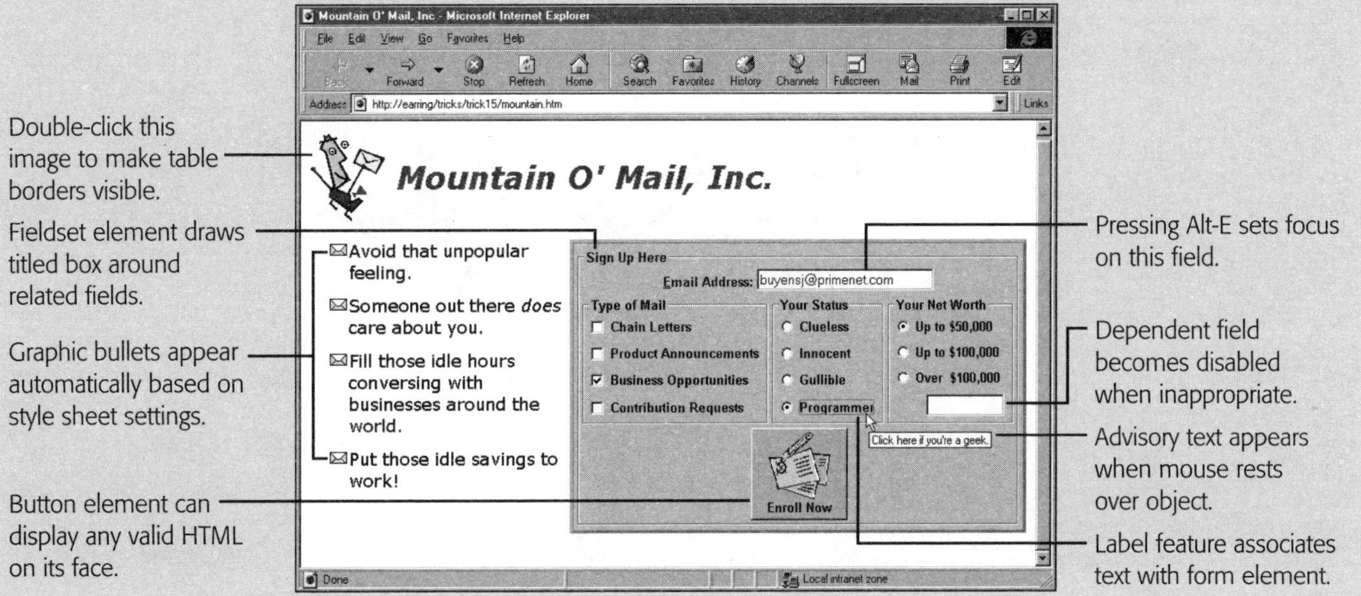

Double-click this image to make table borders visible.

Fieldset element draws titled box around related fields.

Graphic bullets appear automatically based on style sheet settings.

Button element can display any valid HTML on its face.

Pressing Alt-E sets focus on this field.

Dependent field becomes disabled when inappropriate.

Advisory text appears when mouse rests over object.

Label feature associates text with form element.

Note: Notice the dotted line, indicating focus, that surrounds the Programmer label in Figure 15-1. This appears because the browser considers the label text and its associated control as one selectable unit. In other forms in this book, such as Ahab's Anchor Asylum and Coffee Break Deli, the focus lines surround only the control.

of receiving input—only when that radio button is selected. In any other case, it's grayed out, incapable of receiving the focus, and incapable of receiving input. In short, it's *disabled*.

The Enroll Now button contains an image, something ordinary HTML push buttons can't do. This is an example of IE4's new button element, which, on the face of it (so to speak), can display any valid HTML.

Page Layout Details

Six HTML tables organize the Mountain O' Mail page. The largest contains only one row and two cells. Of these, the left cell contains the bullet list and the right one the entire form layout.

Tip: To see all six tables in the Mountain O' Mail page, open it with Internet Explorer and double-click the mail carrier in the upper-left corner.

The five remaining tables are all within the form layout. The outermost of these, a one-row, one-column job, provides the beveled outline, the gray background, and nothing else. The next table is three rows by three columns, and it fits just inside the Sign Up Here fieldset. In rows 1 and 3 all three cells are merged, so the Email Address arrangement and the Enroll Now button can be centered. The last three tables organize the form controls and labels within the Type of Mail, Your Status, and Your Net Worth fieldsets.

Graphic Bullets

The code that defines the graphic bullets appears within a style sheet in the <HEAD> section:

```
LI { list-style-image: url(../images/envelope.gif) ;
     text-indent: -4px ; margin-bottom: 12px; }
```

Assigning this style to the type LI assigns it to every <LI> (list item) tag on the page. This is fine for the Mountain O' Mail page, because there's only one list. If there were several lists, and each were to have different bullets, we could've defined a class instead and coded the CLASS= attribute within each <LI> tag.

Tip: The *text-indent* CSS property controls the indentation of the first line of a paragraph. Positive values indent the first line (like normal text paragraphs) and negative values outdent the first line (like numbered or bulleted lists).

As you can see, specifying the bullet image is no big deal. Just code *list-style-image: url()* within the style sheet, inserting the image's location between the parentheses. This is very cool except for two disgusting little details. First, you might think the browser would automatically indent the list items based on the width of the image. Well, I'm sorry, but no; it uses the same indentation it would for a character bullet. That's why I had to code *text-indent: -4px* in the sample code: to manually override the default indentation.

Tip: If a browser doesn't support graphic bullets, it simply ignores the *list-style-image* CSS property and displays ordinary text bullets instead.

The second disgusting little detail pertains to image positioning. You can't. The browser aligns the bottom of the image with the bottom of the first line of text, and your choices are basically like it or lump it. Any changes you make will have to modify the image itself: enlarging it, shrinking it, adding transparent pixels to the top, bottom, or sides. But all these are image editor changes, not flexibility within CSS. Oh well, maybe next release.

The Fieldset Element

Defining a fieldset is simplicity itself; just surround the desired content with a <FIELDSET>…</FIELDSET> tag pair. (These are new tags introduced with IE4.) This draws the familiar user interface box around the enclosed area. To provide a visible title, enclose the desired text within two more new tags, <LEGEND> and </LEGEND>, somewhere within the fieldset. Here's an example:

```
<fieldset>
<legend>Visible Title Text Goes Here</legend>
    <!-- Enclosed content goes here -->
</fieldset>
```

 Tip: If a browser doesn't support the <FIELDSET> and <LEGEND> tags, it just ignores them. Any text that appears between <LEGEND> and </LEGEND> will then, of course, appear as normal text; the browser ignores the tags but not the content between them.

All this is very cool except for two more of those disgusting little, um, details. First, a fieldset doesn't minimize its width the way a table cell does. Take the case of a paragraph containing one word, for example. The browser considers the paragraph as wide as the entire browser window, as you can see by giving the paragraph a background color. The background extends all the way from the browser's left margin to its right. If you put the same one-word paragraph inside a table cell, however, it's only as wide as the one word.

If you have a couple of form fields, not in a table but snuggled against the left margin, you might think that a fieldset enclosing them might be just wide enough to enclose the widest visible content. Think again; you'll almost certainly find that the fieldset extends all the way across the page. Fortunately, the solution is simple; put the fieldset inside a table cell and *then* put your content inside the fieldset.

The other nasty nuisance with fieldsets pertains to background colors. You might expect that a fieldset's background color would only apply to its interior. Ah, but no; it also applies to the area just outside the visible box, and because there's no border around the outer area, this tends to give the fieldset a rather unfinished look. Again, the solution is relatively simple; put the fieldset inside something that does provide an order border, such as the ubiquitous table cell. This is another reason why, in the Mountain O' Mail page, the Sign Up Here fieldset appears within a table cell.

A third detail, but not so disgusting, involves the height of the three side-by-side fieldsets: Type of Mail, Your Status, and Your Net Worth. These areas aren't naturally the same size, and therefore, lacking any other correction, their bottom

Caution: Transparent GIFs are great for reserving white space in a Web page, but they only guarantee minimum dimensions, not maximum ones. Suppose, for example, a transparent image 100 pixels wide and some other content are in the same container—a table cell, perhaps. The image guarantees the container will never be narrower than 100 pixels, but it can't stop the other content from making the container wider. This is a difficult problem because the size of those content elements may be outside your control: the browser's windows size and various font sizes, for example. The more oversize your transparent GIF, the less likely these uncontrollable factors will affect your layout, but the more excess white space you will have. The trade-off is a judgment call you'll have to decide for yourself.

Tip: Browsers that don't support the <LABEL> and </LABEL> tags will simply ignore them. Any content between those tags will, of course, appear as normal text.

edges wouldn't align evenly. Ugly, ugly, ugly. The correction I chose is my old favorite, the transparent GIF file. The layout table within each fieldset contains an extra column at the right, a column of one cell vertically spanning all four rows. That cell contains a transparent GIF file sized 1 pixel wide and 105 pixels high. The 105 pixels just slightly exceeds the natural height of all three tables, and thus expands each table to the same height. This, in turn, makes each fieldset the same height. Beautiful, beautiful, beautiful.

Form Field Labels

Next up: form field labels. Here are the steps to associate text or any other content as the label of a form field:

1. Identify the form field by coding an ID= attribute within the tag that defines it.

2. Enclose the label content within <LABEL> and </LABEL> tags.

3. Within the <LABEL> tag, code a FOR= attribute specifying the ID you assigned in step 1.

This isn't hard, just repetitious. There are twelve repetitions in the Mountain O' Mail page: one for each check box, one for each radio button, and one for the Email Address check box. Is that pumped or what? Here's a typical example, taken out of context for the sake of simplicity:

```
<input type="checkbox" value="ON" name="ckChain" id="idChain">
<label for="idChain">Chain Letters</label>
```

Access Keys

An access key immediately shifts focus to a designated field. We've already mentioned, for example, that on the Mountain O' Mail page, pressing Alt-E sets focus on the Email Address field. This requires nothing more than the following attribute added within the <INPUT> tag that defines the text box:

```
accesskey="e"
```

Naturally, defining access key shortcuts accomplishes nothing if the user doesn't know they exist. Duh. The normal way of communicating this information is to underline the corresponding character in the field's title and, if you look closely, you'll see that, sure enough, the leading E in Email Address is underlined.

Caution: Access keys defined in a Web page override the browser's normal access key functions. Assigning Alt-E to a form field overrides the browser's normal Alt-E processing, namely opening the Edit menu. (The user can still open the Edit menu by using either the mouse or Alt plus the arrow keys, of course.)

Tip: If you require more precise logic to control underlining, consider passing the text to a Java-Script function that (1) conditionally writes a <U> tag, (2) writes the passed text, and then (3) conditionally writes a </U> tag.

Unfortunately, this isn't automatic; you have to perform the underlining your-self, and this turns out to be trickier than you might have thought.

The simplest way to underline a character is to start and stop underlining with the venerable <U> and </U> tags. Unfortunately, this approach displays the underline even for browsers that don't support the *accesskey* property. Users would see the underline, press the Alt plus *key* combination, get no results, com-plain bitterly, go away, and never be seen again. (OK, maybe in a couple of years, but that's still bad.)

The Mountain O' Mail page illustrates a simple four-step solution to the access key underlining dilemma:

- It marks the "E" in Email Address with <SPAN> and </SPAN> tags.

- It assigns a CSS class named *ND* to this span.

- A style sheet in the <HEAD> section assigns the *text-decoration: underline* property to the *ND* class.

- A subsequent, disabled style sheet overrides the *ND* class with *text-decoration: none*.

Internet Explorer supports both the ACCESSKEY attribute and the *disabled* style sheet property. Supporting the *disabled* property means IE *won't* apply the override in step 4. This means the styles from step 3 will prevail and any text flagged <SPAN CLASS=ND> *will* be underlined.

Netscape Navigator ignores both the ACCESSKEY attribute and the *disabled* style sheet property. Ignoring the *disabled* property means Netscape *will* apply the override in step 4, and any text flagged <SPAN CLASS=ND> *won't* be underlined. Here's some code that illustrates the entire process, again simplified a bit for clarity:

```
<style>
.nd { text-decoration: underline; }
</style>
<style disabled>
.nd { text-decoration: none; }
</style>
    <!-- other content -->
<span class="nd">E</span>-Mail Address:
<input type="text" size="25" name="email"
        accesskey="e">
```

Advisory Text

Advisory text is refreshingly simple and free of disgusting little details. All you have to do is code a TITLE= attribute within the tag that defines any object on the Web page. Whenever the mouse comes to rest over that object (such as the table row defined in the following code) the browser displays the title text as a tool tip (or whatever the user's operating system provides as an alternative). Here's that snippet:

```
<tr title="Enter your Email address here.">
```

Disabled Controls

Tip: The *disabled* property is most useful with form fields that are sometimes inappropriate to enter. A set of radio buttons with an Other choice provides a common example. There's usually a text box associated with the Other choice—a text box that should be disabled unless the user actually chooses Other.

A form element's *disabled* property controls whether or not the field can accept input. As shown below, you can set a field's status to disabled by coding the keyword *disabled* as a tag attribute:

```
<input type="text" name="txt999" size="10" disabled>
```

This is cool but, in and of itself, useless. If the field's always going to be disabled, why display it at all? No, the strength of the *disabled* attribute lies in controlling it from code. When conditions make a given form field irrelevant, you can turn its *disabled* attribute on. When the same field becomes relevant, you can turn its *disabled* attribute off. Here's the statement that turns off the *disabled* property we just defined. Note that *txt999* is the form element's name attribute:

```
document.all.txt999.disabled = 0;
```

Caution: Don't try to modify the *disabled* property if the browser is Netscape Navigator 4 or below; the result is a highly visible error message. Any code that modifies the *disabled* property should first check the browser type.

Typically, you'd include such statements in scripts triggered by element events— *onClick*, *onBlur*, whatever. The statement to turn on disabled status looks just the same, except that it assigns a value of –1.

The Button Element

IE4's new <BUTTON> element provides much more flexibility than a traditional HTML push button. Traditional push buttons are defined by a single tag, an example of which follows:.

```
<input type="button" value="Submit" name="btnEnroll"
       onclick="subForm();">
```

The VALUE= attribute specifies the text that will appear on the button face, and this is just about all the flexibility you get.

Defining the new Button element requires two tags, <BUTTON> and </BUTTON>:

- Attributes that belong to the button as a whole, such as the *name*, *id*, *title*, and *onClick* settings, go inside the <BUTTON> tag.

- Any content you put between the <BUTTON> and </BUTTON> tags appears on the button face.

Here's an example:

```
<button title="Enroll Now" onclick="subForm();">
  <img src="../images/postcrds.gif" align="absmiddle"
      width="66" height="70"><br>
  Enroll Now
  <input type="button" value="Submit" name="btnEnroll"
      onclick="subForm();">
</button>
```

OK, what's wrong with this code? Tip: look at the third and second lines from the bottom; we've got a button within a button here! It's pandemonium in our network! Call the HTML police right away!

Actually, there's a logical explanation. Phew. If a page containing this code gets displayed by a browser that doesn't support the <BUTTON> tag, here's what happens:

- The <BUTTON> and </BUTTON> tags get ignored.

- Everything between those tags, including any <INPUT TYPE="BUTTON"> tags, gets displayed as normal content.

When a browser that *does* support the <BUTTON> tag displays the same code:

- Everything between the <BUTTON> and </BUTTON> tags get displayed on the button face.

- Any <INPUT TYPE="BUTTON"> tags get ignored.

Note: Technically, a browser should never ignore an HTML tag from a previous version, but if you don't tell neither will I.

In short, by coding an old-style button within each new-style button, you ensure that exactly one button will appear no matter what.

More Scripting Techniques

The Mountain O' Mail page contains two more crafty bits so tricky they're invisible. First, the *onBlur* event for each text box runs a routine that eliminates spaces from the entered text. Here's the function, short and sweet:

```
function packText(tbox){
  while (tbox.value.indexOf(" ") >= 0){
    tbox.value =
        tbox.value.replace(" ","");
  }
}
```

To understand the *tbox* argument you must understand how the function itself is called. The <INPUT> tag for each text box contains the following code:

```
onblur="packText(this)"
```

Coding *this* within any tag refers to that tag. Each browser does this in its own way, but that's actually what we want. Who cares about Document Object Models when we can just say *this* and get a valid reference? To make the value of *this* available to a function outside the tag, we pass *this* as an argument. Very elegant, don't you agree?

The function itself runs a *while* loop as long as the text box's value contains at least one space. Within each iteration of the loop, the function replaces the value's first space with nothing. And so it goes until no more spaces remain. *Voilà!*

See Also: The next section in this trick, "You Sent It! We Got It!" presents a simple server-side script that processes data from the Mountain O' Mail page.

Submission and Other Pastimes

When the user submits an HTML form, the browser does three things. It:

1. Assembles the names and values of all form fields using one of two methods—GET or POST—whatever the program in step 2 requires.

2. Specifies the name of a script or program that'll run on the Web server.

3. Transmits these items to the Web server. The Web server runs the program named in step 2, which performs whatever actions the application demands (including sending HTML back to the user).

Note that the program or script that processes your data must *already be on the server*. Furthermore, the server must know it's an executable script or program rather than just another text file or Web page. And finally, whatever that script or program does—send mail, append to a file, update a database, stop on a dime, or give nine cents change—the Web server's security system must permit it.

Many service providers have preinstalled, approved, documented server-side programs available to all users for common tasks. Custom server-side processing obviously requires the cooperation of the Web server's administrator.

The second behind-the-scenes tricky bit occurs when the user clicks whichever button is visible. Neither button submits the HTML form directly; instead, both have *onClick* attributes that run a function called *subForm()*. The *subForm()* function first checks to see whether the Email Address field is blank; if so, the script displays an error message and dies its own personal form of untimely death. If the Email Address contains data, the script displays a warning prompt and then, unless the user strikes Cancel, submits the form.

 Tip: The destination of an HTML form appears in the <FORM> tag, not in the TYPE=SUBMIT button and not in its scripting equivalent, the *submit()* method.

Netscape Navigator Compatibility

I suppose by now you think we've hacked up this simple HTML form so badly that there's no chance of it working with Netscape Navigator. *Au contraire*, it not only displays OK but works just fine. For the proof take a look at Figure 15-2. It's almost scary.

Figure 15-2 looks a bit plain compared to Figure 15-1 but this is expected; Netscape just doesn't have all the IE-specific features we used. Still, despite occasionally having different code for different browsers, it proves you can enhance your site for IE4 users without degrading it for Netscape users.

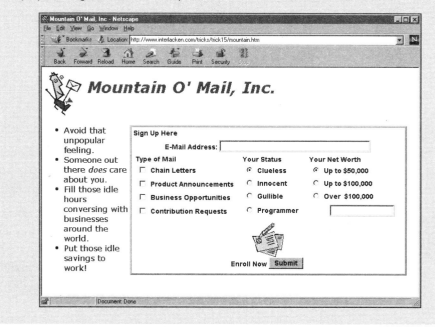

FIGURE 15-2. *Netscape Navigator displays the same page Internet Explorer displayed in Figure 15-1. The IE-specific enhancements, of course, are absent.*

Complete HTML Listing

Life is more than good; it's improving! Fantastic, in fact. Look, here comes the full HTML listing now.

```
<html>
<head>
<title>Mountain O' Mail, Inc</title>
<style>
<!--
```

Continued from previous page

Define style for heading text.

```
H1 { font-family: Verdana, sans-serif;
     font-style: italic; color: #33f; }
```

Define style for unnumbered list. Note bullet image and layout adjustments.

```
LI { list-style-image: url(../images/envelope.gif) ;
     text-indent: -4px ; margin-bottom: 12px; }
```

Define style for the button face.

```
BUTTON { font-family: Arial, san-serif; font-weight:bold; }
```

Define styles for table cells.

```
TD { font-family: Arial, san-serif; font-weight:bold;
     font-size: 80%; }
TH { font-family: Verdana, sans-serif ; font-weight: normal;
     font-size: 110% ;}
```

Define background color for the HTML form.

```
.dialog { background-color: #CCC; }
```

Define underlining for the access key.

```
.nd { text-decoration: underline; }
-->
</style>
<style disabled>
<!--
    LI { text-indent: 0 ; margin-bottom: 0; }
    UL { font-size: 70% }
.dialog { background-color: white; }
   .nd { text-decoration: none; }
-->
</style>
```

Override styles if the browser is Netscape. (Netscape ignores disabled attribute in <STYLE> tag.)

```
<script language="JavaScript">
<!--
function disab999(){
  if (navigator.appName.substring(0,9) == "Microsoft"){
    document.all.txt999.disabled = -1;
  }
}
```

Create function to disable Over $100,000 text box.

```
function enab999(){
  if (navigator.appName.substring(0,9) == "Microsoft"){
    document.all.txt999.disabled = 0;
  }
}
```

Create function to enable Over $100,000 text box.

Trick 15

Continued from previous page

Create function to remove spaces from a text box value.

```
function packText(tbox){
    while (tbox.value.indexOf(" ") >= 0){
        tbox.value =
            tbox.value.replace(" ","");
    }
}
```

Start of Submit function.

```
function subForm(){
```

Point *fld* variable at the email field (as named in each browser).

```
    if (navigator.appName.substring(0,9) == "Microsoft"){
        fld = document.all.email;
    }else{
        fld = document.frm1.email;
    }
```

If the email field is blank, display an error message, put the cursor in the email field, and then exit.

```
    if (fld.value == ""){
        alert("Email Address missing!");
        fld.focus();
        return;
    }
```

Warn the user that Submit won't work if his or her Web server isn't configured.

```
    ans = confirm(
        "This is only going to work if:\n\n" +
        "(1) You're using a Microsoft Web Server.\n" +
        "(2) Active Server Pages are installed.\n" +
        "(3) ../exec/trick15/confirm.asp is present.\n" +
        "(4) ../exec/trick15/confirm.asp is executable.\n\n" +
        "Continue?");
```

Submit form if the user clicked OK.

```
    if (ans){
        document.frm1.submit();
    }
```

End of Submit function.

```
}
```

Reveal table borders.

```
function bordOn(){
    document.all.tab1.border = "2" ;
    document.all.tab2.border = "2" ;
    document.all.tab3.border = "2" ;
    document.all.tab4.border = "2" ;
    document.all.tab5.border = "2" ;
}
```

Continued from previous page

Hide table borders.

```
function bordOff(){
    document.all.tab1.border = "0" ;
    document.all.tab2.border = "0" ;
    document.all.tab3.border = "0" ;
    document.all.tab4.border = "0" ;
    document.all.tab5.border = "0" ;
}
// -->
</script>
</head>
<body bgcolor="#FFFFFF">
```

Start of page heading.
Make table borders visible when
visitor double-clicks image.
Make table borders invisible when
visitor moves mouse off image.
End of page heading.
Start of overall page layout table.

```
<h1>
    <img src="../images/dlvrlttr.gif" alt="Mountain O' Mail"
        align="absmiddle" width="78" height="91"
            ondblclick="bordOn();"
            onmouseout="bordOff();">
    Mountain O' Mail, Inc.</h1>
<table id="tab1" cellpadding="0" cellspacing="0"
        border="0" bordercolor="#000000">
<tr>
    <th align="left" valign="top">
```

Unnumbered list gets
bullets from LI style sheet.

```
    <ul>
    <li>Avoid that unpopular feeling.</li>
    <li>Someone out there <em>does</em> cares about you.</li>
    <li>Fill those idle hours conversing
        with businesses around the world.</li>
    <li>Put those idle savings to work!</li></ul></th>
```

Start of HTML form. Note URL
in *action* property.
Start of one-celled table that
provides form border.
CSS class *"dialog"* controls
background color.

```
    <td valign="top">
    <form name=frm1 method="POST" action="../exec/trick15/confirm.asp">
    <table border="3" cellpadding="4" cellspacing="0">
    <tr>
    <td class="dialog">
```

Continued from previous page

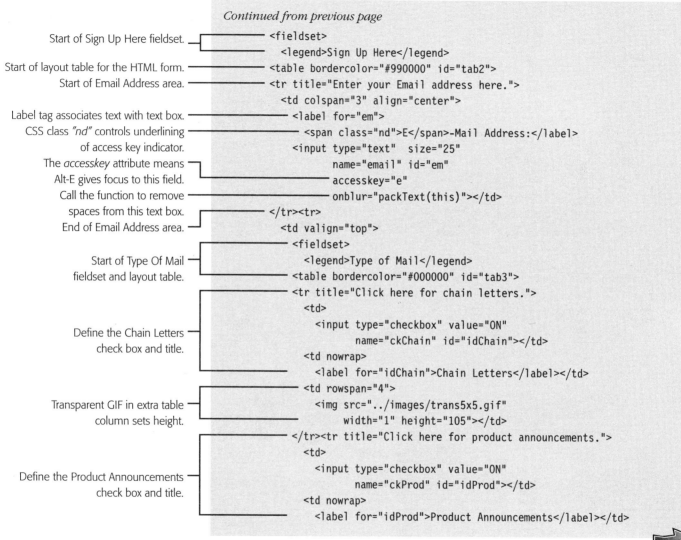

Start of Sign Up Here fieldset.
```
<fieldset>
   <legend>Sign Up Here</legend>
```

Start of layout table for the HTML form.
```
<table bordercolor="#990000" id="tab2">
```

Start of Email Address area.
```
<tr title="Enter your Email address here.">
   <td colspan="3" align="center">
```

Label tag associates text with text box.
```
   <label for="em">
```

CSS class *"nd"* controls underlining of access key indicator.
```
   <span class="nd">E</span>-Mail Address:</label>
<input type="text"  size="25"
```

The *accesskey* attribute means Alt-E gives focus to this field.
```
      name="email" id="em"
      accesskey="e"
```

Call the function to remove spaces from this text box.
```
      onblur="packText(this)"></td>
```

End of Email Address area.
```
</tr><tr>
   <td valign="top">
```

Start of Type Of Mail fieldset and layout table.
```
   <fieldset>
      <legend>Type of Mail</legend>
   <table bordercolor="#000000" id="tab3">
```

```
   <tr title="Click here for chain letters.">
      <td>
```

Define the Chain Letters check box and title.
```
         <input type="checkbox" value="ON"
               name="ckChain" id="idChain"></td>
      <td nowrap>
         <label for="idChain">Chain Letters</label></td>
```

Transparent GIF in extra table column sets height.
```
      <td rowspan="4">
         <img src="../images/trans5x5.gif"
               width="1" height="105"></td>
```

```
   </tr><tr title="Click here for product announcements.">
      <td>
```

Define the Product Announcements check box and title.
```
         <input type="checkbox" value="ON"
               name="ckProd" id="idProd"></td>
      <td nowrap>
         <label for="idProd">Product Announcements</label></td>
```

Continued from previous page

Define the Business Opportunities
check box and title.

```
</tr><tr title="Click here for business opportunities.">
  <td><input type="checkbox" value="ON"
              name="ckBus" id="idBus"></td>
  <td nowrap>
    <label for="idBus">Business Opportunities</label></td>
```

Define the Contribution
requests check box and title.

```
</tr><tr title="Click here for contribution requests.">
  <td>
    <input type="checkbox" value="ON"
            name="ckCont" id="idCont" ></td>
  <td nowrap>
    <label for="idCont">Contribution Requests</label></td>
```

End of Type Of Mail layout
table and fieldset.

```
</table>
</fieldset></td>
<td valign="top">
```

Start of Your Status fieldset
and layout table.

```
<fieldset>
  <legend>Your Status</legend>
<table bordercolor="#000000" id="tab4">
```

Define the Clueless radio button and title.

```
<tr title="Click here if you lack clues.">
  <td>
    <input type="radio" value="clueless" checked
            name="status" id="idClue"></td>
  <td nowrap>
    <label for="idClue">Clueless</label></td>
```

Transparent GIF in extra
table column sets height.

```
<td rowspan="4">
  <img src="../images/trans5x5.gif"
          width="1" height="105"></td>
```

Define the Innocent radio button and title.

```
</tr><tr title="Click here if you're never suspicious.">
  <td>
    <input type="radio" value="innocent"
            name="status" id="idInno"></td>
  <td nowrap>
    <label for="idInno">Innocent</label></td>
```

Trick 15

Continued from previous page

Define the Gullible radio button and title.

```html
</tr><tr title="Click here if you're easily deceived.">
    <td>
        <input type="radio" value="gullible"
                name="status" id="idGull"></td>
    <td nowrap>
        <label for="idGull">Gullible</label></td>
```

Define the Programmer radio button and title.

```html
</tr><tr title="Click here if you're a geek.">
    <td>
        <input type="radio" value="programmer"
                name="status" id="idProg"></td>
    <td nowrap>
        <label for="idProg">Programmer</label>
        </td></tr>
```

End of Your Status layout table and fieldset.

```html
</table>
</fieldset></td>
<td valign="top">
```

Start of Your Net Worth fieldset and layout table.

```html
<fieldset>
    <legend>Your Net Worth</legend>
<table bordercolor="#000000" id="tab5">
```

Define the Up To $50,000 radio button and title.

```html
<tr title="Click here for assets up to $50,000.">
    <td>
        <input type="radio" value="to50k" checked
                name="worth" id="id50k"
                onclick="disab999();"></td>
    <td nowrap>
        <label for="id50k">Up to $50,000</label></td>
```

Transparent GIF in extra table column sets height.

```html
    <td rowspan="4">
        <img src="../images/trans5x5.gif"
            width="1" height="105"></td>
```

Define the Up To $100,000 radio button and title.

```html
</tr><tr title="Click here for assets $50,001 to $100,000.">
    <td>
        <input type="radio" value="to100k"
                name="worth" id="id100k"
                onclick="disab999()"></td>
```

Continued from previous page

```
                                <td onclick=" disab999();" nowrap>
                                    <label for="id100k">Up to $100,000</label></td>
                            </tr><tr title="Click here for assets over $100,000.">
                                <td>
                                    <input type="radio" value="to999k"
                                            name="worth" id="id999k"
                                            onclick="enab999();"></td>
                                <td onclick="enab999();" nowrap>
                                    <label for="id999k">Over  $100,000</label></td>
                            </tr><tr title="Enter net worth if over $100,000.">
                                <td> </td>
                                <td nowrap>  
                                    <input type="text" name="txt999" size="10" disabled
                                        onblur="packText(this)"></td></tr>
                            </table>
                            </fieldset></td>
                        </tr><tr>
                            <td colspan="3" align="center">
                            <button title="Enroll Now" onclick="subForm();">
                                <img src="../images/postcrds.gif" align="absmiddle"
                                        width="66" height="70"><br>
                                Enroll Now
                                <input type="button" value="Submit" name="btnEnroll"
                                        onclick="subForm();">
                            </button></td>
                        </tr>
                        </table>
                    </fieldset></td></tr>
                </table>
            </form>
            </td>
        </tr>
    </table>
    </body>
</html>
```

Define the Over $100,000 radio button and title.

Define the text box for Over $100,000 amount.

Call the function to remove spaces from this text box.

End of Your Net Worth layout table and fieldset.

Start of IE4 Button object.

Provide standard button for browsers that don't understand IE's Button object.

End of IE4 Button object.

End of layout table for the HTML form.

End of Sign Up Here fieldset.

End of one-celled table that provides form border.

End of HTML form.

End of overall page layout table.

A common question regarding browser-specific features is whether to use them at all. If they don't work the same for everyone, the reasoning goes, why bother? Another question though, equally valid, is why hold back some users if enhancing their experience involves no degradation for the others? If your goal is to provide the highest quality experience for every Web visitor, taking full advantage of browser features is a must.

Dynamic Style Sheets in Internet Explorer

If your memory is keen, you'll remember several examples that used disabled style sheets to provide different CSS settings under Internet Explorer and Netscape Navigator. Basically, the approach was this:

- Code up a style sheet that's correct from an Internet Explorer point of view.

- Create a second style sheet that contains any overrides needed for Netscape Navigator, taking care to include the DISABLED keyword inside the <STYLE> tag.

Internet Explorer ignores any style sheet coded <STYLE DISABLED>, but Netscape (at least through version 4) processes such style sheets normally. Therefore, any overrides you put in a disabled style sheet apply only to Netscape.

This approach has two big advantages. First, it doesn't required any JavaScript coding: of HTML, CSS, and JavaScript, you only have to know the first two. Second, it works.

Enquiring minds want to know, however, what will happen if Netscape Navigator ever starts honoring the DISABLED attribute (as the World Wide Web consortium says it should). Also, using a disabled style sheet doesn't permit calculating style properties at runtime—choosing different sizes depending on the size of the browser window, for example.

Internet Explorer supports dynamic styles in a very powerful way:

- The *document* object has a *styleSheets* collection that represents each <STYLE> tag in the document. You can access a particular style sheet numerically, as in *document.styleSheets[0]* (the first style sheet in the document), or by id, as in *documents.styleSheets.garish* (assuming you coded <STYLE ID="garish">.

- Each member of *styleSheets* has a *rules* collection that contains a member for each rule in the style sheet. Well, almost. If you code multiple selectors on a single style rule, Internet Explorer actually stores multiple rules, one for each selector. The following code would create two consecutive rule entries in the *document.styleSheets.garish* collection:

```
<STYLE ID="garish">
 H1, P { font-family: sans-serif; }
</STYLE>
```

To access a particular rule within a *styleSheets* collection, use a numeric subscript. The following expression accesses the H1 rule for the *garish* style sheet above:

```
document.styleSheets.garish.rules[0]
```

Use this expression to determine the number of rules in the *garish* *styleSheets* collection:

```
document.styleSheets.garish.rules.length
```

- The rules in a *styleSheets* collection have all the normal CSS properties, named with the convention of removing all hyphens and capitalizing the next letter.

Well, this is pretty cool. Any time we want—even after the Web page is on display—JavaScript code can change any style rule. Internet Explorer will then redraw whatever portions of the Web page are affected. We could put the following code on a button element, for example, and it would change the color of whatever content used the first rule in the first style sheet in the document:

```
onclick="document.styleSheets[0].rules[0].color = 'red';"
```

Of course, in real life, we want to access style sheet rules by selector rather than numeric subscript. This requires searching through the *rules* collection looking for the selector we want. The selector name appears in a property called *selectorText*. If the rule in *document.styleSheets[0].rules[0]* pertained to the H1 selector, the expression *document.styleSheets[0].rules[0].selectorText* would contain the characters H1.

Quick, before you fuzz over, let's look at an example. This function changes any property of any CSS selector to any value you specify. Pretty good for eight lines of code! Here goes:

```
function setStyle(sel, prop, val){
  for (i=1; i < document.styleSheets[0].rules.length; i++){
    if (document.styleSheets[0].rules[i].selectorText == sel){
      document.styleSheets[0].rules[i].style[prop] = val;
      return;
    }
  document.styleSheets[0].addRule(sel, prop + ": " + val);
  }
}
```

The code to invoke this function would look like this:

```
setStyle("TH", "fontFamily", "sans-serif")
```

The *for* loop just after the *function* statement loops through all the rules in the *styleSheets* collection, starting from the end and working toward the beginning. We start from the bottom because it's perfectly valid to have two rules for the same selector—two H2 rules, for example—and if we modified the first rule, the second rule might override that property anyway. This behavior makes it preferable to find and modify the *last* rule for a selector.

The *if* statement checks to see whether the current rule matches the first argument passed to the function (TH, for example). If it does match, the statement just after the *if* modifies the property named in the second argument, giving it the value specified in the third.

Once we locate the rule for the specified selector and change the specified property, the *return* statement exits the function. If no rule matching the given selector is present, the last statement in the function (not counting the closing curly braces) *adds* a rule, on the fly, with the given selector. By default, new rules go at the end of the collection; if you want a new rule to go somewhere else, code its position as a third argument.

Despite the long-winded explanation, the *setStyle()* function provides an easy way to override CSS properties tuned for Netscape Navigator, substituting properties tuned for Internet Explorer. Here's the step-by step:

Tip: As shown, the *setStyle()* function always modifies the first style sheet in a document. To modify a different style sheet, change the subscript immediately following *document.styleSheets*.

Tip: The *document.styleSheets[x].removeRule(y)* method removes a rule from a *styleSheets* collection. Replace *x* with the identity of the style sheet—either its numeric position or its id value—and *y* with the number of the rule.

1. Code a normal style sheet with the values you want for Netscape Navigator.

2. In a subsequent <SCRIPT> section, test for Internet Explorer and, if found, call *setStyle()* once for each CSS selector and property you want to override.

Here's the code, using the *setStyle()* function, that's equivalent to the <STYLE DISABLED> approach used in the Mountain O' Mail page. For simplicity, I've omitted any rules that don't require an override:

```
<style type="text/css">
LI { list-style-image: url(../images/envelope.gif) ;
     text-indent: 0 ; margin-bottom:0; }
UL {font-size: 70%; }
.dialog { background-color: white; }
.nd { text-decoration: none; }
-->
</style>
<script language="JavaScript">
if (navigator.appName.substring(0,9) == "Microsoft"){
  setStyle("LI","textIndent","-4px");
  setStyle("LI","marginBottom","12px");
  setStyle("UL","fontSize","100%");
  setStyle(".dialog","backgroundColor","#CCC");
  setStyle(".nd","textDecoration","underline");
}
</script>
```

The ability to change styles while a page is on display can lead to some interesting animation effects. You could try to keep the visitor awake by using a timer to change the background color or the default font once a second, for example. Tread carefully, though; it's much easier to be obnoxious than cool, here.

Dynamic Style Sheets in Netscape Navigator

One good thing about the Web: choices abound. Netscape Navigator, starting with version 4, also provides a way to modify CSS properties from JavaScript. Of course, Netscape and Microsoft chose to implement their respective features completely differently. Netscape's version came first, but Microsoft's is more powerful. Choice is good, though; keep telling yourself that.

Netscape calls its approach JASS—JavaScript Accessible Style Sheets. JASS defines style sheets not with normal CSS syntax, but with JavaScript statements. This means program logic can change a page's style sheets based on any information available to the browser—information such as *navigator.appName*, the name of the browser. This sounds very cool except for two major restrictions:

- Netscape Navigator is the only browser that supports JASS.

- All JASS statements must execute *before* the browser starts displaying the body of the Web page.

If it bothers you to depend on Netscape Navigator's ignoring the disabled attribute in a <STYLE > tag, you can accomplish the same thing by using JASS. Here's the JASS code that's equivalent to the <SCRIPT DISABLED> section in the Mountain O' Mail page:

```
<style type = "text/JavaScript">
  if (navigator.appName == "Netscape"){
    tags.LI.textIndent = "0";
    tags.LI.marginBottom = "0";
    tags.UL.fontSize = "70%";
    classes.dialog.all.backgroundColor = "white";
    classes.nd.all.textDecoration = "none";
  }
</style>
```

Note the extra parameter *type="text/JavaScript"* in the <STYLE> tag; this marks the style sheet as JASS. The *if* statement is superfluous for now, but might be needed if Internet Explorer ever supports JASS. It also illustrates support for programmed logic:

- To specify or override a CSS type (the built-in style for a standard HTML tag), prefix the tag identifier with *tags*.

```
tags.LI.textIndent = "0";
```

- To specify or override a CSS class, prefix the class name with *classes* and append it with *all*.

```
classes.dialog.all.backgroundColor = "white";
```

FIGURE 15-3. *Server-side scripts in an Active Server Page generated this Web page as output. The input came from the Mountain O' Mail form.*

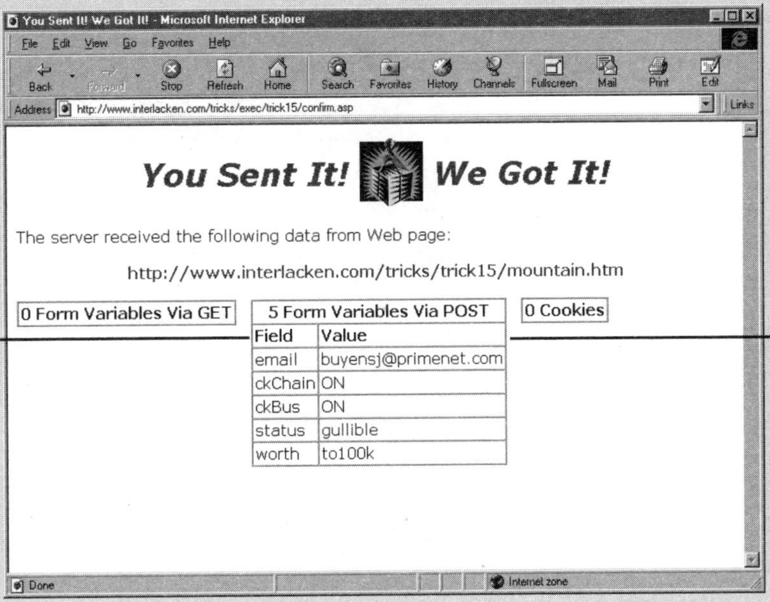
You Sent It! We Got It! - Microsoft Internet Explorer
File Edit View Go Favorites Help
Back Forward Stop Refresh Home Search Favorites History Channels Fullscreen Mail Print Edit
Address http://www.interlacken.com/tricks/exec/trick15/confirm.asp
Links
You Sent It! We Got It!
The server received the following data from Web page:
http://www.interlacken.com/tricks/trick15/mountain.htm
0 Form Variables Via GET
5 Form Variables Via POST
0 Cookies
Field
Value
email
buyensj@primenet.com
ckChain
ON
ckBus
ON
status
gullible
worth
to100k
Done
Internet zone
Field names assigned in HTML.
Values selected by the remote user.

See Also: To learn about running Active Server Pages on your Web server, refer to the sidebar titled "Running and Viewing Active Server Pages" in Trick 2, "Generating Tables Dynamically."

You Sent It! We Got It!

Somewhere before the end of the book it seems fitting to show both sides of HTML forms processing—the browser side and the server side. This is as good a time as any, so let's do it. Figure 15-3 shows the results of processing a Mountain O' Mail submission with an Active Server Page.

Scripting Techniques

An active Server Page, you should recall, is an ordinary Web page with two important changes:

1. The filename extension is *.asp* rather than .htm or .html.

2. The file contains server-side script code within <%...%> markers or <SCRIPT RUNAT=Server> and </SCRIPT> tags.

The server watches for server-side script statements whenever it's delivering an ASP page. Instead of delivering these statements to the remote user, the server executes them. The script can make use of files, databases, and other server-based resources, or it can create output for the remote user. The output appears within the Web page where the script statements originally appeared. By default, ASP pages expect any script code to be VBScript, not JavaScript. Although you can override this, it's best not to. All of Microsoft's ASP examples and documentation are couched in VBScript.

If your HTML form uses the GET method to submit itself to an ASP file, the ASP file sees each form field as an element in the *Request.QueryString* collection. Specifically, if your HTML form contains a field like this:

```
<input type="text" name="hatSize" size="10">
```

an ASP file could access the user-entered value with the expression:

```
Request.QueryString("hatSize")
```

If the HTML form uses the POST method, the ASP file needs to use a slightly different expression:

```
Request.Form("hatSize")
```

Since ASP makes the form data so readily available, your server-side script can do whatever it wants with it. The following statements, for example, would extend a file by one record, containing the *hatSize* and *shoeSize* values from an HTML form. A comma will separate the two values:

```
set fileSys = Server.CreateObject("Scripting.FileSystemObject")
set outFile = fileSys.OpenTextFile(fileName, ForAppending, True)
outFile.WriteLine (Request.Form("hatSize") & _
                   "," & _
                   Request.Form("shoeSize"))
```

Tip: An HTML form uses the GET method if the <FORM> tag contains TYPE="GET" or no TYPE attribute at all.

Tip: An HTML form uses the POST method if TYPE="POST" appears within the <FORM> tag.

Note: Unlike JavaScript, VBScript is sensitive to line endings. If a statement spans multiple lines, each line but the last must end with a continuation character (that is, with an underscore).

Tip: VBScript's *WriteLine* method adds a string of text and a line ending to the end of a file. The *Write* method adds only the string of text.

See Also: The Vicksville Varmints Season Results page in Trick 13, "Reading Data from a File," provides another example of file processing within an Active Server Page.

Note: The *for each* loops that dump the *Request.QueryString* and *Request.Form* collections automatically identify each field using the name assigned by its HTML. For real applications, you'll probably want to display each field value individually and code your own field names as text.

For purposes of this Trick, we'll skip the file processing and just display the form fields back to the user. What's more, we'll do this in a fairly general way that's useful for illustration and debugging. Remember that little *for each...in* drill we used back in Trick 2? We used it to dump the *Request.ServerVariables* collection and produce the Little Egypt ASP Information Pit. Total recall, I'm sure. Anyway, we're going to use it again, this time to dump the *Request.QueryString* collection, the *Request.Form* collection, and just in case a cookie comes along, the *Request.Cookies* collection.

The code to dump the *Request.QueryString* collection follows, and the code to dump the others is very similar. The statements between *for each* and *next* run once for each member of the collection, with the *field* variable receiving each name in turn:

```
for each field in Request.QueryString
  response.write "<tr>"
  response.write    "<td>" & field & "</td>"
  response.write    "<td>" & Request.QueryString(field)
  response.write       "</td></tr>"
next
```

That pretty much concludes the interesting part of this page; there are four tables, one to display each collection and one to arrange the others side by side. The page uses this expression:

```
<% =Request.ServerVariables("HTTP_REFERER") %>
```

to display the URL of the page that submitted the form, and it uses expressions like this:

```
Request.QueryString.Count
```

to get and display the number of items in each collection.

Complete HTML Listing

OK, that's it; any more detail would be boring. You asked for it; you got it; here it lies in all its integrated glory. I speak, of course, of the full HTML listing. Well, why not?

```
<html>
<title>You Sent It! We Got It!</title>
<head>
<style>
<!--
  H1  { font-family: Verdana, sans-serif;
        font-style: italic; color: #33f; }
  P   { font-family: Verdana, sans-serif }
  TD  { font-family: Verdana, sans-serif }
  TH  { font-family: Verdana, sans-serif }
  .ref { font-weight: bold; color: #33f; }
-->
</style>
</head>
<body>
<h1 align="center">
You Sent It!
<img src="../../images/received.gif" alt="Received"
     align="absmiddle" WIDTH="66" HEIGHT="70">
We Got It!</h1>
<p>The server received the following data from Web page:</p>
<p align="center" class="ref">
<% =Request.ServerVariables("HTTP_REFERER") %></p>
<table border="0" cellpadding="0" cellspacing="0">
  <tr>
    <td valign="top">
      <table border=1 cellspacing=0 cellpadding=2>
      <tr>
        <th colspan=2>
          <% = Request.QueryString.count%>
          Form Variables Via GET</th></tr>
      <% if Request.QueryString.Count > 0 then
           response.write "<tr>"
           response.write    "<th align=left>Field</th>"
           response.write    "<th align=left>Value</th></tr>"
```

Define text styles.

Display page heading.

Display the URL of the page
that submitted the form.

Start of overall page layout table.

Start of *Request.QueryString*
collection table.

Display size of *Request.QueryString*
collection.

Emit headings for *Request.*
QueryString members (if any).

Continued from previous page

Display each member of
Request.QueryString collection.

```
for each field in Request.QueryString
    response.write "<tr>"
    response.write    "<td>" & field & "</td>"
    response.write    "<td>" & Request.QueryString(field)
    response.write       "</td></tr>"
next
end if
%>
```

End of *Request.QueryString*
collection table.

```
</table></td>
<td valign="top">
    <img src="../../images/trans5x5.gif" width="15" height="5"></td>
<td valign="top">
```

Start of *Request.Form* collection table.

```
<table border=1 cellspacing=0 cellpadding=2>
<tr>
```

Display size of *Request.Form* collection.

```
<th colspan=2>
    <% = Request.form.count %>
    Form Variables Via POST</th></tr>
```

Write headings for *Request.Form*
members (if any).

```
<%if Request.Form.Count > 0 then
    response.write "<tr>"
    response.write    "<th align=left>Field</th>"
    response.write    "<th align=left>Value</th></tr>"
```

Display each member of
Request.Form collection.

```
for each field in Request.Form
    response.write "<tr>"
    response.write "<td>" & field & "</td>"
    response.write "<td>" & Request.Form(field)
    response.write    "</td></tr>"
next
end if
%>
```

End of *Request.Form* collection table.

```
</table></td>
<td valign="top">
    <img src="../../images/trans5x5.gif" width="15" height="5"></td>
<td valign="top">
```

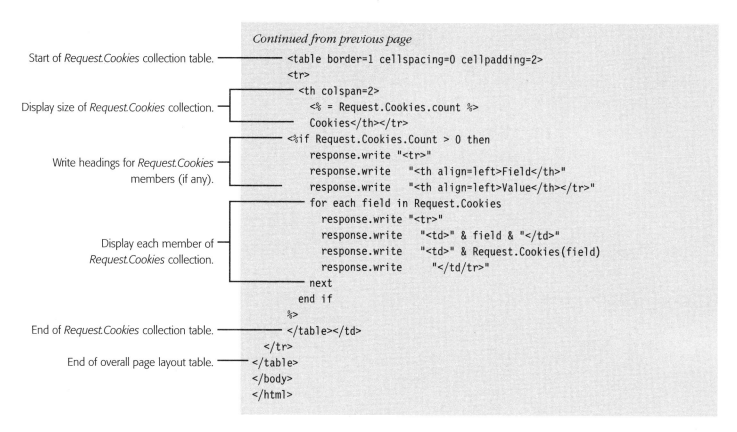

Continued from previous page

Start of *Request.Cookies* collection table.

Display size of *Request.Cookies* collection.

Write headings for *Request.Cookies* members (if any).

Display each member of *Request.Cookies* collection.

End of *Request.Cookies* collection table.

End of overall page layout table.

```
<table border=1 cellspacing=0 cellpadding=2>
<tr>
  <th colspan=2>
    <% = Request.Cookies.count %>
    Cookies</th></tr>
<%if Request.Cookies.Count > 0 then
  response.write "<tr>"
  response.write   "<th align=left>Field</th>"
  response.write   "<th align=left>Value</th></tr>"
  for each field in Request.Cookies
    response.write "<tr>"
    response.write   "<td>" & field & "</td>"
    response.write   "<td>" & Request.Cookies(field)
    response.write       "</td/tr>"
  next
end if
%>
</table></td>
</tr>
</table>
</body>
</html>
```

If your environment supports Active Server Pages, you can use it as a general-purpose HTML form tester. Simply change the ACTION= attribute in the <FORM> tag to

```
action="/tricks/exec/trick15/confirm.asp"
```

or the equivalent, depending on your server's operating conventions. Clicking a button defined like this will then submit your input to the You Sent It! We Got It! page:

```
<input type="submit">
```

If you can't run Active Server Pages, perhaps you can use one of the Perl examples as a guide to writing your own program. The On-Track Messenger Service page in Trick 13 shows how to retrieve a form variable (named *date*) submitted with TYPE=GET coded in the <FORM> tag. Examples of such programs are freely available on the Web—tens or hundreds of thousands of them—as are examples using TYPE=POST as well.

Afterword: Good Coding and Good Luck

First of all, thanks for sticking it out and meeting me here at the end of the book. I hope your head is spinning, not in confusion but in a new awareness of the technologies that bring new life to today's best Web pages. I hope your arsenal of tools is expanded and, even if you don't understand all the details yet, you understand the big picture of how HTML, CSS, and scripting can work together. That's what this book is all about: the big picture, presented in a practical way.

An attractive and functional design makes your pages the equal of others; to stand out, your pages need interactivity as well. Get crazy. Be bold. Do something no one else has done. Make your Web visitors pause in awe as they soak up your message.

When you see a Web page that does something you like, try your browser's View Source command and decipher what the designer has done. If you understood most of this book, you'll understand most of what you find on the Web.

Never slow down; the Web will pass you in an instant. But at the same time, never doubt the scale of what one person can accomplish, given the Web and its millions of denizens. And never stop looking for new tricks.

Index

About the Author

Jim Buyens is the senior PC-LAN administrator for AG Communication Systems, a leading provider of telephone switching equipment and software. An early champion of TCP/IP connectivity, he administers a worldwide corporate network that includes over 40 Microsoft Windows NT Servers and 1800 client PCs. He was an early champion of World Wide Web applications for intranet use, and he administers a corporate Web site at *http://www.agcs.com*.

Jim achieved a Bachelor of Science degree in Computer Science at Purdue University in 1971 and a Master of Business Administration at Arizona State University in 1992. When not administering a network or writing books, he enjoys NHL hockey, NBA and WNBA basketball, and building theatrical scenery. He resides with his family in Phoenix, Arizona.

He is also the author of *Building Net Sites With Windows NT* (Addison-Wesley, 1996), and *Running Microsoft FrontPage 98* (Microsoft Press, 1997).

Contacting the Author

Hearing from happy readers is always a welcome and pleasant experience, and hearing from the others is important as well. My e-mail address is:

buyensj@primenet.com

I'm most interested in your impressions of this book: what you liked or disliked about it, what questions it did or didn't answer, what you found superfluous, and what you'd like to see added in any future books of this type. I'll post errors, omissions, and corrections on my Web site at:

http://www.interlacken.com

The home page for *Stupid Web Tricks* is:

http://www.interlacken.com/swt

Please understand I'm just one person and I can't provide comprehensive technical support or Web page repair service—not even for readers. Please try other channels first, including the following newsgroups:

comp.infosystems.www.authoring.html

comp.infosystems.www.authoring.stylesheets

comp.lang.javascript

comp.lang.perl.misc

microsoft.public.inetsdk.programming.scripting.vbscript

and the following Microsoft Web locations:

http://www.microsoft.com/ie/

http://www.microsoft.com/sitebuilder/

If all else fails, please write. I watch the newsgroups when I have time, but even so it's interesting to know what problems users are experiencing and, therefore, how the book could be more useful in the next iteration. I can't promise complete answers to every question, but I'll try to provide useful suggestions at least.

MICROSOFT LICENSE AGREEMENT

Stupid Web Tricks Companion CD

- **Support Services.** Microsoft may, but is not obligated to, provide you with support services related to the SOFTWARE PRODUCT ("Support Services"). Use of Support Services is governed by the Microsoft policies and programs described in the user manual, in "on-line" documentation, and/or in other Microsoft-provided materials. Any supplemental software code provided to you as part of the Support Services shall be considered part of the SOFTWARE PRODUCT and subject to the terms and conditions of this EULA. With respect to technical information you provide to Microsoft as part of the Support Services, Microsoft may use such information for its business purposes, including for product support and development. Microsoft will not utilize such technical information in a form that personally identifies you.

- **Software Transfer.** You may permanently transfer all of your rights under this EULA, provided you retain no copies, you transfer all of the SOFTWARE PRODUCT (including all component parts, the media and printed materials, any upgrades, this EULA, and, if applicable, the Certificate of Authenticity), **and** the recipient agrees to the terms of this EULA.

- **Termination.** Without prejudice to any other rights, Microsoft may terminate this EULA if you fail to comply with the terms and conditions of this EULA. In such event, you must destroy all copies of the SOFTWARE PRODUCT and all of its component parts.

3. **COPYRIGHT.** All title and copyrights in and to the SOFTWARE PRODUCT (including but not limited to any images, photographs, animations, video, audio, music, text, SAMPLE CODE, REDISTRIBUTABLES, and "applets" incorporated into the SOFTWARE PRODUCT) and any copies of the SOFTWARE PRODUCT are owned by Microsoft or its suppliers. The SOFTWARE PRODUCT is protected by copyright laws and international treaty provisions. Therefore, you must treat the SOFTWARE PRODUCT like any other copyrighted material **except** that you may install the SOFTWARE PRODUCT on a single computer provided you keep the original solely for backup or archival purposes. You may not copy the printed materials accompanying the SOFTWARE PRODUCT.

4. **U.S. GOVERNMENT RESTRICTED RIGHTS.** The SOFTWARE PRODUCT and documentation are provided with RESTRICTED RIGHTS. Use, duplication, or disclosure by the Government is subject to restrictions as set forth in subparagraph (c)(1)(ii) of the Rights in Technical Data and Computer Software clause at DFARS 252.227-7013 or subparagraphs (c)(1) and (2) of the Commercial Computer Software—Restricted Rights at 48 CFR 52.227-19, as applicable. Manufacturer is Microsoft Corporation/One Microsoft Way/Redmond, WA 98052-6399.

5. **EXPORT RESTRICTIONS.** You agree that you will not export or re-export the SOFTWARE PRODUCT, any part thereof, or any process or service that is the direct product of the SOFTWARE PRODUCT (the foregoing collectively referred to as the "Restricted Components"), to any country, person, entity, or end user subject to U.S. export restrictions. You specifically agree not to export or re-export any of the Restricted Components (i) to any country to which the U.S. has embargoed or restricted the export of goods or services, which currently include, but are not necessarily limited to, Cuba, Iran, Iraq, Libya, North Korea, Sudan, and Syria, or to any national of any such country, wherever located, who intends to transmit or transport the Restricted Components back to such country; (ii) to any end user who you know or have reason to know will utilize the Restricted Components in the design, development, or production of nuclear, chemical, or biological weapons; or (iii) to any end user who has been prohibited from participating in U.S. export transactions by any federal agency of the U.S. government. You warrant and represent that neither the BXA nor any other U.S. federal agency has suspended, revoked, or denied your export privileges.

DISCLAIMER OF WARRANTY

NO WARRANTIES OR CONDITIONS. MICROSOFT EXPRESSLY DISCLAIMS ANY WARRANTY OR CONDITION FOR THE SOFTWARE PRODUCT. THE SOFTWARE PRODUCT AND ANY RELATED DOCUMENTATION IS PROVIDED "AS IS" WITHOUT WARRANTY OR CONDITION OF ANY KIND, EITHER EXPRESS OR IMPLIED, INCLUDING, WITHOUT LIMITATION, THE IMPLIED WARRANTIES OF MERCHANTABILITY, FITNESS FOR A PARTICULAR PURPOSE, OR NONINFRINGEMENT. THE ENTIRE RISK ARISING OUT OF USE OR PERFORMANCE OF THE SOFTWARE PRODUCT REMAINS WITH YOU.

LIMITATION OF LIABILITY. TO THE MAXIMUM EXTENT PERMITTED BY APPLICABLE LAW, IN NO EVENT SHALL MICROSOFT OR ITS SUPPLIERS BE LIABLE FOR ANY SPECIAL, INCIDENTAL, INDIRECT, OR CONSEQUENTIAL DAMAGES WHATSOEVER (INCLUDING, WITHOUT LIMITATION, DAMAGES FOR LOSS OF BUSINESS PROFITS, BUSINESS INTERRUPTION, LOSS OF BUSINESS INFORMATION, OR ANY OTHER PECUNIARY LOSS) ARISING OUT OF THE USE OF OR INABILITY TO USE THE SOFTWARE PRODUCT OR THE PROVISION OF OR FAILURE TO PROVIDE SUPPORT SERVICES, EVEN IF MICROSOFT HAS BEEN ADVISED OF THE POSSIBILITY OF SUCH DAMAGES. IN ANY CASE, MICROSOFT'S ENTIRE LIABILITY UNDER ANY PROVISION OF THIS EULA SHALL BE LIMITED TO THE GREATER OF THE AMOUNT ACTUALLY PAID BY YOU FOR THE SOFTWARE PRODUCT OR US$5.00; PROVIDED, HOWEVER, IF YOU HAVE ENTERED INTO A MICROSOFT SUPPORT SERVICES AGREEMENT, MICROSOFT'S ENTIRE LIABILITY REGARDING SUPPORT SERVICES SHALL BE GOVERNED BY THE TERMS OF THAT AGREEMENT. BECAUSE SOME STATES AND JURISDICTIONS DO NOT ALLOW THE EXCLUSION OR LIMITATION OF LIABILITY, THE ABOVE LIMITATION MAY NOT APPLY TO YOU.

MISCELLANEOUS

This EULA is governed by the laws of the State of Washington USA, except and only to the extent that applicable law mandates governing law of a different jurisdiction.

Should you have any questions concerning this EULA, or if you desire to contact Microsoft for any reason, please contact the Microsoft subsidiary serving your country, or write: Microsoft Sales Information Center/One Microsoft Way/Redmond, WA 98052-6399.

Register Today!

Return this
Stupid Web Tricks
registration card today

Microsoft *Press*
mspress.microsoft.com

OWNER REGISTRATION CARD   1-57231-922-4

STUPID WEB TRICKS

_____   _____   _____
FIRST NAME   MIDDLE INITIAL   LAST NAME

_____
INSTITUTION OR COMPANY NAME

_____
ADDRESS

_____

_____   _____   _____
CITY   STATE   ZIP

                                                ( )
_____ _____
E-MAIL ADDRESS   PHONE NUMBER

U.S. and Canada addresses only. Fill in information above and mail postage-free.
Please mail only the bottom half of this page.

For information about Microsoft Press®
products, visit our Web site at
mspress.microsoft.com

Microsoft *Press*

NO POSTAGE
NECESSARY
IF MAILED
IN THE
UNITED STATES

BUSINESS REPLY MAIL

FIRST-CLASS MAIL   PERMIT NO. 108   REDMOND WA

POSTAGE WILL BE PAID BY ADDRESSEE

MICROSOFT PRESS
PO BOX 97017
REDMOND, WA 98073-9830